GOVERNMENT AND POLITICS
[1940–2006]

PATRON

TUN DR MAHATHIR MOHAMAD

Editorial Advisory board

CHAIRMAN
Tan Sri Dato' Seri (Dr) Ahmad Sarji bin Abdul Hamid

MEMBERS OF THE BOARD
Tan Sri Dato' Dr Ahmad Mustaffa Babjee
Prof. Dato' Dr Asmah Haji Omar
Puan Azah Aziz
Dr Peter M. Kedit
Dato' Dr T. Marimuthu
Ms Patricia Regis
Tan Sri Dato' Dr Wan Mohd Zahid Mohd Noordin
Dato' Mohd Yusof bin Hitam
Mr P. C. Shivadas

The *Encyclopedia of Malaysia* was first conceived by Editions Didier Millet and Datin Paduka Marina Mahathir. The Editorial Advisory Board, made up of distinguished figures drawn from academic and public life, was constituted in March 1994. The project was publicly announced in October that year, and eight months later the first sponsors were in place. In 1996, the structure of the content was agreed; later that year the appointment of Volume Editors and the commissioning of authors were substantially complete, and materials for the work were beginning to flow in. By mid-2006, 11 volumes were completed for publication. Upon completion, the series will consist of 16 volumes.

The Publishers wish to thank the following people for their contribution to the first seven volumes:
Dato' Seri Anwar Ibrahim,
who acted as Chairman of the Editorial Advisory Board;
and
the late Tan Sri Dato' Dr Noordin Sopiee
Tan Sri Datuk Augustine S. H. Ong
the late Tan Sri Zain Azraai
Datuk Datin Paduka Zakiah Hanum bt Abdul Hamid
Datin Noor Azlina Yunus

EDITORIAL TEAM

Series Editorial Team

PUBLISHER
Didier Millet

GENERAL MANAGER
Charles Orwin

PROJECT COORDINATOR
Marina Mahathir

EDITORIAL DIRECTOR
Timothy Auger

PROJECT MANAGER
Martin Cross

PRODUCTION MANAGER
Sin Kam Cheong

DESIGN DIRECTOR
Annie Teo

EDITORS
Kiri Cowie
Shoba Devan
Deborah Koh Leng Hoon
Gabrielle Low

ASSISTANT EDITOR
Chang Yan Yi

DESIGNERS
Muamar Ghadafi bin Ali
Theivani A/P Nadaraju
Yusri bin Din

Volume Editorial Team

VOLUME COORDINATOR
Martin Cross

EDITORS
Stephen Chin
E. Ravinderen Kandiappan

ASSISTANT EDITOR
Chang Yan Yi

EDITORIAL CONSULTANT
Assoc. Prof. Dr James Chin

DESIGNERS
Lawrence Kok
Yusri bin Din

ILLUSTRATORS
Chai Kah Yune
Lim Joo
Tan Hong Yew
Wong Lek Min

SPONSORS

The *Encyclopedia of Malaysia* was made possible thanks to the generous and enlightened support of the following organizations:

- DRB-HICOM BERHAD
- MAHKOTA TECHNOLOGIES SDN BHD
- MALAYAN UNITED INDUSTRIES BERHAD
- MALAYSIA NATIONAL INSURANCE BERHAD
- MINISTRY OF EDUCATION MALAYSIA
- NEW STRAITS TIMES PRESS (MALAYSIA) BERHAD
- TRADEWINDS CORPORATION BERHAD
- PETRONAS BERHAD
- UEM WORLD BERHAD
- STAR PUBLICATIONS (MALAYSIA) BERHAD
- SUNWAY GROUP
- TENAGA NASIONAL BERHAD

- UNITED OVERSEAS BANK GROUP
- YAYASAN ALBUKHARY
- YTL CORPORATION BERHAD

PNB GROUP OF COMPANIES
- PERMODALAN NASIONAL BERHAD
- NCB HOLDINGS BERHAD
- GOLDEN HOPE PLANTATIONS BERHAD
- SIME DARBY BERHAD
- MALAYAN BANKING BERHAD
- MNI HOLDINGS BERHAD
- PERNEC CORPORATION BERHAD

CONTRIBUTORS

Dr Adnan Haji Nawang
Universiti Pendidikan Sultan Idris

Ahmad Sarji bin Abdul Hamid
Badan Warisan Malaysia

Prof. Dr Cheah Boon Kheng
Universiti Sains Malaysia (retired)

Paddy Bowie
Paddy Schubert Sdn Bhd

Assoc. Prof. Dr James Chin
Universiti Malaysia Sarawak

Mark Disney
Education Quarterly

Assoc. Prof. Dr Hari Singh
Universiti Kebangsaan Malaysia

Dr T. N. Harper
Magdelene College, Cambridge

Dr Heng Pek Khoon
American University, Washington DC

Jamshah Mustapa
Polis Diraja Malaysia

Prof. Dr Jayum A. Jawan
Universiti Putra Malaysia

Prof. Dr Johan Saravanamuttu
Universiti Sains Malaysia

Dr Mohd Kamarulnizam Abdullah
Universiti Kebangsaan Malaysia

Khairy Jamaluddin
Deputy Leader, UMNO Youth

Dr Khong Kim Hoong
HELP Institute

Prof. Emeritus Dr Khoo Kay Kim
University of Malaya

Assoc. Prof. Dr Paul Kratoska
National University of Singapore

Prof. Dr Diane K. Mauzy
University of British Columbia

Prof. Emeritus R. S. Milne
University of British Columbia

Mohamed Jawhar Hassan
Institute of Strategic and International Studies, Malaysia

Mohd Zahidi bin Hj Zainuddin
Malaysian Armed Forces (retired)

Adjunct Prof. Muhammad Ghazali Shafie
Universiti Kebangsaan Malaysia

Prof. Dr Nik Anuar Nik Mahmud
Universiti Kebangsaan Malaysia

Nik Mohamed Nik Mohd Salleh
Malaysian Historical Society

Nina Adlan
Education Quarterly

Omar Mohd Hashim
Election Commission (retired)

Prof. Dr Phang Siew Nooi
Universiti Malaya

Prof. Dr Ramlah Adam
Universiti Malaya

Assoc. Prof. Dr R. H. W. Reece
Murdoch University, Australia

Prof. Dr Shad Saleem Faruqi
Universiti Teknologi MARA

Assoc. Prof. Dr B. H. Shafruddin
Universiti Brunei Darussalam

P. C. Shivadas
New Straits Times Press (Malaysia) Bhd

Prof. Dr Richard Stubbs
McMaster University, Ontario

Eddie Toh
Singapore Business Times

Prof. Dr Visu Sinnadurai
Universiti Malaya (Adjunct Professor)

Dr Wan Mohd Zahid Mohd Noordin
Federal Power Sdn Bhd

Dr Meredith Weiss
Georgetown University, Washington

Prof. Dr Wu Min Aun
Charles Darwin University, Australia

Prof. Dr Zakaria Haji Ahmad
Universiti Kebangsaan Malaysia

THE ENCYCLOPEDIA OF

MALAYSIA

Volume 11

GOVERNMENT AND POLITICS

[1940–2006]

Volume Editor

Prof. Dato' Dr Zakaria Haji Ahmad

Universiti Kebangsaan Malaysia

ARCHIPELAGO PRESS

Contents

ABOVE: Tunku Abdul Rahman Putra's entourage receiving a rousing welcome in Melaka on his return from the Merdeka Mission in 1956.

FAR RIGHT: Regalia of the Yang di-Pertuan Agong (Paramount Ruler or King) and Raja Permaisuri Agong (Consort to the Yang di-Pertuan Agong) used on royal ceremonial occasions.

TITLE PAGE: The Prime Minister's Office (also known as the Perdana Putra Complex) is located in Precinct One, Putrajaya. The offices of the Prime Minister, Deputy Prime Minister and Chief Secretary to the Government are situated in this office complex.

HALF TITLE PAGE: Tunku Abdul Rahman Putra joins the festivities on the eve of Merdeka Day, 31 August 1957.

Introduction

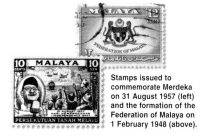

Stamps issued to commemorate Merdeka on 31 August 1957 (left) and the formation of the Federation of Malaya on 1 February 1948 (above).

Home Guard recruits during the Emergency, 1951.

This volume tells the story of Malaysia's history since 1940, and so follows on from Early Modern History, *already published in this series. The emphasis is on the political conception and development of Malaysia. The economic story must be told in parallel, and is covered in a separate volume; that said, the two dimensions cannot be separated entirely, and many of the issues covered in this book have an economic aspect. Malaysia has been in existence since 1963, the volume also covers the political phases that preceded it, including the Malayan Union and the Federation of Malaya.*

Early beginnings

Malaysia's origins can be traced back to the period around World War II. Prior to that, the British colonial administration had a firm grip on *Tanah Melayu* (the Malay states) and the northern Borneo territories. The beginnings of nationalistic sentiment were seen in uprisings and rebellions in some states, and nationalism was in the air as war approached. The Japanese Occupation dispelled any remaining notions of intrinsic British superiority. Whatever the other effects of the Occupation were, and many of them were devastating, it helped up to a point to foster the sense of nationalism. Section One of this volume therefore traces the political genesis of Malaysia. Sadly, one of the war's by-products was to pit against each other, in its aftermath, the various races that had come to call the country home. The immediate post-war situation triggered ethnic unrest and, more notably, the 12-year communist insurgency.

Against this complex background, the volume traces the process whereby the Malays, Chinese, and Indians set aside their differences to form the Alliance coalition and seek 'Merdeka'. Sure enough, independence was granted to the Federation of Malaya, later to become Malaysia. The fact that independence was attained peacefully, certainly so far as the majority of the population were concerned, without violence and bloodshed, must be regarded as a historic achievement on the part of all involved. Individual coverage is also given to Dato' Onn bin Jaafar, who played a particularly crucial role in uniting the Malays, firing them with nationalistic passion and setting the independence movement into motion.

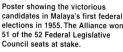

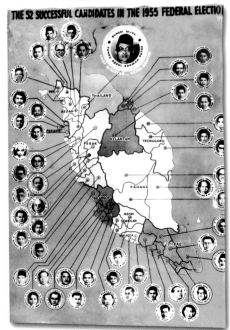

Poster showing the victorious candidates in Malaya's first federal elections in 1955. The Alliance won 51 of the 52 Federal Legislative Council seats at stake.

In Section Two, we explore the issue of diversity. The section shows how the nation's first formula for racial collaboration worked successfully for 12 years before ending tragically with the events of 13 May 1969. This date marked a watershed in Malaysian politics. Later, in 1974, the Alliance formula was expanded into a larger political coalition of the United Malays National Organisation (UMNO) and other parties with the formation of the Barisan Nasional (National Front). Affirmative action and the Malaysia Incorporated

RIGHT: Alliance Party Chairman and UMNO President Tunku Abdul Rahman Putra addresses an Alliance meeting in 1959. In the foreground are (from left) Tun Abdul Razak Hussein (UMNO Deputy President), Tun Tan Siew Sin (MCA President) and Tun V. T. Sambanthan (MIC President).

Sarawak Barisan Nasional billboard, 1995.

The Yang di-Pertuan Agong (Paramount Ruler or King), leads a procession of dignitaries into Parliament House to open the first parliamentary session of 2004.

BELOW: Prime Minister Dato' Seri Dr Mahathir opening Cyberjaya Technology City in July 1999.

BOTTOM: Dr Mahathir hands over papers to his successor, Dato' Seri Abdullah Ahmad Badawi, at the Prime Minister's Office, Putrajaya, 31 October 2003.

policies were instituted to improve the social and economic position of the Malay community.

Government institutions and administration

In Section Three, the spotlight falls on the three branches of government: the legislature, the executive and the judiciary. Focusing on the executive, each of Malaysia's five Prime Ministers is featured. Despite their initial rise to political prominence as head of their ethnic-based political party, Malaysia's Prime Ministers have assumed a broader role looking after the welfare of all races.

Section Four covers the nation's security and administrative institutions, to a large extent modelled on colonial British predecessors. Since Independence, these institutions have evolved to suit Malaysia's own requirements, and provide the nation with a framework of stability on the basis of law and order.

Section Five examines the nation's electoral politics and party system, which are a robust component of Malaysia's public life. This testing of the public will brings to the country's institutions a basis of democratic legitimacy. Malaysia's system of coalition politics revolves around a single dominant partner, the United Malays National Organisation (UMNO). The winning formula has been UMNO's willingness to share power and its due regard to the interests of non-Malay parties, in both the Malay Peninsula and in Sabah and Sarawak. From this section of the volume emerges a clear picture of the complexities faced by a succession of Malaysian governments.

Social institutions and foreign policy

A positive indication that a nation is maturing is its social development. In Section Six, a range of related social topics is examined. For example, the section traces the development of interest and advocacy groups, and the way the flow of information and the media affects the nation's life. As society organizes itself on the basis of a diverse range of interests, it changes, and the lines of communalism which have defined many groups in Malaysian society for decades begin to blur.

It is important to be reminded of the international political atmosphere which prevailed when the Federation of Malaya, and then Malaysia, was born. For example, the Emergency cannot be understood without reference to the broader issue of communism in world affairs, and political developments in China. Many newly independent nations found themselves awkwardly positioned between the two superpowers of the day, the United States of America and the Soviet Union. But this polarity represented also an opportunity for countries such as Malaysia, which has blossomed internationally. Since its formation, Malaysia's international prominence has increased, thanks in no small part to the nation's consistent foreign policy and the global vision of its leaders.

Section Seven explores the evolution of foreign policy as well as the way in which Malaysia has matured into a confident and vocal champion of Third World and Islamic causes.

A volume such as this cannot examine all aspects of such a complex story in detail; hence a bibliography has been included. In it are listed sources of information for anyone wishing to follow up a line of interest.

Chronology

Pre-World War II

Perlis · SIAM · Kedah · Penang · Kelantan · Terengganu · Perak · Pahang · Selangor · Negeri Sembilan · Melaka · Johor · SINGAPORE · Strait of Melaka · South China Sea · BRUNEI · British North Borneo · Sarawak

0   100 km

- Federated Malay States
- Straits Settlements
- Unfederated Malay States
- Brooke-administered
- British Protectorate

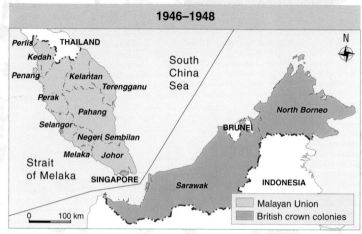

1946–1948

Perlis · THAILAND · Kedah · Penang · Kelantan · Terengganu · Perak · Pahang · Selangor · Negeri Sembilan · Melaka · Johor · SINGAPORE · Strait of Melaka · South China Sea · BRUNEI · North Borneo · Sarawak · INDONESIA

0   100 km

- Malayan Union
- British crown colonies

1940s

1940 Some 150 members of the anti-colonial Kesatuan Melayu Muda (KMM, or Young Malay Union) arrested and imprisoned.

1941 Japan invades and occupies Malaya, British North Borneo (now Sabah) and Sarawak in 68 days.

1942 Japanese soldiers launch *sook ching*, executing thousands of Chinese in Singapore and Malaya.

1943 The Kinabalu Guerrilla Force attacks Japanese facilities in Jesselton (at the time renamed 'Api' by the Japanese). They are captured and executed.

1945 The United States of America drops atomic bombs on Hiroshima and Nagasaki, forcing Japan's surrender.

1945 Britain regains control over territories in the Malay Peninsula and northern Borneo; establishment of the British Military Administration (in Sarawak the Australian Military Administration).

1945 Vyner Brooke cedes control over Sarawak to the British Crown.

1945 The Malayan Union, merging all the Malay states into a single entity, is proposed. The Sultans are pressured into ceding their sovereignty.

1945 The Malayan Democratic Union (MDU) political party is formed to champion self-government and equality of the races.

1946 Shortage of supplies and revenge attacks cause ethnic clashes.

1946 The Malayan Union is established in the face of widespread Malay opposition.

1946 The United Malays National Organisation (UMNO) is formed to unite the Malays in protest against the Malayan Union.

1946 Sarawak and North Borneo are made British crown colonies.

The National Monument in Kuala Lumpur commemorates the fallen soldiers who died in the defence of the nation.

1946 A new constitution is drawn up to replace the Malayan Union.

1946 The Malayan Indian Congress (MIC) is founded.

1947 The All Malaya Council of Joint Action (AMCJA) and Pusat Tenaga Rakyat (PUTERA) organize a nationwide *hartal* to demonstrate opposition to the proposed constitution.

1948 The Malayan Union Order in Council is revoked; the Federation of Malaya Agreement takes its place. The Federation of Malaya comes into existence.

1948 The Malayan Communist Party (MCP) launches its armed insurgency, marking the beginning of the 12-year Emergency period.

1949 Malayan Chinese Association (MCA) founded.

1949 British Governor of Sarawak, Duncan Stewart, is assassinated in Sarawak.

1950s

1950 The Briggs Plan is introduced and New Villages are established to deprive the communists of supplies and support.

1951 The first municipal election in Penang.

1951 Onn Jaafar leaves UMNO to form the Independence of Malaya Party (IMP).

1951 British High Commissioner Henry Gurney is assassinated by communist terrorists in an ambush, on his way to Fraser's Hill.

1952 Gerald Templer replaces Gurney and advocates a 'hearts and minds' strategy to win over the Malay Peninsula's population and deny support to the communists.

1952 The Kuala Lumpur municipal election: UMNO and MCA form an informal alliance.

1953 UMNO–MCA Alliance is formally established.

1954 State elections are held in the Peninsula.

1954 Onn Jaafar leaves IMP and forms Parti Negara.

1954 MIC joins the Alliance.

1955 The first general election for seats in the Federal Legislative Council is held. The Alliance wins 51 out of 52 seats. After the election, the first Cabinet is formed comprising elected and official members with Tunku Abdul Rahman Putra as Chief Minister.

1955 Baling Talks are held between government and communist leaders, with a view to ending the Emergency. The talks are unsuccessful.

1956 Merdeka mission led by Tunku Abdul Rahman Putra goes to London for talks on independence.

1957 Malaya gains independence (see 'Proclamations of nationhood').

1960s

1960 The Emergency ends.

1961 Tunku Abdul Rahman Putra proposes the idea of a new federation: Malaysia.

Prime Minister Tunku Abdul Rahman Putra and the first Cabinet of the Federation of Malaya, 1957.

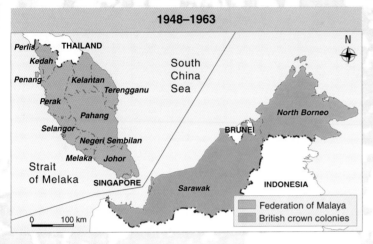

1948–1963	

Perlis — THAILAND
Kedah
Penang — Kelantan
Terengganu
Perak
Pahang
Selangor
Negeri Sembilan
Melaka — Johor
Strait of Melaka — SINGAPORE
South China Sea
North Borneo
BRUNEI
Sarawak
INDONESIA
N
0 100 km

Federation of Malaya
British crown colonies

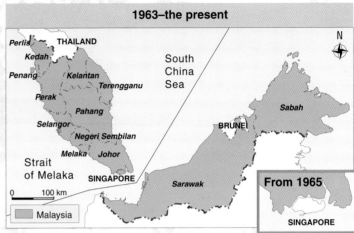

1963–the present	

Perlis — THAILAND
Kedah
Penang — Kelantan
Terengganu
Perak
Pahang
Selangor
Negeri Sembilan
Melaka — Johor
Strait of Melaka — SINGAPORE
South China Sea
Sabah
BRUNEI
Sarawak
N
0 100 km

Malaysia

From 1965
SINGAPORE

1961 The Malaysia Solidarity Consultative Committee, headed by Donald Stephens, is formed.

1962 The Cobbold Commission confirms the willingness of Sarawak and North Borneo to join the Malaysian federation.

1962 Indonesia and the Philippines protest against Malaysia; the Philippines makes territorial claim to North Borneo.

1963 North Borneo is renamed Sabah.

1963 The United Nations confirms willingness of Sarawak and Sabah to join Malaysia.

1963 Sabah, Sarawak, Singapore and the Federation of Malaya are federated to form Malaysia (see 'Proclamations of nationhood').

1963 Indonesia launches *Konfrontasi* (Confrontation) and armed incursions into Malaysian territory.

1963 Television broadcasts are introduced; Radio Televisyen Malaysia (RTM) is formed.

1965 Singapore Prime Minister Lee Kuan Yew launches the Malaysia Solidarity Convention and advocates a 'Malaysian Malaysia'.

1965 Parliament enacts the Constitution and Malaysia (Singapore Amendment) Act to expel Singapore from Malaysia.

1966 Indonesia declares end to *Konfrontasi*.

1966 Malaysia resumes diplomatic ties with the Philippines.

1967 Malaysia resumes diplomatic ties with Indonesia.

1967 The Association of Southeast Asian Nations (ASEAN) is formed, comprising Indonesia, Malaysia, the Philippines, Singapore and Thailand.

1969 Following the general election, the 13 May tragedy leads to the declaration of a state of emergency and the suspension of Parliament. Malaysia is administered by the National Operations Council.

1970s

1970 Tunku Abdul Rahman Putra retires; Tun Abdul Razak bin Dato' Hussein becomes Malaysia's second Prime Minister.

1970 The *Rukunegara* (National ideology) is introduced as a pillar of national identity. Amendments are made to the Constitution to remove sensitive issues from public discussion.

1970 The New Economic Policy is launched.

1971 The National Operations Council is disbanded and parliamentary democracy restored.

1974 The Alliance extends its coalition to include additional parties and is renamed Barisan Nasional (National Front).

1974 Malaysia establishes diplomatic ties with China.

1974 The communist insurgency in Sarawak ends with the signing of a declaration at Simanggang. The town is renamed Sri Aman in honour of the agreement.

1976 Death of Prime Minister Tun Abdul Razak. Dato' Hussein bin Dato' Onn becomes third Prime Minister.

1976 First ASEAN Heads of Government meeting is held in Bali. The Treaty of Amity and Cooperation is signed.

1980s

1981 Dato' Hussein Onn retires as Prime Minister; he is succeeded by Dato' Seri Dr Mahathir bin Mohamad.

1984 Brunei Darussalam becomes the sixth member of ASEAN.

1987 UMNO is deregistered, UMNO Baru formed and Semangat 46 created.

1987 The Lord President and two Supreme Court judges are dismissed.

1989 The MCP formally ceases its struggle.

1990s

1990 Vision 2020 is launched.

1993 Federal Constitution is amended to create a Special Court for the Malay Rulers.

1997–8 The Asian Financial Crisis strikes with serious implications for the economy. The government introduces capital controls and establishes Danaharta and Danamodal and debt restructuring committees.

2000s

2003 Dr Mahathir steps down on 31 October and is succeeded by Dato' Seri Abdullah Ahmad Badawi as the fifth Prime Minister.

2004 Eleventh general election is held; Barisan Nasional increases its parliamentary majority.

The Putra Mosque and Prime Minister's Office in Putrajaya, the new administrative capital of Malaysia.

The Yang di-Pertuan Agong (Paramount Ruler or King) inspecting a guard of honour before opening the first sitting of the 11th parliamentary session at Parliament House, 2004.

PROCLAMATION
OF
INDEPENDENCE

In the name of God, the Compassionate, the Merciful. Praise be to God, the Lord of the Universe and may the blessings and peace of God be upon His Messengers.

WHEREAS the time has now arrived when the people of the Persekutuan Tanah Melayu will assume the status of a free independent and sovereign nation among the nations of the World

AND WHEREAS by an agreement styled the Federation of Malaya Agreement, 1957, between Her Majesty the Queen and Their Highnesses the Rulers of the Malay States it was agreed that the Malay States of Johore, Pahang, Negri Sembilan, Selangor, Kedah, Perlis, Kelantan, Trengganu and Perak and the former Settlements of Malacca and Penang should as from the 31st day of August, 1957, be formed into a new Federation of States by the name of Persekutuan Tanah Melayu

AND WHEREAS it was further agreed between the parties to the said agreement that the Settlements of Malacca and Penang aforesaid should as from the said date cease to form part of Her Majesty's dominions and that Her Majesty should cease to exercise any sovereignty over them

AND WHEREAS it was further agreed by the parties aforesaid that the Federation of Malaya Agreement, 1948, and all other agreements subsisting between Her Majesty the Queen and Their Highnesses the Rulers or any one of them immediately before the said date should be revoked as from that date and that all powers and jurisdiction of Her Majesty or of the Parliament of the United Kingdom in or in respect of the Settlements aforesaid or the Malay States or the Federation as a whole should come to an end

AND WHEREAS effect has been given to the Federation of Malaya Agreement, 1957, by Her Majesty the Queen, Their Highnesses the Rulers, the Parliament of the United Kingdom and the Legislatures of the Federation and of the Malay States

AND WHEREAS a constitution for the Government of the Persekutuan Tanah Melayu has been established as the supreme law thereof

AND WHEREAS by the Federal Constitution aforesaid provision is made to safeguard the rights and prerogatives of Their Highnesses the Rulers and the fundamental rights and liberties of the people and to provide for the peaceful and orderly advancement of the Persekutuan Tanah Melayu as a constitutional monarchy based on Parliamentary democracy

AND WHEREAS the Federal Constitution aforesaid having been approved by an Ordinance of the Federal Legislatures, by the Enactments of the Malay States and by resolutions of the Legislatures of Malacca and Penang has come into force on the 31st day of August 1957, aforesaid

NOW In the name of God the Compassionate, the Merciful, I, TUNKU ABDUL RAHMAN PUTRA ibni AL-MARHUM SULTAN ABDUL HAMID HALIMSHAH, PRIME MINISTER OF THE PERSEKUTUAN TANAH MELAYU, with the concurrence and approval of Their Highnesses the Rulers of the Malay States do hereby proclaim and declare on behalf of the people of the Persekutuan Tanah Melayu that as from the thirty first day of August, nineteen hundred and fifty seven, the Persekutuan Tanah Melayu comprising the States of Johore, Pahang, Negri Sembilan, Selangor, Kedah, Perlis, Kelantan, Trengganu, Perak, Malacca and Penang is and with God's blessing shall be for ever a sovereign democratic and independent State founded upon the principles of liberty and justice and ever seeking the welfare and happiness of its people and the maintenance of a just peace among all nations.

Kuala Lumpur,
31st. Day of August, 1957.

Prime Minister.

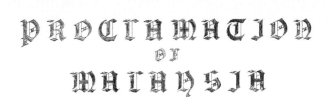

PROCLAMATION OF MALAYSIA

In the name of God, the Compassionate, the Merciful.

Praise be to God, the Lord of the Universe, and may the benediction and peace of God be upon Our Leader Muhammad and upon all His Relations and Friends.

WHEREAS by an Agreement made on the Ninth day of July in the year one thousand nine hundred and sixty-three between the Federation of Malaya, the United Kingdom, North Borneo, Sarawak and Singapore it was agreed that there shall be federated the States of Sabah, Sarawak and Singapore with the Federation of Malaya comprising the States of Pahang, Trengganu, Kedah, Johore, Negri Sembilan, Kelantan, Selangor, Perak, Perlis, Penang and Malacca, and that the Federation shall thereafter be called "Malaysia":

AND WHEREAS it has been agreed by the parties to the said Agreement that as from the establishment of Malaysia the States of Sabah, Sarawak and Singapore shall cease to be colonies of Her Majesty the Queen and Her Majesty the Queen shall relinquish Her sovereignty and jurisdiction in respect of the three States:

AND WHEREAS there has been promulgated a Constitution for Malaysia which shall be the supreme law therein:

AND WHEREAS by the Constitution aforesaid provision has been made for the safeguarding of the rights and prerogatives of Their Highnesses the Rulers and the fundamental rights and liberties of subjects and for the promotion of peace and harmony in Malaysia as a constitutional monarchy based upon parliamentary democracy:

AND WHEREAS the Constitution aforesaid having been approved by a law passed by the Parliaments of the Federation of Malaya and of the United Kingdom has come into force on the Sixteenth day of September in the year one thousand nine hundred and sixty-three:

NOW in the name of God the Compassionate, the Merciful, I, TUNKU ABDUL RAHMAN PUTRA AL-HAJ IBNI ALMARHUM SULTAN ABDUL HAMID HALIM SHAH, Prime Minister of Malaysia, with the concurrence and approval of His Majesty the Yang di-Pertuan Agong of the Federation of Malaya, His Excellency the Yang di-Pertuan Negara of Singapore, His Excellency the Yang di-Pertua Negara of Sabah and His Excellency the Governor of Sarawak DO HEREBY DECLARE AND PROCLAIM on behalf of the peoples of Malaysia that as from the Sixteenth day of September in the year one thousand nine hundred and sixty-three, corresponding to the Twentyeighth day of Rabi'ul Akhir in the year of the Hijrah one thousand three hundred and eighty-three, that MALAYSIA comprising the States of Pahang, Trengganu, Kedah, Johore, Negri Sembilan, Kelantan, Selangor, Perak, Perlis, Penang, Malacca, Singapore, Sabah and Sarawak shall by the Grace of God, the Lord of the Universe, forever be an independent and sovereign democratic State founded upon liberty and justice, ever seeking to defend and uphold peace and harmony among its peoples and to perpetuate peace among nations.

Kuala Lumpur,
Sixteenth day of September, 1963.

Prime Minister.

A

UNTOK MENGINGATI
JASA
PAHLAWAN-PAHLAWAN
YANG GUGOR

TO
OUR
GLORIOUS
DEAD

1914–1918
1939–1945
1948–1960

6

Malay paratroopers with their British Malay-speaking Liaison Officer, Major Hasler, in Alor Star, October 1945.

Sarawak Malay National Union members protest against cession to the British Crown, 1947.

Memorial to fallen soldiers of World Wars I and II and the Emergency in Kuala Lumpur.

An armed roadblock in a rubber estate, set up to halt supplies to communist terrorists, 1950.

High Commissioner of the Federation of Malaya, Sir Donald MacGillivray, signing the Report of the Constitutional Commission, 1956.

The first Yang di-Pertuan Agong (Paramount Ruler or King), the Yang di-Pertuan Besar of Negeri Sembilan, signing the Federation of Malaya Independence Agreement on 5 August 1957.

The Duke of Gloucester handing over the instruments of Independence to Tunku Abdul Rahman Putra at the Merdeka Stadium on 31 August 1957, signifying the nation's independence.

THE QUEST FOR NATIONHOOD

This section explores the dawn of political consciousness in Malaysia and the struggle for independence. Malaysia is racially diverse, and each ethnic group demanded self-government in different terms.

First day cover issued on 31 August 1957 commemorating the birth of the independent Federation of Malaya.

A constant issue in Malayan, and later Malaysian, politics has been the rights of the indigenous Malays. The massive influx of migrant workers in the 19th and 20th centuries had threatened the status quo. Britain was not wholly responsible for this. Even before the British arrived, large numbers of Chinese workers had already been attracted by the Malay Peninsula's abundant natural resources. Their presence and its consequences were among the factors that led to British intervention in the Peninsula.

Nationalism among the Malays first emerged with the advent of large-scale education (see 'Nationalism: The Malay struggle'). The experience and aftermath of World War II intensified this desire for self-determination. When Britain decided to create the Malayan Union after the war, it unwittingly unleashed even more powerful forces for change (see 'The Malayan Union'). The United Malays National Organisation (UMNO), created in response to this, remains Malaysia's dominant political force until today (see 'Dato' Onn bin Jaafar').

As for the non-Malay population, descendants of migrant workers or traders who had settled in the Peninsula years earlier wanted citizenship rights, equality and a voice in government (see 'Nationalism: non-Malays in the Peninsula'). While the Peranakan had become naturalized and adapted to local customs and languages, many other descendants of migrants had maintained their cultural practices and allegiance to their country of origin. This raised fear and suspicion among the Malays. World War II, followed by the communist insurgency (see 'The Emergency'), widened the rift. A certain distrust was slow to die away, and one of Malaysia's great achievements is that all the major races were able to strike a workable compromise as a basis for Independence (see 'Merdeka! Attaining Independence' and 'A constitutional state').

MALAYSIA

16.9.63

Poster commemorating the birth of Malaysia in 1963.

Nationalism in Sabah and Sarawak took a different path to that of the Peninsula (see 'Precursors to nationalism: The armed resistance' and 'Nationalism in northern Borneo'). Political awareness in these states began to develop only when Britain announced plans to grant self-government to its colonies.

Having achieved Independence for Malaya, Tunku Abdul Rahman Putra decided to form a larger federation, Malaysia (see 'The idea of Malaysia'), despite fierce reactions from several quarters (see 'External opposition to Malaysia'). However, a number of unresolved issues eventually led to Singapore's separation from Malaysia (see 'The formation of Malaysia').

Precursors to nationalism:
The armed resistance

The Pangkor Treaty of 1874 enabled the British to achieve authority in the Malay states. Constitutionally, the states were to be 'protected' sovereign states, retaining their Malay Rulers. Practically, however, the British Resident could extend his control as far as the British wished. This prompted armed opposition from the Malays. British colonial manoeuvring also engendered resistance in the northern Borneo states.

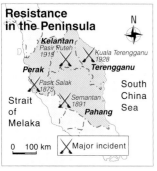

Sultan Abdullah, Ruler of Perak, was implicated in the killing of J. W. W. Birch. Deposed by the British, he was exiled to the Seychelles from 1877 until 1893.

Artist's impression of Maharaja Lela, c. 1875.

J. W. W. Birch in 1874, the year before his murder.

Resistance in the Peninsula

Kelantan
Pasir Puteh 1915
Kuala Terengganu 1928
Perak
Terengganu
Pasir Salak 1875
Semantan 1891
South China Sea
Strait of Melaka
Pahang
0   100 km
Major incident

Latent nationalism

Armed resistance to British colonialism, though sporadic, unorganized and uncoordinated in nature, spearheaded the birth and development of nationalism. This was seen in the revolts against the British in several states between 1875 and 1946.

These uprisings, although led for the most part by Malay Chiefs disgruntled by their loss of power, prestige and privileges, also represented resistance by the local population against British intervention. In nearly all cases, these 'rebel' leaders have come to be regarded as nationalists and heroes.

The Perak war, 1875

Malay uprisings or armed resistance occurred at the very outset when the British established their colonial regime in Perak, through the Pangkor Treaty of 1874. The new regime deprived the Sultan and the Malay Chiefs of their traditional rights and privileges and administrative powers. It also caused the loss of their main sources of income and this, coupled with the friction between Malay rule and British advice and the unpopular personality of the first British Resident, J. W. W. Birch (supposedly an intolerant, arrogant and impatient man who was scornful of Malay society, customs and traditions), led to great resentment.

On 2 November 1875, the posting of notice of a controversial enactment at Pasir Salak served as a signal for the attack by the territorial chief Maharaja Lela's hired assassins, Pandak Induk and Seputum, on Birch, who was killed. Frank Swettenham, a young British officer who was also in Perak, escaped downriver. The British brought in nearly 3000 troops from Penang, Singapore, India and Hong Kong to deal with the Malay warriors, who were later either captured or surrendered themselves. The Maharaja Lela, Pandak Induk and Seputum were hanged. Sultan Abdullah, the Laksamana, the Shah Bandar and Menteri Ngah Ibrahim were later exiled to the Seychelles in the Indian Ocean. Thus ended the Perak war.

The Pahang war, 1891–1895

In Pahang, the establishment of the Residential System in 1888 was resisted with an open revolt. As in Perak, the transition from the old regime to the new one of British colonial administration incited resistance from those whose power and privileges suffered from the changes. Here the British faced an even more serious revolt led by Bahaman, the Chief of Semantan District. In 1891, he mounted a campaign of disobedience, inciting his people to defy all state regulations, and followed later in the same year by his proclamation of an intention to resist the colonial administration by force of arms. He attacked and put to flight a British expedition sent to reinforce the police force in his district. He and his followers then overran the Lubok Trua police station.

The Pahang war lasted for four years and in the course of the struggle, Bahaman was joined by other patriotic leaders, notably Tok Gajah and Mat Kilau. They waged a classic guerrilla campaign against the British forces. Although the British succeeded in first containing and then suppressing the rebellion, they never managed to capture the principal leaders who fled to Kelantan and Terengganu where they were given sanctuary. Tok Gajah and Mat Kilau settled down in Ulu Terengganu whereas Bahaman and his followers, numbering about 100 in all, were taken by the Siamese to Bangkok in 1896. They later moved to live in Chiang Mai in Siam, under Siamese protection. Eventually Bahaman passed away and was buried there.

Mat Kilau (above) and Tok Gajah (inset), Malay leaders during the Pahang war, 1891–5. Mat Kilau lived until 1970.

The Mat Salleh revolt in British North Borneo, 1895

In British North Borneo (now Sabah), the most extensive movement against the British was the Mat Salleh revolt, which erupted in 1895 and lasted until 1903. The introduction by the British of a new tax on imported rice to help finance a cross-country railway exacerbated general discontent which helped trigger the revolt led by Mat Salleh, an impressive man of

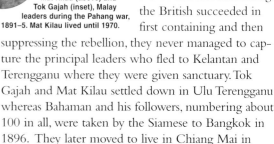

British response to Malay armed resistance

In countering the Malay revolts, the British employed several methods. First, by deploying troops and policemen to deal with the Malay patriots. In Perak, following the murder of J. W. W. Birch, the British deployed a strong force brought in from Penang, Singapore, Hong Kong and India. Second, by surrounding Malay villages and making them restricted areas to deprive the patriots of food and harbourage. This method was effectively used during the Pahang war in 1895. Third, by imposing a naval blockade of Perak and Pahang. Fourth, by razing or burning down the villages of the main leaders of the Malay patriots, as well as other villages whose inhabitants were suspected of being sympathetic to the patriots. This fourth method was used in Perak and Kelantan.

The Malay patriots, on the other hand, in response to the British onslaught, used their usual tactics of refusing a pitched battle, and instead harassed the British columns by ambush, finally cutting the lines of communications. When running short of supplies, the British troops retreated to their main bases and the Malay patriots attacked the retreating column, felling large trees across their path. In some cases, British heavy weaponry had to be spiked and even abandoned.

ABOVE: A contemporaneous etching of the British attack on Kota Lama, Perak, 1876.

LEFT: The British forces ascended the Perak River in praus in order to attack Malay stockades during the Perak war, February 1876.

---

mixed Bajau and Suluk parentage. Although he was eventually killed by the British in 1900, jungle warfare continued for another three years.

The Kelantan revolt, 1915

The next major revolt occurred in Kelantan in 1915 and was led by Haji Mat Hassan Munas, popularly known as Tok Janggut, because he sported a heavy beard (*janggut* is the Malay word for beard). The first outbreak of revolt occurred in the Pasir Puteh District on 29 April 1915, where an anti-land-tax movement developed in opposition to the recently introduced land tax. A police team was sent to arrest Tok Janggut, who knifed one of them to death with his kris while the rest fled. A large crowd then went on to sack the office of the District Officer, symbol of alien rule. The District Officer, Encik Latiff, a Malay from Singapore, had to flee for safety to Kota Bharu. The bungalows and property of European planters were also looted and burned by the crowd.

The Sultan was pressured by the British to declare Tok Janggut a traitor. The British brought in 200 sepoy (Indian) soldiers and some European volunteers belonging to the Malay States Guides from Singapore. Pasir Puteh was recaptured and Tok Janggut killed during the ensuing gun battle. His followers demoralized, the rebellion came to an end. Other leaders fled, particularly to Siam and Terengganu. Engku Besar, the local chief, fled to Siam where he later died. Ibrahim Teleng was executed by the British. Penghulu Deraman, Penghulu Adam and Pak Nik Seman were sentenced to imprisonment.

The Terengganu revolt, 1928

Haji Abdul Rahman, the leader of the Terengganu revolt, who disapproved of the Sultan's acceptance of British control, had been gaining support from the Malay peasants. For more than a year, there had been reports of opposition to British rule in various parts of the state.

Then, in April 1928, Malay patriots, comprising mainly peasants in several areas, were reported to be arming themselves and openly defying the authorities. In Kuala Terengganu, a party of armed police had to open fire on the patriots, who were armed with muzzle-loading shotguns, spears, parangs, and kris, wounding many. One of the 11 killed was their leader, also nicknamed Tok Janggut. Reinforcements arrived from Kuala Lumpur, but the danger was over. They arrested the leaders of the Malay patriots and re-established authority in the interior (*ulu*). Haji Abdul Rahman was sent under escort to Singapore and thence to Mecca, and other leaders were sentenced to varying terms of imprisonment.

Opposition to Sarawak becoming a crown colony, 1949

Malay nationalism in Sarawak was triggered by the decision of the British government to make the state a crown colony on 1 July 1946. Most Malays opposed the move of cession. The climax came on 3 December 1949 when the second Governor of Sarawak, Duncan Stewart, was stabbed to death by a young Malay, Rosly Dhoby, at Sibu (see 'Nationalism in northern Borneo').

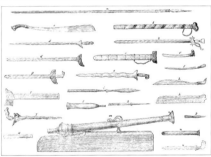

TOP: The body of Haji Mat Hassan Munas, better known as Tok Janggut, martyred in Kampong Dalam Pupoh, Kelantan, 1915.

ABOVE: Weapons used by the Malays, as depicted in the *Illustrated London News*, 26 February 1876.

The northern Borneo states

Resistance in British North Borneo and Sarawak

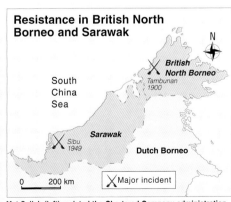

South China Sea

British North Borneo

Tambunan 1900

Sarawak

Sibu 1949

Dutch Borneo

N

0   200 km

✕ Major incident

Mat Salleh (left) resisted the Chartered Company administration in North Borneo. He was captured and killed at Tambunan in 1900. Rosly Dhoby (above right) assassinated Sarawak's British Governor, Duncan Stewart (right), in Sibu in 1949.

Nationalism: The Malay struggle

The Malays became increasingly aware of shortcomings in their socio-economic situation when the British colonial administration introduced education for the Malay community on a significant scale. The Malays' desire to protect their rights and improve their position engendered a new sense of nationalism: they became united as a race rather than as subjects of their respective Sultans. Those engaged in the 'Malay struggle' included groups of religious reformists, conservatives and radicals.

Politically aware Malays protesting against the Malayan Union, 1946.

Colonial government circular dated 16 November 1923 stating that for certain government posts, preference should be given to Malays.

A new awareness

Before World War II, British Malaya was more a geographical than a political entity. For most Malays, society traditionally revolved around the Sultan, the state and, more narrowly, the clan. The idea of a Malayan 'nation' was not common.

Colonial rule altered Malay perceptions. The economy was transformed in the late 19th and the 20th centuries, and there was a huge inflow of Chinese and Indian migrants. Mass education and education abroad were available for the first time. Educated Malays became conscious of the problems affecting their community as a whole. Dissatisfaction and a desire for social change led to the emergence of a sense of nationalism reaching beyond the confines of the state.

The evolution of Malay nationalism

Early Malay nationalism can be seen as the search for the causes of Malay society's economic short-comings and for solutions to overcome them. It took several different forms. Religious reformists saw the problem as the result of deviations from the true teachings of Islam. They advocated the creation of an Islamic kingdom. 'Evolutionary conservatives' were concerned with encroachment by non-Malays and wanted special concessions from the British. They wanted Malay rule, albeit with British values and systems. The 'radicals' considered British colonialism itself as the root of the problem; furthermore, they envisaged the Malay Peninsula as part of a Melayu Raya (Greater Indonesia) (see 'External Opposition to Malaysia').

The nationalist movements faced various challenges. They were out-lawed and some of their leaders were imprisoned. Nevertheless, some of their ideas survived. In particular, the 'conservatives' formed the United Malays National Organisation (UMNO) and went on to wage a successful campaign for Malaya's independence (see 'Merdeka! Attaining Independence'). UMNO continues today in its mission to maintain the Malays' dominant position. Today's Parti Islam Se-Malaysia (PAS) is reminiscent of the 'religious reformists' in wanting to set up its model of an Islamic state. However, there are few traces of the 'radicals' with their ideal of Melayu Raya.

Education as a catalyst for change

Under the British colonial government there arose a need for trained people of local origin to work in the administration of the states. The authorities showed a preference for Malays. Mass education was introduced to fulfil this need. As a result of education, the level of political awareness among the Malays rose. In the event, the specific form taken by their approach to nationalism was greatly influenced by their place of education.

ABOVE: Sultan Idris Training College in the late 1920s.

BELOW: Sultan Ibrahim of Johor at the wheel of a car while studying in England, early 1900s.

BELOW RIGHT: Tunku Abdul Rahman Putra (left) studied in Britain from 1922–31.

Middle Eastern universities
Events in the Middle East towards the end of the 19th century greatly influenced the 'religious reformists'. Religious scholar Sheikh Muhammad Abduh led an Islamic reform or *islah* movement that impacted the entire Muslim world. The movement inspired Malay scholars who studied in the Middle East, notably in Cairo's Al-Azhar University, and returned home to promote reform. Al-Azhar University, which admits only Muslim students, was originally built in 972 CE as a mosque. It expanded over time into a university for religion, Arabic and the metaphysical sciences.

Sultan Idris Training College
This college was established by the colonial administration in 1922 in Tanjung Malim, Perak, for the training of teachers. It proved fertile ground for the seeds of radical nationalism. Grassroots leaders campaigned among 'low class subjects' and the Malay-educated, especially schoolteachers and journalists. They were strongly anti-colonial and in favour of purging Malaya of British influence. They also saw themselves as part of a greater Malay nation and sought unity with Indonesia.

British universities
Many aristocratic Malays were groomed by the British for the Malayan Civil Service and sent to study in Britain. They considered themselves part of the establishment and argued for reforms from within the system. They were characterized by loyalty to their respective sultans and to the British Crown. The colonial administration maintained a friendly attitude toward them.

Malay nationalism: the forces working for change

Evolutionary conservatives

Kesatuan Melayu Singapura (KMS), or Singapore Malay Union, was formed in 1926. It encouraged Malays to advance themselves politically, socially, educationally and economically.

The primary concern of the KMS was the large presence of Chinese and Indian migrant workers. The KMS regarded these groups as transient labourers who should return to their own countries at an appropriate time.

The KMS wanted Malays to be given priority for openings in education and jobs in the civil service. It also argued that land should be reserved specially for Malays and safeguards put in place against encroachments by the Chinese and Indians. The party inspired the formation of similar organizations in Pahang, Selangor and Negeri Sembilan.

The first congress of 'conservative' Johor Malay organizations held in early 1946.

Reformists and the Malay press

Syed Sheikh Al-Hadi co-founded the journal Al-Imam.

Sheikh Tahir Jalaluddin graduated from Cairo's Al-Azhar University.

Malay scholars, such as Sheikh Tahir Jalaluddin, who returned from studies in the Middle East in the first quarter of the 20th century, perceived Malay society to be backward, mired in superstitions and animistic beliefs. They urged Malays to embrace the true principles of Islam.

Publications such as *Al-Imam* (The Leader), *Warta Negara* (National News) and *Saudara* (Comrade) advocated modern education, rationalism and adaptation of Western technology. They championed women's rights to education and participation in social affairs, and the equality of all men before God, and argued that these were compatible with the teachings of Islam. They also criticized the aristocratic 'establishment' or *Kaum Tua* (Old Faction) for self-indulgence and for not leading Malay society forward.

Since members of this *Kaum Muda* (Youth Faction) attacked the religious authorities, they were given neither positions in the religious establishment, nor facilities to preach their message. In some states, their publications were banned. As a result of these curbs on their activities, the reformists set up religious schools in the Straits Settlements.

The radicals

Radical movements such as the Kesatuan Melayu Muda (KMM, or Young Malay Union) opposed colonialism and considered the Sultans, Malay aristocrats and British-educated Malays in general as allies of the British who compromised their positions in exchange for pensions and positions in the bureaucracy. Inspired by Indonesia's nationalists, they sought merger with Indonesia.

Dr Burhanuddin Al-Helmi, born in 1911.

KMM radical, Dato' Ishak Haji Muhammad, known as Pak Sako. 'Sako' was how the Japanese pronounced his name, Ishak, during the Occupation.

Among the outspoken radicals of the KMM were Ibrahim Yaakob, Tan Melaka, Dato' Ishak Haji Muhammad (Pak Sako), Ahmad Boestamam and Dr Burhanuddin Al-Helmi. The authorities viewed the KMM with great suspicion, and in 1940–1, 150 of its members were arrested and imprisoned.

Ibrahim Yaakob was one of the KMM members arrested by the British authorities in 1941.

The Japanese Occupation shattered the illusion of British invincibility and boosted the nationalists' confidence. Several KMM leaders founded Kesatuan Rakyat Indonesia Semenanjung (KRIS), or the Peninsular Indonesian People's Union, with the intention of declaring Malayan independence as part of an independent Indonesia. However, Japan's unexpected surrender thwarted the plan, and Indonesia declared its independence without Malaya.

The radical leaders nevertheless continued to champion Malaya's independence, first through UMNO and later by forming Pusat Tenaga Rakyat (PUTERA). However, PUTERA failed to gain support as it was perceived to be communist-influenced and pro-Indonesia.

Za'ba

Zainal Abidin Ahmad, better known as Za'ba, began his career as a teacher at the English College in Johor Bahru before transferring to the prestigious Malay College in Kuala Kangsar, Perak.

An articulate writer, from 1916 onwards he wrote hundreds of articles in both the Malay and English press highlighting the Malay situation and the plight of colonized Muslims throughout the world. His famous articles 'The Poverty of the Malays' and 'The Salvation of the Malays', which appeared in *The Malay Mail* in November 1923, caused him to be transferred almost immediately to Sultan Idris Training College (SITC) in Tanjung Malim, Perak. This was the climax of earlier disciplinary action whereby he was denied any increase to his salary for five years from 1918.

Za'ba (1895–1973)

He was closely involved in the *Kaum Muda* (Youth Faction) and organized several related associations. Notably, while at the Malay College he arranged a meeting of over 100 English-educated *Kaum Muda* members to organize a lecture tour of the Malay states by Khwaja Kamaluddin, proprietor of *The Islamic Review*, who was based in England.

At SITC, Za'ba continued his struggle by focusing on the development of the Malay language, closely watched by his superiors and the Special Branch. After World War II he was made Chairman of the Organizing Committee of the Malay Congress which established UMNO. A founder member of UMNO, he later resigned to focus on his academic work.

Women nationalists

A number of women broke traditional norms to protest against the Malayan Union, led by a few prominent individuals from Perak, Johor and Negeri Sembilan. When UMNO was formed in 1946, women leaders joined their respective state associations to formulate the UMNO Charter. They later became the core of UMNO's Women's Movement. Female nationalists rallied crucial voter support for the Alliance in the 1955 elections and for the independence movement. Fatimah Hashim (now Tun) and Aishah Ghani (now Tan Sri) later served as Ministers in government. Among the most prominent women nationalists were Datin Puteh Mariah Ibrahim Rashid, the first Chief of UMNO's Women's Movement, and Dato' Halimahton Abdul Majid, who rallied anti-Malayan Union protests.

ABOVE: Datin Puteh Mariah Ibrahim Rashid, UMNO Women's Chief from 1946–50.

LEFT: Protest against the proposed Malayan Union in 1946.

Nationalism: Non-Malays in the Peninsula

The non-Malays in the Peninsula approached nationalism in different ways. Many Chinese and Indian migrant workers were transient; after a time they returned to their respective homelands. Even those who did settle in the Peninsula often maintained certain loyalties to their homeland. It was only after World War II that the majority of these ethnic groups developed a greater sense of belonging to the Peninsula.

Peranakan (Straits Chinese) wedding party, 1929. The Peranakans are descendants of Chinese traders who arrived in the Malay Peninsula before the 18th century.

A multi-ethnic mix

The diverse, multi-ethnic nature of Malaysia makes an account of non-Malay nationalism rather complex. Historically, members of each community identified principally with their own ethnic group in almost all aspects of social and economic life. The various ethnic communities have responded in different ways to political, economic and social changes within and outside the country.

As in most plural environments, the less developed communities often felt disadvantaged, and their struggle for advancement was often expressed in ethnic terms. Communalism, not ideology, was the main political force in this multi-ethnic society.

Attitudes of a migrant population

The Chinese and Indian communities who migrated to Malaya in the late 19th and early 20th century were different from earlier settlers such as the Peranakan (Straits Chinese) or Chitty Indians who were generally assimilated into the local culture. They came in large enough numbers to form their own distinct communities and retained their own culture. As a consequence, the focus of their loyalties and sense of national identity tended to remain with their respective homelands. However, their descendants began to consider the Peninsula as their home and developed a different sense of identity.

Political awakening

After World War II, the tide of global opinion ran against colonialism. A sense of political awareness began to form in the Malay Peninsula, and political parties were formed. The creation of the United Malays National Organisation (UMNO) in protest against the Malayan Union (see 'The Malayan Union') prompted non-Malays to organize themselves and seek political representation. The parties that resulted favoured equal rights for all races, and opposed the administrative practice of categorizing people as Malay and non-Malay, so as to legitimize their members' entitlement to stay in their new homeland.

Outpost nationalism

In the 19th and early 20th centuries, large numbers of Chinese arrived in the Malay Peninsula, having left their homelands in the Fujian and Guangdong provinces in hope of better economic prospects, and to avoid political instability and natural disasters.

Indians were also recruited to work in Malaya, as a result of the labour policy of the colonial administration which was assisted by factors such as food and work shortages, drought, land taxes and discrimination associated with the caste system. Most Indian labourers came from Tamil Nadu and Andhra Pradesh in south India, while English-educated Malayalees (from Kerala in south India) and Ceylonese (from what is now Sri Lanka) were hired as clerks, hospital assistants, railway stationmasters, and labour overseers.

Most of these migrant workers looked upon the Malay Peninsula as a temporary workplace; their long-term ambition was to save enough money to return home. Loyalties therefore remained strongly directed towards their countries of origin; attitudes to nationalism among many non-Malays tended to reflect that of nationalist movements in the countries they originated from.

Among the Chinese, there was excitement when Chinese nationalists overthrew the Manchurian, or Qing, dynasty in 1911; indeed, many Chinese in Malaya were active members of the Kuomintang, a coalition of anti-Manchu secret society factions formed in China, which existed as a legal registered society in the Peninsula until 1925. When Japan invaded Manchuria in September 1931 and later went to

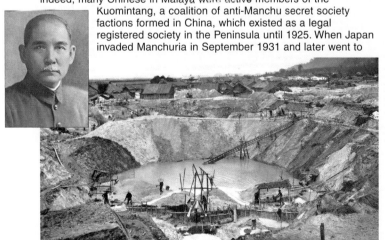

Future Indian Prime Minister Jawaharlal Nehru during his visit to Kuala Lumpur in 1946.

war with China in 1937, there was an outpouring of anger—Japanese goods were boycotted, anti-Japanese demonstrations held and money collected for the China Relief Fund.

Indians in Malaya identified with the Independence movement in India. The Indian Independence League recruited members and organized activities in Malaya. Indian nationalist Subhas Chandra Bose set up the Indian National Army in the Peninsula during World War II to recruit Indians, training them to fight the British for India's independence. These organizations created a strong feeling of Indian nationalism that transcended religion and class. Even after the war, Indian political leaders maintained close links with India's Congress Party and attended its annual meetings.

Left: Tin mine operated by Chinese labourers in Kampar, Perak, 1906.

Left inset: Kuomintang leader Sun Yat Sen visited the Malay Peninsula in 1900 to get support for the revolutionary cause, and revisited seven times between 1905 and 1911.

Right: Indian women grading sheets of rubber. Many Indians worked in the rubber industry.

Many of these parties, such as the All Malaya Council of Joint Action (AMCJA), were considered left-wing organizations because of their radical views and methods. They were willing to call for strikes and street protests to apply pressure on the colonial authorities. The employment of these tactics caused concern among the Malays, who were doubtful of the non-Malays' intentions.

Pre-war social and political organizations

In addition to the so-called secret societies, the Kuomintang and the Malayan Communist Party, several other influential organizations were established by the Malayan Chinese prior to World War II. Among these were the Chinese Chambers of Commerce. In February 1947, the Associated Chinese Chambers of Commerce was formed.

Colonel Lee Hau Sik, head of the Associated Chinese Chambers of Commerce, 1947.

The Peranakan community established politically inclined organizations such as the Straits Chinese British Association (SCBA) in Singapore and in Melaka in 1900, and in 1920 in Penang. The main activity of the SCBA was to promote the interest of those Chinese who were British citizens. After the war, its political influence declined due to its close association with the waning colonial era.

S. N. Veerasamy, who organized the CIAM, was a member of the Federal Council of the Federated Malay States.

Local Indian activism started in the early 20th century with the formation of associations such as the Taiping Indian Association and the Selangor Indian Association, which focused in particular on the concerns of plantation workers. Early local Indian political organizations included the Gadr Party, which focused on the northern Indian community, particularly those working in the police force and the sepoys. The Central Indian Association of Malaya (CIAM), organized in 1936 by S. N. Veerasamy, initially promoted the interests of the Indian community by forwarding demands to the British for better public sector employment opportunities and wider participation in policy-making bodies. It also strove to unite the Indians in the Peninsula and to forge closer ties with the nationalist movement in India.

From 1946–7, the Malayan Democratic Union emerged as the leading representative of non-Malay nationalism. However, it disbanded in 1948.

The early Chinese press

Chinese newspapers such as *Thien Nan Shih Pao* and *Kong See Boo Poe* were established as early as the late 19th century. Among the proprietors of these publications was English-educated Dr Lim Boon Keng, who was attracted to the reformist ideas that emerged from China. He published the bilingual newspaper *The Straits Chinese Herald* to disseminate reformist ideas among the Peranakan (Straits Chinese) in the Straits Settlements. With the same objective he also revived publication of the *Sing Po* newspaper which changed its name to *Ju Shin Pau* in 1899.

Newspaper proprietor Dr Lim Boon Keng was a prominent social activist, and co-founded the Straits Chinese British Association.

An 1897 edition of Kong See Boo Poe, printed in Kuala Lumpur.

The relatively small Peranakan community were more attracted to locally moulded and Malaya-oriented politics, and published several newspapers in the Baba Malay creole. These included *Bintang Timor* (1884–5), *Kabar Selalu* (1925), *Kabar Uchapan Baru* (1926–31), *Bintang Peranakan* (1930–1) and *Sri Peranakan* (1932).

The All Malaya Council of Joint Action and beyond

Tan Cheng Lock and the formation of the AMCJA

Wealthy Peranakan Chinese businessman Tan Cheng Lock was an influential champion of Malayan nationalism among the Chinese. While in India during World War II, he formed the Overseas Chinese Association of India. In a memorandum to the Colonial Office, he asked for citizenship to be automatically granted to those born in the Malay Peninsula (based on the principle of *jus soli,* under which a person's citizenship is determined by the place of his birth) and less strict citizenship requirements for those not born in the Peninsula. These proposals were incorporated into the Malayan Union.

Tan Cheng Lock (5 April 1883–13 December 1960).

In response to the Malays' protest against the terms of the Malayan Union, Tan formed the All Malaya Council of Joint Action (AMCJA) with other non-Malay parties such as the Malayan Democratic Union (MDU), Malayan Indian Congress (MIC), the Pan-Malayan Federation of Trade Unions (PMFTU) and the Malayan People's Anti-Japanese Army Ex-comrades Association.

The PUTERA–AMCJA alliance

Eurasian Gerald de Cruz served as Secretary of the AMCJA.

In March 1947 the AMCJA joined forces with the Malay-based Pusat Tenaga Rakyat (PUTERA) which comprised Parti Kebangsaan Melayu Malaya (PKMM) and its youth and women's wings. PUTERA was formed by Dr Burhanuddin Al-Helmi who disagreed with UMNO's views and left the umbrella organization (see 'Nationalism: The Malay struggle'). Dr Burhanuddin became PUTERA–AMCJA President with Tan Cheng Lock as Deputy President.

The PUTERA–AMCJA coalition presented a counter-proposal for a new constitution but it was rejected by the British government. In 1948, the PMFTU staged a strike involving 260,000 people and was promptly outlawed by the British. Many of its members were arrested. Those who escaped reportedly joined the Malayan Communist Party in its armed struggle (see 'The Emergency'). This tarnished PUTERA–AMCJA's image and the coalition collapsed: the MDU dissolved itself voluntarily and the PKMM pulled out of the coalition when the local media accused it of being a communist tool.

After the AMCJA

Tan Cheng Lock went on to set up the Malayan Chinese Association (MCA) in 1949 as a political alternative to the communists, with Tun Leong Yew Koh and Colonel H. S. Lee. The British administration encouraged the MCA's leaders to play an active political role in an attempt to offer a moderate alternative to the Malayan Communist Party (MCP). The MCA was a key player in the relocation of Chinese settlers into 'New Villages'; it helped in the process and raised funds for additional aid to the villagers (see 'The Emergency resolved').

Some members of both the MCA, such as Tan Cheng Lock and his son Tan Siew Sin, and of the MIC, collaborated with Onn Jaafar's Independence of Malaya Party (IMP) as its non-communal stance was compatible with their agenda of securing non-Malay rights in a post-independence Malaya. However, the relationship was unstable, as Onn was against granting citizenship on the principle of *jus soli.*

Both the MCA and the MIC eventually collaborated with UMNO to form the Alliance, a key factor in winning Independence (see 'Merdeka! Attaining Independence'). They remain major components of the Barisan Nasional coalition that followed the Alliance.

An UMNO–MCA parade in support of having a majority of elected representatives in the first Federal Legislative Council election, 1954.

Nationalism in northern Borneo

In the Malay Peninsula, nationalism gained strength following the end of World War II. In northern Borneo, on the other hand, nationalistic feelings were stimulated only when the proposal for the formation of Malaysia was aired in 1961.

The *North Borneo News and Sabah Times*, dated 29 June 1962, reports on the response to the Cobbold Commission, appointed to ascertain the views of the people of Sarawak and North Borneo on the formation of Malaysia.

Crest of the Colony of North Borneo.

North Borneo: Chartered company to crown colony

In 1878, the Sultan of Sulu ceded parts of North Borneo (now Sabah) to a British syndicate formed by Alfred Dent. The British North Borneo Company was formed to take over the concession and received a charter from Queen Victoria in 1881. The British North Borneo Chartered Company's (BNBCC) administration was generally peaceful. Several warriors such as Mat Salleh, Mat Sator, Syerif Osman, Antenom, Si Gunting and Pak Musa, however, led uprisings in the late 19th and early 20th centuries which were suppressed by the authorities. That was the extent of nationalism until World War II.

A sense of state identity was engendered as the people of North Borneo mounted a dramatic but tragically doomed resistance against the Japanese (see 'The Japanese Occupation of northern Borneo'). During the war, serious infrastructural damage was inflicted on the state, and when the war ended, restoration was clearly beyond the BNBCC's resources. The territory was turned over to the British Crown in 1946.

Sir Malcolm MacDonald reading the Proclamation in Council which declared North Borneo a British crown colony, July 1946.

The Sarawak position

Sarawak was ruled by the Brooke dynasty for a century, from 1841 to 1941. The first White Rajah

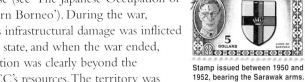

Stamp issued between 1950 and 1952, bearing the Sarawak arms.

(king), English adventurer James Brooke, was followed by Charles and finally Vyner Brooke, who between them extended their territorial control to cover present-day Sarawak. At the end of World War II, Vyner Brooke returned temporarily to rule Sarawak, but again, the cost of post-war reconstruction was beyond his resources. Sarawak was then ceded to the British government in 1946.

The transfer of Sarawak from the Brookes to the British government was not entirely smooth. A spirit of nationalism manifested itself in the form of the anti-cession movement. The anti-cessionists demanded instead the full independence of Sarawak.

The issue gave rise to the formation of two associations, the Malays National Union of Sarawak (MNUS) and the Dayak Association of Sarawak (DAS). At the height of the anti-cession movement, the second governor, Duncan Stewart, was killed in Sibu (see 'Precursors to nationalism: The armed resistance). However, the movement was soon effectively quelled.

Some members of the Chinese community, on the other hand, sided with the British. They hoped that a change in status would provide a more

The cession of Sarawak

RIGHT: Vyner Brooke signs the Instrument of Cession at Kuching, May 1946. Seated to his left is C. W. Dawson, the British Representative.

BELOW: Anti-cession protesters greet Rajah Vyner Brooke on his visit to a Malay kampong in Kuching, 1946.

The assassination of Duncan Stewart

The second governor of Sarawak, Duncan Stewart, was stabbed by a young Malay student teacher named Rosly Dhoby in Sibu in 1949. He died one week later in Singapore. Rosly and three accomplices were subsequently convicted and sentenced to death. The anti-cessionists abandoned their campaign soon after.

ABOVE RIGHT: Rosly Dhoby under arrest in Sibu, December 1949.

RIGHT: Painting of the assassination.

conducive business environment. The working-class Chinese were generally inclined to a leftist ideology and were in any case at the time more concerned with events in mainland China.

Attitudes to colonial rule

Other than the Sarawak anti-cession movement, there was little by way of active nationalist movements in North Borneo and Sarawak under early British rule. Ironically, after the end of World War II, efforts were initiated by the British colonial authorities themselves to speed up the move towards self-government.

In North Borneo, the authorities introduced an expansion of local governance in 1950, when an Executive and a Legislative Council were established. Later, District Councils and local authorities were established to give greater participation in governance to the local people.

In Sarawak, the constitution of 1941 that was introduced by Vyner Brooke (but which had hardly come into effect when the Japanese attacked) was re-enacted. By this constitution, a legislative body, the Council Negeri (State Council), and an executive body, the Supreme Council, were introduced.

Notably, the native population groups of both states had been left largely out of education during most of the Chartered Company's and the Brookes' rule. Few people could fully grasp the change in the status of these territories from being protectorates to entities directly governed by the British.

A catalyst for political awareness

The announcement of a plan to form Malaysia (see 'The formation of Malaysia') composed of the Federation of Malaya, Singapore, North Borneo, Sarawak and Brunei provided a catalyst, stimulated political consciousness, and increased political activities in North Borneo and Sarawak.

Many political parties began to emerge, to represent dissent from the proposal (see 'Barisan component parties'). The people were equally divided between those who supported, objected to, and were indifferent (as a result of limited access to the media) to the proposal. Besides, the campaign to promote the formation of Malaysia was mostly confined to urban areas. Nevertheless, the proposal to form Malaysia put the people of the two states at a crossroads; it forced them to take a position that was to affect their political future.

Sabah and Sarawak political leaders Datu Mustapha Harun, Donald Stephens and Stephen Kalong Ningkan, 1964.

Political parties in Sarawak

Datu Bujang bin Tunku Othman, first President of the BARJASA party, 1962.

Various political parties emerged in Sarawak shortly after the Malaysia proposal was made in May 1961 (see 'The idea of Malaysia'). They included PANAS (Parti Negara Sarawak) and BARJASA (Barisan Rakyat Jati Sarawak) among the Malay and Melanau communities. The existence of these two parties reflected the cleavage in Malay-Melanau society between the traditional leaders who founded PANAS and the educated leaders in BARJASA. The former were closely associated with government, both that of the Brookes and later the colonial administration. Similar divisions existed in the Iban community, which was also courted by two political parties with differing backgrounds: PESAKA (Parti Pesaka Anak Sarawak) led by the traditional community leaders, and SNAP (Sarawak National Party) led by the educated leaders. In time, however, these native political parties supported the concept of Malaysia.

The politically active Chinese were mostly against the formation of Malaysia. The leading Chinese-based political party, SUPP (Sarawak United People's Party), led the opposition to the proposal, arguing that Sarawak should be independent first before deciding to join the federation. In fact, some SUPP leaders were committed leftists and saw the Malaysia proposal as an imperialist plot hatched in London.

SNAP Secretary-General Stephen Kalong Ningkan (right) speaking at the first open rally of the Sarawak Alliance, held in support of independence through Malaysia, December 1962.

Political parties in Sabah

Chief Minister-designate Fuad Stephens (centre) bids farewell to the last British Governor of North Borneo, Sir William Goode, 15 September 1963.

In Sabah, the formation of political parties was, as in Sarawak, part of the response to the May 1961 Malaysia proposal. The first party, the United National Kadazan Organization (UNKO), was formed in August 1961, led by Donald Stephens. USNO (United Sabah National Organization) was formed in December 1961 by Datu Mustapha Harun; its members were mainly indigenous Muslims. UPMO (United Pasok Momogun Organisation) was formed by Orang Kaya-kaya Datuk G. S. Sundang, former Vice-President of UNKO, in January 1962. The Chinese community was divided between two parties, the Democratic Party led by Peter Chin and the United Party led by Khoo Siak Chiew. These two parties merged in October 1962 to form the Borneo Utara (North Borneo) National Party (BUNAP). When North Borneo became Sabah with the formation of Malaysia, BUNAP was renamed SANAP, which eventually became the Sabah Chinese Association (SCA) in 1965.

All these parties helped to unite Sabahans in their expression of support for Malaysia. For the 1962 local government elections, they came together under the coalition banner, the Sabah Alliance (see 'The Barisan Nasional framework'), led jointly by leading political figures Donald Stephens and Datu Mustapha Harun.

The people of Sabah supported the formation of Malaysia, as evidenced by this rally in September 1968.

The Japanese invasion

As World War II was being waged in Europe, Japan joined the German-Italian Axis alliance in September 1940. The Japanese made a surprise invasion of the Malay Peninsula and northern Borneo in December 1941. Both territories were quickly overrun, and the British defence forces suffered a humiliating defeat.

28 January 1942: Japanese troops cycle past the Federal Secretariat Building in Kuala Lumpur.

Lieutenant Adnan Saidi led a group of Malay Regiment soldiers who defended their post to the last man in Pasir Panjang, Singapore, shortly before the British surrender.

Japanese preparations

The Japanese sought to conquer northern Borneo to control its strategically important oil resources. Serious preparation by the Japanese for the invasion of the Malay Peninsula had begun in January 1941, which was carried out in Formosa (now Taiwan). Rehearsals were held on the island of Hainan which the Japanese had annexed in 1939.

Japan's imperial ambitions

Japan planned to build an Asian empire to gain access to resources it lacked, such as oil, tin and rubber. Concerned over Japan's ambitions, Britain, the United States and Holland froze Japanese assets.

In 1940–1, the United States (US) banned the export of strategic minerals and equipment, oil, steel and scrap iron to Japan, and demanded the withdrawal of Japanese forces from French Indochina and northern China. Japan had to either abandon its dreams of an empire, or make itself more self-sufficient by seizing new territories.

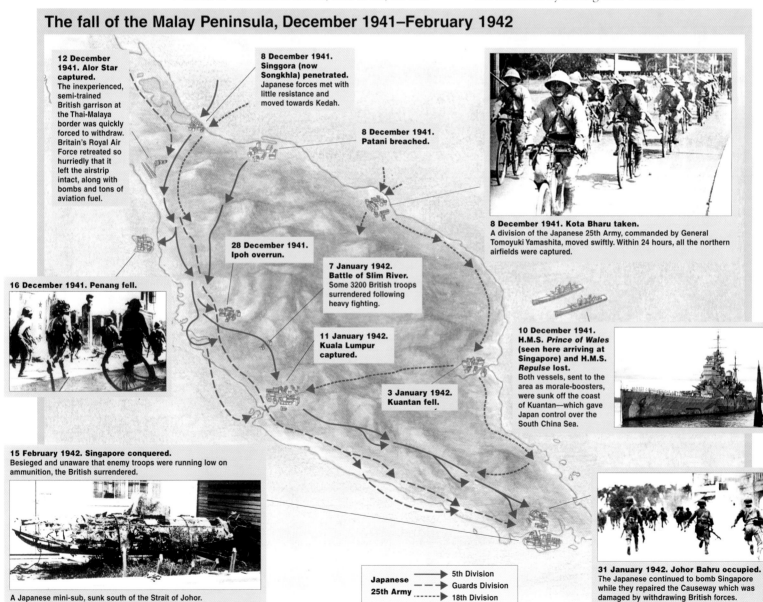

The fall of the Malay Peninsula, December 1941–February 1942

12 December 1941. Alor Star captured.
The inexperienced, semi-trained British garrison at the Thai-Malaya border was quickly forced to withdraw. Britain's Royal Air Force retreated so hurriedly that it left the airstrip intact, along with bombs and tons of aviation fuel.

8 December 1941. Singgora (now Songkhla) penetrated.
Japanese forces met with little resistance and moved towards Kedah.

8 December 1941. Patani breached.

8 December 1941. Kota Bharu taken.
A division of the Japanese 25th Army, commanded by General Tomoyuki Yamashita, moved swiftly. Within 24 hours, all the northern airfields were captured.

28 December 1941. Ipoh overrun.

16 December 1941. Penang fell.

7 January 1942. Battle of Slim River.
Some 3200 British troops surrendered following heavy fighting.

11 January 1942. Kuala Lumpur captured.

10 December 1941. H.M.S. *Prince of Wales* (seen here arriving at Singapore) and H.M.S. *Repulse* lost.
Both vessels, sent to the area as morale-boosters, were sunk off the coast of Kuantan—which gave Japan control over the South China Sea.

3 January 1942. Kuantan fell.

15 February 1942. Singapore conquered.
Besieged and unaware that enemy troops were running low on ammunition, the British surrendered.

A Japanese mini-sub, sunk south of the Strait of Johor.

31 January 1942. Johor Bahru occupied.
The Japanese continued to bomb Singapore while they repaired the Causeway which was damaged by withdrawing British forces.

Japanese 25th Army
→ 5th Division
→ Guards Division
→ 18th Division

Since British and Dutch forces were engaged in Europe, and US forces were not mobilized, Japan opted for a military campaign. On 8 December 1941, Japan declared war on Britain, the US and Holland. Earlier that day Japanese forces invaded the Malay Peninsula and launched a surprise attack on the US Pacific Fleet anchored at Pearl Harbor.

The invasion

War came to Malaya in the afternoon of 8 December 1941, some two and a half hours before the attack on Pearl Harbor, when Japanese forces landed at Pantai Sabak (Sabak Beach) near Kota Bharu in the state of Kelantan in the north of the Peninsula. Another beachhead was opened in southern Thailand, and the Japanese army moved swiftly down and across the Peninsula. British morale crumbled two days later when Japanese aircraft sank their two largest warships, H.M.S. *Repulse* and H.M.S. *Prince of Wales*.

It took 68 days for the Japanese, with a force of some 70,000, to capture the Malay Peninsula and

The *Straits Times* of 8 December 1941 (left) reporting the beginning of the invasion, and the last issue of the *Straits Times* until after the war (below), dated 15 February 1942.

Singapore. This was one of the most decisive victories of World War II. Northern Borneo fell shortly after the Peninsula. The Japanese met little resistance, and Sarawak and British North Borneo fell by the end of January 1942.

The island of Singapore had been commonly assumed to be well-defended. The British military authorities had erroneously concluded that the Malay Peninsula, being covered with jungle and rubber estates, would thwart the advance of the Japanese army.

The invasion of northern Borneo, December 1941–January 1942

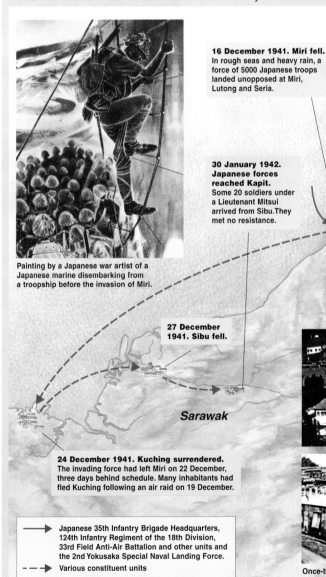

Painting by a Japanese war artist of a Japanese marine disembarking from a troopship before the invasion of Miri.

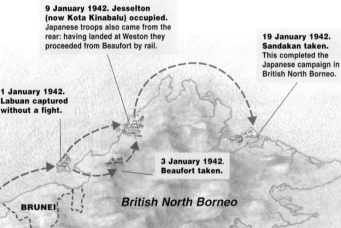

16 December 1941. Miri fell.
In rough seas and heavy rain, a force of 5000 Japanese troops landed unopposed at Miri, Lutong and Seria.

9 January 1942. Jesselton (now Kota Kinabalu) occupied.
Japanese troops also came from the rear: having landed at Weston they proceeded from Beaufort by rail.

19 January 1942. Sandakan taken.
This completed the Japanese campaign in British North Borneo.

1 January 1942. Labuan captured without a fight.

30 January 1942. Japanese forces reached Kapit.
Some 20 soldiers under a Lieutenant Mitsui arrived from Sibu. They met no resistance.

3 January 1942. Beaufort taken.

BRUNEI

British North Borneo

27 December 1941. Sibu fell.

Sarawak

24 December 1941. Kuching surrendered.
The invading force had left Miri on 22 December, three days behind schedule. Many inhabitants had fled Kuching following an air raid on 19 December.

→ Japanese 35th Infantry Brigade Headquarters, 124th Infantry Regiment of the 18th Division, 33rd Field Anti-Air Battalion and other units and the 2nd Yokusaka Special Naval Landing Force.

-→ Various constituent units

Once-thriving Sandakan before (top), and after (above) the war.

The Japanese Occupation of the Malay Peninsula

The Japanese moved swiftly and harshly to re-establish law and order in the Malay Peninsula. The pre-existing British administrative machinery was kept largely intact, while the Malay Rulers retained a reduced role. Life was extremely difficult; the population faced a daily struggle for survival. Racial tensions were created by Japanese policies.

Japanese Governor Marquis Tokugawa Yoshichika inspecting an army honour guard at the Istana (Palace), Klang, 1942.

The Malay Peninsula under the Japanese

Perlis and Kedah · THAILAND · Kelántan · Penang · Terengganu · South China Sea · Perak · Pahang · Selangor · Negeri Sembilan and Melaka · Strait of Melaka · Johor · Syonan (SINGAPORE)

0   100 km

Ceded by Japan to Thailand, August 1943–August 1945.

Japanese control

The Japanese took immediate steps to impose law and order; in some locations by means of terror and cruelty, and practices such as the decapitation of criminals. The Japanese conscripted young men, mostly Malays, into police and volunteer forces to assist the Japanese army. They also organized neighbourhood associations to control crime and maintain security. A new administrative system for the Peninsula was introduced, although for practical purposes many of the colonial administrative institutions established by the British were retained.

Generally, the Japanese were hostile to all pro-British individuals or groups. Anyone suspected of British sympathies was rounded up, then imprisoned, interrogated and sometimes summarily executed. Torture was often used; most notorious was the 'water torture' where water would be pumped through a victim's mouth until his stomach was bloated: then the interrogator would step on his abdomen, often causing extensive, and fatal, internal organ damage.

Racial polarization

Although this was not the deliberate aim, Japanese policies created animosity between the Malays and

As Japanese armies moved south through the Peninsula, they created Peace Preservation Committees to handle food control, sanitation and public services. Following the British surrender, the Peninsula and Sumatra became a 'Special Defence Area', an 'integral territory' of Japan that did not fall under the Greater East Asia Ministry.

A Department of Military Administration under Japan's 25th Army handled administrative affairs until April 1943, when the Southern Army moved its headquarters to Singapore and took charge of the Peninsula.

Chinese. The Chinese were heavily discriminated against, while Malays dominated the bureaucracy and served in the defence forces that attacked the Chinese-dominated resistance movement. Inter-ethnic clashes between pro-Japanese volunteer forces and resistance guerrillas were inevitable. As a result, many Chinese considered Malays to be instruments of the Japanese occupiers.

The Japanese use of violence created a climate of brutality among civilians and also in the resistance movement, which was to be expressed in reprisals after the war ended.

In the Peninsula as elsewhere, the Japanese Occupation, initially touted by some as the agent of liberation in European-colonized Asia, left a legacy more negative than positive.

Attitudes toward the invaders

Malay members of Force 136 unit with Lieutenant Colonel P. J. G. Dobree (standing, eighth from the left).

The Indian dimension

Japan used Indian nationalism as a weapon against the British. In July 1943, Subhas Chandra Bose, former Indian National Congress president, fled India to avoid prosecution for his militant views and arrived in Malaya. He set up the Provisional Government of Azad Hind (Free India). The military campaign by Bose's 'Indian National Army' and

Japanese forces in Imphal, northeast India, was defeated by Allied forces.

Indian sentiments toward the Japanese later changed, as food became scarce and Indian labourers were forced to work in inhuman conditions on the infamous Thailand-Burma railway, which came to be known as the 'Death Railway'.

The Malays

The Japanese initially adopted a friendly, 'pro-Malay' policy. As a result, the Malay response to the occupation was largely passive. However, to prevent any premature stirrings of Malay nationalism, the invaders changed their tactics, and even banned the pro-Japanese Kesatuan Melayu Muda (Young Malay Union),

which had considered merger with Indonesia (see 'Nationalism: The Malay Struggle).

Malay resentment was further provoked in 1943 when the Japanese ceded Kedah, Perlis, Kelantan and Terengganu to Thailand in recognition of that country's cooperation during the invasion.

Resisting the Japanese

At the outbreak of war, the British recruited Chinese volunteers for operations behind enemy lines. Units of the Malayan People's Anti-Japanese Army (MPAJA) were formed when communists and pro-Kuomintang (Nationalist Party of China) organizations offered their cooperation. The Malays, through the Royal Malay Regiment, took part in the British-led resistance to the invasion. Plans for guerrilla resistance came to fruition in 1944 with the formation of Force 136 in Perak, Kedah, Pahang and Kelantan. The MPAJA then came under the authority of Force 136. However, the Malay resistance forces never saw military action, as Japan surrendered in August 1945.

In January 1944 administrative responsibility passed to a new 29th Army, which was placed under a new 7th Area Army three months later.

Civil administration remained in the hands of the pre-war bureaucracy throughout the occupation, with Japanese officials filling senior positions. The Japanese authorities told administrators to respect the 'customs, habits, and religions' of the inhabitants, allow free enterprise, popularize *Nippon-go* (Japanese language), and arrange for local political participation. At the same time, they subjected people they considered hostile to considerable brutality.

The Japanese divided the Malay Peninsula into 10 provinces, which coincided for the most part with the pre-war states and settlements; each province had a Japanese Governor. Singapore became the Syonan Special Municipality under a Japanese mayor. Provinces had considerable autonomy, and laws or regulations varied from place to place. In March 1942 civilians were appointed as governors of the provincial administrations. The Marquis Tokugawa Yoshichika became Civil Governor of Malaya, but the Malayan Military Administration remained in overall charge. The central military administration began operations with four bureaus, and by the end of the 1942 had 11 bureaus overseeing 25 departments. The most notable was the General Affairs Bureau,

which carried out coordinating functions and handled local administration and finance. The Japanese appointed local men to senior positions in departments where they had previously served, but they retained the top posts. The number of Japanese available to staff the administration was insufficient, and many of the men sent to Malaya knew nothing of local languages and customs. Advisory Councils created in the latter part of 1943 gave an illusion of popular participation but had no power to pass legislation or formulate policy.

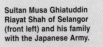

The Japanese administration respected Islamic practices and gave time off for Friday prayers.

The Malay Sultans

The Japanese initially planned to strip the Sultans of their political authority, but later decided to use them to promote reconstruction and build support. In 1943, the Sultans were made official advisors to their respective governors.

Sultan Musa Ghiatuddin Riayat Shah of Selangor (front left) and his family with the Japanese Army.

Life under Japanese rule

The Peninsula's economy suffered severely after the invasion because retreating British forces had destroyed roads, bridges and factories. The rubber and tin industries ground to a halt when their principal export markets were cut off. Essential supplies grew scarce and inflation soared.

The Japanese administration resorted to the rampant over-issue of currency notes which had very little value and bore no serial number. No one, not even the Japanese, knew how much currency was issued. This led to further inflation.

The people had to cultivate their own foodstuff for survival. Rationing and other restrictions were imposed on the sale of most consumer goods, such as rice, sugar, salt, flour, matches and soap. The result was a pervasive 'black market'.

The authorities introduced 'Grow More Food' programmes. A substantial portion of the urban population, mostly Chinese, migrated to rural areas to grow food. This was the root of the post-war 'Chinese squatter problem'. The squatters became an important source of food, supplies and intelligence for the communists during the Emergency (see 'The Emergency').

Japanese currency, known locally as 'banana money'.

Education

In schools, stress was laid on Emperor worship, *Nippon-go* (Japanese language), music and history. The *Nippon seishin* (Japanese spirit) was extolled. In April 1942, Malay and Tamil schools were reopened and only Japanese, Malay and Tamil languages were allowed. Malay was promoted ahead of English.

Chinese schools were allowed to reopen in October 1942, but prohibited from using Chinese as a medium of instruction. In 1943, the Japanese relented and allowed Chinese to be taught for three hours a week. However, a year later, the ban was re-imposed and only *Nippon-go* was allowed. Courses in Japanese were obligatory in technical, administrative, medical, and normal teachers' schools called *kunrenjo* (training schools).

Cartoon from *Malai Sinpo*, an English-language newspaper set up by the Japanese. It was captioned '*Malai-go* (Malay language) for *Nippon-jin* (Japanese people)—an object lesson'.

Sook ching

The Japanese had never forgiven the overseas Chinese for their anti-Japanese activities when Japan invaded China in 1937. The administration therefore forced the Overseas Chinese Association to pay a tribute to Japan (see 'The Japanese Occupation of northern Borneo').

Colonel Masanobu Tsuji decided to purge all anti-Japanese elements before he left the Peninsula. Starting on 18 February 1942, between 6000 and 25,000 Chinese were massacred in Singapore. Japanese troops then extended the so-called *sook ching*

Colonel Masanobu Tsuji, largely blamed for the *sook ching*.

(clean-up) operation to Negeri Sembilan, Melaka, Johor and Pahang and killed over 20,000 Chinese. The true numbers are still unknown, as testimonies at war tribunals were inconsistent as evidence had been destroyed—corpses were thrown into the sea or left in the open to be preyed on by wild animals. *Sook ching* struck terror into the hearts of

the Chinese and hundreds fled into the jungle to join the MPAJA (Malayan People's Anti-Japanese Army). After the war, the Malayan Chinese demanded compensation and apologies from the Japanese government. A 'gift of atonement' or 'blood debt', of RM25 million for the financing of the purchase of two ships, finally arrived during the government of Tunku Abdul Rahman Putra.

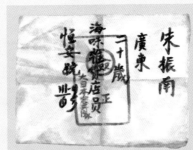

The 'mark of life'

When the Japanese army carried out *sook ching*, many Chinese, mostly men between 15 and 50 years old, were rounded up by the *kempeitai* (secret police). Screening methods were arbitrary. A person's age, physical appearance and profession could be sufficient 'evidence' of his being anti-Japanese. Those declared innocent were given a mark on their foreheads, arms or a piece of cloth (left).

The Japanese Occupation of northern Borneo

The Japanese combined Sarawak, Brunei and North Borneo (now Sabah) into a single military administrative unit, headquartered for much of the war in Kuching and then in Jesselton. Many pre-war institutions continued to operate and several new institutions were introduced. Relations with the indigenous people deteriorated as the war progressed; the Japanese acted harshly against resistance.

Government during the Occupation

As well as redeliniating northern Borneo into five provinces (*shu*), the Japanese renamed several towns and the island of Labuan. The latter became *Maedashima* ('the Island of Maeda') after Marquis Maeda, first Commander of *Boruneo Kita*, following his death in an air crash in June 1942.

Wartime Sarawak

The Japanese invaders' first priority was to secure essential military resources, particularly the oil fields of Miri and Brunei. British forces had damaged oil pumping and processing facilities before they surrendered. Many pre-war government institutions and services were allowed to continue.

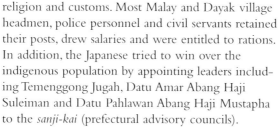

Japanese Prime Minister Hideki Tojo arriving at Kuching airfield, 7 July 1943. He paid a surprise visit as part of a tour of the occupied countries.

Japanese officials dominated the civil service. The Malays and Dayaks were given autonomy in matters of religion and customs. Most Malay and Dayak village headmen, police personnel and civil servants retained their posts, drew salaries and were entitled to rations. In addition, the Japanese tried to win over the indigenous population by appointing leaders including Temenggong Jugah, Datu Amar Abang Haji Suleiman and Datu Pahlawan Abang Haji Mustapha to the *sanji-kai* (prefectural advisory councils).

By late 1944, the Japanese war effort was not going well, and anti-Japanese sentiment grew. Shipping problems created shortages of various necessities and imported items. The local population was forced to hand over foodstuffs and supply labour to the Japanese.

People were recruited to the *jikeidan* (local vigilante association) and every longhouse household was made

Transition

Upon the occupation of Sarawak, a preliminary form of civil administration was established until a more permanent form could be devised. In Kuching, a *gunsei-bu* (military administration board) was established. The civil court system was re-established in November 1943.

In North Borneo, the Resident of the state's west coast and the Commander of the Armed Constabulary met the Japanese when they arrived at Beaufort on 3 January 1942, and were removed to Brunei for questioning. In Jesselton (now Kota Kinabalu), the Japanese produced a document, purportedly signed by the two officials, which stated that the dignity of civil servants would be upheld and that laws of the former government would be enforced, other than those which were anti-Japanese. European officials of the West Coast Residency continued to serve until 16 May 1942 when they were arrested and interned. When the Japanese reached Sandakan, then the seat of government, the Governor issued orders to all European officials to take no part in the Japanese administration except for certain limited cases.

responsible for local security. Despite threats of severe punishment, longhouses in the Limbang area in northern Sarawak provided shelter and protection to downed American airmen in late 1944.

Wartime North Borneo

The Kadazandusun, Murut and other natives suffered as the Japanese soldiers frequently shot or seized their livestock. Their resentment mounted when army garrisons were set up in Ranau, Keningau, Tenom, Beaufort and Pensiangan for the purposes of control of the population.

Tributary money

The Japanese treated the Chinese as enemies due to their pre-war anti-Japanese activities. The invaders forced the Overseas Chinese Association in the Malay Peninsula to raise 50 million Straits Dollars as a tribute of 'atonement' to Japan. As most of its properties and assets were destroyed during the war, the association had to borrow $21.5 million from the Yokohama Specie Bank.

In North Borneo and Sarawak, a similar demand was made. Although it remains unclear exactly how much was ultimately collected, the burden was undoubtedly extremely heavy. The Northern Borneo Overseas Chinese Association was formed to record Chinese assets and collect donations.

Receipt for donation to the Japanese-sponsored Overseas Chinese Defence Fund.

Japanese demands

Chinese in the Malay Peninsula	$50 million
Chinese in Sarawak	$1 million from Kuching $700,000 from Sibu $300,000 from Miri
Chinese in North Borneo	$600,000 from the west $400,000 from the east

The Api rebellion

On 9 October 1943, the eve of the Double Tenth National Day of China, over 300 youths called the Kinabalu Guerrilla Defence Force (KGDF) started an uprising in Api (Jesselton, now Kota Kinabalu). They had learned that the Japanese would conscript 3000 Chinese men for heavy labour and seize Chinese women to provide sexual services as 'comfort women'.

The KGDF attacked Japanese offices, police stations, wharfs and warehouses, and killed about 50 Japanese. Japanese retribution was swift and savage, with reinforcements, including aircraft, sent from Kuching. Severe reprisals were taken against the local population. KGDF leader Albert Kwok (Guo Hengnan) surrendered on 19 December 1943, hoping this would end the reprisals. A month later, he and 175 others were beheaded on the Petagas bridge near Api. A further 131 were sent to Labuan, of whom only nine survived. Another 96 detainees were tortured and, on 5 May 1944, executed at the Batu Tiga prison camp.

Albert Kwok (Guo Hengnan) was born in Kuching and educated in China. He settled in Jesselton in late 1940, having escaped the Japanese invasion of Shanghai.

Japanese administrative policy

Japanese policy was to govern Sarawak, Brunei and North Borneo as a single entity, *Boruneo Kita*, meaning 'Northern Borneo' in Japanese and 'Our Borneo' in Malay. *Boruneo Kita* was divided into five *shu*, or provinces. At the apex of the *Boruneo Kita* administration was the Commander of the Japanese Defence Forces. Beneath him, a Director General, appointed before the invasion and answerable directly to the Commander, headed each *shu*. Under each Director General were a number of *ken* or prefectures each with a locally-appointed head.

Government was divided into five departments: *kampei-tai* (military police), administration (including the maritime and communications bureaux), industry, finance and accounts, and intelligence. The control and administration of the vitally important oilfields of Miri and Seria were the direct responsibility of Tokyo headquarters. The large protective force originally stationed near the oilfields led to it becoming the military administration's first *Boruneo Kita* headquarters. However, at the whim of the first Commander, Marquis Maeda, the headquarters were moved to Kuching in June 1942.

Official circular stating the correct protocol to be observed towards senior Japanese officers.

The establishment of the Borneo Defence Force headquarters in Kuching marked a change in the military administration; government became more formal. Social control through the *kempei-tai* and *jikeidan* (local vigilante association) became harsher. With offices in all major population centres, the dreaded *kempei-tai* relied on physical force and intimidation to control the population. It was accountable only to the local Commander-in-Chief and the Japanese War Ministry. The *jikeidan* supplemented the *kempei-tai*. This association was based on the traditional Japanese system of group responsibility for individual action. All urban and semi-rural areas were divided into sections of thirty households (or in the interior, one longhouse). Regular night patrols and air raid drills were organized, and each section leader had to report on the movements of their section members, on petty crimes and anti-Japanese talk or actions. It thus served as an informal intelligence-gathering network, and was also used by the Japanese to mobilize forced labour and collect 'subscriptions'. Above the local sections was a complex hierarchy, with members of the local elites appointed to some higher positions.

It was only in late 1943 that a proper civil affairs policy for *Boruneo Kita* was announced. In a military decree of 1 October 1943, a system of *ken-sanji-kai* (prefectural advisory councils) was established. The head of each prefecture nominated a maximum of 15 *ken-sanji* (councillors) from the indigenous leadership who were to provide advice on policy formulation and assist in policy implementation. Chinese and Indians were limited to temporary membership. The *sanji* were, however, only required to meet twice a year, suggesting that they formed merely a peripheral part of the government structure.

Japanese scientific expedition at the summit of Mount Kinabalu, June 1943. This formed the basis of a propaganda film, *Kinabalu-san*.

Also in late 1943, a training programme was commenced in Kuching for future Japanese-educated leaders. The intention was that once promising graduates had completed the course in Kuching, they would be sent to Japan prior to being deployed throughout the *Boruneo Kita* administration. However, this latter part of the plan was ultimately frustrated by the increasing threat of Allied aircraft.

The Japanese *gunsei-bu* (military administration board) and local staff, Kuching, c. May 1942.

Large gangs of local labourers were drafted to improve roads and construct airstrips. Under a forced labour system, even civil servants and Chinese *towkay* (businessmen) had to work at least two hours on roads and airports every day, before and after office hours.

The Chinese in North Borneo and Sarawak also suffered from *sook ching*, and were warned not to engage in any anti-Japanese activities (see 'The Japanese Occupation of the Malay Peninsula'). Several Chinese leaders were arrested and some organizations were disbanded. Many Chinese businesses were taken over by Japanese companies. Most of the Chinese fled to the countryside to protect their womenfolk, avoid labour conscription and to grow food.

The serious shortage of labour led the Japanese to conscript some 20,000 *romusha* (labourers) from Java. Thousands died from starvation, malaria, dysentery, beri-beri, malnutrition and the bad working conditions. The Japanese relied on the local population to build and repair military installations, such as bridges and airfields.

Living conditions had deteriorated in North Borneo which led to the various communities uniting to support the Api rebellion in October 1943.

The impact of the Japanese Occupation in northern Borneo

When the war ended in September 1945, latent inter-ethnic tensions surfaced. In the brief interregnum before Allied forces returned, clashes took place. In Kanowit, the Dayak beheaded 23 Chinese who were branded as traitors. In Kuching, the Chinese rioted against Malays who had worked closely with the Japanese regime.

Rajah Vyner Brooke and the British North Borneo Chartered Company ceded control of their territories to the British Crown after the war. The oppressive character of the Japanese Occupation became an indirect catalyst for nationalism, leading to a desire for independence.

Plaque commemorating the forced march of Australian and British prisoners from the Sandakan Prisoner of War camp to Ranau just before the war ended. Only six of the 2434 prisoners survived. A cemetery in Labuan contains the graves of some of those who died.

The British Military Administration

After the Japanese surrender on 15 August 1945, the British reoccupied the Malay Peninsula. They governed the Peninsula and North Borneo through a military administration until 1 April 1946. Sarawak was run by an Australian military administration. The population had to confront the chaotic aftermath of war, including chronic food shortages and social disorder. It was also a time of intense political competition.

Supreme Allied Commander South East Asia Lord Louis Mountbatten proclaims the institution of the British Military Administration of the Malay Peninsula in Singapore on 15 August 1945.

Unexpected victory

The Allied Forces planned to retake the Peninsula with 'Operation Zipper', a series of amphibious landings on the west coast starting on 9 September 1945. This was pre-empted by Japan's unexpected surrender after the United States of America dropped atomic bombs on Hiroshima and Nagasaki. The first landings were brought forward, but the bulk of the British forces arrived only on 9 September.

There was therefore an interregnum of 25 days, during which time other forces made a bid for power. The Malayan Communist Party's paramilitary arm, the Malayan People's Anti-Japanese Army (MPAJA), 'liberated' many towns in the Peninsula. They were fêted by some, feared by many others. MPAJA 'kangaroo courts' imposed brutal reprisals on those

A Japanese General surrenders his samurai sword to General Messervy at a ceremony to formally hand over power held on 22 February 1946 at British Army Headquarters, Victoria Institution, Kuala Lumpur.

who had been seen to 'collaborate' with the Japanese. British liaison officers working with the guerrillas were unable to restrain them. These vendettas hit all communities, but when Malay officials and police were attacked, ethnic clashes between Chinese and Malays ensued, especially (from August 1945) in parts of Perak and Johor. Thousands of people fled their homes as a result.

Against this backdrop, Lord Louis Mountbatten, the Supreme Allied Commander South East Asia, established the British Military Administration (BMA) in September 1945. He was based in Singapore and Major-General Ralph Hone became responsible for the Peninsula as the Chief Civil Affairs Officer.

The BMA was designed to be a 'caretaker' administration, operating until a more permanent

Government structure

Civil affairs were planned by Brigadier H. C. Willan, designated Deputy Chief Civil Affairs Officer, Malay Peninsula. A Civil Affairs Headquarters was established at the Federal Secretariat in Kuala Lumpur. The initial staff was very small, but was gradually increased—in particular when the headquarters merged with the pan-Malayan headquarters of the Chief Civil Affairs Officer in October 1945.

The Peninsula was divided into nine regions each under the control of a Senior Civil Affairs Officer with the rank of either Colonel or Lieutenant Colonel. The Malay Rulers had no official role in the administration. Civil Affairs Officers were established as District Officers as soon as they became available. Headquarters quickly set up departments to cover the major aspects of the administration. Fortunately, the Government Printing Works in Kuala Lumpur had been left intact. This greatly aided the administration's efficiency.

Division of the Peninsula into regions

THAILAND
South China Sea

1 Kedah
Perlis
2 Penang
Perak
Kelantan 7
Terengganu 8
3
9
Pahang
Strait of Melaka
Selangor 4
Negeri Sembilan
5 Melaka
Johor 6

0   200 km

The nine regions under the British Military Administration followed the pre-war division of the country into states and settlements, with only minor changes to boundaries.

Dealings with the communists

During the occupation, the British had no choice but to accept the Malayan Communist Party (MCP) and its Malayan People's Anti-Japanese Army (MPAJA) as allies. When the war ended, the MPAJA were treated as heroes and participated in a victory parade in London. The British supplied training and weapons to the MPAJA, and arms were hidden away in the jungles in anticipation of Operation Zipper. Although the BMA later disarmed the MPAJA, most of the weapons were not recovered and were used later (see 'The Emergency'). Although the MCP had some 7000 men under arms, it did not exploit British weakness and launch a revolutionary struggle at this time. Its forces were scattered and poorly coordinated, and its leadership, who were mostly Chinese, feared Malay resistance.

The MCP was legalized when the BMA allowed the lapse of pre-war legislation on the registration of societies and trade unions, and control of the press. Encouraged, the MCP sought to widen its political support through a 'United Front' of leftist parties, trade unions and youth movements.

However, relations between the BMA and the MCP rapidly deteriorated, particularly after the latter organized industrial action in December 1945 and January 1946. The MCP had planned a general strike, to mark the anniversary of the fall of Singapore, on 15 February 1946. This resulted in confrontation with the administration.

Victory Day parade in Kuala Lumpur, 13 September 1945.

Immediate steps were taken to re-establish the court system to its pre-war stature, particularly as crime levels in the aftermath of the war were extremely high. The photograph shows Colonel J.G. Adams (seated top row), President of the Superior Court, with local court officials, at the Ipoh High Court, 1945.

Japanese soldiers lay down their swords at the Kuala Lumpur airport, September 1945.

civil government could be established. Its role was to prevent disease and disorder and re-establish basic services. However, from the outset, it had to deal with a major social and economic crisis, and could not avoid involvement in a volatile political situation.

Food shortage

Daily life was dominated by scrambles for scarce supplies. The war had ruined the regional rice trade. Little rice was flowing in from Burma (now Myanmar) and Thailand. Attempts to increase domestic production failed to compensate for the shortages. The 1945 harvest yielded only one-third of the 1940 crop. Malnutrition was widespread and there was a rise of endemic diseases such as malaria.

The BMA instituted strict food-control measures, which forced black market prices way above the official price. Indeed, the BMA was remembered by many Malayans as the 'Black Market Administration'; there were food riots in a number of towns.

Resettlement and rehabilitation

The war had seen massive movements of people, moving both on their own initiative and under compulsion. Those whom the Japanese had used as forced labour now struggled to return home. Over 80,000 Malayans of all races had been sent to Thailand for railway construction; an estimated 30,000 died there. Many Chinese—perhaps as many

as 400,000—had fled Malaya's towns for the fringes of rubber estates and forests, where they formed the majority of the now illegal 'squatters', growing food for their families and for the market. The British responded with relief measures and schemes for growing food. However, resources were inadequate to cope with the scale of the crisis.

The administration placed a high priority on the rehabilitation of the estates and mines. The war had put enormous financial stress on imperial Britain, which needed Malaya more than ever as an economic resource. Yet labour was in short supply and labourers were unwilling to accept pre-war wages and conditions.

The black market

The British Military Administration had to deal with severe shortages of basic supplies; a rampant black market had developed during the Japanese Occupation. Below are the prices of some commodities based on an informal survey taken in Ipoh, regarded as the cheapest town in Malaya to live in prior to the war.

The situation in Sarawak

The British Military Administration covered the states of Peninsular Malaya as well as North Borneo. It did not extend to Sarawak. The Japanese in Sarawak surrendered on 11 September 1945 to Australian forces. Sarawak was then placed under Australian military administration until the return of Vyner Brooke, who resumed his role as the Rajah on 15 April 1946.

Japanese Major-General Yamamura surrenders to Australia's Brigadier General Eastick at Kuching on 11 September 1945.

Following the Japanese surrender in 1945, army rations including canned food and cigarettes were sold by Chinese hawkers in central Kuala Lumpur.

Onlookers gather at the Lee Rubber building in Kuala Lumpur as a Japanese war criminal is brought to trial, January 1946.

Inflation and the black market

Goods	Unit	Pre-war, Dec. 1941 Straits Dollar	Dec. 1944	July 1945	End of war, Aug. 1945
			Japanese scrip (banana money)		
Rice	Per kati	0.06	8.20	36.00	75.00
Sugar	Per kati	0.08	18.00	72.00	120.00
Salt	Per kati	0.015	9.50	22.00	28.00
Eggs	Each	0.03	1.25	8.50	35.00
Tiger balm	1/2 oz	0.45	15.00	35.00	45.00
Lorry tyre	Each	65.00	25,000.00	55,000.00	75,000.00
Petrol	Per gallon	0.85	55.00	160.00	185.00
Refrigerator	Each	500.00	6000.00	17,000.00	35,000.00

Notes: The Japanese scrip, which replaced the Straits Dollar, started on par value; 1 kati = 604.79 grams.
Source: *Malaya Upside Down* by Chin Kee Onn.

The Malayan Union

The British Military Administration ended with the establishment of the short-lived Malayan Union, known officially as **Persatuan Melayu,** *which was designed to consolidate British control and improve governmental efficiency. However, the British government anticipated neither a fierce awakening of Malay nationalism, nor a lack of active support on the part of non-Malays who would have benefited from the Union.*

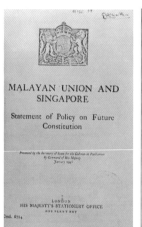

The Malayan Union policy statement presented to the British parliament in January 1946.

Sir Harold MacMichael (left) persuaded each Malay Ruler to sign an agreement such as that below.

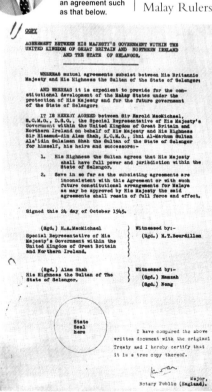

A scheme to unite the Malay states

When the colonial government resumed rule over the Malay Peninsula through the British Military Administration, it decided to consolidate all the states into a single entity. The Malayan Union, first announced in October 1945, merged the nine Federated and Unfederated Malay States together with the British Straits Settlements, except Singapore. The latter was excluded due to its strategic importance and its mainly Chinese population which would upset the population balance of the Peninsula.

The Malayan Union scheme effectively abolished state sovereignty. The Union was to be headed by a Governor who would in turn appoint his own Legislative Council. The Council would enact laws without the approval of the Malay Rulers, who were to be in charge only of Islamic matters and Malay customs. A Commissioner Resident would be appointed to run each state. Citizenship would be granted to anyone born in the country after the establishment of the Malayan Union, or who was then over the age of 18 and had lived in Malaya for more than a decade.

Existing treaties recognized the Malay Rulers' sovereignty and British officials were designated as 'advisers' only. New treaties therefore had to be arranged. A day after the scheme was announced in London, Sir Harold MacMichael arrived in the Peninsula to conclude formal agreements with each Malay Ruler (see document to the left) whereby jurisdiction would be ceded to the British Crown. MacMichael had no difficulty in securing the new treaties very quickly: if the Malay Rulers refused, they could be accused of being Japanese collaborators and lose their 'office'. Within two months, MacMichael had achieved his aim.

The Malays' reaction

The restriction of the Malay Rulers' powers and of the Malays' special privileges provoked a strong reaction

Why the Malayan Union?

Historians have identified various motives behind Britain's Malayan Union plan. Some saw it as a shift in colonial policy: to create a basic political infrastructure leading to eventual self-rule and at the same time replace the inefficient multi-state administrative system with a centralized system. Some aspects of the plan may have been, in part, an acknowledgement of the role of those Chinese who fought on the British side in the war. It has also been suggested that the plan was designed to pre-empt attempts in Malaya to form a Melayu Raya (Greater Indonesia). The nationalist movement in the East Indies that led to the uprising against Dutch colonial administration worried the British. A distinct political identity would help differentiate the Peninsular Malays from the Indonesians.

Perhaps more importantly, the British government needed to legalize its unauthorized use during World War II of large sums of money held on trust for the Malay States by the Crown Agents in London. Indeed, one of the key components of the Malayan Union scheme was the transfer of all assets and liabilities of Malaya to the British government, and in April 1946, Malayan Union Ordinance No. 1/46 barred 'legal proceedings in respect of certain payments made and acts, done or under authority of the Secretary of State for the Colonies or the Crown Agents, during the war period'.

> ### The Malayan Union
> Perlis THAILAND N
> Kedah
> Kelantan
> Penang Terengganu
> Perak
> Pahang
> Selangor Negeri Sembilan
> Melaka Johor
> 0 — 100 km SINGAPORE

that the British had not anticipated. Initially the response was ambivalence and resignation. The people lacked information and the post-war political situation and prospects were not clearly understood. But as awareness of the implications set in, the Malayan Union scheme came to be widely condemned across the political spectrum, from the Malay Rulers to the *ulama* (Muslim scholars) and teachers and the population at large.

Many Malays were jolted into political activity and ethnic awareness and began to feel a heightened sense of nationalism. While the *negeri* (state) remained important to them, it was no longer the main focus of their loyalty. For perhaps the first time, the idea that Malays in other states shared the same political fate led many to recognize a sense of nationalism on a Peninsula-wide basis.

The British response

The British government, unwilling to back down under pressure, initially ignored the widespread hostility to the scheme. The Malayan Union was implemented on 1 April 1946 amidst almost total boycott. However, the British government was soon forced to reassess its position.

The Chinese, on whom the British had counted for support, did not show much enthusiasm for the Union, despite the new citizenship privileges.

At the same time, opposition from the Malays, with some support from the Malay Rulers, became ever more widespread and intense. The Malays, hitherto assumed by the British to be unable to

The Federated Malay States flag continued to be used during the short-lived Malayan Union.

ABOVE: Governor-General designate Sir Malcolm MacDonald (centre) is greeted on his arrival in Kuala Lumpur by Governor Sir Edward Gent (right), May 1946.

LEFT: Colonial Secretary George Hall directed Lt Col. David Rees-Williams and Captain L. D. Gammans, who were on their way to Sarawak, to report on the reaction to the Malayan Union. The photograph shows their reception in Tapah, Perak, by UMNO members.

act in political unison, even threatened to renounce their loyalty to their respective Rulers if they were to co-operate with the British. The British were also alarmed by reports that the Malays' attitude was undergoing a broader change: from being specifically anti-Malayan Union, many were becoming generally anti-British.

The demise of the Malayan Union

The Governor of the Malayan Union, Sir Edward Gent, decided against using force to perpetuate British rule. He favoured the development of a stable base of popular support.

Gent decided to work with the United Malays National Organisation (UMNO) and the Malay Rulers, rather than with the (Malayan Communist Party (MCP) or the Parti Kebangsaan Melayu Malaya (Malay Nationalist Party). The former were considered 'safe opposition' as their immediate priority was to persuade the British to consider their views and revise the constitutional structure. The latter parties wanted an end to British rule.

The Governor-General designate, Malcolm MacDonald, supported Gent. He felt that giving concessions to the Malay Rulers and UMNO would not fundamentally endanger British political,

economic and military interests. It might even help Britain strengthen its position in the Peninsula.

MacDonald convinced his government that the Malays' demand for the return of sovereignty to the Malay Rulers and a tightening of citizenship laws for the Chinese and Indians could be accommodated. The Colonial Office finally consented to negotiate with UMNO and the Malay Rulers to work out a new, mutually acceptable framework of government. Two months after its inauguration, the Malayan Union was as good as dead, as a working committee representing UMNO, the Malay Rulers and the colonial administration set to work on the new federal structure that would replace it.

Sir Edward Gent taking the salute of the Bihar Regiment prior to his installation as Governor of the Malayan Union on 1 April 1946. In a brief 20-minute ceremony the British Military Administration was brought to an end, the Malayan Union inaugurated and the Governor installed.

British hierarchy in Southeast Asia

The position of Governor-General was created by the British in 1944, together with that of Special Commissioner, who was in charge of foreign affairs. These two positions covered all five of the Southeast Asian territories in which Britain had a direct interest: the Malay Peninsula, Singapore, North Borneo, Brunei and Sarawak. Malcolm MacDonald was appointed Governor-General in 1945, while Lord Killearn was appointed Special Commissioner. The positions of Governor-General and Special Commissioner were subsequently combined in 1948, and the position renamed Commissioner-General.

The British official who headed each of the five territories (in the case of the Malayan Union this was the Governor) reported to the Governor-General.

Why the Malayan Union failed

United Malays National Organisation

The Malays objected to the loss of sovereignty of their Rulers who were the object of their loyalty. They also feared that they would be overwhelmed by the Chinese and Indians if citizenship and the right to stay permanently in the Peninsula were granted more widely.

The protests and demonstrations against the proposed Union by several Malay groups in various states led to the formation of an umbrella organization, the United Malays National Organisation (UMNO), headed

Dato' Onn Jaafar, UMNO leader 1946–51.

by Dato' Onn Jaafar. Onn wrote a letter of objection to the British prime minister; local women formed opposition groups; and many Malays wrapped white cloth around their *songkok* (cap), a symbol of mourning.

UMNO demanded a return to the pre-war political structure of British indirect rule. It organized a boycott of the colonial government when the Malayan Union was implemented in April 1946.

Representatives of political parties from all over the Malay Peninsula gathered at Istana Besar, Johor to officially form UMNO on 11 May 1946.

Royal opposition

The Malay Rulers were unhappy with the severe curtailment of their authority, even on matters pertaining to Islam. They feared for their states' integrity and the future of the Malays.

The Malay Rulers took up the issue with the Colonial Office in London, by writing letters of objection and waging a public relations campaign in Britain with the help of former Malayan Civil Service officers including Sir Frank Swettenham, Sir George Maxwell and Sir Richard Winstedt.

Tuanku Abdul Rahman, Yang di-Pertuan Besar of Negeri Sembilan, one of the Rulers opposed to the Malayan Union.

Dato' Onn bin Jaafar

As the leading Malay politician of his time, Dato' Onn bin Jaafar did much to forge the Malays of the Peninsula into a unified community. The Malay newspaper Utusan Melayu *called him the 'new Hang Tuah', after the legendary Malay hero. A talented administrator with experience of journalism, Onn seemed destined to lead Malaya to independence and become its first Prime Minister. However, he was also a man of mercurial personality, tinged with impatience and perhaps over-confidence, and this ultimately cost him the opportunity of becoming the nation's leader.*

Dato' Onn, then Menteri Besar of Johor, speaking at the first meeting of the Federal Legislative Council in Kuala Lumpur in February 1948.

Profile	
1895	Born in Bukit Gambir.
1903 –10	Studied at Aldeburgh Lodge School, Suffolk, England.
1936 –45	Johor District Officer; member of Johor State Council.
1946	Founder-President, UMNO.
1946 –50	Johor Menteri Besar.
1951	Appointed Member for Home Affairs.
1951	Left UMNO, formed IMP.
1954	Formed Parti Negara.
1962	Passed away.

Dato' Onn, while Menteri Besar of Johor, with his sister Azizah Jaafar at an UMNO event.

Pupils at a Malay school with Dato' Onn, who visited their school as Member for Home Affairs.

Member of the Malay aristocracy

Onn was the son of Dato' Jaafar Haji Muhammad, who served as Johor's Menteri Besar (Chief Minister) for 46 years. His mother was Roquaiya Hanim, who was Turkish. Following the death of her second husband, she became Dato' Jaafar's fourth sequent wife. She bore him seven children, of whom Onn was the sixth.

Born in 1895 at Bukit Gambir, near Johor Bahru, Onn briefly attended a Malay school before he was adopted by Sultan Ibrahim and received tutoring at the palace. In the period 1903–10, Onn together with the Sultan's three sons attended Aldeburgh Lodge School in Suffolk, England. Onn won prizes for English and French, and excelled at sports, winning the school sports championship cup for three consecutive years. He then attended the Malay College at Kuala Kangsar, Perak, where most sons of the Malay aristocracy were educated.

Onn was married four times and had four sons and four daughters, the most famous being Tun Hussein Onn, Malaysia's third Prime Minister.

Journalist and government servant

Onn published two early Malay newspapers while living in Singapore. Later, he spent most of his life in government service. He held numerous posts in Johor, including publicity officer, State Food Controller (1941–5), District Officer, member of the Johor State Council (1936–45) and Menteri Besar (1946–50). He also held several Federal positions, including Member for Home Affairs in the Federal Legislative Council, and in 1951 became Chairman of the Rural and Industrial Development Authority.

Onn had performed well in the civil service, but politics was the arena in which he excelled. In January 1946 when Britain announced the Malayan Union with broadly equal citizenship rights for all ethnic communities (see 'The Malayan Union'), Onn initiated a meeting in Kuala Lumpur of 41 Malay associations from across the Malay Peninsula, named the Pan Malayan Malay Congress, with the aim of co-ordinating action against the Malayan Union. The congress decided to form a central organization for the protection of Malay interests. In May 1946, the United Malays National Organisation (UMNO) was inaugurated, with Onn as its founder and first President.

Travelling from state to state, Onn, a skilled orator, led rallies and demonstrations against the Malayan Union. He initiated an UMNO-led boycott of the British administration and persuaded the Malay Rulers to renege on the 'unjust treaties' that threatened to take away *Tanah Melayu* (the Malay states).

Three months after the Malayan Union was promulgated, UMNO, the Malay Rulers and the British agreed on the main points of a new political scheme to replace the Malayan Union—a federation with safeguards for the Malays. The Federation of Malaya, inaugurated in February 1948, marked a substantial victory for the Malays. It established UMNO as the dominant political force in the land and Onn as its undisputed leader.

Moving towards Independence

From 1949 to 1950, Onn expanded his activities to include a greater degree of engagement with other

Delegates, including Dato' Onn (front row, ninth from left), at the Pan-Malayan Malay Congress held on 2–4 March 1946, at the Sultan Sulaiman Club in Kampung Baru, Kuala Lumpur. The Congress agreed to establish UMNO, and the slogan *Hidup Melayu!* ('Long live the Malays!') was first used.

Dato' Onn leaves UMNO

'If we desire to be on par with our neighbouring countries, if we desire to be on par with countries that are free, then there is only one way that is open to us, in my view. That is, to claim that independence together, each community supporting and working with the other. There is no other way.'

The final speech made by Dato' Onn as Head of UMNO, at its General Assembly held in Kuala Lumpur's Majestic Hotel, 25 August 1951.

RIGHT: Dato' Onn resigning from UMNO at the Roof Garden, Majestic Hotel, Kuala Lumpur, 25 August 1951. The party's General Assembly then went on to elect his deputy, Tunku Abdul Rahman Putra, seated to his left, to succeed him.

Dato' Onn as Independence of Malaya Party (IMP) president, at an early IMP rally, 1951.

Dato' Onn as President of Parti Negara, 1958.

BELOW: Prime Minister Tunku Abdul Rahman Putra with Dato' Onn after the opening of Parliament in 1959.

BOTTOM: Dato' Onn was accorded a state funeral in Johor Bahru in recognition of his contribution to the nation, 1962.

races. He met with various ethnic leaders to study the causes of ethnic conflict and to recommend solutions. The forum for these discussions was the Communities Liaison Committee (CLC). The CLC was important in the political development of the country. It set a precedent for the seeking of solutions through bargaining and negotiation among leaders. These meetings led to two reports that established some of the key parameters which later formed part of the independence Constitution. However, the CLC's significance was not apparent at the time. The reports attracted little public support and the Malay press was hostile.

Onn's interaction with other ethnic leaders in the CLC altered his perception of the non-Malays. He increasingly came to believe that the surest route to independence would be through the creation of a multi-ethnic party. Accordingly, he began to pressure his own party to adopt a broader view, embracing the interests of non-Malays. Onn encountered resistance. In early 1950, he tried to persuade UMNO to adopt a more liberal position with respect to granting citizenship to non-Malays. He resigned from UMNO, thus forcing the party reluctantly to accept his terms in order to bring him back.

Sir Gerald Templer, British High Commissioner making Dato' Onn a Knight Commander of the Order of the British Empire at a ceremony in 1953.

Seemingly unaware of the dangerous ground he was treading, Onn, in late 1950, insisted that the party accept all races as its members. Once again, he tried to run roughshod over the widespread opposition in the party—he insisted they accept his demands or he would resign. This time, however, no one appealed for him to reconsider his resignation. In August 1951, he left UMNO.

The end of a career

From that point on, Onn's political career began to slide. The final phase began with the ideals of a multi-ethnic Independence of Malaya Party (IMP) and ended, somewhat bitterly, with Parti Negara (National Party).

The IMP was inaugurated in September 1951 with great fanfare, amidst predictions that it would soon dominate the political scene. However, it soon became apparent that strong Malay support was not forthcoming. The Chinese, from whom Onn expected to draw support for his multi-ethnic platform, in general backed away. The Malayan Chinese Association (MCA) was badly split on the issue and eventually withdrew its support for the IMP. The MCA formed an ad hoc alliance with UMNO.

At the 1952 municipal council elections in Kuala Lumpur, the IMP only won two of 12 seats, losing badly to the UMNO-MCA alliance. In the six municipal council elections that followed, it won only one seat and none in Johor Bahru. Thereafter, the IMP languished and in due course Onn abandoned it to form another new party.

Parti Negara was formed in 1954 with Onn as President. Although it claimed to be non-ethnic, its political line was communalistic. The party presented itself as a communal goad to UMNO. In the first general election in 1955, Parti Negara lost every seat contested. Onn suffered a humiliating defeat in his home constituency of Johor Bahru.

Parti Negara was a broken party thereafter, but Onn persisted. He lost again in a by-election in 1957. In 1959, the party won only one federal seat, contested by Onn, and four state seats in Terengganu. When Onn died in January 1962, the Alliance recaptured his seat in the ensuing by-election. Parti Negara faded into obscurity.

His legacy

As founder of UMNO and leader of the anti-Malayan Union movement, Onn was the first major Malay politician of the post-war era. Although he did not become the first post-Independence leader, he laid the foundation for independence and demonstrated the viability of multi-ethnic accommodation, and thereby secured an important place in history.

The Federation of Malaya

Stung by the vehement rejection of the Malayan Union by the Malays and the generally unenthusiastic response of other groups, the British government decided to work with the Malay Rulers and UMNO on an alternative. The Federation of Malaya proposal satisfied the three parties' interests, but met with opposition from non-Malays, radicals and communists, who did not participate in the discussions. This time, the British government ignored the objections and stuck to its plans.

The Federation flag flies between the Union Jack and the Selangor state flag outside the government offices in Kuala Lumpur, 1948.

Federation of Malaya

Perlis
Kedah
Penang
Kelantan
Perak
Terengganu
Pahang
Selangor
Negeri Sembilan
Melaka
Johor
South China Sea
Strait of Melaka
0 100 km
N

The initial proposal

When it became apparent that the Malayan Union scheme would fail, the British government had to act quickly to prevent losing the support of the people of the Malay Peninsula. It needed allies who could quell the opposition and would support its rule: these were the Malay Rulers and UMNO.

On 25 July 1946, a working committee was formed to draw up proposals for a federal structure. The terms of reference by which the working committee was guided included the fact that a strong central government was needed to ensure effective administration, while maintaining the individuality of each of the Malay States and of the Straits Settlements. Further, the new arrangements, in the long term, had to provide the means and prospects of development in the direction of

ultimate self-government. A common form of citizenship was to be introduced which would enable political rights to be extended to all those who regarded the Peninsula as their real home and as the object of their loyalty. Also, the agreement needed to preserve the dignity of the Malay Rulers and to protect and preserve the special position and rights of the Malays.

The British government conditionally approved the first draft agreement for a federation of Malay States on 24 December 1946. The proposed federation would be headed by a British High Commissioner, and restored the status of the Malay Rulers to the position prior to World War II. The Malays were also given representation in the new Legislative Council that was to be established.

Local opposition

While the committee was developing the new Constitution, other organizations were very unhappy with their exclusion and the secrecy of the closed-door meetings. As it seemed to them, the process had the air of a British conspiracy to perpetuate colonial rule in Malaya.

The recommendations of the working committee confirmed their worst fears and spurred them into action. Non-Malay opposition parties formed a coalition with the name 'All Malaya Council of Joint Action' (AMCJA) to coordinate their opposition (see 'Nationalism: Non-Malays in the Peninsula'). The AMCJA then joined forces with the Malay Nationalist Party to become PUTERA–AMCJA.

The enlarged coalition drafted an alternative constitution entitled 'The People's Constitutional Proposals' which among other things proposed that all members of the legislature should be elected by citizens, rather than appointed as recommended by the working committee. PUTERA–AMCJA planned to exert pressure on the British government on a scale similar to earlier opposition to the Malayan Union. Protest meetings, demonstrations and mass rallies were organized to show the masses' support for their proposals and their dissatisfaction with the working committee's

The working committee

A working committee comprising six British officials, four representatives from the Malay Rulers and two UMNO officials was formed to determine the details of what would become the Federation of Malaya agreement. The draft agreement was completed on 18 November 1946.

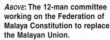

ABOVE: The 12-man committee working on the Federation of Malaya Constitution to replace the Malayan Union.

LEFT: The working committee at the Plenary Conference of the Constitutional Proposals for Malaya at King's House (now part of Carcosa Seri Negara), November 1946.

1. Sir Theodore Adams	Adviser to Their Highnesses
2. Mr K. K. O'Connor	Attorney General (representing the colonial administration)
3. Mr A. T. Newboult	Chief Secretary (representing the colonial administration)
4. Dato' Onn bin Jaafar	Representative of United Malays National Organisation (UMNO)
5. Tuan Haji Muhammad Sheriff bin Osman, Secretary to Government, Kedah	Representative of Their Highnesses
6. Raja Kamarulzaman bin Raja Mansur, Raja Kechil Tengah, Perak	Representative of Their Highnesses
7. Mr D. C. Watherston	Secretary to the Committee
8. Sir Ralph Hone	Observer for His Excellency the Governor-General
9. Mr W. D. Godsall	Financial Secretary (representing the colonial administration)
10. Dato' Nik Ahmed Kamil bin Mahmud, Dato' Sri Setia Raja Kelantan	Representative of Their Highnesses
11. Dato' Hamzah bin Abdullah Orang Kaya Menteri, Selangor	Representative of Their Highnesses
12. Dato' Abdul Rahman bin Muhammad Yasin	Representative of UMNO
13. Dato' R. St. J. Braddell	Legal Adviser to UMNO
14. Dr W. Linehan	Representing the colonial administration

(1) Signing the Federation of Malaya Agreement, 1 February 1948. (2) Sultan Ibrahim ibni Al-Marhum Sultan Mohamed IV of Kelantan signs the Federation of Malaya Agreement. (3) High Commissioner Sir Edward Gent calls for cooperation and racial tolerance at the conclusion of the signing of the Federation of Malaya Agreement.

The terms of the Federation

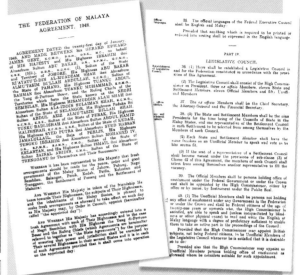

The text of the Federation of Malaya Agreement. The preamble provided that 'progress should be made towards eventual self-government...'.

- In many ways, the structure of government was similar to the Federated Malay States before World War II, except that it would now include all the states in the Peninsula. Singapore would not, however, be included.

- A High Commissioner would replace the position of Governor and essentially retain all his predecessor's powers, except those touching on Malay customs and Islam. These would be returned to the Sultans.

- The Sultans would regain their pre-war positions as constitutional monarchs.

- Federal Executive and Legislative Councils would be set up, with members appointed by the High Commissioner. The Federal Legislative Council would comprise 50 members. All of the Malay Menteri Besar (Chief Ministers) from the nine State Councils and two representatives from the Settlement Councils (Resident Commissioners) would automatically become members.

- Non-Malays would be given federal citizenship, but according to much stricter conditions than under the Malayan Union. Previously, non-Malays had no political status: they were subjects of neither the Sultans nor the British Crown. To become citizens, they would now be required to have lived in the Peninsula for 15 years and be adequately fluent in either Malay or English.

Membership of the Federal Legislative Council

Chinese 14
Malays 22
Indians 7
Europeans 5
Ceylonese 1
Eurasians 1

The official seal of the Federation of Malaya.

draft, and force the British government to back down. However, when the British showed no signs of accommodation, PUTERA–AMCJA decided to escalate the confrontation and called for a nationwide *hartal* (complete stoppage of economic activity) on 20 October 1947. Shops and businesses were closed and the nation came to a standstill.

Politically, the *hartal* was satisfying to the coalition as it demonstrated PUTERA–AMCJA's influence, and raised the political consciousness of the 'man in the street'.

Ironically, the *hartal*'s success worked against PUTERA–AMCJA. The coalition's membership, which included the Malayan Communist Party, the radical Pan-Malayan Federation of Trade Unions and the pro-Indonesia Malay Nationalist Party, gave an impression to the British that PUTERA–AMCJA were influenced by communists and out to wreck British rule. The British dismissed the *hartal* as a subversive act and a challenge to its power and authority, rather than a legitimate demonstration of opposition to the federation.

The outcome

By dealing exclusively with UMNO and the Malay Rulers, the British had indicated clearly whom they were prepared to work with, and what their constitutional policy was. However, to defuse criticisms of partiality, the government announced that a final decision would not be made until all interested parties had had the opportunity to express their views.

A consultative committee was set up to receive representations that would be forwarded to London for consideration. The committee sent its report to the British Colonial Office in March 1947. Four months later, the British government confirmed its final decision on the structure of the new Federation of Malaya with the publication of the revised constitutional proposals. Except for some minor details, the proposals were the same as those outlined in the draft agreement.

The British pushed ahead to implement the new plan. The Malayan Union Order in Council was revoked. Fresh agreements were signed with the Rulers and on 1 February 1948, the Federation of Malaya was inaugurated.

The Emergency

The Emergency lasted from June 1948 to July 1960. It pitted the British colonial administration and, later, the Malayan government, against the Malayan Communist Party (MCP), its rural-based guerrilla army and mostly ethnic-Chinese supporters. The MCP gained strength in the first few years of the Emergency but was unable to defeat the government forces. By the end of 1951, the two sides were deadlocked in an uneasy stalemate.

Military map showing the deployment of security forces at the height of the Emergency, 1950.

Why 'Emergency'?
It was an emergency, rather than a 'war', that was declared by the colonial administration against the MCP. This was for several reasons:

- The MCP guerrillas were considered a small group of 'bandit' law-breakers. Such law-and-order problems had previously been handled by means of emergency regulations.

- There was no external hostile attack, although some historians have argued that the communist offensive was orchestrated at the Calcutta Youth Conference in 1948, and was inspired by international communism.

- Malayan industries could rely upon London insurance firms to cover losses of stocks and equipment in riots and civilian activities during an emergency, but not in a civil or international war. A declaration of war could have ruined them.

- The Colonial Office rejected calls to impose martial law in December 1950, fearing problems similar to those experienced in Palestine, and citing difficulties in finding military personnel to manage administrative functions such as the court system.

- Under emergency regulations, the High Commissioner was granted extraordinary powers. Declaring war would have removed these powers and hampered the government campaign.

Origins of the Emergency

The Emergency was the sequel to the economic and social turmoil of the Japanese Occupation and the MCP's decision to wage an armed struggle to oust the British colonial government (see 'The Japanese Occupation of the Malay Peninsula' and 'The British Military Administration'). Furthermore, constitutional changes introduced after the war by the British alienated some sections of the population (see 'The Malayan Union').

The communists took advantage of this discontent. The MCP's membership initially saw themselves as 'peaceful agitators' but gradually shifted towards a policy of 'armed struggle'.

The British administration tried to curb the influence of communism by arresting MCP members and restricting trade union activities and that of other communist-front and satellite organizations.

Change of MCP tactics

MCP Secretary-General Chin Peng was encouraged to take up arms by the Calcutta Youth Conference of February 1948. Here the Soviet Union had urged communist parties in Asia to resist imperialism actively. The Chinese Communist Party had also waged a successful guerrilla war against their Kuomintang opponents in China.

A guerrilla war broke out in Malaya on 16 June 1948 when three planters were murdered in two attacks in the Sungei Siput area of Perak. When a state of emergency was declared, the MCP moved its cells into the jungle. Its strategy was to force the British out of rural areas, expand its own army in these 'liberated' areas, and attack towns, villages and communication lines. China and the Soviet Union would then pressure Britain to give independence to Malaya under an MCP government.

The communists found support particularly among the rural Chinese, some of whom were unhappy with

Communist attacks

1. A stage bus lies burnt following an attack.

2. Fuel depot ablaze after a terrorist attack.

3. In an attempt to disable the economy, rubber trees were hacked and damaged.

4. Train derailment.

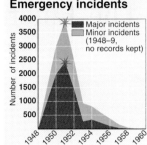

Number of incidents

■ Major incidents
■ Minor incidents
(1948–9,
no records kept)

1948 1950 1952 1954 1956 1958 1960

LEFT: Roadblocks were set up to curb the transport and sale of supplies to communists.

their living conditions, and many of whom lived on the jungle fringe. The MCP used kinship and friendship networks to source recruits, supplies and money. It used murder, torture and other forms of intimidation as methods of control. The MCP failed, however, to attract Malay support, communism being antithetical to Islam.

Poor counter–measures

The British initially treated the problem as criminal rather than political. Their strategy was to eliminate the guerrillas and punish their supporters. However, they had little knowledge of the communist leaders or their support organizations. Thus, the entire Chinese community became suspect in their eyes.

During large-scale sweeps through the jungle, soldiers shot many of those who fled, guilty or otherwise. Houses and even villages belonging to the Chinese were destroyed. People living near 'black areas' of communist activity were detained or deported wholesale.

The administration's ill-conceived strategy drove many Chinese to support the communists. From 1000 or so guerrillas in 1948, the MCP army grew to over 8000 by the end of 1951. Similarly, guerrilla attacks rose from just under 1500 (1949) to nearly 4800 (1950) and then over 6000 (1951).

Stalemate

By the end of 1951, there was stalemate. The MCP could not sustain its attacks on government forces. The Malays distrusted the communists and were

Measures to prevent the smuggling of food to the communists extended to body searches; sometimes in makeshift cabins as on the right of the picture.

supportive of the British. The MCP had inexperienced leadership and poor communications, and their violence and intimidation were resented.

On its side, the government could not effectively counter the insurgency. Its failure was underscored by the assassination of Sir Henry Gurney in 1951. Intense guerrilla warfare appeared inevitable for years to come.

However, the arrival of Sir Gerald Templer, and the success of the Briggs Plan, tipped the balance against the communists (see 'The Emergency resolved').

Treachery within communist ranks

From 1936 to 1947, when the MCP was headed by Secretary-General Lai Tek, it was reluctant to use violence. As top political and military commander of the MCP and Malayan People's Anti-Japanese Army (MPAJA), Lai Tek was much admired and respected as the 'Lenin of Malaya' by the younger leaders.

Unknown to party members, Lai Tek had been a British secret agent since 1934. He was engaged to 'strategically mislead' the MCP and so serve British strategic interests. He rose up the ranks within five years, with help from the British colonial authorities who arrested or deported his rivals.

Before working for the British, Lai Tek alias Mr Wright, served as a secret agent for the French Sûreté in Indochina until his cover was 'blown'. During the Japanese Occupation, Lai Tek became a triple-agent, working also for the Japanese. When the war turned against Japan, Lai Tek switched sides back to the British.

Rare picture of Lai Tek, whose photograph was not publicly seen until 1984.

Just as the MCP began to suspect his treachery in 1947, Lai Tek absconded with a huge amount of party funds and fled to Hong Kong. His fate is shrouded in mystery. Some believed he was recalled by the British Special Branch or returned to North Vietnam. According to Chin Peng, Lai Tek was spotted by a group of Chinese and Thai communists in late 1947 who apparently strangled him to death in a Bangkok hotel.

Lai Tek's betrayal left a lasting impact within the party and bred insecurity and distrust among its leaders.

The death of Henry Gurney

The communists assassinated High Commissioner Sir Henry Lovell Goldsworthy Gurney (left) in October 1951.

Sir Henry and Lady Gurney were travelling in the official Rolls-Royce to Fraser's Hill when their convoy was ambushed two miles short of the Gap (the foothill entrance to the hill resort). Sir Henry was shot down by heavy automatic gunfire.

The Straits Times

TROOPS SEARCH AMBUSH AREA

ABOVE: *The Straits Times* report on the incident.

LEFT: Gurney's bullet-ridden car is now in the Penang Museum.

The Emergency resolved

The government's fight against the communist insurgency gained renewed energy with the arrival of Sir Gerald Templer. Meanwhile, the Malayan Communist Party (MCP) had decided to change its strategy. By the time the Alliance government won the 1955 federal elections, the communists were prepared to surrender and join mainstream politics. However, the government rejected their terms, and, although destined for defeat, the MCP continued hostilities until 1960.

Sir Gerald Templer energized the colonial administration with his strong personality. Guerrilla activity decreased markedly following his arrival in 1952.

Emergency laws
Numerous laws were passed during the Emergency period to deal with the situation. These included the National Services Ordinance 1952 and the Land (Group Settlement Areas) Act 1960.

New strategies

The administration's fight against the communist insurgency was rejuvenated in February 1952 when Sir Gerald Templer replaced the assassinated Sir Henry Gurney as High Commissioner and Director of Operations.

Building on the efforts of Gurney and former Director of Operations Lieutenant General Briggs, Templer advocated a 'hearts and minds' strategy that emphasized a coordinated effort on all fronts—social, economic, political, cultural and military—to gain the support of all sections of the population. He addressed the grievances of Malayans while punishing those who supported the communists. The aim was to isolate the guerrillas from their base of support and make them vulnerable to the operations of the security forces.

Templer's new strategy proved successful. The general population offered information on the MCP and its support organizations. A steady stream of guerrillas surrendered and further boosted the government's intelligence resources. The security forces used the information to lay ambushes or

Security forces that defeated the communists

1. Members of the Home Guard.
2. Commonwealth troops included those from Fiji.
3. Malay Special Constable inspecting a car.
4. The Malay Regiment.
5. Sarawak Rangers.

directly attack guerrilla camps. The security forces even lived in the jungle for weeks on end in order to ambush the guerrillas. The increased military, police and administrative pressure forced the guerrillas deep into the jungle; the MCP eventually moved its headquarters to the Thai border region.

Change of heart
The 'hearts and minds' approach coincided with a change in the MCP's strategy. Its leaders had evaluated their failure to make a decisive break-through in the guerrilla campaign and issued secret

---

Hearts and minds: strategies that beat the communists

The Sultan of Kedah (centre) proclaims a 'white area' at Alor Star on 20 February 1954.

'White areas'
Areas that were considered free of guerrillas were to be designated as 'white areas'; here the emergency regulations were lifted, so that the inhabitants could enjoy a relatively normal life. This policy was designed to encourage cooperation with the government.

Restriction on movement and food
General restrictions were placed on all Malayans with regard to travel and the movement of goods. In selected areas, strict controls on foodstuffs and other essential supplies—culminating in the food denial operations that commenced in 1956—were implemented and enforced, with civil service support, to deprive the guerrillas of vital supplies.

C. C. Too, Head of Psychological Warfare, was aided by British Intelligence.

Propaganda
A major propaganda offensive was mounted. Millions of leaflets were distributed urging the communists to quit and the population to stop supporting them. Tours by mobile film projection units were organized. Surrendered guerrillas were brought forward by the authorities to give speeches, and the country's radio services were expanded to spread the propaganda message.

Poster issued by the Federal Information Department.

Penalties for communist sympathizers
The British colonial administration imposed severe penalties on communist sympathizers. Villages and towns that remained uncooperative to the government would be subjected to curfews, and any individuals found to support the MCP were imprisoned.

A public display of anti-communism.

directives to downgrade the military struggle. Equal priority was to be given to mobilizing the masses politically. The consequent reduction in guerrilla attacks in 1952 coincided with the start of the 'hearts and minds' campaign (see 'The Emergency').

Political irrelevance

The MCP's political efforts were hampered by the rapid growth of Malaya's political parties. Malaya's political process accelerated with the first municipal elections in December 1951. The first nationally significant elections were those held in Kuala Lumpur in February 1952. These were followed by village council elections in many parts of Malaya, and state elections in late 1954.

A wide range of political parties was formed, and competed vigorously in the run up to the first federal elections in July 1955. Significantly, criticism of the British and calls for independence were voiced through the legitimate political process.

The MCP became increasingly irrelevant. It responded by elevating some of the few Malay and Indian members to senior party positions to present a multi-racial image to Malayans. The Central Committee also offered to negotiate an end to the fighting. As a result, the Baling Talks were held on 28 and 29 December 1955. The MCP sought to leave the jungle and be recognized as a legitimate political party, but Tunku Abdul Rahman Putra would not agree to some of its demands; the talks broke down.

With Malaya's Independence on 31 August 1957, the communists became totally isolated. Mass surrenders and government pressure caused the eventual collapse of the guerrilla army. On 31 July 1960 the Emergency officially ended.

The Baling Talks

During the 1955 general elections, the Alliance coalition campaigned on a peace programme to end the Emergency quickly. Keeping to his word, a victorious Tunku Abdul Rahman Putra offered amnesty to communist insurgents who surrendered.

On 7 October 1955, the communists requested a meeting with the Tunku. The meeting was held in Baling, Kedah, on 28 December. The government delegation comprised the Tunku, Singapore Chief Minister David Marshall and MCA leader Dato' Tan Cheng Lock, while the communists were represented by Chin Peng, Chen Tien and Rashid Mydin.

During negotiations, Chin Peng questioned the status of the Tunku's government; it was still controlled by the British. The MCP offered to cease hostilities and disband its armed units if Britain agreed to transfer power of internal security, national defence and self-determination to the Alliance government.

In effect, the MCP demanded Malaya's independence. This presented Tunku Abdul Rahman Putra with a strong bargaining counter in pressing Britain for independence (see 'Merdeka! Malaya's Independence').

Nevertheless, the Baling Talks ended in stalemate the following day because the Tunku rejected Chin Peng's demands that the MCP be recognized as a legitimate political party in exchange for ending its armed struggle. Chin Peng also wanted the government to waive its demand that all ex-communists be screened by the police.

Conducting Officer J. L. H. Davis accompanies Chin Peng's party to the talks.

David Marshall, Tan Cheng Lock and Tunku Abdul Rahman Putra walk to the meeting.

A Malayan Air Force contingent saluting the Yang di-Pertuan Agong outside the Federal Secretariat Building, Kuala Lumpur, during the victory parade held on 1 August 1960 to celebrate the end of the Emergency.

The Briggs Plan

Popularly known as the Briggs Plan, the 'Federation Plan for the Elimination of the Communist Organisation and Armed Forces in Malaya' report was presented to the British Defence Co-ordination Committee in May 1950. The plan was to clear the country from south to north.

Even before the tabling of the plan, Briggs began to put into place an operations room command structure to oversee implementation of the plan. In April 1951 a Federal War Council (later merged by Templer with the Executive Council) and a chain of State, Settlement and District War Executive Committees (SWECs and DWECs) were established: the former to produce policy and provide resources, the latter to execute the policies—'to wage war in their own territories'. The new structure effectively by-passed the existing, somewhat cumbersome, state administration.

Lieutenant General Sir Harold Briggs, appointed in a civilian capacity as Director of Operations in March 1950. The position allowed him to coordinate the actions of the police and the armed forces.

The plan's key points

1. Domination of populated areas; building up feeling of complete security in these areas, thereby obtaining increased information from all sources.

2. Breaking up the communists' essential human infrastructure, the *Min Yuen* (Masses Organization), within populated areas.

3. By means of (1) and (2), isolating the guerrillas from their food, information and supply organizations.

4. Destroying the guerrillas by forcing them to attack the security forces on their own ground.

Resettlement and New Villages

To cut off the guerrillas' supply lines and places of refuge, some 600,000 Chinese squatters living in the jungle fringes were moved into New Villages. Resettlement began in the state of Johor on 1 June 1950 and worked northwards.

By December 1951, 385,000 people were resettled into 509 New Villages and given land and homes. Revenues arising from the Korean War boom were used to provide basic amenities: clean water, schools, community centres and basic medical care. Home Guard brigades comprising locals and the police were set up to protect these barbed-wire-ringed settlements.

The Village Councils Bill, passed by the Federal Legislative Council in May 1952, enfranchised the Chinese in these New Villages.

ABOVE RIGHT: Relocation in progress.

RIGHT: A resettlement village, c.1952.

Merdeka!
Attaining Independence

After World War II ended, the global climate favoured an end to colonialism. It was only a matter of time before the British crown colonies and protectorates, including Malaya, would be granted self-government and subsequently Independence.

Tunku Abdul Rahman Putra being greeted by crowds in front of A'Famosa, Melaka, on his return from London in February, 1956.

TOP: The Datuk Panglima Bukit Gantang of Perak, Dato' Haji Abdul Wahab (right), one of the representatives from the Malay Rulers, seated beside Tunku Abdul Rahman Putra at the Independence Agreement signing ceremony in London.

BELOW: Tunku Abdul Rahman Putra announcing the date of Independence at Bandar Hilir, Melaka, 20 February 1956. To his left is Melaka UMNO Chairman Abdul Ghafar Baba (now Tun).

Popular support

Although the British government worked exclusively with the Sultans and UMNO to formulate the Federation of Malaya Agreement, it indicated a preference to have the various ethnic groups participate in the administration. It encouraged various factions to work together and adopt a non-ethnic stand.

Dato' Onn Jaafar's Independence of Malaya Party (IMP) competed with his former party, UMNO, for the support of Malays, non-Malays, and the British authorities. The IMP sponsored a National Conference in 1953 with the support of the Malayan Indian Congress (MIC) and the Straits Chinese British Association. The conference called for municipal and state elections to be held before the federal elections, scheduled for late 1956. It also proposed that elected members be given minority status in the new 90-member Federal Legislative Council. The MIC found the conference to be too conservative and withdrew its delegates.

UMNO, under Tunku Abdul Rahman Putra's leadership, changed its slogan from '*Hidup Melayu!*' (Long live the Malays) to 'Merdeka!' (Independence) to give its members a broader, non-ethnic perspective. UMNO also simultaneously sponsored a

National Convention, attended by the Pan-Malayan Islamic Party (PMIP), the Peninsular Malay Union and the Persatuan Persetiaan Melayu Kelantan (Kelantan Loyal Malays Association). The convention endorsed an earlier pact between UMNO and MCA: it proposed that 75 seats in the Federal Legislative Council be given to elective members, and demanded elections by the end of 1954.

The British government showed an inclination towards Onn. The Federal Elections Committee, set up in 1953, comprised mostly people close to Onn. The committee endorsed the proposals made at the IMP's National Conference and recommended minority status for elected members in the council.

In response, the UMNO-MCA alliance sent a delegation (the first Merdeka mission), comprising Tunku Abdul Rahman Putra, H. S. Lee, Dato' Abdul Razak Hussein and T. H. Tan, to London to put its case. Oliver Lyttelton, the Secretary of State for the Colonies, initially refused to meet them. The parties did, however, finally meet, and agreed on a ratio of 52 elected to 46 appointed members in the Federal Legislative Council, with the majority party in the council to be consulted on the nomination of seven of the appointees.

Landslide victory

In the first federal elections, held in 1955, the Alliance, the MIC now in its ranks, won 51 of the 52 seats contested. This huge majority gave the Alliance

Slow boat to London

The second Merdeka mission: Tunku Abdul Rahman Putra had the delegation travel to London by sea, and so gave himself ample opportunity to discuss the forthcoming negotiations with all the representatives. The M.V. *Asia* left Singapore on 1 January 1956. By the time it reached Karachi, a common position had been reached. Arrangements were then changed, and the delegation went on to London by air.

The second Merdeka mission to London, comprising the Alliance representatives (AR) and the Rulers' representatives (RR), from left: Dato Nik Ahmed Kamil (RR), Tun Dr Ismail Abdul Rahman (AR), T. H. Tan (Alliance Secretary General), Dato' Haji Abdul Wahab (RR), Tunku Abdul Rahman Putra (AR), Dato' Mohd Seth (RR), Abdul Kadir Shamsuddin (Secretary to the Mission), H. S. Lee (AR), Dato' Abdul Aziz A. Majid (RR), Dato' Abdul Razak Hussein (AR).

Tunku Abdul Rahman Putra signs the Independence Agreement in London, watched by British Secretary of State for the Colonies, Alan Lennox-Boyd, 8 February 1956.

Above: Tunku Abdul Rahman Putra raises his hand and shouts 'Merdeka!' (Independence) on 31 August 1957.

Right: The Proclamation of Independence was made at the newly completed Merdeka Stadium in Kuala Lumpur.

Far right: A parade was held in Kuala Lumpur, the capital city, to celebrate Merdeka, 31 August 1957.

the mandate to negotiate independence. Tunku Abdul Rahman Putra was appointed Chief Minister under High Commissioner Sir Donald MacGillivray.

Discussions on self-government and the possibility of independence began in August 1955 when the new Secretary of State for the Colonies, Alan Lennox-Boyd, visited Kuala Lumpur. Subsequently, the second Merdeka mission, comprising four representatives of the Alliance and four from the Malay Rulers, left for London in January 1956.

It was decided at the meeting that an independent Commonwealth Constitutional Commission be appointed to examine the changes needed in the constitution and all their ramifications. Lord Reid chaired the Commission, which included Sir Ivor Jennings (Britain), Sir William McKell (Australia), Mr B. Malik (India) and Justice Abdul Hamid (Pakistan).

The Reid Commission first met at the end of June 1956 and invited associations and individuals in Malaya to submit memoranda. Members of the public could also make verbal statements. Of the 131 memoranda received, the most important were from the Sultans and the Alliance who raised several concerns and aired numerous grievances. However, the leaders agreed that such differences should not be allowed to delay the achievement of independence; they could be settled after the birth of the new nation-state.

The Commission's proposals were next sent to a Working Committee in February 1957, chaired by High Commissioner MacGillivray. The committee's recommendations were then sent to the British government and the Conference of Rulers. A final constitutional conference was held in May 1957 in London to address issues raised by the Commission.

Merdeka!

On 31 August 1957, the Federation of Malaya ceased to be a British protectorate and became a state with Tunku Abdul Rahman Putra as its first Prime Minister. Parliament comprised those members who had been elected in the 1955 elections.

The pen used to sign the Merdeka Agreement.

The national anthem

'Negaraku' ('My country'), adapted from the Perak state anthem, was chosen as the national anthem on 5 August 1957 by a committee headed by Chief Minister Tunku Abdul Rahman Putra.

A new musical arrangement, with a livelier beat, was adopted in 1992, and another in 2003, with the beginning of the tune returned to its original pace. The lyrics translate as follows:

My country, the land where my blood is spilt
The people live in unity and prosperity
May God bestow His blessings and happiness upon us
May our King reign in peace.

The idea of Malaysia

After Malaya's Independence, Prime Minister Tunku Abdul Rahman Putra grew increasingly concerned about communism, seen as a very real threat at the time. Although he had initially rejected the idea of merging Malaya with other British colonies, he reassessed the position, and sought a union with Brunei, North Borneo, Sarawak and Singapore.

Protests were held in Kuching against the Malaysia concept, 1962.

The 17 August 1963 edition of *The Sarawak Tribune* reported the arrival of the United Nations team sent to verify whether the people of North Borneo and Sarawak wished to join Malaysia.

The Sarawak Tribune

U.N. TEAM ARRIVES

Crowds Along Airport Route Shout

Anti - Malaysia Greetings

Idea of a merger

Tunku Abdul Rahman Putra's proposal for the formation of Malaysia in May 1961 came as a surprise to many, because he had initially rejected the idea of merging Malaya with Singapore. His party, the United Malays National Organisation (UMNO), was concerned that the Malays would, in such an event, become a minority and lose their special privileges; non-Malays, only 50 per cent of Malaya's population, made up 80 per cent of Singapore's.

Motivations for forming Malaysia

Events in Singapore in 1961 may have been a factor in prompting the Tunku to reassess his position. It appeared that communist parties were gaining ground in Singapore where the ruling People's Action Party suffered defeats in two crucial by-elections, thus suggesting that communists could possibly win a Singapore general election. In the climate of the time, the neutralization of any communist threat was a priority.

The Malayan government also learned of a communist plan involving Indonesia and China, whereby the region would be divided between them. An expanded federation that incorporated the Borneo territories would scuttle this plan.

Vision of Malaysia

'Malaya... cannot stand alone. Sooner or later, she should have an understanding with Britain and the peoples of Singapore, North Borneo, Sarawak and Brunei. It is premature for me to say how this closer understanding can be brought about, but it is inevitable that we should look ahead to this objective and think of a plan whereby these territories can be brought together in political and economic cooperation.'

Tunku Abdul Rahman Putra, giving a speech at the Foreign Correspondents Association, 27 May 1961.

Acceptance of the idea

The Malaysia proposal seemed to be a strategically sound solution to a number of issues. It would help dilute the Chinese presence in Singapore; curb the communist threat; provide economic and political support for the Borneo territories; and hasten the territories' independence. After all, these states shared a similar cultural heritage and a legacy of British colonial rule. Although initially reluctant, the British government eventually supported the proposal.

The Borneo response

Initially, local leaders in North Borneo (now Sabah) and Sarawak were opposed to the idea of Malaysia. Some had hoped for an independent state comprising Sabah, Brunei and Sarawak. The Sarawak United People's Party was especially ferocious in its opposition to the federation, and organised mass demonstrations. In North Borneo, Donald Stephens, a senior indigenous leader, was also sceptical.

However, the British colonial authorities were able to use their influence among the indigenous groupings to gain support for the proposal. Singapore's Lee Kuan Yew, one of the new federation's strongest supporters, also attended a series of meetings of the Malaysia Solidarity Consultative Committee (MSCC) to drum up support. Stephens in Sabah, and other key leaders in Sarawak, changed their minds and finally decided to support the merger, subject to a number of safeguards known as the 'Twenty Points'.

The communist threat

Fear of communism was prevalent in Southeast Asia after World War II. The Soviet Union and China boasted of their intention to sweep across the world, overwhelming capitalism; and the 'domino theory' of states in the region falling to communism was rife.

In Singapore, granted self-rule in 1959, the ruling People's Action Party (PAP) was in danger of losing its majority to the communist-linked Socialist Front. PAP Secretary-General Lee Kuan Yew asked Tunku Abdul Rahman Putra for help. With a merger, it was hoped that pro-communist, anti-Malaya elements could be removed.

Malaya found a Chinese map outlining its proposed hegemony over the mainland of Asia, leaving the islands to Indonesia. By forming Malaysia—effectively splitting up Borneo and merging northern Borneo politically with the mainland—such a scheme would be thwarted.

Confiscated communist propaganda.

Communist elements were suspected of organizing and inciting anti-Malaysia protests in Sarawak.

Attitudes to the Malaysia proposal

Other involved parties
British government response to the Malaysia proposal was initially cautious, for fear that it might compromise the Southeast Asia Treaty Organisation (SEATO) pact (see 'External opposition to Malaysia'). British Governors in Borneo preferred the idea of merging their territories into a North Borneo federation as a first step, before considering the formation of Malaysia. Left-wing groups, particularly Singapore's Socialist Front, the Malayan Labour Party and Sarawak United People's Party, objected to the stridently anti-communist stance of Malaya's Alliance government. Objections came also from Indonesia and the Philippines (see 'External opposition to Malaysia'). The photograph shows anti-Malaysia slogans in Sarawak.

North Borneo (Sabah) and Sarawak
Local leaders such as Sarawak Iban leader Temenggong Jugah (left) and Datu Mustapha Harun (right), himself of Suluk descent, feared being 'colonized' by Malaya and becoming minorities in the new Federation. They were also concerned about the communist threat and being dominated by the Chinese community.

Brunei
Sultan Sir Omar Ali Saifuddin supported the Malaysia plan. However, Parti Rakyat (People's Party) preferred a union with Indonesia to form Indonesia Raya (Greater Indonesia). Its president, A. M. Azahari, staged a revolt in December 1962 to overthrow the Sultan but failed. Brunei eventually opted out of the merger when issues regarding the monarchy and oil revenues could not be resolved. The photograph shows rebels in custody.

Singapore
The Singapore government of Lee Kuan Yew (right) and Singapore's first Chief Minister, David Marshall, supported the idea. A referendum found that a majority of Singaporeans endorsed it, convinced that a fully independent Singapore could not stand on its own economically. The merger would give Singapore guaranteed access to the natural and human resources offered by a Malaysian common market.

PHILIPPINES

South China Sea

Peninsular Malaysia

BRUNEI

North Borneo

Sarawak

SINGAPORE

INDONESIA

N

0   800 km

Seeking consensus

Stage One
The Malaysia Solidarity Consultative Committee was formed to recommend general conditions for federation. Leaders such as Donald Stephens and Temenggong Jugah, who initially resisted the idea, agreed to it subject to certain safeguards.

Stage Two
Public opinion was sought. The Cobbold Commission held 50 meetings in Sarawak and North Borneo with some 4000 individuals representing 690 groups. It reported that one-third of the population endorsed Malaysia; one-third favoured the idea with safeguards in place; the remainder wanted either independence before joining Malaysia or continued British rule. In Singapore, 71 per cent of the population supported the merger.

The Malaysian Commission of Enquiry, popularly known as the Cobbold Commission after its Chairman, Lord Cobbold (centre). Standing with him are Commission members (from left): Sir Anthony Abell, Ghazali Shafie, Dato' Wong Pow Nee, and Sir David Watherston. The Commission was appointed by the British and Malayan governments to ascertain the views of the people of Sarawak and North Borneo on the proposed inclusion of these two territories in Malaysia.

Stage Three
Lord Lansdowne chaired an inter-governmental committee to formulate Malaysia's Constitution. North Borneo and Sarawak proposed the 'Twenty Points' while Singapore forwarded its own requirements. The final round of negotiations was held in London in July 1963 and Malaysia was set to be introduced on 31 August.

Lord Lansdowne (right) with British High Commissioner, Sir Geoffrey Tory.

The 'Twenty Points' for North Borneo (Sabah) and Sarawak

- **Religion**
  National religion: Islam.
  Sabah and Sarawak: No state religion.

- **Language**
  National language: Malay.
  Sabah and Sarawak: English allowed.

- **Constitution**
  New Constitution, not amendment to Malaya's Constitution.

- **Right of secession**
  Neither state can secede from the Federation.

- **Head of Federation**
  State Heads are not eligible to be Yang di-Pertuan Agong.

- **State Heads**
  Yang di-Pertua Negeri.

- **Names of states**
  Sabah and Sarawak.

- **State governments**
  Ministerial system; Chief Ministers elected by Legislative Council.

- **Representation in Federal Parliament**
  To be based on population, size and potential of the states, and no less than Singapore.

- **Indigenous races**
  To enjoy special rights analogous to Malays in Malaya.

- **'Borneonization'**
  The civil service of Sabah and Sarawak to be run by staff from those two states.

- **Name**
  Malaysia, not Melayu Raya.

- **Constitutional changes**
  No amendments, modification, or withdrawal of special safeguards without agreement from the state governments of Sabah and Sarawak.

- **Immigration**
  Entry into Malaysia:
  Federal Government control.
  Entry into Sabah and Sarawak:
  State government control.

- **British civil service officers**
  To remain until replaced by staff from Sabah and Sarawak.

- **Citizenship**
  Granted to anyone born in Sabah or Sarawak after Malaysia's formation; and special terms for those born before.

- **Tariffs and finance**
  Sabah and Sarawak to retain control of own finances, development, taxation, tariffs and loans.

- **Transitional period**
  Legislative powers to rest with state government until 1970.

- **Education**
  Existing system to be retained, under control of Sabah and Sarawak.

- **Control over land, forests and local government**
  Powers of National Land Council and National Council of Local Government do not apply.

The principal members of the MSCC (Malaysia Solidarity Consultative Committee) chaired by Donald Stephens (seated centre). The Committee was formed to collect views and opinions on Malaysia in the northern Borneo territories, as well as to disseminate information, to encourage discussion on Malaysia and to promote activities to expedite its realization.

43

The formation of Malaysia

Creating a nation-state comprising diverse ethnic, economic and cultural elements proved to be a complicated exercise. Every member state's interests had to be protected in the search for common ground. However, the Malaysia Agreement demonstrated that compromise and concession could lead a diverse group of peoples towards a common destiny. On 16 September 1963 began the story of Malaysia as it is known today.

The Proclamation of Malaysia document signed by Tunku Abdul Rahman Putra.

Birth of Malaysia

Malaysia became a reality two years after Tunku Abdul Rahman Putra mooted the idea (see 'The idea of Malaysia'). Leaders from Britain, Malaya, Singapore and the British Borneo territories met in London and signed the Malaysia Agreement on 10 July 1963.

The timing originally planned for the creation of Malaysia would have been perfect: 31 August 1963 coincided with Malaya's independence. However, the Tunku chose to delay the inauguration by 16 days to allow United Nations Secretary-General U Thant to complete his report on the wishes of North Borneo and Sarawak as regards the formation of Malaysia (see 'The idea of Malaysia' and 'External opposition to Malaysia'). Nevertheless, North Borneo was granted self-governing status on 31 August, and changed its name to Sabah.

Brunei decided against joining Malaysia, a result of the failure of the parties to reach agreement on at least two key terms. First, the issue of the seniority of the Sultan of Brunei Sir Omar Ali Saifuddin in the election process of the Yang di-Pertuan Agong (Paramount Ruler or King), especially in view of the Sultan's position as head of the Malay World's oldest sultanate; and second, Brunei's unwillingness to surrender control over its rich oil revenues after a proposed period of 10 years.

Uniting a diverse country

Forging a viable Malaysian nation-state out of such disparate ethnic, linguistic and religious elements was, not surprisingly, highly problematic. The ruling Alliance government needed to forge a multi-racial Malaysia, albeit one defined by its basic Malay ethnic, linguistic and Islamic characteristics. Although member states were given certain autonomy, the Federal Government strongly opposed any moves that challenged its basic policies.

A crisis erupted in Sarawak in 1966 when its Chief Minister, Stephen Kalong Ningkan, provoked the ire of BARJASA (one of the component parties in the Sarawak Alliance) when he tried to implement new Land Bills that would enable non-Bumiputera to acquire native lands. He also resisted federal policies on language and education, and the use of federal funds to construct more mosques in Sarawak.

In June 1966, the Sarawak state Governor dismissed Ningkan based on a letter expressing 'no confidence' in him signed by 21 of the 42 members of the State Assembly. However, he was reinstated by the

States and Federal Territories of Malaysia

The 13 states, and the Federal Territories of Kuala Lumpur, Labuan and Putrajaya (created in 1973, 1984 and 2001 respectively), have their own flags and crests.

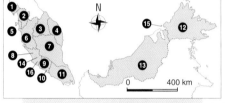

Name	Flag	Crest
1. Perlis		
2. Kedah		
3. Kelantan		
4. Terengganu		
5. Pulau Pinang		
6. Perak		
7. Pahang		
8. Selangor		
9. Negeri Sembilan		
10. Melaka		
11. Johor		
12. Sabah		
13. Sarawak		
14. Kuala Lumpur		
15. Labuan		Federal Territories
16. Putrajaya		

Emblems of a nation
The national flag
The design for the Malayan flag was chosen after a competition in 1949. The flag was first raised at the Sultan of Selangor's palace on 26 May 1950. When Malaysia was formed, the original 11 stripes and 11 points of the star became 14. After Singapore's departure, the design was retained to represent the unity of the states with the Federal Government.

The Malaysian coat of arms
The coat of arms of Malaysia incorporates a star and crescent, symbols of Islam. The star has 14-points representing the equal status of the federation's 13 states and their unity with the Federal Government.

The shield contains five kris which represent the former Unfederated Malay States, and four coloured panels—red, black, white and yellow—that represent the former Federated Malay States.
-The betel tree and Penang Bridge represent Penang; the Melaka tree, Melaka state. Sabah and Sarawak are symbolized by the crests to the left and right respectively of the *bunga raya* or Hibiscus, the national flower. The five petals of the *bunga raya* symbolise the *Rukunegara* while the colour red represents courage.

The tigers are retained from the Federation of Malaya's armorial design. The scroll is royal yellow, colour of the Sultans, and bears the motto *Bersekutu Bertambah Mutu* ('Unity is Strength') in both the Romanized and Jawi scripts.

High Court in Borneo which ruled the dismissal unconstitutional. The Federal Government intervened by declaring a state of emergency in Sarawak and amending the state constitution to allow for such dismissals. The incident showed that the Borneo states were expected to govern in a manner that would not be detrimental to local Bumiputera or federal policies aimed at nation-building and national integration.

While not altogether free of tensions or differences in federal–state relations, integrating Sabah and Sarawak into the Malaysian body politic has been successfully achieved. However, the union with Singapore proved unsuccessful; the state separated from Malaysia after less than two years. Singapore and Malaysia now cooperate as independent nations.

The Malaysia Proclamation was read in all four territories of the federation: (1) in Kuala Lumpur's Merdeka Stadium by Prime Minister Tunku Abdul Rahman Putra witnessed by the Malay Rulers (right); (2) in Singapore by the state's first Prime Minister, Lee Kuan Yew; (3) in Kuching, Sarawak, by Federal Government representative Khir Johari—with him were the new Governor of Sarawak Datu Abang Haji Openg and Chief Minister Stephen Kalong Ningkan; and (4) in Kota Kinabalu, Sabah, by Sabah Chief Minister Dato' Donald Stephens, beside whom are seated the first Governor of Sabah Tun Mustapha Harun and Deputy Prime Minister Tun Abdul Razak.

My dear Chin Chye,

I am writing to tell you that I have given the matter of our break with Singapore my utmost consideration and I find that in the interest of our friendship and the security and peace of Malaysia as a whole, there is absolutely no other way out. If I were strong enough and able to exercise complete control of the situation I might perhaps have delayed action, but I am not, and so while I am able to counsel tolerance and patience, I think the amicable settlement of our differences in this way is the only possible way out. I request you most earnestly to agree.

Kind regards,

Yours sincerely,
Tunku Abdul Rahman

Separation of Singapore from Malaysia

Serious disagreements with Singapore surfaced soon after Malaysia was formed. Several key issues had not been satisfactorily resolved. For example, no date had been fixed for the imposition of customs duties on imports from Singapore to other parts of Malaysia. The Federal Government was under pressure from Chinese businessmen in the Peninsula to introduce them quickly while their counterparts in Singapore resisted the move.

In addition to these disagreements, riots broke out in Singapore for a number of reasons including serious ethnic differences. The demand for a 'Malaysian Malaysia' in particular, and the combined factors mentioned above, led the Tunku, in June 1965, to decide on separation.

On 6 August 1965, the Tunku and his Cabinet informed Lee Kuan Yew of the decision to separate Singapore from Malaysia. Three days later, on 9 August 1965, the Federal Parliament passed a Bill approving separation, with 126 votes in favour and none against. The Singapore representatives were absent. That same day, Lee Kuan Yew issued a Proclamation declaring Singapore a sovereign and independent nation.

Tunku Abdul Rahman Putra explained the decision to separate in his handwritten letter to Dr Toh Chin Chye, Deputy Prime Minister of Singapore (above). Dr Toh replied by letter dated 8 August 1965 (right).

8th August 1965

My dear Tunku,

I thank you for your undated letter which I received yesterday explaining your position and your solution to the present difficulties that have arisen between the central government and the Singapore government. It is indeed sad that in your view our problems can be solved only by asking Singapore to quit Malaysia and this barely two years from the day Malaysia was inaugurated.

My colleagues and I would prefer that Singapore remain in Malaysia and we felt that there could be other solutions to the present impasse. However as you have indicated that the situation does not lend itself to any other workable settlement and as you have impressed upon me that Singapore remaining in Malaysia will lead to a situation you may not be able to control, we have no alternative but to be resigned to your wish that Singapore leaves the Federation of Malaysia.

I and my colleagues had rejoiced at the re-unification of Singapore with Malaya in September 1963. It has come as a blow to us that the peace and security of Malaysia can only be served by the expulsion of Singapore from Malaysia. If this is the price for peace in Malaya and Singapore then we must accept it however agonising our inner feelings may be. Although lasting unification of Singapore and Malaya has not been achieved this time, nevertheless it is my profound belief that future generations will succeed where we have failed.

In order that my friends and political colleagues in the other states of Malaya and especially those in the Malaysia Solidarity Movement may know my true feelings on this matter I may have at some future time to tell them of the true position.

With kind regards,

Yours sincerely,
Toh Chin Chye

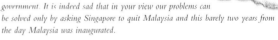

External opposition to Malaysia

The birth of Malaysia faced two external challenges. The Philippines laid claim to North Borneo; a communist-influenced Indonesia accused Malaysia of colonialism in disguise. When diplomatic attempts to block the formation of Malaysia failed, Indonesia became more aggressive and until 1966 waged an undeclared war against Malaysia.

Indonesian opposition

When Tunku Abdul Rahman Putra proposed the formation of Malaysia, Indonesia did not raise any objections. Its foreign minister, Subandrio, even made two public statements offering Indonesia's good wishes. However, the Indonesian stance changed dramatically after the influential Partai Komunis Indonesia (PKI) condemned the new Malaysia as a form of neo-colonialism designed to suppress 'democratic and patriotic movements'.

This confirmed Malaysia's fears that China and Indonesia's communists had formed a pact aimed at establishing a hegemony over the mainland of Asia and the Southeast Asian archipelago respectively. The inclusion of the Borneo territories within Malaysia would complicate their plans (see 'The idea of Malaysia').

The Philippines and North Borneo

The president of the Philippines, Diosdado Macapagal, opposed Malaysia's formation and renewed a claim to the eastern part of North Borneo (formerly part of the Sultan of Sulu's domain). Earlier, as a congressman, Macapagal had negotiated the return of Turtle Islands or Tawi-Tawi from the British authorities. He had also initiated claims on North Borneo without his then government's support.

Macapagal sent his vice president, Emmanuel Pelaez, to London to press the Philippines' territorial claims. However, while this was under way, he made a national speech contradicting Pelaez's claims and saying he wanted North Borneo for security reasons. Pelaez returned home empty-handed.

1. A caricature of President Sukarno crowing that Malaysia would be crushed before 1 January 1965.

2. In May 1963, Sukarno agreed to meet Tunku Abdul Rahman Putra privately in Tokyo. The talks ended in an agreement to start negotiations between the foreign ministers of Indonesia, Malaya and the Philippines in Manila the following week.

3. Dr Radakrishna Ramani (right), Deputy Permanent Representative to the United Nations, talking with UN Secretary-General U Thant in 1963.

4. Indonesian weapons and equipment captured in Sarawak in early 1964. The arms included 66 automatic weapons and some 18,000 rounds of ammunition.

Caricature dated 14 September 1963 that depicts Presidents Sukarno and Macapagal reneging on their agreement in the Manila Accord to welcome Malaysia once an independent and impartial authority ascertained the support of the peoples of Sabah and Sarawak.

MAPHILINDO

Macapagal found common cause with Indonesia's President Sukarno, who was preparing his policy of *Konfrontasi* (Confrontation). Invoking the sentiment of unity based on ethnicity, Macapagal proposed the idea of MAPHILINDO, comprising Malaya, the Philippines and Indonesia. Malaya was not persuaded, as the idea seemed too restrictive, and specifically related to Malaya, but not Malaysia. The Philippines then urged that the Malaysia plan be referred to the International Court of Justice (ICJ).

Malaya saw MAPHILINDO and the ICJ proposal as attempts to frustrate and delay plans for the creation of Malaysia. There was a fear that any delay might allow Singapore to fall under communist influence and demand independence as a separate nation.

The British response

Britain's Colonial Office initially opposed the idea of Malaysia. It would have preferred first to merge Singapore with Malaya; then create a federation of Borneo territories with the Sultan of Brunei as its constitutional ruler; and finally persuade both

Konfrontasi (Confrontation)

Despite UN Secretary-General U Thant's report favouring the formation of Malaysia, both the Philippines and Indonesia continued their protests. The Philippines downgraded its embassy in Kuala Lumpur to a consulate while Indonesia broke diplomatic ties and declared a campaign to *ganyang* (crush) Malaysia.

Indonesia revived Kesatuan Melayu Muda (Young Malay Union) under Ibrahim Yaakob's leadership to oppose the formation of Malaysia. Volunteers from Partai Komunis Indonesia (PKI) were sent on raids into Malaysia, followed by regular troops in 1964.

The Malaysian Armed Forces worked with British and Commonwealth forces from Australia and New Zealand to repel the attackers. Most of the fighting was confined to Borneo as the Indonesians could safely retreat to Kalimantan. Several incursions were also attempted on Peninsular Malaysia. The raiders believed in their government's propaganda and expected locals to welcome them as liberators and form guerrilla groups. This never materialized.

Malaysia protested to the UN Security Council, which voted nine against two to condemn Indonesia, but the Soviet Union vetoed the resolution. Indonesia left the United Nations when Malaysia was voted into the Security Council in 1965.

By the end of 1965, anti-communist popular uprisings and military action led to the fall of PKI. In 1966, General Suharto overthrew Sukarno in a coup. His army turned their weapons on the communists at the border. On 25 May 1966, Indonesian army officers flew to Malaysia offering to end *Konfrontasi*. A peace agreement was signed on 11 August 1966.

Local newspaper headlines during the Confrontation.

The proclamation of emergency

A proclamation of emergency was made under Article 150 of the Federal Constitution by the Yang di-Pertuan Agong on 3 September 1964. Pursuant to this, the Emergency (Essential Powers) Act 1964 received the Royal Assent on 17 September 1964 and empowered the Yang di-Pertuan Agong to make any regulations that he considered desirable or expedient for securing the public safety, the defence of the Federation, the maintenance of public order and of supplies, and services essential to the life of the community.

Numerous regulations were passed in accordance with the emergency powers. Among them were the Emergency (Tenants Registration) Regulations 1965. These applied only to certain areas of Malaysia. In each of these areas a headman was appointed. The headman was made responsible for preparing and keeping a list of tenants, and tenants were required to keep a list of persons residing in their premises. By the Essential (Emergency Service) (Volunteer Armed Forces) Regulations 1964, members of the volunteer armed forces were to continue in service even if they were otherwise due to be released or discharged.

A large number of other regulations were passed pursuant to the Act including those relating to the suspension of local government elections, the registration of fishing craft and crews, the prohibition of strikes and certain proscribed industrial actions, and the carrying of firearms and ammunition.

29 December 1963. Kalabakan. Moving some 30 miles into Sabah, guerrillas caught Malaysian troops off guard during prayers and killed them. British, Malay and Gurkha troops captured or killed all but six.

12 April 1963. Tebedu police post. Even before Britain relinquished Sarawak, a small Indonesian party, the 'Army of North Borneo', attacked the post and killed a policeman.

25 October 1964. Johor-Melaka boundary. Fifty-two Indonesian troops landed in a raid. Three were captured and the remainder were killed.

17 August 1964. Southwest coast of Johor. Indonesian paratroopers launched an amphibious raid.

28 September 1963. Outpost at Long Jawi. Indonesian-sponsored guerrillas penetrated 35 miles into Sarawak to attack the outpost. Returning to camp, they were decimated by British Gurkha troops.

10 March 1964. Singapore A bomb exploded within MacDonald House. Three people were killed and 33 others injured. Two Indonesian marines were subsequently found guilty of the bombing and sentenced to death.

Tun Abdul Razak and Indonesian Foreign Minister Dr Adam Malik sign the peace treaty ending the Confrontation, 11 August 1966. Standing between them is General Suharto.

federations to merge. The Malaysia plan effectively preempted that scenario.

Britain was also committed to the Southeast Asia Treaty Organisation (SEATO), which was never part of Malaya or Malaysia's plans. The British Commissioner in Southeast Asia, Lord Selkirk, feared that, with the creation of Malaysia, SEATO could lose the strategic use of Singapore as a base.

The British decided to assess the wishes of the people of North Borneo and Sarawak, and sent a commission led by Lord Cobbold to investigate (see 'The idea of Malaysia'). Despite the Cobbold Commission's report favouring the Malaysia plan,

the Philippines and Indonesia insisted at a tripartite summit in Manila on verification by the United Nations before they would accept Malaysia. They said they would welcome Malaysia once the United Nations' Secretary-General, U Thant, was able to confirm the wishes of the people of the two Borneo states. Two teams—one to North Borneo and the other to Sarawak—were sent with Malayan, Indonesian and Filipino officials attached.

U Thant was unable to produce his report by the date originally planned, and it did not appear until 14 September. For this reason the Malayan government decided to make 16 September Malaysia Day.

A constitutional state

Democratic idealism coupled with the realities of Malaya's political, economic and ethnic situation in 1957 influenced those who wrote the Constitution of the Federation of Malaya. The Constitution provides the basis for a multi-racial and multi-religious society, and serves as the foundation for the rule of law. Importantly, the Constitution, as amended in 1963 upon the formation of Malaysia, recognizes the special rights of the indigenous peoples of Sabah and Sarawak in addition to the pre-existing special rights of the Malays.

The Reid Commission

In 1956, the Reid Commission was appointed to draft Malaya's Constitution. The commission comprised (1) Lord Reid (United Kingdom), (2) Sir Ivor Jennings (United Kingdom), (3) Sir William McKell (Australia), (4) B. Malik (India), (5) Justice Abdul Hamid (Pakistan).

The Federal Constitution came into being on 31 August 1957.

New beginnings

Work on Malaya's Constitution began after the Alliance won by a landslide in the 1955 Federal Legislative Council elections and demanded independence from the British (see 'The Alliance' and 'Merdeka! Malaya's Independence').

With the formation of Malaysia in 1963, the Constitution was amended to include provisions relating to Sabah and Sarawak; and to Singapore, which was eventually excluded from the federation in 1965 (see 'The formation of Malaysia').

The status of the Constitution

Malaysia is bound by a written constitution. The 183 Articles and 13 Schedules that make up the Federal Constitution embody many features appropriate to maintaining strong central government while maintaining safeguards for a democratic and plural society.

Articles 4(1) and 162(6) affirm the supremacy of the basic law over all pre- and post-independence laws. The superior courts are empowered to nullify legislative and executive actions that violate the Constitution. Since 1957, there have been judicial reviews of government action, even though this safeguard is mitigated by wide-ranging powers given to Parliament in order to combat subversion and emergencies.

Constitutional integrity

There are provisions in Malaysia's Constitution which are entrenched and cannot be repealed without a two-thirds parliamentary majority. Furthermore, the consent of the Conference of Rulers is mandatory for changes in 10 politically sensitive areas. Any amendments to the rights of Sabah and Sarawak require the agreement of the Yang di-Pertua Negeri of those states.

From Malaya's Independence to date, there have been 44 constitutional amendments, including the transformation of Malaya into Malaysia in 1963.

Main features of the Federal Constitution

System of government

A Federal Government and 13 state governments possess legislative, executive, judicial and financial powers. Federal and state legislative assemblies are elected. The Federal Parliament comprises two chambers: the Dewan Rakyat (House of Representatives) and the Dewan Negara (Senate) (see 'The federal legislature'). State Assemblies have only one chamber. The political executive is part of the legislature and can be removed by elected representatives on a vote of no-confidence.

Parliament House in Kuala Lumpur was built in 1963.

Special privileges of the Bumiputera

Article 153 prescribes policies for preserving the privileges of Malays and the indigenous peoples of Sabah and Sarawak, collectively known as Bumiputera (natives). A number of features indigenous to the Malay Archipelago are incorporated. Among them are the sovereignty of the Malay Sultanates, the status of Islam as the religion of the federation, Malay privileges, reservation land, Malay as the official language and special protection for Malay customary laws. However, the Constitution also provides special rights and protection for the other communities within Malaysia, such as citizenship rights and the freedom to practise any religion, learn native languages, observe cultural practices, establish vernacular schools and participate in business and other economic activities.

Poster promoting the use of the Malay language.

The judiciary

The Constitution addresses such matters as the status of the courts and the appointment of judges. The judiciary enjoys many constitutional safeguards, in matters of appointment and dismissal. The terms and conditions of a judge's service cannot be altered to his or her detriment. Courts have the power to punish for contempt. Judges also enjoy absolute immunity in respect of their judicial actions.

Sultan Salahuddin Abdul Aziz Shah court complex, Shah Alam, Selangor.

The constitutional status of Islam

The Constitution states that Islam is the religion of the federation but other religions may be practised in peace and harmony. Related provisions are also included in the Constitution which allow the promotion of Islamic education, the setting up of Islamic religious and economic institutions, and the establishment of *syariah* (Islamic law) courts administering Islamic religious laws binding on all Muslims.

In some areas, the life of Muslims is regulated by Malay *adat* (custom). Criminal law is entirely secular and applies to the whole community, determined by provisions enacted by the elected Federal legislatures. Non-Muslims are subject only to secular law.

LEFT: Masjid Negara, the National Mosque, was built in 1965, the brainchild of Prime Minister Tunku Abdul Rahman Putra.

RIGHT: Muslim prayers are often recited at official functions attended by both Muslims and non-Muslims.

Constitutional monarchy

Except in a narrow area permitted by the Constitution, the Yang di-Pertuan Agong is required to act in accordance with the advice of the Prime Minister (see 'Constitutional monarchy'). The Conference of Rulers elects one of the Rulers as Yang di-Pertuan Agong (Paramount Ruler or King).

The first Yang di-Pertuan Agong, Tuanku Abdul Rahman Ibni Tuanku Muhammad, who reigned from 31 August 1957 to 1 April 1960.

Constitutional definition of a Malay

Before Independence, Malays were readily identified according to their birthplace and ethnicity. The framers of the Constitution, however, had to adopt a definition that distinguished the term 'Malay' from people of Malay stock from other countries.

According to Article 160 of the Federal Constitution, a Malay is defined as a person who professes the Muslim religion, habitually speaks Malay, conforms to Malay custom, and was either born in the Federation before Merdeka Day, or born of parents, one of whom was born in the Federation, or was on Merdeka Day domiciled in the Federation. Offspring of such a person also qualify. For the purposes of the Constitution, a person does not need to be of Malay ethnic origin to be a 'Malay'. Conversely, an ethnic Malay who does not profess the Islamic faith, for example, may be considered a 'non-Malay'.

Elections

The Constitution provides for periodic elections, universal adult suffrage run by an independent Election Commission. Each parliamentary constituency returns one MP to the Dewan Rakyat, although rural constituencies may have smaller populations than urban constituencies.

Election clerks counting ballot papers at a vote-counting centre in Kuala Lumpur during the 1964 general election.

Constitutional guarantees

Articles 5 to 13 of the Constitution establish a number of 'fundamental' rights such as personal liberty; abolition of slavery and forced labour; protection against retrospective criminal laws and repeated trials; equality before the law; freedom of movement; right to free speech, assembly and association; freedom of religion; rights in respect of education; and rights to property. These rights fall into two broad categories. Some, such as the right to property, are protected against Parliament's legislative power. Others, such as freedom of speech, are shielded only against executive arbitrariness. However, Parliament has the power to impose restrictions on a number of grounds. Thus, personal liberty can be restricted 'in accordance with law'.

The Internal Security Act provides for 'preventive detention': any person deemed a threat to national peace and security may be detained indefinitely by order of the Minister of Internal Security. Freedom of speech is circumscribed by laws such as the Sedition Act, the Printing Presses and Publications Act and the Official Secrets Act (see 'National security'). Thus, 'fundamental liberties' are granted insofar as they do not pose a threat to the nation's peace and security.

Civil service and armed forces

The Constitution provides for a number of public services together with mechanisms of control (see 'Institutions of state and national security'). Civil servants are required to keep out of politics and their terms are unaffected by the rise and fall of governments. They enjoy safeguards against arbitrary dismissal or reduction in rank. The armed forces are under civilian control.

Anti-subversion powers

When the Constitution was drafted, the threat of communism in the region was very real. The Constitution, through Articles 149–151, armed Parliament and the executive with overriding powers to combat subversion and emergency. These special powers are still in force today and have been employed extensively to control perceived threats to public order and national security. The nationwide emergencies declared in 1964 and 1969 have never been officially revoked.

The 1948–60 Emergency: a communist surrenders.

Minister of Defence Dato' Sri Mohd Najib Tun Abdul Razak (now also Deputy Prime Minister) addresses troops during armed forces exercises in Pasir Putih, Kelantan, in October 2002.

UNDI-LAH PERIKATAN

UNITY IN DIVERSITY

The Federation of Malaya was governed on the basis of a power-sharing arrangement, essentially the formula that had earned 'Merdeka' (see 'The Alliance formula'). For a time, the situation appeared stable; the nation looked to the future with confidence. The communist insurgency was in decline.

However, with the expansion of the federation to form Malaysia came factors which made the situation more complex, and the formula came under threat. Socio-economic development did not proceed at an equal pace among all the ethnic groups—among the Malays, it was relatively slow. Furthermore, non-Malays clamoured for a greater share of political power. Increasing racial tension was a factor in Singapore's exit from Malaysia, but even after this dramatic event, the underlying issues remained.

The tensions culminated in the tragic events of 1969 (see 'The 13 May 1969 tragedy'). This episode proved to be a watershed in Malaysian politics. Parliament was suspended and a council was established to take total control of the nation. The Constitution was amended to include safeguards against future unrest. Affirmative action policies were instituted to address socio-economic imbalances (see 'The National Operations Council' and 'Economic policies'). Malaysia's political landscape, formerly characterized by inter-racial bargaining and compromise, became one where the Malays, specifically through UMNO, clearly became the politically dominant players.

Department of National Unity and Integration publications: *Jiran* ('Neighbour'), and *Perpaduan* ('Unity').

However, after the events of 13 May 1969, the Alliance coalition was expanded to include a number of former opposition parties (see 'The Barisan Nasional framework'). Divisive issues were addressed within the system rather than through public confrontation. Power-sharing remains a key feature of this coalition today: every major ethnic group is represented in the Cabinet. This formula for managing ethnic diversity has brought peace and harmony for over 47 years since the Federation's inception, first under the Alliance and since 1973 under a Barisan Nasional government.

The Federal Government has also had to manage territorial diversity, especially in its relationship with Sabah and Sarawak. These states have special provisions within the Federation, as compared with the Peninsular states (see 'The idea of Malaysia' and 'Federal-state relations'), and a cultural and ethnic composition that differs from that of the Peninsula.

The Barisan Nasional coalition formula in Malaysia differs from that in other countries as the number of Cabinet seats to be given to major political parties is more or less decided in advance, whereas in other countries it is often based on a scramble for seats after the election results are declared.

The country's various ethnic groups (including the three largest—Malay, Chinese and Indian) are united as citizens, although local politics remain communally based.

1. Alliance rally at Sulaiman Court, Kuala Lumpur, April 1969.

2. From right: Sabah Yang di-Pertua Negeri Tun Sakaran Dandai, Barisan Nasional Chairman Dato' Seri Abdullah Ahmad Badawi, Sabah Chief Minister Datuk Seri Musa Aman, UMNO Information Chief Tan Sri Muhammad Muhd Taib and State Barisan Nasional leaders at a 'breaking of fast' function at Kota Kinabalu, held in November 2004.

3. Prime Minister Dr Mahathir Mohamad being greeted on arrival at Mulu Airport in Sarawak, May 1995.

The Alliance

Following the creation of the Federation of Malaya, local—and later national—elections were held. It was a coalition of Malay, Chinese and Indian political parties, known as the Alliance, which succeeded in capturing the popular vote.

The Alliance 'sailing boat' logo.

A jubilant Tunku Abdul Rahman Putra lifted by supporters in Alor Star. The Alliance won a landslide victory in the parliamentary and state elections of April 1964.

Aftermath of the Malayan Union

A working committee was set up in July 1946 to formulate an acceptable alternative governmental and political structure to the ailing Malayan Union. It comprised representatives of the Malay Rulers, the United Malays National Organisation (UMNO) and the government. Non-Malay organizations were not invited to participate; several of them formed a coalition, the All-Malaya Council of Joint Action (AMCJA), to submit proposals on the future Malayan constitution. Their exclusion from the working committee raised fears among the non-Malays, especially the Chinese, over their social and cultural identity and resulted in strikes and trade boycotts in some places.

Notwithstanding opposition to the Federation Agreement (which became the Constitution for Malaya), the Federation of Malaya was established in 1948. Soon after, the Malayan Communist Party (MCP)—the majority of whose members were Chinese—launched an armed insurgency (see 'The Emergency'). A Communities Liaison Committee was established to channel Chinese support away from the MCP. Committee members included leaders from both the non-Malay and Malay communities, one of whom was Dato' Onn bin Jaafar.

The birth of the Alliance

Dato' Onn had hoped to achieve multiracial unity by opening up UMNO membership to non-Malays, but this idea was strongly rejected by party members. Dato' Onn left UMNO in 1951 and formed a multiracial political party, the Independence of Malaya Party (IMP).

Tunku Abdul Rahman Putra, who took over from Dato' Onn as Yang di-Pertua of UMNO, faced the challenge of undermining the IMP's political

How the Alliance worked

The Alliance enabled the United Malays National Organisation (UMNO), the Malayan Chinese Association (MCA) and the Malayan Indian Congress (MIC)—each representing a distinct ethnic group—to work together, while continuing to represent the interests of their respective members.

The MCA agreed to accept Malay political dominance, but in return sought assurances from UMNO over the position and role of the Chinese community in politics and the economy. The MCA were satisfied that the status quo between the three main ethnic groups would be maintained and that through the Alliance, Chinese business and economic interests would be protected.

The MIC, formed in 1946, signed a secret pact to support the ad-hoc alliance in the 1952 Kuala Lumpur municipal council elections. The MIC formally joined the Alliance in 1954, further strengthening the coalition.

1. Prime Minister Tunku Abdul Rahman Putra addressing the UMNO Conference, 1963. Seated to his right are Alliance leaders Deputy Prime Minister Tun Abdul Razak, MCA President Tun Tan Siew Sin and MIC President Tun Sambanthan.

2. Tun Abdul Razak speaking at an Alliance function in Sentul, Kuala Lumpur in 1964.

3. MCA leader Tan Cheng Lock addressing an Alliance election rally in 1955.

4. Tun V. T. Sambanthan, the MIC's fifth President, led the party from 1955 to 1973.

5. Tan Sri V. Manickavasagam, President of the MIC from 1973 to 1979.

6. Tun Tan Siew Sin, President of the MCA from 1961 to 1974.

ABOVE: *The Straits Times* of 28 July 1955.

RIGHT: The Tunku seated in a boat resembling the Alliance logo after his success in the 1964 election.

influence. The Malayan Chinese Association (MCA) had unexpectedly agreed to join the IMP by integrating MCA members into the IMP. This put UMNO's political position in jeopardy. However, the proposed IMP-MCA integration failed to take off due to a personality clash between Dato' Onn and MCA President Tan Cheng Lock.

Shortly before the Kuala Lumpur municipal council elections in February 1952, UMNO Elections Committee Chairman Dato' Yahya bin Sheikh Ahmad and MCA Selangor Branch Chairman Colonel H. S. Lee formed an electoral understanding to face the IMP's challenge. This cooperation was a success, winning nine of the 12 seats contested; the IMP secured only two.

The relationship between UMNO and the MCA was formalized in 1953 as the Alliance, and in 1954 the Malayan Indian Congress (MIC) joined. The Alliance swept to a landslide victory in the 1955 general election, winning 51 of the 52 Federal Legislative Council seats contested. The election was a crucial test of the Tunku's leadership, especially concerning the distribution of constituencies among candidates from the Alliance's three member parties. UMNO members demanded that 90 per cent of candidates had to be Malays, but a consensus was ultimately achieved whereby UMNO fielded 35 candidates, the MCA 15 and the MIC two.

Strength and respect

A major strength of the Alliance was the relationship between the three political parties—UMNO, the MCA and the MIC—each of which represented the interests of a distinct racial group.

The parties respected the role played by each ethnic group in the development of the country and the maintenance of social harmony. This respect was inherent in the accommodative stance of the parties and made possible the bargaining process that was an integral and key feature of the Alliance, particularly on the sensitive issues of education, religion, language and citizenship.

The consequences of 1969

As a result of the 13 May 1969 incident (see 'The 13 May 1969 tragedy'), there was an increase in politicking. In order to reduce this, efforts were

made by Tun Abdul Razak and political parties, including those in Sabah and Sarawak, to broaden the Alliance coalition formula (see 'The Barisan Nasional framework'). Since then, the 'Alliance formula' has worked well and has brought about harmony in the country.

Tunku Abdul Rahman Putra addresses an Alliance rally at Sulaiman Court, Kuala Lumpur in April 1969. Seated next to him are Deputy Prime Minister Tun Abdul Razak Hussein and MIC leader Tun V. T. Sambanthan.

The Sabah and Sarawak Alliances

ABOVE: Sabah Yang di-Pertua Negeri Datu Mustapha Harun is seen launching 'Malaysian Solidarity Week' in Jesselton (now Kota Kinabalu), 1964. The Sabah Alliance Party, established in 1962, followed the example of the Malay Peninsula's Alliance Party.

LEFT: An early meeting of the Sarawak Alliance, formed in 1962. The Sarawak Alliance initially consisted of Parti Negara Sarawak, Barisan Rakyat Jati Sarawak, Sarawak National Party, Parti Pesaka Anak Sarawak and the Sarawak Chinese Associaton.

The 13 May 1969 tragedy

On the evening of Tuesday, 13 May 1969, three days after a keenly contested general election, the nation was shaken by serious racial disturbances. These continued for several weeks and, although they were mainly restricted to Kuala Lumpur, were described by Tun Abdul Razak as a national tragedy. A state of emergency was declared and the National Operations Council was established to restore order.

The Federal Reserve Unit of the Royal Malaysia Police was mobilized to control the unrest.

Events leading to 13 May 1969

A bitter election campaign was fought by various political parties prior to the general election of 10 May 1969. Party leaders stoked racial and religious sentiments in order to win support. Parti Islam Se-Malaysia (PAS) accused the United Malays National Organisation (UMNO) of selling the rights of the Malays to the Chinese, while the Democratic Action Party (DAP) accused the MCA of giving in to UMNO. The DAP promoted the concept of 'Malaysian Malaysia' which would deprive the Malays of their special rights under the Constitution. Both the DAP and the People's Progressive Party objected to Malay as the national language and proposed multi-lingualism in its stead.

Senior Alliance politicians, including Prime Minister Tunku Abdul Rahman Putra, accused the People's Action Party of Singapore of involvement in the campaign, as it had done during the 1964 general election campaign.

The run-up to the election was marred by two deaths: that of an UMNO election agent, who was killed by a group of armed Chinese youths in Penang and that of a member of the Labour Party of Malaya (LPM), who was killed in Kepong, Selangor.

There was a contrast in the handling of these two deaths. The UMNO worker was buried without publicity, while the LPM member was honoured at a parade on 9 May when some 3000 LPM members marched from Kuala Lumpur to Kepong, violating regulations and trying to provoke incidents with the police. Participants

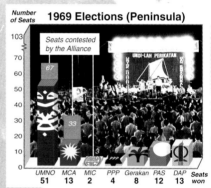

1969 Elections (Peninsula)

Number of Seats — Seats contested by the Alliance

	UMNO	MCA	MIC	PPP	Gerakan	PAS	DAP
Seats won	51	13	2	4	8	12	13

Official reasons

'The eruption of violence on May 13 was the result of an interplay of forces.... These include a generation gap and differences in interpretation of the constitutional structure by the different races in the country....; the incitement, intemperate statements and provocative behaviour of certain racialist party members and supporters during the recent General Elections; the part played by the Malayan Communist Party (MCP) and secret societies in inciting racial feelings and suspicion; and the anxious, and later desperate, mood of the Malays with a background of Sino-Malay distrust, and recently, just after the General Elections, as a result of racial insults and threats to their future survival in their own country.'

Extract from *The May 13 Tragedy, a Report by the National Operations Council*, October 1969.

Flashpoints

Violence was focused in Kuala Lumpur, and erupted in only a limited number of other locations. There were no disturbances in Sabah or Sarawak.

sang Communist songs, waved red flags, and called upon the people to boycott the general election.

Amidst this tension, the general election was held on 10 May 1969. Election day itself passed without incident; the results the following day showed that the opposition had tied with the Alliance for control of the Selangor state legislature.

On 12 May, thousands of Chinese marched through Kuala Lumpur and parading through the predominantly Malay areas of Kampung Baru and Kampung Pandan, they hurled insults of a racial nature.

The events of 13 May

Members of UMNO Youth gathered in Kuala Lumpur at the residence of Selangor Menteri Besar, Dato' Harun bin Haji Idris, on 13 May and demanded that they too should hold a victory celebration: at the national level the Alliance had gained a majority in Parliament, albeit a reduced one, and in Selangor it had gained the majority by cooperating with the sole independent candidate.

While the UMNO Youth members were gathered in the compound of the Menteri Besar's residence, two cars containing a number of Chinese suddenly drew up. The Chinese asked the gathering to disperse, saying that the residence now belonged to the opposition leader. Meanwhile, news arrived that Chinese groups had attacked Malays in Setapak. This triggered a wave of violence resulting in loss of life and property.

The Malay version of the Emergency (Essential Powers) Ordinance of 16 May 1969. In English it stated: 'By reason of the existence of a grave emergency threatening the security of Malaysia, a Proclamation of Emergency has been issued'.

Declaration of emergency

Many people in Kuala Lumpur were caught in the midst of the racial violence. Dozens were injured and even killed; houses were burnt, and lorries and cars wrecked. The violence was largely limited to

Burnt-out and overturned cars along Jalan Raja Abdullah, Kuala Lumpur, shortly after 13 May 1969.

RIGHT: The only way members of the public could leave their homes during the curfew was with a pass such as this. The round-the-clock curfew imposed on 13 May was gradually relaxed. Within a month it extended only to late night hours.

The scale of the tragedy: 13 May–31 July 1969

	Malays	Indians	Chinese	Others	Total
Deaths (in parentheses, by gunshots)	25 (10)	13 (6)	143 (35)	15 (1)	196 (52)
Injuries caused by firearms	37	17	125	1	180
Injuries by other weapons	90	9	145	15	259
Arrests leading to court charges	1133	1470	2907	51	5561

Source: *The May 13 Tragedy, a Report by the National Operations Council*, October 1969.

Kuala Lumpur, although isolated skirmishes occurred in Melaka, Perak and Penang.

The government ordered an immediate round-the-clock curfew throughout the state of Selangor (which at the time included Kuala Lumpur). Security forces took control of the situation: 2000 Malay Regiment soldiers and 3600 police officers were deployed. Over 300 Chinese families were moved to refugee centres at the Merdeka Stadium and the Tiong Nam Settlement.

On 14 May 1969, a state of emergency was declared throughout the country, and on 16 May the National Operations Council (NOC) was established by proclamation of the Yang di-Pertuan Agong and headed by Tun Abdul Razak. With Parliament suspended, the NOC became the supreme decision-making body for the next 18 months. State and District Operations Councils took over state and local government.

The NOC implemented security measures to restore law and order in the country, including the establishment of an unarmed Vigilante Corps, a territorial army, and police force battalions. The restoration of order in the country, although not immediately accomplished, was gradually achieved. Curfews continued in most parts of the country, but were gradually scaled back. Peace was restored in the affected areas within two months. In February 1971 parliamentary rule was re-established.

Reporting the tragedy

From 15 to 17 May, the government ordered the suspension of newspaper publishing. On 22 May, publications produced by political parties were banned. Just the day before, censorship—of matters deemed prejudicial to public order, or national security—was introduced under the Essential (Newspapers and other publication) Regulations 1969. These regulations empowered the authorities to require the submission of any matter intended for printing or publishing for scrutiny and clearance, and enabled them to open, examine and, if necessary, seize post, telegrams and printed matter. The penalty for offences under the regulations was a fine of M$10,000 or three years imprisonment or both.

Despite the risk of publications being proscribed, the foreign media remained undeterred. For example, *Life* magazine published an article in July 1969 by Peter Simms entitled 'A Quiet Coup in Kuala Lumpur' which was considered by Tunku Abdul Rahman Putra to contain misstatements of fact, distortions of truth, deliberate omissions, fantastic conclusions and pontifical prophesies. The issue containing the article was not banned from sale in Malaysia, however.

The Straits Times headlines: the 15 May edition (above right) was published but not widely distributed; that of 16 May (right) is the Singapore edition, as the Malaysian press was by then suspended.

ABOVE: Tunku Abdul Rahman Putra (left) reassures community leaders at a relief centre in Kuala Lumpur on 17 May 1969.

LEFT: Tun Abdul Razak (right) and Tan Sri (now Tun) Muhammad Ghazali Shafie (dark shirt) visit Kampung Datuk Keramat to see food distribution by goodwill committees.

Accounts of the tragedy

1. Prime Minister Tunku Abdul Rahman Putra published his personal account of the tragedy, *May 13: Before and After*, in late September 1969.

2. The National Operations Council published its official report on 9 October 1969.

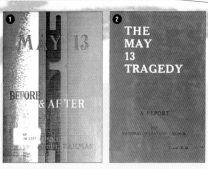

The National Operations Council

Three days after the tragedy of 13 May 1969, Parliament was suspended and responsibility for the running of the country transferred to the National Operations Council (NOC) led by Tun Abdul Razak. The NOC succeeded in restoring order and implemented policies designed to promote national unity. It also introduced measures to protect the special position of the Malays. The NOC had a lasting impact on Malaysia's government, economy and social order.

Formation

On the evening of 13 May 1969, serious rioting broke out in Kuala Lumpur. A state of emergency was declared on 14 May by the Yang di-Pertuan Agong on the advice of Prime Minister Tunku Abdul Rahman Putra. Two days later, the Yang di-Pertuan Agong, by virtue of Article 150 of the Federal Constitution, empowered himself to make regulations to deal with the emergency and to create the office of Director of Operations and establish the National Operations Council (NOC). The Yang di-Pertuan

Prime Minister Tunku Abdul Rahman Putra (fourth from left) and National Operations Council Director of Operations Tun Abdul Razak (to the Tunku's right) meeting with Heads of the State Operations Councils.

The Department of National Unity

The Department of National Unity was set up by the National Operations Council. Its main tasks was to forge unity and harmony. Led by Tun V. T. Sambanthan, the Department was essentially a research, monitoring and evaluation agency with the mandate to conduct reseach into the most fundamental issues of Malaysian society, particularly pertaining to community relations.

In 1972, the Department was merged with the National Goodwill Office to form the Ministry of National Unity. This ministry coordinated the functions of the National Unity Advisory Council and the Goodwill Councils at federal, state and district levels. In 1990, a Ministry of National Unity and Community Development was formed. In 2004, the Department of National Unity was moved to the Prime Minister's Department.

An important part of the department's efforts to strengthen national unity was the Rukun Tetangga (Neighbourhood Committee) ('RT') programme launched in 1975. RT was initially a self-help scheme under which certain residential areas were designated as RT zones the residents of which would look after their own safety and welfare. The concept was expanded in 2001 to include community development, such as social outreach efforts aimed at specific target groups like disabled persons, single mothers and drug addicts.

Agong then delegated all of his powers under the Constitution and other written laws to the Director of Operations to be exercised by the Director as he might think fit, subject to the proviso that the Director of Operations had to exercize those powers in accordance with the advice of the Prime Minister.

Deputy Prime Minister Tun Abdul Razak bin Dato' Hussein was appointed as the Director of Operations and the other members of the NOC were appointed, with its executive arm headed by Lieutenant General Dato' Ibrahim Ismail. State and District Operations Committees were also established to assume the roles of state and local governments respectively.

Policies

The NOC formulated and implemented policies designed to restore harmony and goodwill among Malaysia's diverse communities. On 17 July 1969 a National Goodwill Council was formed under the chairmanship of Tunku Abdul Rahman Putra. State and local goodwill committees were also set up around the country. The function of these committees was to promote goodwill among the various communities, to study social and public welfare problems and coordinate with the appropriate government agencies, and to assist in social and charitable work. A tangible success of the committees was to convince refugees from the events of 13 May to return to their homes. The committees also held goodwill markets and goodwill parties, encouraging neighbours of various races to become better acquainted with one another.

Prime Minister Tunku Abdul Rahman Putra (seated second from left) addressing the inaugural session of the 67-member National Consultative Council in the Senate Chamber Parliament, 27 January 1970.

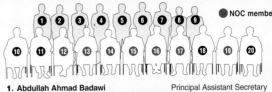

● NOC members

1. Abdullah Ahmad Badawi	Principal Assistant Secretary
2. C. C. Too	Director of Psychological Warfare
3. Deputy Superintendent Yahya Yeop Ishak	Royal Malaysia Police
4. Superintendent Mohammed Hanif Omar	Royal Malaysia Police
5. Mohd Amir Ya'acob	Assistant Secretary
6. Lieutenant Colonel Wan Ismail Wan Salleh	Ministry of Defence
7. Lieutenant Colonel Ghazali Che Mat	Ministry of Defence
8. Mohd Yusoff bin Abdul Rashid	Legal Advisor
9. Shariff Buruk	Press Relations Officer
10. Azizan Zainul Abidin	Principal Assistant Secretary
11. Tan Sri Mohd Salleh Ismael	Inspector-General of Police
12. Tan Sri Muhammad Ghazali Shafie	Permanent Secretary, Ministry of Foreign Affairs
13. Tun V. T. Sambanthan	Minister for Works, Posts and Telecommunications
14. Tun (Dr) Ismail bin Dato' Abdul Rahman	Minister of Home Affairs
15. Tun Abdul Razak bin Dato' Hussein	Director of Operations
16. Tun Tan Siew Sin	Special Functions Minister
17. Hamzah Dato' Abu Samah	Minister of Information and Broadcasting
18. Lieutenant General Dato' Ibrahim bin Ismail	Chief Executive Officer
19. Tan Sri Abdul Kadir Shamsuddin	Chief Civil Affairs Officer
20. Abdul Rahman Hamidon	Secretary

Note: The eighth member of the NOC, General Tan Sri Tunku Osman Tunku Mohd Jewa, Chief of Armed Forces Staff, was not present for the photograph.

Subsequently, the Department of National Unity was set up to carry out and coordinate activities for the promotion of national unity and solidarity. A National Consultative Council was then formed to establish guidelines for interracial cooperation and social integration for the growth of national identity. The Department of National Unity drafted the *Rukunegara* (National Ideology) which was then submitted for deliberation to the National Consultative Council.

The setting up of the National Goodwill Council, the Department of National Unity and the National Consultative Council reflected the serious efforts taken by the NOC to improve the social relations at the heart of national unity.

Tun Abdul Razak laid out the basis of a New Economic Policy to build a more dynamic, coherent, progressive and just society (see 'Economic policies'). He was of the view that there could be no real unity among the people while the gap between rich and poor was so wide. He emphasized the need to provide greater opportunities in rural areas and to reduce unemployment in both rural and urban areas. He also called for more aggressive land development schemes so as to improve the lot of the Malays. Chinese industrialists were exhorted to employ an appropriate percentage of Malays. At the same time, efforts were made to attract foreign capital, a move that was intended to benefit the Chinese community as much as that of the Malays.

Steps were also taken to enhance the education system. A new education policy was announced on 10 July 1969: Malay was to be introduced in stages to replace English as the medium of instruction in government schools.

Another step taken by the NOC was the removal of sensitive issues—the 'entrenched provisions' of the Constitution—from public discourse. It became an offence to question Malay rights, the national language, the sovereignty of the Malay Rulers and citizenship. These changes to the law were made to ensure that racial sensitivities would not again be used for political provocation.

Successful conclusion

The NOC was able to restore quickly peace and confidence. Parliamentary government was reintroduced in February 1971.

The *Rukunegara*

Formally proclaimed by the Yang di-Pertuan Agong on 31 August 1970, the *Rukunegara* (National Ideology) sought to balance development with good values and is intended for both the government and citizens.

LEFT: It is common practice for school students to take the oath of *Rukunegara* during morning assembly.

OUR NATION, MALAYSIA,
being dedicated:
    to achieving a greater unity
      of all her peoples;
    to maintaining a
      democratic way of life;
    to creating a just society in which the
      wealth of the nation shall be equitably shared;
    to ensuring a liberal approach to her
      rich and diverse cultural traditions;
    to building a progressive society which shall be oriented
    to modern science and technology;

WE, her peoples, pledge our united efforts to attain these ends guided by these principles:

    Belief in God
    Loyalty to King and Country
    Upholding the Constitution
    Rule of Law
    Good Behaviour and Morality

Laws passed

While Parliament was suspended, Director of Operations Tun Abdul Razak bin Dato' Hussein enacted federal laws in the form of regulations. The earlier regulations were for the most part directly related to the events of 13 May 1969, and included the Emergency (Essential Powers) Ordinance 1969, the Essential (Requisition of Property other than Land) Regulations 1969, the Police (Mobilisation of Reserve) Order 1969, the Essential (Procedure for Deprivation of Citizenship) Regulations 1969 and the Essential (Disposal of Dead Bodies and Dispensation of Inquests and Death Inquiries) Regulations 1969.

By 1970, the NOC began to pass regulations relating to the ordinary functions of government such as the establishment of free trade zones and of the Tourism Development Council.

Mission accomplished: Tun Abdul Razak chairs the last NOC meeting on 7 February 1971.

Economic policies

As a consequence of the events of May 1969, the government implemented the bold New Economic Policy (NEP) which aimed to achieve national unity by eliminating poverty and restructuring society. Overall, the 20-year NEP was a success, although it did not meet all its targets. Subsequent policies have continued the broad aims of the NEP.

National Economic Consultative Council Chairman Tan Sri Muhammad Ghazali Shafie (right) presenting the MAPEN 1 report, which assessed the success of the New Economic Policy, to Prime Minister Dr Mahathir Mohamad in 1991.

The New Economic Policy (1971–1990)

In June 1971, the Federal Government launched the New Economic Policy (NEP), the main objective of which was to foster national unity. This 20-year plan incorporated a two-fold policy agenda: poverty eradication and societal restructuring.

The main focus of poverty eradication was to reduce the number of hardcore poor. This was to be achieved by raising income levels and increasing employment opportunities for all Malaysians regardless of race. Measures included the introduction of modern techniques and better use of facilities in the agricultural sector. There was also a shift towards high-productivity economic activities such as land development schemes, fishing, commerce, industry and modern services. Financial and technical assistance, education and training opportunities were provided and new government agencies were established. The role and scope of existing government agencies such as the Federal Land Development Agency (FELDA) and Majlis Amanah Rakyat (MARA or Council of Trust for the Indigenous People) were strengthened and broadened. By 1973, FELDA had resettled nearly 174,000 people, mostly Malays, as part of its land development scheme. In the same year, MARA sponsored more than 5000 Malay students to study locally and abroad.

The other major component of the NEP was the restructuring of society regardless of race. This included the reduction and eventual elimination of identification of race with economic function. As part of this, efforts were made to modernize the rural economy and to create a Bumiputera Commercial and Industrial Community to enable the Malays and other indigenous people to become full partners in all aspects of economic life.

The NEP aimed to increase the Bumiputera share of the economy to 30 per cent, and at the

Top: Tun Abdul Razak (third from left) addressing Permanent Secretaries on the Second Malaysia Plan, February 1970.

Above: Dato' Hussein Onn (left) and Tun Ismail Mohd Ali, the Chairman of PNB, at the launch of Amanah Saham Nasional, a unit trust fund for Bumiputera individuals, 1981.

Objectives of the New Economic Policy

- Reduce and eventually eradicate poverty by raising income levels and increasing work opportunities for all Malaysians, irrespective of race.

- Restructure society to correct economic imbalances, to reduce and eventually eliminate the identification of race with economic function.
  - Modernize rural life
  - Promote rapid and balanced growth of urban activities
  - Create a Malay Commercial and Industrial Community.

- Benchmarks for success
  - Occupations of Malaysians to reflect the country's racial composition
  - Bumiputera to own 30 per cent of corporate share capital.

The New Economic Policy was laid out in the Second Malaysia Plan.

Some organizations established under the New Economic Policy

Organization	Year
Food Industries of Malaysia (FIMA)	1971
Lembaga Kemajuan Ikan Malaysia (LKIM) (Fisheries Development Authority of Malaysia)	1971
Lembaga Padi dan Beras Negara (LPN)	1971
Malaysian Rubber Development Corporation (MARDEC)	1971
Pahang State Agricultural Development Corporation (Pahang SADC)	1971
Sabah Economic Development Corporation	1971
Southeast Pahang Development Corporation (DARA)	1971
Urban Development Authority (UDA)	1971
Komplex Kewangan Berhad	1972
Sarawak Economic Development Corporation	1972
Selangor State Agricultural Development Corporation (Selangor-SADC)	1972
Southeast Johor Development Authority (KEJORA)	1972
Central Terengganu Development Authority (KETENGAH)	1973
Perlis State Development Corporation	1973
Rubber Industry Smallholders' Development Authority (RISDA)	1973
Farmers' Organisation Authority	1973
Petroliam Nasional Berhad (PETRONAS)	1974
Permodalan Nasional Berhad(PNB) (National Equity Corporation)	1978
Yayasan Pelaburan Bumiputera (YBP) (Bumiputera Investment Foundation)	1978
Heavy Industries Corporation of Malaysia (HICOM)	1980

Permodalan Nasional Berhad (PNB or National Equity Corporation) headquarters in Kuala Lumpur.

The Rubber Industry Smallholders' Development Authority (RISDA) building in Kuala Lumpur.

Left: PETRONAS Melaka Refinery Complex. PETRONAS is wholly owned by the Government.

Right: Wisma SEDCO, Kota Kinabalu, Sabah. SEDCO is a state-owned agency that stimulates the development of Sabah.

same time increase the share of the non-Malays to 40 per cent. This reallocation of the economy was to be made possible by a reduction of the stake held by foreigners to 30 per cent.

Direct government participation in the economy was increased with the setting up of state-owned enterprises and the establishment of joint ventures with the private sector. Malay entrepreneurs were given assistance in the form of licenses, contracts and credit facilities. This led to the creation of *Melayu Korporat* (Corporate Malays) who went on to cooperate and compete successfully with established non-Malay businesses.

On 19 January 1989, the National Economic Consultative Council (NECC) was formed to evaluate the progress of NEP. The NECC found that the NEP had succeeded in reducing poverty and, to some extent, in reducing the economic imbalances between the three main ethnic groups. However, Bumiputera corporate share ownership amounted to 20.3 per cent and not 30 per cent as targeted. Other major challenges also remained including urban poverty and the declining socioeconomic standing of the Indian community. Measures recommended by the NECC included the provision of more equitable educational opportunities.

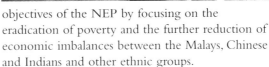

The second and third Outline Perspective Plans that contain the National Development Policy and National Vision Policy.

objectives of the NEP by focusing on the eradication of poverty and the further reduction of economic imbalances between the Malays, Chinese and Indians and other ethnic groups.

The government took steps to create more Bumiputera entrepreneurs. One of the mechanisms for doing this was by identifying particular Malay industrialists to lead certain economic sectors. The success of this plan was, however, hampered by the effects of the Asian Financial Crisis of 1997–8.

Several well-known Bumiputera corporate figures required government assistance, and the government had to intervene to restructure government-linked companies and major Bumiputera-controlled assets. These circumstances overshadowed the overall success of the NDP, which reduced the poverty level from 16.5 per cent in 1990 to 7.5 per cent in 1999.

ABOVE LEFT: Chinese-controlled companies such as YTL have flourished under the government's successive economic policies.

ABOVE: Foreign-owned companies, particularly those involved in the electronics sector, such as Sony, have invested in Malaysia.

Objectives of the National Development Policy

- Continue objectives of the NEP.
- Emphasize eradication of hard-core poverty.
- Reduce relative poverty, and improve access of lower-income groups to better social services and opportunities.
- Develop an active Bumiputera Commercial and Industrial Community (BCIC) to increase Bumiputera participation in modern sectors of the economy.
- Enlist the private sector to create growth opportunities.
- Promote human resource and entrepreneurial skills development.

Objectives of the National Vision Policy

- Build a resilient nation.
- Promote an equitable society.
- Sustain high economic growth.
- Enhancing competitiveness.
- Develop a knowledge-based economy.
- Strengthen human resource development.
- Pursue environmentally sustainable development.

The New Development Policy (1991–2000)

As a continuation of the NEP, the government launched the New Development Policy (NDP) in 1991. This 10-year programme continued the

Privatization

In 1983, the government introduced the policy of privatization. The objectives of privatization included reducing the government's financial and administrative burden, enhancing efficiency and productivity, facilitating economic growth, reducing government involvement in the economy, and precipitating the achievement of the goals of the New Economic Policy.

Privatization has taken several forms including 'build-operate' (where a company is licensed to build and to manage a project), 'build-operate-transfer' (where a company is given an agreed period to build and to operate a project after which the project is transferred to the government), asset sales and management

Northport, a privatized entity.

buy-outs. In some cases, privatization has been achieved in two stages, with corporatization (ie. with the institution granted control of human resources and limited financial control) occurring prior to full privatization.

Between 1983 and 2004, 485 government bodies were privatized (139 of which were new projects). This saved the government capital expenditure of RM138.9 billion and, by 2004, RM7.8 billion in annual operating expenditure. In 2004, over 113,000 employees worked for privatized organizations.

The National Vision Policy (2000–2010)

A new National Vision Policy (NVP), was introduced following the review of the NDP undertaken by the Second National Economic Consultative Council in 2000. With the overriding objective of maintaining national unity, the aim of the National Vision Policy (NVP) was to establish a progressive and prosperous society. The policy focused on building a resilient and competitive nation, although socioeconomic development policies would continue to be given priority. Economic growth was to be promoted alongside efforts aimed at restructuring marginalized elements of society, eradicating hardcore poverty and empowering human resource development among the Orang Asli, the Bumiputera communities of Sabah and Sarawak, and also among the Indians.

The target of the NVP is to reduce the social, economic, and regional imbalances among the various ethnic groups. One aspect of this policy is the development of a knowledge-based society; others include the desire to increase domestic investment and to develop indigenous capacity while still attracting foreign investment in strategic areas such as information technology.

Tan Sri Ahmad Sarji bin Abdul Hamid (right), Chairman of the Second National Economic Consultative Council presenting the report to Prime Minister Dr Mahathir Mohamad at Putrajaya in 2000.

The Barisan Nasional framework

In 1974, an enlarged political coalition—which included former opposition parties and parties from Sabah and Sarawak—was formed. Known as the Barisan Nasional (National Front), it has proved to be a success, winning at least two thirds of all parliamentary seats at each general election that it has contested.

Signboard for the office of a Barisan Nasional Member of Parliament incorporating the Barisan logo of a pair of scales (*dacing*) to represent balance, and slogan 'Vision. Justice. Efficiency.'

Tun Abdul Razak (second from left), seen here chairing a Barisan Nasional meeting in June 1974, is credited as being the architect of the Barisan Nasional.

The formation of Barisan Nasional

Heeding the advice of his predecessor, Tunku Abdul Rahman Putra, to share power, Tun Abdul Razak set about enlarging the Alliance.

In the Peninsula, the People's Progressive Party (PPP), which almost gained control of Perak in 1969, and Parti Gerakan Rakyat Malaysia (Gerakan), which won control of Penang, joined the Alliance in 1972. Parti Islam Se-Malaysia (PAS), which had won in Kelantan, formed a coalition with the Alliance in 1973. In Sarawak, a Sarawak Alliance–SUPP coalition was formed in 1970, although the Sarawak Alliance lapsed in 1974. The Sabah Alliance was formed in 1962.

In early 1974, Tun Abdul Razak held a series of high-level talks with leaders of the Alliance member parties to work out a common strategy

and platform for the general election anticipated later in the year. The adoption of a common symbol for all Barisan Nasional parties—the scales of justice (*dacing*)—was announced in April 1974, and the Barisan Nasional was registered on 1 June 1974, just two months before the general election. Member parties of the Barisan Nasional at that time included PBB (being the Sarawak Alliance's sole remaining member), SUPP, and the Sabah Alliance.

The Barisan Nasional formula and framework are similar to those of the Alliance, although the dominance of UMNO is even more apparent. In particular, the President of UMNO automatically becomes Barisan Nasional Chairman. The overriding objective of the Barisan Nasional is to foster and maintain a united and harmonious Malaysian nation.

Challenges

The Barisan Nasional has faced several political challenges over the years. PAS withdrew from the Barisan in 1977, and Sabah-based Parti Bersatu Sabah (PBS), withdrew in 1985. However, PBS lost its control of the state in the 1986 state elections.

The strongest political challenge to Barisan Nasional came in February 1988, when UMNO was deregistered as a political party by the High Court of Malaysia. This followed a highly charged contest

Barisan over the years

The membership of the Barisan Nasional coalition has grown over the years to include parties from all major ethnic groups. It has won large majorities, with over two-thirds of parliamentary seats, in each of the eight general elections from 1974 to 2004.

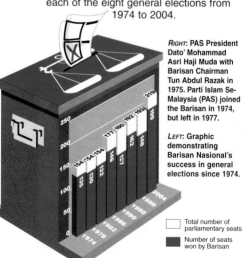

Right: PAS President Dato' Mohammad Asri Haji Muda with Barisan Chairman Tun Abdul Razak in 1975. Parti Islam Se-Malaysia (PAS) joined the Barisan in 1974, but left in 1977.

Left: Graphic demonstrating Barisan Nasional's success in general elections since 1974.

Growth of the coalition

Alliance (1969)	Barisan Nasional (1974)	Barisan Nasional (2005)
UMNO	UMNO	UMNO
MCA	MCA	MCA
MIC	MIC	MIC
	PAS	PPP
	PPP	Gerakan
	Gerakan	SUPP
	SUPP	PBB
	PBB	PRS
	Sabah Alliance	SPDP
		SAPP
		PBS
		LDP
		PBRS
		UPKO
3	9	14

□ Total number of parliamentary seats
■ Number of seats won by Barisan

Dato' Hussein Onn (second from left) chairing a meeting of the Barisan Nasional Council. Seated with him are Dr Mahathir Mohamad (left), Ghafar Baba (second from right) and MCA President Datuk Lee San Choon, June 1978.

Component parties

1. Prime Minister Dato' Seri Dr Mahathir Mohamad officiated at the MCA's 49th Annual General Meeting, August 2002.

2. Dr Mahathir waving to the crowd at the MIC's 1999 Annual General Assembly.

3. Prime Minister Dato' Seri Abdullah Ahmad Badawi meets component party leaders after chairing a BN Sabah meeting, November 2004 (from left), PBS President Datuk Joseph Pairin Kitingan, UPKO President Tan Sri Bernard Dompok, and UMNO State Liaison Chief Datuk Seri Musa Aman (far right).

4. Dr Mahathir at the 2003 Annual General Meeting of SUPP standing beside Sarawak Barisan President, Pehin Seri Tan Sri Haji Abdul Taib bin Mahmud.

for the UMNO presidency between 'Team A' (led by Dato'Seri Dr Mahathir Mohamad) and 'Team B' (led by Tengku Razaleigh Hamzah). Despite UMNO's deregistration, the Barisan Nasional remained intact, being temporarily chaired by Datuk Seri Dr Ling Liong Sik, then President of the MCA, which formed the second largest component party. Dr Mahathir later formed UMNO Baru (New UMNO), and Tengku Razaleigh formed Semangat '46 and went into opposition. Although the Barisan National retained its two-thirds majority in the 1990 general election, the state of Kelantan was lost to opposition party PAS.

The Barisan Nasional was unable to recapture Kelantan from the opposition in the 1999 general election, and in addition lost the state of Terrengganu to PAS. The Barisan Nasional did however retain its two-third's parliamentary majority.

A successful formula

The Barisan Nasional's most conspicuous success has been its ability to maintain a two-thirds parliamentary majority at each of the eight general elections that it has contested. Two-thirds is the majority required to amend the Constitution. The Barisan Nasional, through Parliament, has thus been able to effect constitutional changes. For example, in 2001 the Federal Constitution was amended to eliminate discrimination based on gender.

Barisan component parties cooperate closely as the allocation of constituencies between them is pre-determined, and each component party supports all Barisan Nasional candidates regardless of which component party they represent. Often a non-Malay Barisan Nasional candidate is fielded in a Malay-dominated constituency.

As with the allocation of parliamentary seats, the appointment of Cabinet members is also pre-determined. In this manner, power is shared between the parties, ethnic groups and states.

Barisan Nasional leaders presenting the coalition's manifesto at the Putra World Trade Centre, Kuala Lumpur, March 2004. From left: SUPP President Tan Sri George Chan, MCA President Datuk Seri Ong Ka Ting, Barisan Deputy Chairman Dato' Sri Najib Tun Razak, Barisan Chairman Dato' Seri Abdullah Ahmad Badawi, MIC President Dato' Seri S. Samy Vellu and Barisan Secretary-General Tan Sri Khalil Yaakob.

Barisan Nasional slogans

1974: *The People's Front for Happier Malaysia*

1978: *The Man You Can Trust*

1982: *Clean; Efficient; Trustworthy*

1986: *Tradition Nurtures the People*

1990: *Towards Peace, Stability and Prosperity*

1995: *Vision. Justice. Efficiency*

1999: *Unity. Progress. Freedom*

2004: *Excellence. Glory. Distinction*

Federal–state relations

Malaysia has a federal system of government, with both the federation and its constituent states having governments. The Federal Constitution provides for a strong Federal Government in relation to those of the states. This relationship has been further reinforced as a result of a party political system dominated by the Barisan Nasional. Several national institutions have been established to enhance federal-state relations, which have generally been harmonious.

The Prime Minister's Department, Putrajaya.

Constitutional framework

At Malaya's Independence in 1957, the Federal Constitution created a strong central, or federal, government, while giving the states some measure of autonomy. Constitutionally, the status of the states and their relationships with the Federal Government and each other were equal. The Constitution of the Federation of Malaya contained articles designed to preserve the legacy of the Peninsular Malay states and sultanates, symbols of Malay power and legitimacy. The Malay Rulers and their states continue to attract strong loyalties, among both Malays and non-Malays.

When Malaysia was formed in 1963, the new Constitution retained the original's core organizational provisions but conferred additional rights and powers upon Singapore, Sabah and Sarawak. Special measures to ensure the rights and dominance of the indigenous peoples of Sabah and Sarawak were preserved.

The first two articles of the Federal Constitution identify the 13 states of the federation and the three Federal Territories, and empower Parliament to admit other states to the federation. The Federal and state governments work together through a number of institutions to implement policies, minimize overlapping responsibilities and resolve conflicts.

The Federal Government, through the Yang di-Pertuan Agong, is granted special powers by Article 150 of the Constitution to issue a proclamation of emergency in the event that the security, economic life or public order of the federation is threatened by a grave emergency. While such a proclamation is in force the executive authority of the federation extends to any matter within the legislative authority of a state and to the giving of directions to the government of a state. To date, the Federal Government has exercised such powers upon the proclamation of emergencies on two occasions: in 1966 with regard to Sarawak, and in 1977–8 in Kelantan.

Royal influence on federal-state relations has gradually reduced. The Yang di-Pertuan Agong's power to withhold or delay (for more than 30 days) the grant of royal assent to federal legislation was removed in 1984. Several of the state constitutions have been similarly amended vis-à-vis the grant of royal assent by their respective Rulers.

The Gua Musang headquarters of Lembaga Kemajuan Kelantan Selatan (KESEDAR, the South Kelantan Development Board), established in 1978.

Party politics

The operation of and relationships between political parties shaped federal-state relations from the beginning. The Alliance and its successor, the Barisan Nasional, have been in control of the Federal Government since Independence. They have also controlled most of the state governments.

Issues arising between the Federal Government and UMNO- or Barisan-led states are frequently resolved through internal party political mechanisms and processes. The states have generally deferred to the Federal Government's decisions.

Opposition parties have, at various times, taken control of certain states, for example PAS in Kelantan and Terengganu, Gerakan (prior to its joining the Barisan Nasional) in Penang and PBS in Sabah. This has resulted in federal-state tensions. The Federal Government has sometimes deployed its financial, administrative and constitutional resources (including emergency powers) to assert its influence.

The Johor State Secretariat building, Johor Bahru.

Special provisions for Sabah and Sarawak

The plan to form the federation known as Malaysia was initially treated with some scepticism by the political leaders, native chiefs and a significant minority of the populations of Sabah and Sarawak. As a result, various safeguards were established in respect of the relationship between these two states and the rest of the federation. The most important of these were included in the 'Twenty Points' published by the Inter-Governmental Committee (IGC) in February 1963, and subsequently incorporated in the Malaysia Agreement and the Federal Constitution (see 'The idea of Malaysia').

Wisma Bapa Malaysia, Kuching (left) and Wisma Innoprise, Kota Kinabalu (right) house the offices of the Chief Ministers of Sarawak and Sabah respectively.

Federal Secretaries and Federal Development Departments

The posts of Federal Secretary for the states of Sabah and Sarawak were created in 1963, responsible for coordinating the administrative functions of government departments and public corporations in the states concerned. The Federal Secretary also facilitates the implementation of federal-funded projects. His main responsibility is to strengthen relations between the Federal and state governments. The posts of Federal Secretary for each of Sabah and Sarawak were abolished in 1982 and recreated in 1990.

The Federal Development Departments of Sabah and Kelantan were established in 1991 in response to the loss of those states to opposition parties in the 1990 general election. Formed to take over the tasks and duties of the former State Development Offices, the departments coordinate and monitor the implementation of federal development projects in their respective states.

Opening ceremony of the Pahang State Assembly, officiated by the Sultan of Pahang, April 2003. The assembly can legislate for matters on the state list.

The division of legislative power

Schedule Nine of the Federal Constitution contains three legislative lists identifying the respective legislative powers of Parliament and the state legislatures: the federal, state and concurrent lists. The concurrent list includes those matters in respect of which both Parliament and the state legislatures may make laws.

In addition, Article 76 of the Constitution empowers Parliament to make laws (subject to certain exclusions) with respect to matters enumerated in the state list for the purpose of implementing any treaty, agreement or convention between the federation and any other country, or any decision of an international organization of which the federation is a member; for the purpose of uniformity of the laws of two or more states; or if requested by the legislative assembly of any state.

Article 77 of the Constitution states that the legislature of a state shall have power to make laws with respect to any matters not enumerated in any of the three lists, and which is not a matter in respect of which Parliament has power to make laws.

Federal list

1. External affairs
2. Defence of the federation or any part thereof
3. Internal security
4. Civil and criminal law and procedure and the administration of justice
5. Federal citizenship and naturalization; aliens
6. The machinery of government, subject to the state list
7. Finance
8. Trade, commerce and industry
9. Shipping, navigation and fisheries
10. Communication and transport
11. Federal works and power
12. Surveys, inquiries and research
13. Education
14. Medicine and health including sanitation in the federal capital
15. Labour and social security
16. Welfare of the aborigines
17. Professional occupations other than those specifically enumerated
18. Holidays other than state holidays; standard of time
19. Unincorporated societies
20. Control of agricultural pests; protection against such pests; prevention of plant diseases
21. Newspapers; publications; publishers; printing and printing presses
22. Censorship
23. Subject to part of item 5 of the state list: theatres; cinemas; cinematograph films; places of public amusements
25. Co-operative societies
25A. Tourism
26. Subject to item 9A of the concurrent list, prevention and extinguishment of fire, including fire services and fire brigades
27. All matters relating to the Federal Territories.

State list

1. Islamic law and personal and family law of persons professing the religion of Islam, except with respect to the Federal Territories; *wakafs* (Muslim religious bodies), charitable and religious trusts; Malay customs; Islamic religious revenue; Islamic public places of worship; *syariah* courts
2. Land, except in relation to the Federal Territories
3. Agriculture and forestry, except with respect to the Federal Territories
4. Local government outside the Federal Territories
5. Other services of a local character, except with respect to the Federal Territories
6. State works and water
7. Machinery of state government, subject to the federal list
8. State holidays
9. Creation of offences in respect of any matters included in the state list or dealt with by state law, proof of State law or of things done thereunder, and proof of any matter for purposes of state law
10. Inquiries for state purposes
11. Indemnity in respect of any matters in the state list or dealt with in state law
12. Turtles and riverine fishing
12A. Libraries, museums, ancient and historical monuments and records and archaeological sites and remains, other than those declared to be federal by or under federal law

Supplement to state list for states of Sabah and Sarawak

13. Native law and custom
14. Incorporation of authorities and other bodies set up by state law, if incorporated directly by state law, and regulation and winding-up of corporations so created.
15. Ports and harbours, other than those declared to be federal by or under federal law; regulation of traffic by water in ports and harbours or on rivers wholly within the state, except traffic in federal ports or harbours; foreshores
16. Cadastral land surveys
17. In Sabah, the Sabah Railway

Concurrent list

1. Social welfare; social services subject to the federal and state lists (excluding the Sabah and Sarawak supplement); protection of women, children and young persons
2. Scholarships
3. Protection of wild animals and wild birds; National Parks
4. Animal husbandry; prevention of cruelty to animals; veterinary services; animal quarantine
5. Town and country planning, except for the federal capital
6. Vagrancy and itinerant hawkers
7. Public health, sanitation (excluding sanitation in the federal capital) and the prevention of diseases
8. Drainage and irrigation
9. Rehabilitation of mining land and land which has suffered soil erosion
9A. Fire safety measures and fire precautions in the construction and maintenance of buildings
9B. Culture and sports
9C. Housing and provisions for housing accommodation, improvement trusts

Supplement to concurrent list for states of Sabah and Sarawak

10. Personal law relating to marriage, divorce, guardianship, maintenance, adoption, legitimacy, family law, gifts or succession, testate or intestate
11. Adulteration of foodstuffs and other goods
12. Shipping under 15 registered tons, including the carriage of passengers and goods by such shipping; maritime and estuarine fishing and fisheries
13. The production, distribution and water supply of water power and electricity generated by water power
14. Agricultural and forestry research, control of agricultural pests, and protection against such pests; prevention of plant diseases
15. Charities and charitable trusts and institutions in the state and their trustees
16. Theatres; cinemas; cinematograph films; places of public amusement
17. Elections to the state assembly held during the period of indirect elections
18. In Sabah until the end of the year 1970 (but not in Sarawak), medicine and health, including matters specified in part of item 14 of the federal list

Seremban District and Land Office, Negeri Sembilan.

Syariah Court at Petaling Jaya, Selangor.

Federal-state institutions

The Constitution provides for the establishment of federal-state institutions to address competing responsibilities and foster cooperative federalism. At the highest level is the Conference of Rulers (see 'Constitutional monarchy'). Other bodies include the National Finance Council (NFC), National Land Council (NLC), National Council for Local Government (NCLG). These powerful institutions include representatives from both Federal and state governments.

The NFC is consulted on financial matters, notably the raising of loans, securing grants from the federal government, the assignment of taxes and fees to the states. The NLC advises on all matters relating to natural resources such as land, mining, forestry, and agriculture. The NLC absorbed the National Forestry Council (set up in 1971) in 1992. The NCLG covers local government policies and regulations.

Policies formulated by the NLC and NCLG are binding on both Federal and state governments, except for Sabah and Sarawak, which accordingly have no voting powers in the councils.

The control of financial resources

The Federal Government controls Malaysia's richest and most productive revenue sources as well as major areas of expenditure. The extent of this control was demonstrated in October 2000 when the Federal Government nullified the royalty agreement between national petroleum company Petroliam Nasional Berhad (PETRONAS) and the Terengganu state government, controlled by opposition party Parti Islam Se-Malaysia (PAS). Royalty payments to the state were replaced with direct and special payments made by the Federal Government.

PETRONAS oil rig off the Terengganu coast.

State governments typically enjoy minor revenue bases such as agriculture, mining, manufacturing, trade and tourism. Large-scale federal financial transfers are inevitable, and are provided for constitutionally. Each state is thus to a degree financially dependent on the Federal Government, although the degree depends on its fiscal capacity.

Malaysia Plans

The Federal Government carries out national development projects primarily through five-year 'Malaysia Plans'. These reflect federal perspectives and direction, not least in terms of financial expenditure and allocation, and hence determine which state gets what, when and how.

SYSTEM OF GOVERNMENT

Malaysia's system of government provides institutional ballast and stability to a country only independent since 1957. With strong genetic links to the British 'Westminster' and 'Whitehall' models, the system has nevertheless been adapted to suit Malaysia's particular circumstances.

The 20 Ringgit note (discontinued in 1998) bore an image of Bank Negara Malaysia (Central Bank of Malaysia), established by the government in 1958 to issue currency and act as a banker and financial adviser to the government.

The effective functioning of the Malaysian system of government is attributable to the Constitutional Rulers, and to the three key branches of government: the legislature, the executive, and the judiciary. The doctrine of the separation of these three 'powers' is guaranteed by the Federal Constitution.

By virtue of Malaysia's status as a federal nation, each of the key branches of government is represented at the federal level and, at least to some extent, at the state level, as are the Rulers. The focus of this section of the volume is, however, on the federal level alone.

The interplay of the various branches of government is testimony to an orderly political process in which the government's writ is large and regarded as essential. Indeed, Malaysia has an authoritative and working system of government once the roles of the civil service, police and armed forces are taken into account (see 'Institutions of State and National Security').

Malaysia is a constitutional monarchy. The Yang di-Pertuan Agong (Paramount Ruler or King) is an elective position and the object of loyalty of the population of a multi-racial nation (see 'Constitutional monarchy').

At the federal level, representation of the *rakyat* (people) is fulfilled by the Dewan Rakyat (House of Representatives) supported by the Dewan Negara (Senate) (see 'The federal legislature'). However, in the Malaysian context it is the apportionment of executive responsibility to Ministers in the Cabinet that in practice forms the core of the political system. The judiciary (and the administration of justice) represents the third pillar of the governmental system.

As the nation's chief executive, the Prime Minister of Malaysia is the embodiment of elective political power and of the aspirations of the body politic. The Prime Ministerial role impacts substantially on the nation's political, economic and social fabric. Begin-ning with Tunku Abdul Rahman Putra, who was also the first and only Chief Minister of a self-governing Federation of Malaya before Independence was achieved in 1957, he and his successors have had their personality and their ideas stamped on the various phases of the country's development.

The former Prime Minister's Department building in Jalan Dato' Onn, Kuala Lumpur in 1995. In 1999, the department moved to the federal administrative capital of Putrajaya.

Constitutional monarchy

Malaysia has a unique system of monarchy: a Yang di-Pertuan Agong (Paramount Ruler or King) is elected for a period of five years from among the nine Malay Rulers. While the role of traditional rulers in democracies may have diminished, the Malay Rulers and Yang di-Pertuan Agong remain potent symbols of Malay political power. The traditions of the individual states are thus integrated with the federation.

The Raja of Perlis, Tuanku Syed Sirajuddin, signs the Oath of Office Document as the 12th Yang di-Pertuan Agong at Istana Negara in December 2001.

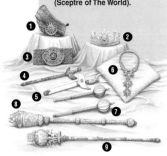

Royal regalia

Full regalia is used by the Yang di-Pertuan Agong and Raja Permaisuri Agong on royal ceremonial occasions.

1. *Tengkolok Diraja* (The Royal Headdress)
2. *Gandik Diraja* (The Royal Tiara)
3. *Pending Diraja* (The Royal Waist Buckle)
4. *Keris Panjang Diraja* (The Royal Long Kris)
5. *Keris Pendek Diraja* (The Royal Short Kris)
6. *Kalung Diraja* (The Royal Necklace)
7. *Cokmar* (The Maces)
8. *Cogan Agama* (Sceptre of Religion)
9. *Cogan Alam* (Sceptre of The World).

His Majesty the Yang di-Pertuan Agong

A constitutional monarch reigns but does not rule, and is essentially a ceremonial Head of State. Thus the traditional status of monarch is reconciled with a modern state system, within the provisions of the Federal Constitution.

The Head of State of Malaysia is the Yang di-Pertuan Agong. His consort is known as the Raja Permaisuri Agong and takes precedence immediately after him. Both are full sovereigns with the titles 'His Majesty' and 'Her Majesty' respectively.

The Yang di-Pertuan Agong's powers fall into three categories: acting on the advice of the Cabinet or Prime Minister; acting on the advice of other organizations such as the Pardons Board and Religious Affairs Council; and discretionary functions, including the appointment of a Prime Minister. As the fountain of honour, he bestows federal awards.

Election of the Yang di-Pertuan Agong

The Yang di-Pertuan Agong is elected by secret ballot at the Conference of Rulers from among Malaysia's nine Malay Rulers and holds office for five years. Thus, all the Rulers have a chance to serve as Yang di-Pertuan Agong. Once the original list of Rulers in line for the office is exhausted, a new one is instituted—though the order is not necessarily based on seniority or the previous sequence.

The extension of the process of democracy to the very highest level, namely the election of the

Head of State, was the idea of Tunku Abdul Rahman Putra, the nation's first Prime Minister.

Once appointed, the Yang di-Pertuan Agong ceases to exercise his functions as Ruler of his particular state, other than those as Head of Islam. A Regent will usually be appointed in his place.

The Conference of Rulers also elects a Deputy Head of State, the Timbalan Yang di-Pertuan Agong, who performs the King's duties in the event of the latter's incapacity due to illness, or absence from the Federation. At other times, the Timbalan Yang di-Pertuan Agong continues to perform his function as head of his own state.

The Timbalan Yang di-Pertuan Agong does not automatically become the next Yang di-Pertuan Agong. In the event of the Yang di-Pertuan Agong's death or resignation, the Conference convenes and each Ruler may offer himself for the position. A secret ballot is taken, and the first to receive five or more votes is chosen.

Hereditary state Rulers

The Malay Rulers are Heads of State for their respective states. They are also Constitutional Rulers, acting on the advice of their respective state governments. Unlike the office of the Yang di-Pertuan Agong, that of the Malay Ruler is

The Conference of Rulers in 1948 (top) and in 2004 (left). The Conference must be consulted on, among other things, the appointment of judges, the Attorney-General, the Election Commission and the Public Services Commission.

The Conference of Rulers

The Conference of Rulers comprises the nine Rulers of the Malay States. One of its main functions is to elect the Yang di-Pertuan Agong and his Timbalan (Deputy).

As each Sultan is also head of Islam in his respective state, the Conference also serves as a platform for making decisions concerning Islam for the whole nation. For example, the Conference determines the dates for starting and ending the fasting month of Ramadan; and the festive months of *Syawal* (marked by Hari Raya Aidilfitri) and *Zulhijjah* (Hari Raya Aidiladha).

First-day cover published in 1997 to commemorate the first century of the Conference of Rulers.

The Conference is also attended by the Yang di-Pertua Negeri, with the Chief Ministers of each state acting as advisors. They do not participate in matters concerning the election of the Yang di-Pertuan Agong.

The consent of the Conference is required on matters pertaining to the Rulers' position and privileges, territorial integrity of the states and the federation, the special privileges of Bumiputera and citizenship, and amendments to the Federal Constitution. In theory this gives the Sultans a degree of authority within the political process—a check on executive power.

His Majesty the Yang di-Pertuan Agong—from Independence to the present

1st Yang di-Pertuan Agong
Almarhum Tuanku Abdul
Rahman Ibni Almarhum
Tuanku Muhammad.

Negeri Sembilan
31 Aug. 1957–1 Apr. 1960

2nd Yang di-Pertuan Agong
Almarhum Tuanku Hisamuddin
Alam Shah Al-Haj Ibni
Almarhum Sultan Alaiddin
Sulaiman Shah.

Selangor
14 Apr. 1960–1 Sept. 1960

3rd Yang di-Pertuan Agong
Almarhum Tuanku Syed Putra
Al-Haj Ibni Almarhum Syed
Hassan Jamalullail.

Perlis
21 Sept. 1960–20 Sept. 1965

4th Yang di-Pertuan Agong
Almarhum Tuanku Ismail
Nasiruddin Shah Ibni
Almarhum Sultan Zainal
Abidin.

Terengganu
21 Sept. 1965–20 Sept. 1970

5th Yang di-Pertuan Agong
Al-Sultan Almu'tasimu Billahi
Muhibbuddin Tuanku Alhaj
Abdul Halim Mu'adzam Shah
Ibni Almarhum Sultan Badlishah.

Kedah
21 Sept. 1970–20 Sept. 1975

6th Yang di-Pertuan Agong
Almarhum Tuanku Yahya Petra
Ibni Almarhum Sultan Ibrahim.

Kelantan
21 Sept. 1975–29 Mar. 1979

7th Yang di-Pertuan Agong
Sultan Haji Ahmad Shah
Al-Musta'in Billah Ibni
Almarhum Sultan Abu Bakar
Ri'ayatuddin Al-mu'adzam Shah.

Pahang
26 Apr. 1979–25 Apr. 1984

8th Yang di-Pertuan Agong
Sultan Iskandar Ibni Almarhum
Sultan Ismail.

Johor
26 Apr. 1984–25 Apr. 1989

9th Yang di-Pertuan Agong
Sultan Azlan Muhibbuddin Shah
Ibni Almarhum Sultan Yussuf
Izzuddin Shah Ghafarullahu-lah.

Perak
26 Apr. 1989–25 Apr. 1994

10th Yang di-Pertuan Agong
Tuanku Ja'afar Ibni Almarhum
Tuanku Abdul Rahman.

Negeri Sembilan
26 Apr. 1994–25 Apr. 1999

11th Yang di-Pertuan Agong
Almarhum Sultan Salahuddin
Abdul Aziz Shah Alhaj Ibni
Almarhum Sultan Hisamuddin
Alam Shah Alhaj.

Selangor
26 Apr. 1999–21 Nov. 2001

12th Yang di-Pertuan Agong
Tuanku Syed Sirajuddin Ibni
Almarhum Tuanku Syed Putra
Jamalullail.

Perlis
13 Dec. 2001–present

hereditary, although the system of succession varies from state to state. The non-royal states—Penang, Melaka, Sabah and Sarawak—are each headed by a Yang di-Pertua Negeri, who is federally appointed after consultation with the respective Chief Minister, and holds office for four years.

Prior to British rule, beginning in Perak in 1874, the Malay Rulers had wide-ranging powers. These became circumscribed under the British. They became Rulers-in-Council, and participated in the governance of their respective states in this capacity,

giving their assent to Ordinances and Acts passed by the State Councils. Upon Independence, they gave their assent to legislation passed by the state legislative assemblies.

The Malay Rulers retain their role as fountains of honour in their respective states, through the granting of honours and awards.

Additionally, the Malay Rulers are heads of Islam in their states, while the Yang di-Pertuan Agong assumes this function for Penang, Melaka, Sabah and Sarawak.

The Yang di-Pertua Negeri
In the four states of Melaka, Penang, Sabah and Sarawak, the Yang di-Pertua Negeri assumes the position of Head of State. The Federal Constitution specifies, however, that the Malay Rulers take precedence over the Yang di-Pertua Negeri.

Formerly known as Governors, the Yang di-Pertua Negeri exercise their executive powers in accordance with their respective state's Constitution. Generally, they make decisions based on the advice of the State Cabinet or the Chief Minister. However, each Yang di-Pertua Negeri has the authority to order the sitting and dissolution of his respective State Legislative Assembly. In addition, the assent of the Yang di-Pertua Negeri is required on every law and regulation approved by the State Legislative Assembly.

Sarawak Yang di-Pertua Negeri Tun Abang Muhammad Salahuddin (second from right) arrives for the opening of the 2004 State Legislative Assembly sitting.

Landmark constitutional amendments
There have been two important amendments to the Federal Constitution which have modified the constitutional monarchy (see 'A constitutional state'). The first was in 1983, which stipulated that the Yang di-Pertuan Agong shall assent to Parliamentary Bills within 30 days of their being presented to him. This is done by his causing the Public Seal of the Federation to be affixed to the Bill. If a Bill is not assented to by the Yang di-Pertuan Agong within the specified 30 days, it automatically becomes law as if it had been assented to.

Until the enactment of the Constitutional (Amendment) Act 1993, the Malay Rulers were immune from criminal prosecution. The amendments to the Constitution created a Special Court in which any proceedings by or against the Yang di-Pertuan Agong or the Ruler of a state in his personal capacity could be brought. The Special Court, which has its registry in Kuala Lumpur, comprises the Chief Justice of the Federal Court, the two Chief Judges of the High Courts, and two persons who have held office as judge of the Federal Court or a High Court appointed by the Conference of Rulers. Proceedings in the Special Court are decided in accordance with the majority vote of the members.

1. The Public Seal of the Federation, kept at the Yang di-Pertuan Agong's official residence, Istana Negara (National Palace).

2. When affixed to a Parliamentary Bill, the seal signifies the Yang di-Pertuan Agong's assent to the Bill, which thereby becomes law.

The federal legislature

Legislative authority is vested in Parliament, which comprises the Yang di-Pertuan Agong, the House of Representatives (Dewan Rakyat) and the Senate (Dewan Negara). The power to make laws is exercised by Bills being passed by both houses of Parliament and assented to by the Yang di-Pertuan Agong.

The Dewan Rakyat in session.

First day cover issued on 12 September 1959 commemorating the inauguration of Parliament.

Functions of Parliament

Parliament's main function is law-making. It is considered supreme and has the power to make or unmake any law. Bills usually originate from the Dewan Rakyat, and may relate to any subject under the Federal Constitution for which laws can be enacted, including matters that fall within the concurrent list (see 'Federal-state relations'). One of the most important roles played by Parliament is the approval of the annual budget and five-yearly development plans.

Parliament is also a forum where government policies can be scrutinized and debated. When a Bill is introduced in Parliament, it is closely examined. At each parliamentary sitting, one hour is set aside for oral questions. It is common practice for Members of Parliament (MPs) to question Ministers on various aspect of government administration. An MP may seek information or use questions to expose weaknesses in government. Ministers are, however, entitled to have notice and to give written replies.

MPs may also seek to air the grievances of their local constituencies by proposing motions for debate in Parliament.

Parliamentary privilege and procedures

All proceedings in Parliament are 'privileged', subject to certain limitations specified in the Constitution. That means that MPs have complete freedom of speech and are not exposed to court action for things that are said in Parliament. This helps to ensure that, as representatives of the people, they can carry out their duties without fear or favour.

Parliamentary procedures are regulated by the Dewan concerned and cannot be questioned in any court of law. The procedures are based on Standing Orders. If precedents are not to be found in the Standing Orders, the Speaker may make a new ruling, guided by similar practices in other Commonwealth countries. The Speaker's rulings are final.

The Standing Orders also prescribe the proper decorum required of the MPs. For example, MPs must refrain from personal attacks. Words of treason and sedition that can incite ill feelings between religious and ethnic communities are disallowed. Abuses of privileges are subject to punishment by the Committee of Privileges. An MP may be ejected from Parliament or suspended for misconduct.

All proceedings in Parliament are conducted in Malay, the official language since the National Language Act was passed in 1967. The Speaker, however, may grant permission to a member to speak in English.

Decisions and motions

Decisions in Parliament are usually made by a simple majority. However, in cases where amendments are made to the Constitution or a Bill is introduced to cancel the reservation of land for Malays, a two-thirds majority is required. When the Election Commission delimits and creates new constituencies, at least half of all members must approve it.

An MP may put forward a motion to discuss parliamentary decisions. Generally, 14 days'

Parliament

The third Yang di-Pertuan Agong Tuanku Syed Putra Al-Haj Ibni Syed Hassan Jamalullail officially opening the new Parliament building on 21 November 1963.

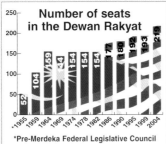

Number of seats in the Dewan Rakyat

Year	Seats
*1955	52
1959	104
1964	159
1969	144
1974	154
1978	154
1982	154
1986	177
1990	180
1995	192
1999	193
2004	219

*Pre-Merdeka Federal Legislative Council

(1) The Dewan Rakyat
The Dewan Rakyat directly represents the electorate and has a maximum term of five years. Each member is elected by a constituency.

(2) The Dewan Negara
The Dewan Negara has 70 members. Each state nominates two persons. The remaining 44 are appointed by the Yang di-Pertuan Agong on the advice of the Prime Minister, including two from the Federal Territory of Kuala Lumpur and one each from the Federal Territories of Labuan and Putrajaya. Senators hold office for three-year renewable terms. They are not affected by general elections.

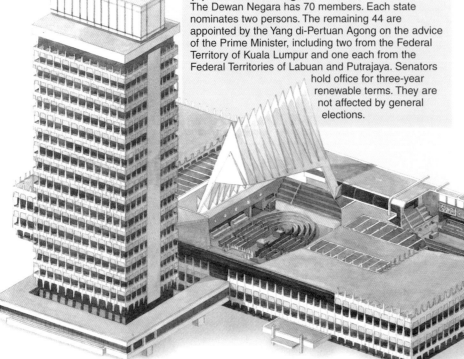

How laws are made

Every law starts out as a draft, called a Bill. Although most Bills originate in the Dewan Rakyat, a Bill can be introduced in either house. There are several types of Bills.

- **Private Member's Bill:** A Bill introduced by an individual Member of Parliament (MP).

- **Private Bill:** Introduced by the government or a private member, a Private Bill affects only one particular person or group.

- **Hybrid Bill:** While it affects the rights or interests of an individual, a Hybrid Bill also has a general application.

- **Public Bill:** The most common Bill. Introduced by the government, this type concerns public policy and is applicable throughout the country. After getting Cabinet approval, a Minister introduces it to Parliament.

Readings

On its way to becoming law, a Bill goes through two readings, a committee stage and a final reading. The first reading introduces the Bill and nothing is discussed. Before the second reading, copies of the Bill are circulated to MPs. The principles of the Bill are debated at this stage, but no discussion on the details is allowed.

Once a Bill passes the second reading, it goes before the Committee of the Whole House. At this stage, the Dewan Rakyat may debate the details of the Bill but not the general principles. This is a less formal forum where an MP may speak more than once and motions do not need to be seconded.

Changes agreed upon at the committee stage will be incorporated into the Bill and the Minister involved will ask for it to be read a third time.

At the third reading, the Bill is voted on by members without further discussion. The quorum required is 26 excluding the Speaker. Absentees may not vote by proxy.

The approved Bill will then be transmitted to the Dewan Negara. The Bill goes through three readings in the Dewan Negara in a similar process to that in the Dewan Rakyat. Once the Bill is passed, it is forwarded to the Yang di-Pertuan Agong for royal assent—the public seal is affixed on the Bill. This is essentially a formality: even if the Yang di-Pertuan Agong withholds his assent, the Bill will still become law (see 'Constitutional monarchy').

A law becomes effective immediately after the government has gazetted it.

Failure to agree

If the Dewan Negara disagrees with a Bill or makes any amendments to it, the Bill is sent back to the Dewan Rakyat. The latter will decide on whether to accept or reject these counter-proposals and amendments, and reply to the Dewan Negara with its reasons. The Dewan Negara in turn may refuse to accept these reasons, and the matter is turned back to the Dewan Rakyat. This back-and-forth process cannot continue indefinitely: the Dewan Rakyat has the final say, and, at most, the Dewan Negara can only delay the passage of a Bill by one year. With the Supply Bill, the time limit is only one month.

The Supply Bill

Better known as 'the Budget', the Supply Bill outlines the government's fiscal policies for the following year. It is introduced like all other Bills with a few exceptions; copies of the Bill are circulated to the MPs before it is introduced and the second reading may be held at the same sitting. After the second reading, the Dewan Rakyat does not debate the general principles of the Bill until at least two days later. This gives MPs a chance to discuss its contents. The debate is limited to 11 days, after which the Bill goes into committee. The Committee of Supply has 18 days to deliberate and may recommend budgetary reductions, but not increases.

A Dewan Negara sitting.

notice is required; on urgent matters, the Speaker may approve a one-day notice for motions. An MP who is not part of the government may forward a 'motion for the adjournment to discuss a definite matter of urgent public importance' which may be moved within 24 hours. If it is accepted, all other proceedings are suspended while the motion is debated and voted upon. Unlike a Bill, decisions (known as 'resolutions') on a motion are not forwarded to the Dewan Negara. The Dewan Rakyat also has the power to amend schedules in certain Acts, such as the Financial Procedure Ordinance 1957, without the approval of the Dewan Negara.

The Speaker

The Chairman of the Dewan Rakyat ('Dewan') is known as the Speaker. He is elected by the Dewan and does not necessarily have to be a Member of Parliament. The Speaker presides at Dewan sittings and is responsible for ensuring that rules of debate are observed. The Speaker also decides on points of order and his rulings cannot be questioned unless opposed by a majority of the Dewan. When Parliament is dissolved prior to a general election, the Speaker acts as a caretaker until a new government is formed.

Past Speakers

The post of Speaker was first created in 1953 for the Federal Legislative Council, and was appointed by the High Commissioner. Upon Independence in 1957, the speaker was appointed by the Yang di-Pertuan Agong. From the first meeting of the Federal Parliament in 1959, the Dewan Rakyat has elected the Speaker.

1. Dato' Sir Mahmud bin Mat (1953–5)
2. Raja Uda bin Raja Muhammad (later Tun) (1955–7)
3. Dato' Haji Abdul Malek bin Yusof (later Tun) (1957–9)
4. Dato' Haji Mohamad Noah bin Omar (later Tan Sri) (1959–64)
5. Tuan Syed Esa bin Alwee (later Dato') (1964)
6. Dato' Chik Mohamad Yusof bin Sheikh Abdul Rahman (later Tan Sri) (1964–74)
7. Tan Sri Datuk Haji Nik Ahmad Kamil Haji Nik Mahmood (1974–7)
8. Tan Sri Datuk Syed Nasir bin Ismail (later Tun) (1978–82)
9. Tun Dato' Seri (Dr) Mohamed Zahir Haji Ismail (1982–2004)
10. Tan Sri Ramli Ngah Talib (2004–present)

The President

The President of the Dewan Negara (Senate), who is elected from among the Senators, wields similar authority to the Speaker. He, too, is not affected by the dissolution of Parliament. He serves a three-year term, which may be renewed.

Past Presidents

There have been 14 holders of the position since the first session of the first Federal Parliament on 11 September 1959.

1. Dato' Haji Abdul Rahman bin Mohamed Yassin (1959–68)
2. Tuan Syed Sheh bin Syed Hassan Barakbah (later Tun) (1969)
3. Dato' Haji Mohamad Noah bin Omar (later Tan Sri) (1969–70)
4. Tan Sri Haji Abdul Hamid Khan bin Haji Sakhawat Ali Khan (1971–3)
5. Tun Datuk Haji Omar Yoke Lin Ong (1973–80)
6. Tun Ismail Khan (1981–5)
7. Tan Sri Datuk Benedict Stephens (1985–8)
8. Tan Sri Datuk Abang Haji Ahmad Urai bin Datu Hakim Abang Haji Mohideen (1988–90)
9. Tan Sri Dato' Chan Choong Tak (1990–2)
10. Tan Sri Dato' Vadiveloo s/o Govindasamy (1992–5)
11. Dato' Adam bin Kadir (now Tan Sri) (1995–6)
12. Tan Sri Dato' Haji Mohamed bin Ya'acob (1996–2000)
13. Tan Sri Dato' Michael Chen Wing Sum (2000–3)
14. Tan Sri Dato' Seri Dr Abdul Hamid Pawanteh (2003–present)

The federal executive

The Federal Constitution stipulates that the executive authority of Malaysia is vested in the Yang di-Pertuan Agong, and exercisable by him or by the Cabinet or by a Minister authorized by the Cabinet, and that Parliament may by law confer executive functions on other persons.

The first Cabinet meeting after the 2004 general election.

Representative government

Malaysia practises a system of Cabinet government. A Prime Minister (Perdana Menteri) is appointed by the Yang di-Pertuan Agong to preside over the Cabinet. As political chief executive, the Prime Minister holds office on the basis of majority support gained by his party in democratic elections. In Malaysia's present-day political context, executive responsibility for various functions is apportioned to Ministers chosen from the membership of the Barisan Nasional government in the spirit of power-sharing.

Only Ministers are members of the Cabinet. They are drawn from the Dewan Rakyat, and in very few cases from the Dewan Negara, and are appointed, and may be dismissed, by the Yang di-Pertuan Agong acting on the advice of the Prime Minister. The Prime Minister and the Cabinet are ultimately accountable to Parliament.

The first Cabinet meeting of the Federation of Malaya in 1957. Seated (left to right): Abdul Aziz Ishak, V. T. Sambanthan, Abdul Razak Hussein, Tunku Abdul Rahman Putra, Henry H. S. Lee, Sulaiman Abdul Rahman, and Sardon Haji Jubir. Standing (left to right): Omar Ong Yoke Lin, Abdul Rahman Haji Talib, Mohamed Khir Johari, Tan Siew Sin, and Bahaman Samsudin.

Collective responsibility

Although Ministers have direct responsibilities with regard to their respective portfolios, a hallmark of Cabinet government is the doctrine of collective responsibility. This doctrine requires Cabinet members to express support in public for all Cabinet decisions, even those not related to their portfolios. This has contributed greatly to Malaysia's political stability and the inter-ethnic accommodation of political interests.

Ministers holding office are sworn to secrecy in respect of Cabinet deliberations, and have rarely broken ranks with their Cabinet colleagues. Cabinet meetings, held weekly, are also a focal point of government policy implementation, whereby decisions made are transmitted at post-Cabinet meetings of the various ministries.

Ministers are assisted in the discharge of their duties and functions by Deputy Ministers and Parliamentary Secretaries who are members of either the Dewan Rakyat or the Dewan Negara, and are appointed by the Yang di-Pertuan Agong on the advice of the Prime Minister. Deputy Ministers and Parliamentary Secretaries are not members of the Cabinet.

Ministerial portfolios

Executive functions are shared between the Ministers who make up the Cabinet, each of whom is assigned a given portfolio or portfolios. These cover a wide range of policy areas. Each Minister performs functions that are decided by the Cabinet.

Ministers, Deputy Ministers and Parliamentary Secretaries by state (2006)

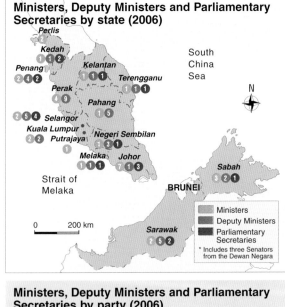

Ministers, Deputy Ministers and Parliamentary Secretaries by party (2006)

Ministerial portfolios

1. Prime Minister's Department
2. Agriculture and Agro-Based Industry
3. Culture, Arts and Heritage
4. Defence
5. Domestic Trade and Consumer Affairs
6. Education
7. Energy, Water and Communications
8. Entrepreneur and Cooperative Development
9. Federal Territories
10. Finance
11. Foreign Affairs
12. Health
13. Higher Education
14. Home Affairs
15. Housing and Local Government
16. Human Resources
17. Information
18. Internal Security
19. International Trade and Industry
20. Natural Resources and Environment
21. Plantation Industries and Commodities
22. Rural and Regional Development
23. Science, Technology and Innovation
24. Tourism
25. Transport
26. Women, Family and Community Development
27. Works
28. Youth and Sports

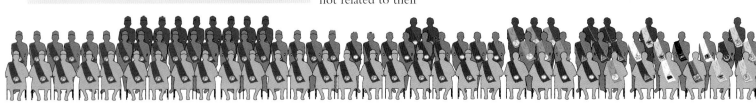

The position of Prime Minister

The Yang di-Pertuan Agong appoints as Prime Minister (Perdana Menteri) the member of the Dewan Rakyat who in his judgment is likely to command the confidence of the majority of members of that house. Naturalized citizens are not entitled to be appointed Prime Minister.

If the Prime Minister ceases to command the confidence of the majority of members of the Dewan Rakyat he must tender the resignation of the Cabinet unless, at his request, the Yang di-Pertuan Agong dissolves Parliament.

Most of the important powers of the Prime Minister are political and conventional, rather than legal, in nature, and are thus not stated categorically in the Constitution.

The Prime Minister is effectively the head of the executive. It is he who determines the members of the Cabinet, and he may use this power to dismiss a Minister to enforce any of the norms underlying Cabinet government, such as

Tunku Abdul Rahman Putra was sworn in as the nation's first Prime Minister on 31 August 1957.

The former Prime Minister's Department, Kuala Lumpur.

collective responsibility. Indeed, he determines the structure of the government as well as government policy, the latter by virtue of his power to decide the agenda of Cabinet business and to determine what legislation will be introduced by the government into Parliament. It is also the Prime Minister who decides the timing of the general election. In addition, he frequently represents the nation in international affairs.

Cabinet government

1. Tunku Abdul Rahman Putra (fourth from left) and members of the Cabinet in the Cabinet Chamber, Kuala Lumpur, August 1959.

2. Tun Abdul Razak (fourth from right) presides at a Cabinet meeting in the Prime Minister's Office, Kuala Lumpur, September 1970.

3. Dato' Hussein Onn (at the head of the table) holds a Cabinet meeting at the Prime Minister's Department, Kuala Lumpur, March 1976.

4. Dr Mahathir (third from left) chairs his last Cabinet meeting in Putrajaya, October, 2003.

Members of the Cabinet

Under the Federal Constitution, Ministers are appointed by the Yang di-Pertuan Agong acting on the advice of the Prime Minister. The Prime Minister has an absolute prerogative as to whom is appointed. In practice, by convention, successive Prime Ministers have ensured that the Cabinet represents all members of the coalition government, such that all the major ethnic groups and all regions are represented in it.

Under the Federal Constitution, a Minister—who can be either an elected Member of Parliament or a Senator—must, before he exercises the functions of his office, take and subscribe in the presence of the Yang di-Pertuan Agong the oath of office and allegiance and the oath of secrecy.

Following the 2004 general election, the Cabinet was expanded from 29 to 33 ministers.

Ministerial oaths

Oath of office and allegiance

'I, ..., having been appointed to the office of .... do solemnly swear (or affirm) that I will faithfully discharge the duties of that office to the best of my ability, that I will bear true faith and allegiance to Malaysia, and will preserve, protect and defend its Constitution.'

Members of the Cabinet take their oaths of office, May 1995.

Oath of secrecy

'I, ..., do solemnly swear (or affirm) that I will not directly or indirectly communicate or reveal to any person any matter which shall be brought under my consideration or shall become known to me as .... except as may be required for the due discharge of my duties as such or as may be specially permitted by the Yang di-Pertuan Agong.'

Chief Minister Tunku Abdul Rahman Putra Al-Haj

Tunku Abdul Rahman Putra Al-Haj is the Father of Independence (Bapa Kemerdekaan). He became the nation's first and only Chief Minister (1955–7) before being appointed Prime Minister upon Independence. Already in his middle years when he was thrust upon the political scene, the Tunku was the right man for high office at a formative time, and set the course for Malaya's, and later Malaysia's, political development.

The Tunku presenting the Report on the Constitutional Proposals for the Federation of Malaya to the Federal Legislative Council on 14 March 1956.

Royal lineage

Tunku Abdul Rahman Putra was born on 8 February 1903 in Alor Star, Kedah, as the youngest son of Sultan Abdul Hamid Halimshah. His mother, Makche Menjelara, was of Thai-Shan parentage. She had been adopted by the Sultan's eldest sister and raised in the palace as a Muslim. She was reputedly the Sultan's favourite wife.

The Tunku's education was varied and prolonged. In 1909, he entered a small English-medium school run by Mohd Iskandar, the father of Dr Mahathir Mohamad. Between 1913 and 1915, he lived in Bangkok with his elder brother Tunku Yusuf, and attended a Thai-medium school. In 1916, he was sent to the English-medium Penang Free School, an elite multi-ethnic institution.

In 1919, the Tunku was awarded a Kedah scholarship to the University of Cambidge in Britain. After passing matriculation in Britain, he was admitted to St Catherine's College, Cambridge in 1922. He had his first taste of racial discrimination when his application to occupy quarters within the college was rejected. When the authorities later learned he was a member of royalty and offered him boarding, he declined. This experience may well have been formative in the Tunku's desire for fairness to all races.

At university, the Tunku acquired a reputation for being a 'playboy', not unusual for students at the time. Nevertheless, he received a Bachelor of Arts in

The Tunku's personal crest depicts a sphinx—from the Greek myth in which a prince solved the Sphinx's riddle and saved his kingdom. The Malay motto *Dibebaskan* means 'freed'.

law and history in 1925. The following year, the Tunku was sent back to Britain to read law at the Inner Temple, London, by his brother, Tunku Ibrahim, who wanted him to become a lawyer or Magistrate. While in London, the Tunku founded the Malay Society of Great Britain.

The Tunku failed his bar examination in 1930 and returned to Malaya to serve in the Kedah civil service. In 1933, he married Meriam, a Thai-Chinese who converted to Islam. In two years, they had a daughter, Tunku Khadijah, and a son, Tunku Ahmad Nerang. Meriam died of malaria soon after their son's birth.

Several months later in Singapore, the Tunku married Violet Coulson, a woman he had known in Britain. This proved to be a short-lived marriage— Violet soon returned to Britain and they divorced not long after.

The Tunku made another attempt to pass the bar examinations in 1938 and passed Part One. The following year, he married Sharifah Rodziah binti Syed Alwi Barakbah. They adopted three children.

World War II forced an interruption to the Tunku's studies and he returned to work in the civil service. When the war ended, he returned to Britain once more and passed his Bar examinations in 1946, at which point, in his words, he celebrated his 'Silver Jubilee as a law student'. He then worked in the legal profession, and in 1950 became the Deputy Public Prosecutor in Kuala Lumpur.

The Tunku (right) with a close friend at Debsurin School in Bangkok, 1914.

RIGHT: Members of the Malay Society of Great Britain, which was founded by the Tunku, in 1926. The Tunku is seated fourth from left.

72

On the election trail

TOP LEFT, LEFT AND ABOVE: The Tunku, President of UMNO and Chairman of the Alliance, campaigning during the first federal election in 1955. The success of both the party and coalition at the polls provided the necessary mandate to form the government, and for the Tunku to be appointed Chief Minister.

Politics and Independence

In 1951, the United Malays National Organisation (UMNO) faced the fearful prospect of the imminent departure of its founder, Dato' Onn bin Jaafar, who had no heir apparent and no rival in the party. Dato' Abdul Razak bin Hussein, who considered

himself too young for the post at this time, suggested the Tunku as a candidate and persuaded him to accept the nomination.

LEFT: The Tunku after graduating as a Barrister at the Inner Temple, London, in 1947.

BELOW: The Tunku (third from left) as a cadet in the Kedah Civil Service posing with fellow cadets at his house in Alor Star, 1931.

The Tunku was virtually unknown nationally, being merely Kedah UMNO's Chairman in 1949 and Kuala Lumpur UMNO representative from 1950, but he was a Malay prince with a civil and legal service background and that counted. On 26 August 1951, he was elected UMNO President. Although not a chauvinist, he understood the strains on Malay unity at that time and gave a strong speech on Malay rights. He said that Malays would decide who 'Malayans' should be.

In the 1952 Kuala Lumpur municipal election, an ad hoc alliance between UMNO and the Malayan Chinese Association (MCA) proved successful, and the Tunku seized the opportunity to form a more permanent coalition of ethnic parties. It was his answer to the need for ethnic harmony. By 1954, a formal national Alliance of UMNO, MCA and the Malayan Indian Congress (MIC) was established.

At the first general election in 1955, the Alliance won 51 of the 52 available seats, a result which convinced the British that independence could work in a multi-racial environment. The Tunku was then appointed the country's Chief Minister and Minister of Home Affairs. In 1956, he led a mission to London for talks with the British government on independence for Malaya. The meeting resulted in the signing of the Independence Agreement at Lancaster House in London on 8 February 1956 and, ultimately, Independence for Malaya on 31 August 1957.

The Tunku, in ceremonial uniform, bidding farewell to Sir Donald MacGillivray, the last British High Commissioner, under whom he had served as Chief Minister, in 1957.

Prime Minister Tunku Abdul Rahman Putra Al-Haj

Appointed the nation's first Prime Minister upon Independence in 1957, Tunku Abdul Rahman Putra went on to become the principal architect of the union of Malaya with Singapore, Sarawak and Sabah, which in 1963 resulted in the creation of Malaysia. He is recognized as the Father of Malaysia (Bapa Malaysia). He steered the new Federation through its first, often difficult, years until his retirement in 1970.

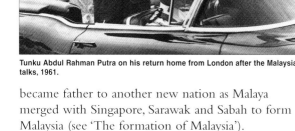

Tunku Abdul Rahman Putra on his return home from London after the Malaysia talks, 1961.

Profile

1957	Prime Minister of the Federation of Malaya.
1958	First President of the Asian Football Confederation.
1963	Prime Minister of Malaysia.
1970	Retired from politics.
1974	PERKIM President.
1980	Magsaysay Award recipient.
1990	Passed away.

The Tunku campaigning in Pulau Langkawi prior to the 1959 elections.

Tumultuous times

Tunku Abdul Rahman Putra Al-Haj's service to the nation did not end at Malaya's Independence. As the nation's first Prime Minister, he sat in the place of the departed British High Commissioner MacGillivray at the first Malayan Cabinet on 10 September 1957, and immediately introduced a new spirit of mutual understanding and confidence. In addition to his responsibilities as Prime Minister, the Tunku also held the External Affairs ministerial portfolio, and immediately set to work in this capacity: just six weeks after Independence an Anglo-Malayan Defence Agreement was signed. In 1960 he attended the Commonwealth Prime Ministers' Meeting, held in London.

In 1961, the Tunku surprised everyone by proposing a new, wider federation (see 'The idea of Malaysia'). There followed a whirl of activity involving Britain and the United Nations. This culminated when in September 1963 the Tunku

> *'From the developments which have already taken place in the growing reality of the Malaysia ideal I am confident that with unity in will and wish we can achieve our goal. Speaking for the government of the Federation of Malaya I say now that we will do everything humanly possible to make the road to the future Malaysia as straight and clear as we can.'*
>
> **Tunku Abdul Rahman Putra, speech to Parliament, 16 October 1961.**

became father to another new nation as Malaya merged with Singapore, Sarawak and Sabah to form Malaysia (see 'The formation of Malaysia').

The rest of the decade was equally tumultuous. First, Indonesia launched a limited military campaign against Malaysia because it objected to the federation's creation (see 'External opposition to Malaysia'). Then, problems developed in political and economic relations between the Federal Government and Chinese-dominated Singapore; challenges to the Alliance and its ethnic-bargaining concept emerged from Singapore's People's Action Party (PAP), and racial riots erupted in the island state. Rather than send in the army to quell the unrest and ask the Malays to make concessions to help the MCA fend off the PAP challenge, the Tunku decided that Singapore had to secede from Malaysia. On 9 August 1965, the Federal Parliament enacted the

1. The winning team on the first anniversary of the international *Pestabola Merdeka* (Independence Football Competition) with the Tunku, who had himself initiated the competition.

2. The Tunku, who practised 'golf diplomacy', playing a round of golf with Tun Abdul Razak, 1958.

3. President Lyndon B. Johnson with the Tunku during the former's visit to Malaysia, 1966.

4. The Tunku entertains Prince Norodom Sihanoukh of Cambodia, December 1962.

The Tunku's achievements

Besides negotiating Independence, and steering the nation's course as Prime Minister of the Federation of Malaya (1957–63) and of Malaysia (1963–70), the Tunku took Malaysia into the international arena. During his premiership, Malaya joined the United Nations and the Commonwealth (both in 1957). He helped establish the Commonwealth's anti-apartheid policy when he moved the resolution to expel the Republic of South Africa from the Commonwealth, and supported the struggles of the peoples of Palestine and the Congo (see 'A global role').

Regionally, the Tunku initiated the Association of Southeast Asia (ASA) in 1961, which comprised Malaya, Thailand and the Philippines. This group was later disbanded to make way for a larger organization, the Association of Southeast Asian Nations (ASEAN), in 1967.

Besides making Islam the official religion, the Tunku also established the Islamic Welfare Organisation (PERKIM) in 1960, to help Muslim converts adjust to their new lives as Muslims. The Tunku was President of PERKIM until a year before his death. In 1961 Malaysia hosted the first International Qur'an Recital Competition, an event that had developed from the time the Tunku organized the first state-level competition in Kedah in 1951.

ABOVE: The Tunku as Secretary-General of the Organization of the Islamic Conference, Jeddah, 1971.

The Tunku sought not only to raise the image of Islam in Malaysia and in the region but also at the international level. In 1969 he helped set up the Organisation of the Islamic Conference (OIC), of which he was the first Secretary-General. Subsequently he initiated the setting up of the Islamic Development Bank as a specialized institution within the OIC. The Tunku was also President of the Regional Islamic Da'wah Council of South East Asia and the Pacific (RISEAP) from 1982 to 1988.

The Tunku at the Commonwealth Prime Ministers' Meeeting in London, February 1961.

Constitution and Malaysia (Singapore Amendment) Act 1965 which effected the separation of Singapore from the federation (see 'The formation of Malaysia').

These incidents eroded the confidence of the people in the government. This eventually contributed to the several factors that resulted in the violence that followed the 1969 elections (see 'The 13 May 1969 tragedy'), as a result of which the Yang di-Pertuan Agong proclaimed a state of emergency, Parliament was suspended and power passed to the National Operations Council. The National Operations Council existed alongside a Cabinet sworn in on 30 May 1969 and headed by the Tunku as Prime Minister (see 'The National Operations Council'). Despite this power-sharing arrangement, from May 1969 until the Tunku's retirement in September 1970, it was National Operations Council Director Tun Abdul Razak bin Hussein who undertook much of the Prime Minister's traditional role. Nevertheless, the Tunku continued during this period to promote inter-communal goodwill through the National Goodwill Council and to fulfil his duties as Head of Government; for example, he received King Faisal of Saudi Arabia on his first state visit to Malaysia in June 1970.

Senior statesman

The Tunku remained active and politically involved during the last 20 years of his life. He headed a number of organizations and emerged as a major political columnist: in this context he could write what others dared not. He also campaigned in the October 1990 elections in support of Semangat 46 during UMNO's most divided period, but was hospitalized, exhausted.

He passed away, aged 87, on 6 December 1990 and was laid to rest at the Langgar Royal Mausoleum in Alor Star.

The Tunku's legacy

The Tunku has come to be known as the 'Father of Malaysia'. He had a gift for reconciliation and a personality that was ideal for promoting accommodation. His ability to relate to people made him a much-needed 'supra-communal arbiter'. As such, he was able to obtain agreement for the 'social contract' between the ethnic groups that convinced the British that Independence could work, and to create the Alliance formula of coalition government.

A warm-hearted man, the Tunku wanted to be remembered as leading the country to Independence without violence, a mission he accomplished. He was nevertheless a staunch anti-communist, and will be remembered for establishing a parliamentary democracy and leading one of the most successful multi-ethnic political arrangements in the world.

ABOVE: The Tunku at his last Cabinet meeting, at Parliament House, 21 September 1970.

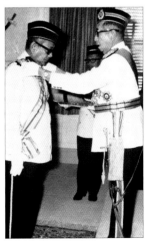

RIGHT: Tuanku Ismail Nasiruddin Shah, the fourth Yang di-Pertuan Agong, presenting the D.M.N. (*Darjah Utama Seri Mahkota Negara* or The Most Exalted Order of the Crown of The Realm) to the Tunku, 2 September 1970.

Prime Minister Tun Abdul Razak bin Dato' Hussein

Malaysia's second Prime Minister (1970–6) is best remembered for his relentless efforts to improve living standards, particularly of the rural population. A talented administrator, diligent worker and astute planner, he instituted reforms in education and rural development, and was the architect of the New Economic Policy. Although his term in office was cut short by illness, Abdul Razak laid a lasting foundation for national development. He is recognized as the Father of Development.

Dato' Abdul Razak (seated, left), as Deputy Prime Minister, with Tunku Abdul Rahman Putra and some Cabinet members, 1957.

Profile

1922	Born in Pulau Keladi, Pahang.
1947	Scholarship to read law in England; King's Scholar.
1950	Graduated as a lawyer.
1951	Deputy President of UMNO.
1952	State Secretary, Pahang.
1955	Resigned from civil service; Acting Menteri Besar of Pahang; Member of Parliament; Minister of Education.
1956	Released Razak Report.
1957	Minister of Defence; Deputy Prime Minister.
1959	Minister of Rural and National Development.
1969	Director, National Operations Council.
1970	Prime Minister.
1974	Formed Barisan Nasional to replace the Alliance Party.
1976	Passed away.

Aristocratic roots

Abdul Razak bin Dato' Hussein was born on 11 March 1922 in his mother's village of Pulau Keladi in Pahang. His father, Dato' Hussein bin Mohd Taib, was the Orang Kaya Indera Shahbandar, one of the four major territorial chiefs of Pahang. His mother, Hajah Teh binti Daud, was Hussein's first wife.

When Abdul Razak was two years old, he was taken to live with his paternal grandparents in Jambu Langgar, six miles from Pekan. He attended a Malay primary school at age six and in 1933, was selected by the Pahang Resident to attend the elite Malay College at Kuala Kangsar, to be trained for the civil service.

He was a bright student and a good sportsman as well. In 1940, he was awarded a scholarship to Raffles College in Singapore. This was his first interaction with non-Malays, and also his first contact with both anti-Malay and anti-British attitudes.

His education was interrupted by World War II. In 1941–5, Abdul Razak served in the Japanese Occupation administration, first as a clerk and later as an interpreter. However, he was also secretly a member of Wataniah, an anti-Japanese resistance force to which he passed information.

After the war, Abdul Razak won a scholarship to study law in Britain. To qualify, he studied Latin privately in Pahang for a year while working full time. In 1947, he entered Lincoln's Inn in London. True to his academic prowess, he became a King's Scholar and passed his law examinations within 18 months. His quest for knowledge was insatiable. While waiting to be called to the Bar and to be granted his licence to practise law, Abdul Razak completed a course in economics and public administration at Cambridge University. He then enrolled at the University of

FEDERAL LEGISLATIVE COUNCIL

Document by which Abdul Razak was appointed a Member of the Federal Legislative Council in March 1951.

London for a degree in economics. He also frequently attended lectures and debates at the London School of Economics, which may have sown the seeds of a life-long concern to eradicate rural poverty. His father's death in 1950 prompted Abdul Razak to return immediately to Pahang and assume the hereditary role of the Orang Kaya Indera Shahbandar. He never completed the economics degree.

Abdul Razak's stay in Britain whetted his appetite for politics. He joined the British Labour Party and the Fabian Society, a left-of-centre think-tank that encouraged open-minded debate on political ideas and policy reforms. He was able to vote in the 1950 British elections although, ironically, he enjoyed no such franchise in his homeland.

Politics and government

Abdul Razak entered the Malayan Civil Service and became the youngest ever State Secretary of Pahang in 1952. In 1955, he was appointed acting Menteri Besar, and eventually became Menteri Besar of Pahang. He rose rapidly in politics. Having joined UMNO in 1950, within only a few months he was elected leader of the UMNO Youth Movement. In August 1951, aged 29, he was elected Deputy President of UMNO.

Abdul Razak left the civil service in 1955 to stand as an Alliance candidate in the first federal election. He won his seat decisively, as he did in the next four elections. His first ministry was education, and his term was noted for the 1956 Razak Report that called for an integrated national system of education with a common syllabus (see 'Primary and secondary education').

Following Malaya's Independence, he became the Deputy Prime Minister, Minister of Defence and Minister of Home Affairs. However, it was as Minister of Rural and National Development from 1959 that Abdul Razak really found his niche.

Rural development

Abdul Razak set up 'operation rooms' from national level down to district level to oversee projects; bureaucratic red tape was slashed by the introduction of 'on-the-spot allocations' and telephone reports instead of written reports in triplicate. He targeted development in roads, electricity, bridges, irrigation

Top: Abdul Razak, as Minister of Defence, welcomes back the men of the initial battalion of the Malayan Special Force to the Congo, 1961.

Above: Abdul Razak toured rural development areas extensively. Here, he inspects young rubber plants at the Sungai Durian new rubber planting scheme, in 1961.

Tun Abdul Razak (seated, third from right), at the conference in Bangkok in which the Malaysian and Indonesian governments declared the Confrontation over, May 1966.

Tun Abdul Razak, as Prime Minister and Director of the National Operations Council, opens the Menteri Besar and Chief Ministers' Conference at the Cabinet room, Prime Minister's office in Kuala Lumpur, October 1970.

The last Alliance Cabinet, 19 December 1972.

1. Tan Sri Ong Yoke Lin (Minister without Portfolio)
2. Tun V. T. Sambanthan (Minister of National Unity)
3. Tun Dr Ismail Al-Haj bin Dato' Abdul Rahman (Deputy Prime Minister and Minister of Home Affairs)
4. Tun Hj. Abdul Razak bin Dato' Hussein (Prime Minister, Minister of Foreign Affairs and Minister of Defence)
5. Tun Tan Siew Sin (Minister of Finance)
6. Tan Sri Hj. Sardon bin Hj. Jubir (Minister of Communications)
7. Encik Mohamed Khir Johari (now Tan Sri) (Minister of Trade and Industry)
8. Tan Sri Muhammad Ghazali bin Shafie (now Tun) (Minister of Special Functions/Information)
9. Tan Sri Hj. Mohd Ghazali bin Hj. Jawi (Minister of Agriculture and Fisheries)
10. Tan Sri V. Manickavasagam (Minister of Labour and Manpower)
11. Tan Sri Fatimah bte Hj. Hashim (Minister of Welfare Services)
12. Datuk Ong Kee Hui (Minister of Technology, Research and Local Government)
13. Dato' Hamzah bin Dato' Abu Samah (Minister of Culture, Youth and Sports)
14. Tan Sri Temenggong Jugah Anak Barieng (later Tun) (Minister of Sarawak Affairs)
15. Tan Sri Lee Siok Yew (Minister of Health)
16. Ahmad Sarji bin Abdul Hamid (now Tan Sri) (Secretary 'A' Division)
17. Tan Sri Abdul Kadir bin Shamsuddin (Secretary to the Cabinet and Chief Secretary to the Government)
18. Datuk Hj. Abdul Taib bin Mahmud (now Pehin Sri Tan Sri) (Minister of Primary Industries)
19. Dato' Hussein bin Onn (later Tun) (Minister of Education)
20. Datuk Hj. Abdul Ghani Gilong (Minister of Works and Power)
21. Abdul Ghaffar bin Baba (now Tun) (Minister of National and Rural Development)
22. Tan Sri Abdul Kadir bin Yusoff (Attorney General)
23. Dr Lim Keng Yaik (now Dato' Seri) (Minister of Special Functions)

canals, drains, health clinics, schools, literacy classes for adults and the construction of *surau*—prayer facilities for Muslims.

He travelled an average of 50,000 miles a year around the country, checking on results. The Federal Land Development Authority (FELDA) was one of his lasting contributions to rural development (see 'The Alliance'). It also earned him the prestigious Magsaysay Award in 1967.

Abdul Razak was also the Tunku's trouble-shooter, handling the details of Singapore's separation in 1965 and the rapprochement with Indonesia after *Konfrontasi*. He was also a major participant in the establishment of the Association of Southeast Asian Nations in 1967.

Prime Minister

When the 13 May 1969 tragedy led to a state of emergency, Abdul Razak was made Director of the National Operations Council (NOC) where he ruled by decree (see 'The 13 May 1969 tragedy' and 'The National Operations Council'). He took firm action to restrain ethnic extremists and made a number of sweeping political and economic changes during this period. He also instituted safeguards to prevent future incitements to racial violence.

He took over as Prime Minister when the Tunku resigned in 1970. Unfortunately, he was also diagnosed with terminal leukaemia. He served as premier for only six years before the illness claimed his life. Abdul Razak did not let his medical condition prevent him from implementing important changes. He recruited new talent into UMNO. He realigned foreign policy to one of neutrality, neutralization and regional cooperation. He also established diplomatic relations with China in 1974 to balance Malaysia's good ties with the West.

Then, he implemented a major coalition-building strategy to make the government more inclusive and reduce politicking. Heeding the Tunku's advice to

'It is important that individually and jointly we should create a deep awareness that we cannot survive for long as independent but isolated peoples unless we also think and act together and unless we prove by deeds that we belong to a family of Southeast Asian nations bound together by ties of friendship and goodwill and imbued with our own ideals and aspirations and determined to shape our own destiny. With the establishment of ASEAN, we have taken a firm and a bold step on that road.'

Tun Abdul Razak, speech as Deputy Prime Minister of Malaysia, at signing of Bangkok Declaration, Bangkok, August 1967.

share power, he brought opposition parties into the coalition and formed the Barisan Nasional in 1974. In addition, he embarked on the New Economic Policy (NEP), a daring economic development strategy of preferential policies to increase opportunities for the Malays while seeking to minimize resentment from other races.

Abdul Razak's legacy

Tun Abdul Razak was at the centre of politics for 30 years. He was task-oriented and an innovator. He was an unselfish team player who nominated the Tunku as President of UMNO and served loyally under him for 20 years. He was a consensus seeker and supreme coalition-builder: the Barisan Nasional's success is testimony to his work. As director of the NOC, he could have turned the country into a dictatorship, but he returned it to democracy. On the resumption of Parliament, in order to maintain racial harmony, he led the move to create the 'entrenched provisions' of the Federal Constitution (see 'The National Operations Council'). Although his time as Prime Minister was short, and he died aged 53 on 16 January 1976, he played an important part in establishing many of the political and economic strategies that contributed to Malaysia's success in later years.

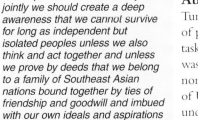

First day cover issued on 14 January 1977 to commemorate the achievements of Tun Abdul Razak.

Abdul Razak, as Director of the National Operations Council, tours the Chow Kit area on 13 May 1970 to reassure the people against a repeat of the tragedy.

BELOW: Abdul Razak, as Minister of Defence and Prime Minister, at the five-nation 'Bersatu Padu' (United) manoeuvres, a Commonwealth joint services exercise, in 1970.

Prime Minister Dato' (later Tun) Hussein bin Dato' Onn

The country's third Prime Minister, Dato' Hussein bin Dato' Onn, served from 1976 to 1981. He continued and built on the policies—both domestic and foreign—established by his predecessors and set high standards of integrity, rectitude and devotion to duty. He is recognized as the Father of Unity.

Hussein Onn speaking at a press conference prior to his departure for Bali, 22 February 1976.

Profile

1922	Born in Johor Bahru, Johor.
1940	Joined Indian Military Academy, India.
1945	Commandant, Johor Bahru Police Depot.
1946	Joined civil service.
1948	Joined UMNO.
1949	UMNO Youth Chief.
1951	Left UMNO; joined IMP.
1968	Returned to UMNO.
1970	Minister of Education.
1973	Deputy Prime Minister; Minister of Trade and Industry.
1974	Minister of Finance; Minister of Coordination of Public Enterprises.
1976	Prime Minister; Minister of Defence.
1981	Retired from politics.
1990	Passed away.

Military man: Hussein Onn with Ibrahim Ismail during military training (above). Captain Hussein receives the Sultan Ibrahim medal from the Regent of Johor in 1949 (below).

Military career

Hussein Onn was born in Johor Bahru on 12 February 1922 and was educated there at the English College (now Sultan Abu Bakar College). He was the eldest son of UMNO founder Dato' Onn bin Jaafar and Datin Halimah Hussein, who had eight children.

Hussein joined the Johor Military Forces as a cadet officer after leaving school. In 1940 he was sent to the Indian Military Academy at Dehra Dun in India. After being commissioned in 1942, Hussein joined the 19th Hyderabad Regiment, and served in the Middle East.

He was then posted to the British Army Intelligence headquarters in New Delhi. Subsequently, he was seconded to be an instructor at the Malayan Police Recruiting and Training Centre in Rawalpindi (then part of India) training fighters for the resistance to the occupying Japanese forces in the Malay Peninsula. Hussein left India for the Peninsula in 1945.

Many of Hussein's virtues were acquired from the military during his time in the armed forces. He valued leadership and national loyalty very highly, and showed a great sense of responsibility to those who served under him. The safety, comfort and welfare of his troops always came first.

After the war, Hussein became the Commandant of the Johor Bahru police depot. He joined the Malay Administrative Service six months later and was posted to the district offices of Kuala Selangor and Klang, Selangor. He also served as Assistant District Officer in Segamat, Johor.

Hussein left the civil service to join his father in politics. He became UMNO Secretary-General and its first Youth Chief at the age of 28. When Onn left UMNO in 1951 to found the Independence of Malaya Party, Hussein followed. However, as support for the new party waned, Hussein left politics, and commenced the study of law at Lincoln's Inn in London.

Hussein was cautious and meticulous by nature. As a student, he is said to have read books carefully, underlining page after page, checking and counter-checking everything. In his opinion, it was better to be safe than sorry.

In 1958 Hussein became a barrister-at-law, and began practice with a Kuala Lumpur law firm.

Rise to the premiership

Hussein rejoined UMNO in 1968 at the behest of Tun Abdul Razak. By June 1969, he had risen to become a Supreme Council member and a Member of Parliament. The following year, he joined the Cabinet as Minister of Education and became UMNO Vice President.

Hussein was made acting Deputy President of UMNO and Deputy Prime Minister following the untimely death in August 1973 of Tun (Dr) Ismail Abdul Rahman. When Abdul Razak passed away on 14 January 1976, Hussein became UMNO acting President three days later—he was later elected unopposed to the post of President of UMNO, in 1978. He was sworn in as Prime Minister on 15 January 1976.

Hussein's rise in politics did not appear to come out of driving ambition. He was not self-seeking, preferring only to do his duty. His rapid promotion has been attributed to the fact that he had the support of Tun Abdul Razak, and that there were few candidates who could match his experience and reputation. Also, his own qualities commanded admiration, including his respect for the rule of law, and his unwillingness to bend the rules for political expediency or to avoid unpopularity. Further, he, more than others at the time, had a firm grounding in the intricacies of local politics as he had been inducted into UMNO politics by his father, Dato' Onn Jaafar.

In particular, Hussein was a deadly foe of corruption. He believed that a country could be destroyed if its leaders were dishonest, untrustworthy or corrupt.

> *'Discipline is the most important thing in human life and has to be the main priority. Self-discipline is also important, especially in society or organizations such as political parties.*
>
> *One of the reasons for UMNO's success is because of the members' obedience and respect for party discipline, and their upholding of its rules and regulations. Indisciplined members will lead to the destruction of the party.'*
>
> **Hussein Onn speaking at a meeting of UMNO Division heads in Kuala Lumpur, 9 December 1977.**

Leadership challenges

Hussein was prepared to assert his authority when necessary. When the Menteri Besar of Kelantan, Dato' Haji Mohamed Nasir, refused to step down from office in October 1977 despite a vote of 'no-confidence' in the state assembly, street protests were sparked in the state capital of Kota Bharu.

To prevent matters from worsening, Hussein advised the Yang di-Pertuan Agong (Paramount Ruler or King) to impose emergency rule in the state, which lasted for a three-month period. Parti Islam Se-Malaysia (PAS) withdrew from the Barisan Nasional in December 1977 following an ultimatum from the latter, and thus took the state of Kelantan into the opposition. Hussein ordered snap state elections to be held. These were won convincingly by the Barisan Nasional and Mohamed Nasir's new party, Berjasa. PAS only managed to win in two of the 36 constituencies.

Hussein's legitimacy as Prime Minister was further endorsed in the 1978 general election. Campaigning on a 'Man Whom You Can Trust' platform, he led the Barisan to a clean sweep of all state legislatures and 130 federal seats out of 154. This also strengthened his position within UMNO.

Hussein was relentless in his fight against corruption. The most prominent case during his premiership was that of Dato' Harun bin Haji Idris, Menteri Besar of Selangor and head of UMNO Youth, who was accused of corruption associated with losses of RM6.5 million incurred by Bank Rakyat. When Hussein took over as Prime Minister, he proceeded with charges. Dato' Harun Idris was subsequently convicted and expelled from UMNO.

As incumbent UMNO President, Hussein was challenged by Sulaiman Palestin; the first time that an UMNO leader had been challenged since Tunku Abdul Rahman Putra. Hussein won the vote comfortably.

Hussein faced a number of distractions on the foreign-relations front during his term as Prime Minister. These included the fall of Saigon to North Vietnamese forces in 1975, and his concern over the 'domino' theory. He also progressed the resolution of the thorny issue of the Philippines' claim over Sabah; in 1976 he had a bilateral meeting with President Marcos at the Bali Summit that took the matter outside of the ASEAN forum.

ABOVE: A kindly and compassionate man, Dato' Hussein Onn chats with a physically-challenged guest at a family day function.

LEFT: Hussein Onn arrives to open the 1979 MIC Annual General Assembly.

'A leader must have integrity. The integrity I mean is not only in the support given to the party struggle, but also in thinking, decision-making and action. Without integrity, a leader will use his position as a commodity to peddle influence and to achieve status, name and riches. He will use the party and the party's struggle just as a means to satisfy his desires. He will take the opportunity to exploit any circumstance or crisis to his own advantage.'

Speech by Hussein Onn at the Sri Gading Division UMNO representatives' meeting in Batu Pahat, Johor, 16 May 1981.

On the economic front he overcame strong opposition to the New Economic Policy from the Associated Chinese Chamber of Commerce and Industry of Malaysia, and went on to tighten the implementation of the NEP under the Third and Fourth Malaysia Plans. Under the Third Malaysia Plan (1976–80), there was internal average Gross Domestic Product (GDP) growth of 8.6 per cent, 1.5 per cent more than under the previous plan.

As UMNO President, Hussein Onn (centre) officiates at the 1977 General Assembly.

End of a career

In May 1981, after undergoing a coronary bypass, he announced his retirement from politics, which took effect in July. He received the title 'Tun' on his retirement. Tun Hussein Onn dedicated his life after retirement to social work. Among his various positions, he was the President of Malaysian Association for the Blind. He died on 29 May 1990, aged 68, in San Francisco.

LEFT: Hussein Onn attends his last Cabinet meeting before retirement from the premiership in 1981.

BELOW: Hussein Onn inspects a Malaysian Armed Forces parade held in his honour prior to his retirement.

Achievements

Despite his brief term, Hussein left his mark as a man who worked for continuity and unity, indeed he came to be known as the 'Father of Unity'.

He worked on rectifying economic imbalances and introduced the successful Amanah Saham Nasional (National Unit Trust scheme). He also devoted time to promoting the Rukun Tetangga (Neighbourhood Committee) drive to bring the various races closer together (see 'The National Operations Council').

Prime Minister Dato' Seri (now Tun) Dr Mahathir bin Mohamad

Malaysia's fourth Prime Minister (1981–2003), Dr Mahathir has been described as the 'Father of Modern Malaysia'. He was a medical doctor. Having had a multi-racial education, he was able to empathize with the views of all sections of the people. His character was shaped by his strict upbringing by a conservative father and by his experiences during the Japanese Occupation. Under his leadership Malaysia was profoundly transformed in terms of economic development, and Dr Mahathir ably articulated its point of view in the global arena.

Dr Mahathir at the East Asian Economic Conference in Singapore, 1999.

Profile

1925	Born in Alor Star, Kedah.
1946	Joined UMNO.
1953	Graduated from King Edward VII College of Medicine, Singapore.
1964	Member of Parliament.
1969	Lost parliamentary seat; expelled from UMNO; wrote *The Malay Dilemma*.
1973	Appointed Senator.
1974	Resigned from Senate to re-enter politics; rejoined UMNO; appointed Minister of Education.
1975	UMNO Vice President.
1976	Deputy Prime Minister.
1978	Minister of Trade and Industry; UMNO Deputy President.
1981	UMNO President; Prime Minister.
2003	Retired from premiership.

Simple beginnings

Mahathir bin Mohamad was born on 20 December 1925 in Seberang Perak, Alor Star in the state of Kedah. He was the ninth and youngest child of Mohamad Iskandar, better known as 'Master Mohamad', a schoolmaster. He was nicknamed 'Che Det', a pseudonym he used in his early journalistic forays at university.

Mahathir received an orthodox Muslim upbringing. These values and beliefs made him, in his own words, a 'true fundamentalist'. His father nurtured his enquiring mind, encouraging him to think for himself and to speak out. The young Mahathir won a scholarship to the Government English School (now Sultan Abdul Hamid College) where he developed a love for the English language and a lifelong belief in education as a way out of poverty.

Fervent nationalist

While at school, Mahathir came to believe that the Malays were a disenfranchised race, effectively dispossessed in their own land by the British and other foreigners. He became a fervent nationalist, fiercely opposed to colonialism.

Dr Mahathir as Education Minister.

The Japanese Occupation interrupted his schooling for three years. To survive, he ran a stall selling fried bananas in Pekan Rabu, Alor Star. This experience enabled him, after he became Prime Minister, to write a primer for the small Malay entrepreneur.

After the war, he returned to school and entered active politics covertly. He would sneak out at night to post pamphlets opposing the Malayan Union—a seditious act from the British standpoint. Mahathir joined the newly formed UMNO party and was present on 11 May 1946 when it was inaugurated, becoming one of its youngest members.

Dr Mahathir graduated in 1953 with an MBBS degree from the University of Malaya in Singapore and practised medicine for 11 years. However, politics was never far from his mind. Many of his patients used to call him 'Dr UMNO'.

Political career

From the time he joined UMNO, Dr Mahathir took 18 years to become a Member of Parliament (for Kota Setar Selatan, Kedah). He went on to criticize the UMNO leadership after the tragedy of 13 May 1969—he had lost his seat in the general election that preceded the tragedy. Following his attack on the leadership, he was expelled from UMNO. During this period, he wrote *The Malay Dilemma*, outlining his views on the plight of the Malays. In March 1972 was invited back into the party due to the efforts of certain UMNO leaders.

In 1974, Mahathir was elected as Member of Parliament for Kubang Pasu, Kedah, and then appointed Minister of Education. While serving as Minister, he played a major part in restructuring the school system (see 'Primary and secondary education').

Mahathir the writer

Some of the books written by Dr Mahathir include:

The Multimedia Super Corridor (1998)
A New Deal for Asia (1999)
Malays Forget Easily (2001)
Reflections on Asia (2002)
Globalization and the New Realities (2002)

The Malay Dilemma

Published in 1970 and initially banned, *The Malay Dilemma* was an influential, albeit scathing, book. It addressed the mindset of the Malay community at the time and analysed the way in which the Malays had become marginalized and apathetic to their condition. It was also critical of the government for its inability to rectify this situation.

By exploring the Malay thought process and way of life, Dr Mahathir attempted to rouse the Malays to become politically and economically more assertive.

1. Dr Mahathir and Parti Bersatu Sabah (PBS) President Datuk Seri Panglima Joseph Pairin Kitingan (on Dr Mahathir's left, with glasses) wave to supporters at the 18th PBS Annual Meeting in Kota Kinabalu, September 2003.

2. The opening of the 50th Malaysian Chinese Association Annual General Assembly, August 2003, officiated by Dr Mahathir. On his left is MCA President Datuk Ong Kah Ting.

3. In his capacity as President of UMNO, Dr Mahathir gives the closing speech at the 54th UMNO General Assembly, 2003.

4. Dr Mahathir, accompanied by Sarawak Chief Minister and Parti Pesaka Bumiputera Bersatu (PBB) President Tan Sri Taib Mahmud (left), meets Orang Ulu chiefs in Kuching, 2002.

In 1975 he was elected Vice President of UMNO, and became Deputy Prime Minister the following year.

The premiership

Dr Mahathir was 55 years of age when he became Prime Minister. His period of leadership was marked by an extraordinary vigour, by a drive to energize the nation. He was considered a liberal idealist and reformist, and two weeks into his office, he began to release detainees who were held under the Internal Security Act (ISA).

Dr Mahathir introduced the values of *Bersih, Cekap dan Amanah* ('Clean, Efficient and Trustworthy') and 'Leadership by Example' into his administration. He was a stickler for punctuality and discipline. Civil servants, including himself, were required to clock in for work and to wear nametags for identification and to promote accountability.

Under Dr Mahathir's administration, the government actively participated in a series of programmes that were intended to bring Islamic principles to bear on public policy. In line with this, Bank Islam Malaysia was established in 1982 and the International Islamic University in 1983.

Dr Mahathir's political style was distinctive. He took bold measures when he felt the situation demanded them. In the early 1980s, he initiated a 'Buy British last' campaign in protest against the abolition of grants for overseas students at British universities (Malaysian students were badly affected) and against restricted landing rights at Heathrow Airport. He urged Malaysians to 'Look East' for models of excellence and to wean themselves from over-dependence on the West.

Leadership challenges

Dr Mahathir's period at Malaysia's helm saw several challenges from within and from abroad. He was almost ousted in an UMNO leadership tussle in 1987

'The world that we have to face in the new decades and centuries will see numerous attempts by the Europeans to colonize us either indirectly or directly. If our country is not attacked, our minds, our culture, our religion and other things will become the target.'

Tun Dr Mahathir's final speech as UMNO President at 54th General Assembly, June 2003.

(see 'The United Malays National Organisation (UMNO)'), and the foreign press was often hostile.

The Asian economic crisis of 1997–8 galvanized Dr Mahathir into restructuring the banking and corporate sectors; and English was reintroduced in schools to make Malaysians more competitive internationally. He also warned Malays against complacency, threatening to remove the 'crutches' unintentionally created by the New Economic Policy.

Track record

Dr Mahathir created a model of capitalism that was concerned not merely with wealth creation but also with wealth distribution. He fostered a society of entrepreneurs with a range of pro-business policies.

Articulated in 1990, Vision 2020 was an aspiration for Malaysia to become a developed nation by the year 2020.

Dr Mahathir received the title 'Tun' from the Yang di-Pertuan Agong in 2003. He will be remembered for fostering social harmony through programmes under the National Development Policy and National Vision Policy. He also championed the cause of Islam, demonstrating that Islam is not incompatible with modernity, and spoke out for third world countries. He was once described as a 'truly global statesman'.

BELOW: Delegates pose with Dr Mahathir at an Organization of Islamic Conference meeting in Kuala Lumpur, 1996.

BOTTOM: Dr Mahathir hands over duties to new Prime Minister Dato' Seri Abdullah Ahmad Badawi on 31 October 2003.

Prime Minister Dato' Seri (now Tun) Dr Mahathir—part two

Malaysia underwent a significant political, social and economic transformation during Dr Mahathir's 22 years as Prime Minister. Throughout that period, he provided visionary leadership to the nation, and on the international stage was a commanding voice for the rights and dignity of the developing world.

One of Dr Mahathir's first initiatives as Prime Minister was a programme of economic self-reliance called Malaysia Boleh ('Malaysia Can').

Dr Mahathir the environmentalist

During his first year in office, Dr Mahathir expressed the view that Antarctica should be the common property of all nations. In 1984, he tabled the first draft resolution in the United Nations to update and conduct research on Antarctica. This timely proposal was passed unanimously.

Later, in 1989 as Chairman of the Commonwealth Conference, he initiated the Langkawi Declaration, which set out a Commonwealth programme of action to deal with environmental problems facing the world.

He also attended the Earth Summit in Rio de Janeiro in 1992, which set goals for reversing some of the planet's most threatening problems such as global warming and species extinction.

His participation in the Earth Summit led to the formulation of the National Biodiversity Policy in 1998. The policy emphasizes the importance of conservation and outlines strategies to protect biodiversity.

Dr Mahathir was the first Prime Minister to lead a delegation to the South Pole, during his eight-day visit to Antarctica, in 2002.

Economic achievements

Dr Mahathir took office in July 1981, mid-way through the New Economic Policy (NEP) (see 'Economic policies'). In 1990, the National Development Policy (NDP) was introduced—with growth rather than social restructuring as its primary objective. This was followed in 2001 by the National Vision Policy, re-emphasizing national unity as the overriding objective, and incorporating key strategies from the NEP and NDP.

In 1983, Dr Mahathir initiated the 'Malaysia Inc.' concept, whereby the government and the private sector cooperated for economic growth, and state-owned and controlled entities were corporatized and privatized to increase productivity and efficiency, while reducing the government's financial and administrative burdens.

In 1984, he initiated the National Agricultural Policy, which facilitated business and development activities by the private sector and producers. The Industrial Master Plan (1985) identified priority industrial product groups for development and export and helped focus government and private sector efforts. He oversaw market liberalization and active promotion of private sector growth with the enactment of the Promotion of Investments Act 1986, which provided incentives for manufacturing, agriculture and tourism, and amendments to the Industrial Coordination Act 1975 to extend exemptions from licensing and reporting requirements.

One of the biggest challenges of Dr Mahathir's tenure came during the Asian Financial Crisis of 1997–8. Dr Mahathir went against conventional wisdom by instituting strict capital controls, pegging the rate of exchange for the Ringgit, and setting up national asset management company Danaharta to reduce the financial sector's non-performing loans. Roundly condemned at the time by many economists worldwide, Dr Mahathir was, in the eyes of many international pundits, later vindicated by results.

Dr Mahathir was awarded the International Real Estate Federation (FIABCI) Award of Distinction for Nation Building in 2004.

Infrastructure development

In his quest for the creation of a modern, industrialized nation, Dr Mahathir promoted the construction of remarkable infrastructure such as the Petronas Twin Towers, the Kuala Lumpur Inter-national Airport and Putrajaya. He was involved in the development of the national airline, highways, ports and container yards, and in 1982, he initiated the plan to utilize the island of Langkawi's natural wealth to transform it into an international tourist resort. Among his most ambitious initiatives was the 1996 launch of the Multimedia Super Corridor, an information and communications technology hub.

International accomplishments

On the global stage, Dr Mahathir demonstrated a sense of international responsibility. In 1990, he proposed the East Asia Economic Caucus (EAEC) to bring together ASEAN and northeast Asia. Initially undermined by pressure from the United States, the grouping took off in 1997 as 'ASEAN Plus Three' (see 'Expanding ties').

Dr Mahathir was a leading voice in the Commonwealth. For example, in 1997 he was instrumental in establishing the Commonwealth Business Council to involve the private sector in the promotion of trade and investment. Malaysia hosted the Commonwealth Games in 1998, and in 1999 was part of the Commonwealth Ministerial Action Group that reconstituted the Harare Declaration.

Dr Mahathir was an outspoken critic of the economic and political domination of the United States and Europe. He criticized the United Nations (UN), calling for the veto powers of the permanent members of the UN Security Council to be abolished and replaced with a more equitable system of representation. He was dedicated to the idea that Asia could compete with the so-called developed nations on an equal footing. Similarly, he was a leading light in the Muslim world, especially in the Organisation of the Islamic Conference (OIC) where he was involved in the introduction of the common trade area, the Islamic arsenal and the Gold Dinar (see 'Foreign affairs').

Dr Mahathir was a champion of the developing world: in the strength of his conviction that developing nations should not be dominated either economically or politically by Western powers.

The Mahathir years

The 1980s

1982: Look East Policy introduced to emulate the work ethic of countries in northeast Asia, especially Japan and Korea.

Dr Mahathir meeting staff at a Yamaha factory during his visit to Japan in 1983.

1982: Standardized time for the whole nation. Clocks in the Peninsula were put forward by 30 minutes to match Sabah and Sarawak.

1983: Announced the policy of privatization to increase productivity and efficiency of services, while reducing the Government's financial and administrative burden.

1983: Announced plans for a national car project.

Dr Mahathir launches Malaysia's first car, the Proton Saga, on 9 July 1985.

1984: Dr Mahathir instrumental in promulgating the National Agricultural Policy.

Dr Mahathir at an exhibition booth at a Muda Agricultural Development Authority service centre in Kedah.

1984: Labuan, previously part of the state of Sabah, is made a Federal Territory.

1987: Elected President of the International Conference on Drug Abuse and Illicit Trafficking.

1989: Hosted Commonwealth Heads of Government Meeting and introduced the Langkawi Declaration on environmental protection.

The 1990s

1990: Elected Chairman of G–15, a group of Asian, African and Latin American developing countries.

1991: Announced Vision 2020 with the aim of Malaysia achieving fully developed country status by 2020.

1991: Instrumental in organizing the first Langkawi International Maritime and Aerospace (LIMA) Exhibition.

1993: Instrumental in introducing Constitutional amendments to remove the immunity of the Malay Rulers from being charged for criminal offences.

Mahathir looking out from the presidential suite of his hotel in Langkawi during LIMA 2003.

Dr Mahathir launches the book *Dealing with the Malaysian Civil Service* with then Chief Secretary to the Government Tan Sri Ahmad Sarji Abdul Hamid, 1993.

1995: Official launch of Putrajaya, destined to become the nation's new administrative capital.

1995: Inauguration of the Langkawi International Dialogue, part of the 'International Dialogue on Smart Partnership' series.

Dr Mahathir with participants at the fifth Langkawi International Dialogue in July, 1999.

Dr Mahathir inspecting the Samsung Electronic Seremban complex in 1997. He was extremely successful at attracting Foreign Direct Investment to Malaysia.

1995: Outline of the Multimedia Super Corridor announced.

1997: Asian Financial Crisis.

Opening ceremony of the Commonwealth Games staged in Kuala Lumpur, 1998.

1998: Imposed currency controls to curb offshore currency speculation in the ringgit and to regulate short-term capital flows.

1999: Officially opened the world's tallest building, the Petronas Twin Towers, in Kuala Lumpur.

1999: Malaysia hosted the penultimate leg of the world Formula One championship, the Petronas Malaysian Grand Prix, for the first time at the newly built Sepang Circuit.

The Prime Minister, accompanied by the Multimedia Super Corridor international advisory panel, officially opens Cyberjaya, the country's 'intelligent city', in July 1999.

The 2000s

2001: Involved in Malaysia–Singapore talks which resolve long-standing disputes, ranging from water supplies to air space. Agreements are also signed to build a new bridge and tunnel.

2002: Announced sudden resignation. Later agreed to remain as UMNO President and Barisan Nasional Chairman until October 2003 to allow for a smooth transition of power.

Dr Mahathir presides as the Chairman of the Organisation of the Islamic Conference, Kuala Lumpur, 2003.

2003: Initiated the Malaysia Microchip project.

Dr Mahathir standing behind a model Liquefied Natural Gas (LNG) carrier following the opening of the Petronas LNG complex in Bintulu, Sarawak, 2003.

Prime Minister Dato' Seri Abdullah Ahmad Badawi

Like his predecessor, Malaysia's fifth Prime Minister (2003–present) Dato' Seri Abdullah Ahmad Badawi came from a relatively modest background. He is a tried and tested leader, an erudite scholar, and a consensus builder. His reputation for accessibility enhances his popularity with the grassroots electorate.

Dato' Seri Abdullah Ahmad Badawi on his first day of office, 3 November 2003.

Profile

1939	Born in Penang.
1964–78	Officer in the Malaysian Civil and Administrative Service.
1978	Member of Parliament for Kepala Batas, Penang; Parliamentary Secretary to the Federal Territory Ministry.
1980	Deputy Minister of Federal Territory Ministry.
1981	Minister in the Prime Minister's Department; UMNO Supreme Council member.
1984	Minister of Education; UMNO Vice President.
1986	Minister of Defence.
1991	Minister of Foreign Affairs.
1996	UMNO Vice President.
1999	Deputy Prime Minister and Minister of Home Affairs.
2000	UMNO Deputy President.
2003	Prime Minister and acting President of UMNO.
2004	President of UMNO.

LEFT: Abdullah (circled) as National Operations Council Principal Assistant Secretary, 1969.

Strong family traditions

Dato' Seri Abdullah Ahmad Badawi, or 'Pak Lah' as he is affectionately known, was born on 26 November 1939 in Kampung Perlis, Bayan Lepas, Penang. He is the eldest child of Haji Ahmad bin Haji Abdullah Fahim (popularly known as Ahmad Badawi) and Kailan binti Hassan, and has three siblings.

Abdullah's family came from a family of educationists with a strong religious background. His father and grandfather were both born in Mecca and spent their younger days there pursuing religious studies. His grandfather started a religious school, Sekolah Menengah Agama Daeratul Maarif Wataniah, in Kepala Batas, at which Abdullah himself took instruction. It was during these formative years that Abdullah's knowledge of Islam was nurtured. This was further strengthened when he pursued a Bachelor of Arts (Honours) degree in Islamic Studies at Universiti Malaya.

There is also a family tradition of political involvement. Abdullah's grandfather, Abdullah Fahim was the first from Seberang Perai to register as an UMNO member, in 1946. His advice was often sought by UMNO leaders, most notably for the date of the country's Independence. Abdullah's father, Ahmad Badawi, became UMNO Youth Chief of the Seberang Perai Division in 1946 and subsequently national Deputy UMNO Youth Chief in 1952. He was elected to the Penang state legislative body as assemblyman for Bertam in 1959 and held his seat until his demise in 1977.

When Tunku Abdul Rahman Putra was looking for a suitable date for Independence, UMNO Youth Chief Sardon Jubir and his deputy, (Abdullah's father) Ahmad Badawi (right), consulted (Abdullah's grandfather) Abdullah Fahim (left), an expert in Islamic astronomy. Abdullah Fahim advised that 31 August 1957 was the most auspicious date.

Government and political experience

Upon graduation in 1964, Abdullah joined the civil service as Assistant Secretary in the Federal Establishment Office (now known as the Public Service Department). In 1969, he was promoted to Principal Assistant Secretary of Public Affairs to the National Operations Council and held the post until 1971 (see 'The National Operations Council'). His commitment towards racial integration in Malaysia was shaped by his experience during these years.

He was later appointed Director-General of the then Culture, Youth and Sports Ministry and was promoted to become the Ministry's Deputy Secretary-General in 1974. In this capacity he actively engaged youths, particularly student leaders whose views commonly contradicted the government's. He has frequently stated his belief that youth is one of the nation's most important assets and is the foundation of the country's future.

Abdullah's strong resolve as Prime Minister to improve the public delivery system can be partly attributed to his experience in the civil service.

Abdullah left government service to pursue a political career in 1978, when he stood for election and won the Kepala Batas parliamentary seat, a seat which he still held in 2005.

Abdullah's involvement in politics came as no surprise based on the strong leadership qualities that he demonstrated during his time as a student. He was active in student politics at university and became President of the Federation of Peninsular Malay Students (Gabungan Pelajat-pelajar Melayu Semenanjung, GPMS) which was actively involved in nationalist issues.

After winning his first election, Abdullah was appointed Parliamentary Secretary to the Federal Territory Ministry. He went on to hold numerous Cabinet posts, beginning with that of Minister in the Prime Minister's department, where he implemented various initiatives under Prime Minister Dato' Seri Dr Mahathir Mohamad such as *Bersih, Cekap dan Amanah* ('Clean, Efficient and Trustworthy') and the *Penerapan Nilai-Nilai Islam* ('Applying Islamic Values') campaign. When he became the Minister of Education, he started intitatives such as the pursuit of science and technology courses by Malays through the Joint Secretariat on Scholarships Abroad programme. He ensured sufficient housing for Ministry personnel in his short stint at the Ministry of Defence.

The UMNO leadership crisis in 1987 led to a short break from the Cabinet for Abdullah. He was dropped from the Cabinet, but remained loyal to UMNO. Dr Mahathir reinstated him to the Cabinet as Minister for Foreign Affairs in 1991, a position that he went on to hold for eight years. With the position of Deputy Prime Minister vacant following the sacking of Dato' Seri Anwar Ibrahim in 1998, Dr Mahathir appointed Abdullah as his deputy in February 1999 and also as Minister of Home Affairs.

Initiatives

Abdullah is a strong advocate of instilling the right mindset, culture, values and attitudes in people, and strongly believes in developing Malaysians in all spheres for the continuous success of the country. In his first two years as Prime Minister, Abdullah called for the reform of the education system to create

Prime Minister Abdullah, in his capacity as President of UMNO, giving the closing speech at the 55th UMNO Annual General Meeting, September 2004.

well-rounded Malaysians. He also pushed for measures to eradicate corruption and reform the civil service, and introduced the National Integrity Plan and Institute of Integrity Malaysia. He commenced measures to improve the performance of government-linked companies and established the Royal Commission to Enhance the Operations and Management of the Royal Malaysia Police. Abdullah also placed great emphasis on developing Malaysian society in line with the concept of Islam Hadhari, which is a long-term effort to ensure that Islam is practised in a more holistic, broader and more diverse context encompassing all aspects of life.

In performing his duties as Chairman of the Organisation of the Islamic Conference and of the Non-Aligned Movement, Abdullah stressed the need for all parties, especially the major powers, to understand the root causes of terrorism and that Islam is a religion of peace. He also encouraged capacity building and greater economic cooperation between Muslim countries in creating wealth and prosperity.

> 'The public sector shoulders the responsibility of ensuring national policies are implemented effectively and must reflect a clean and incorruptible image. Our resolve to have a civil service that is corruption-free should not be weakened by unhealthy practices in the private sector or by parties outside the government that contribute to this disease.'
>
> **Dato' Seri Abdullah Ahmad Badawi, maiden address to Parliament, 2 November 2003.**

Abdullah receiving the final report of the Royal Commission to Enhance the Operations and Management of the Royal Malaysia Police from Commission chairman Tun Mohammed Dzaiddin Haji Abdullah, April 2005.

Prime Minister Abdullah (centre) opens the BioMalaysia 2005 Conference and Showcase in Putrajaya at which he unveiled the National Biotechnology Policy and announced the creation of a Malaysian Biotechnology Corporation.

The 2004 general elections

After hardly five months in office, Prime Minister Dato' Seri Abdullah Ahmad Badawi called a snap general election in March 2004.

The Barisan Nasional's landslide win increased its majority in Parliament, won back control of the opposition heartland of Terengganu from Parti Islam Se-Malaysia (PAS) and came close to unseating PAS from the state of Kelantan. Abdullah's electoral strategy concentrated on development, economic progress, efficiency in the civil service, and clean and transparent government. His success was also attributed to his appeal to voters who supported a moderate version of Islam.

The Star newspaper declares the 2004 election result, 22 March 2004.

Islam Hadhari

In February 2005, Abdullah formally launched a guidebook on Islam Hadhari. He listed 10 general principles of Islam Hadhari, namely:

- Faith and piety in Allah.
- A just and trustworthy government.
- A free and independent people.
- A vigorous pursuit and mastery of knowledge.
- A balanced and comprehensive economic development.
- A good quality of life for the people.
- Protection of the rights of minority groups and women.
- Cultural and moral integrity.
- Safeguarding of natural resources and the environment.
- Strong defence capabilities.

A guidebook which explains the rationale of Islam Hadhari, the meaning of its 10 principles and the steps which need to be taken to implement the policy, was launched by Prime Minister Abdullah Ahmad Badawi in February 2005.

LEFT: The Prime Minister leading UMNO Supreme Council members in Maghrib prayers after breaking fast at Putra World Trade Centre, October 2004.

The judiciary

The judiciary—in its wider sense, including not only the courts but also other elements of the legal establishment—is key to the rule of law as a fundamental tenet of government in Malaysia, and serves as the third branch of government. Alongside the secular court system exists a syariah *court system, applicable only to Muslims, that deals with matters such as family, marriage, property, inheritance and divorce.*

Judicial ceremonial attire
1. High Court Judge
2. Chief Judge of the High Court in Malaya
3. Chief Judge of the High Court in Sabah and Sarawak
4. President of the Court of Appeal
5. Chief Justice of the Federal Court

Judicial courtroom attire
1. Magistrate
2. Sessions Court Judge
3. High Court Judge

Top: The Lord High Chancellor of Great Britain (centre) with Malayan judges after a special sitting of the Kuala Lumpur Supreme Court on 4 September 1957, shortly after Independence.

Above: The Yang di-Pertuan Agong, Tuanku Ja'afar, arrives for the official opening of the Court of Appeal in Kuala Lumpur, 1994.

Upholding the rule of law

In common with many Commonwealth nations, Malaysia's system of government is based on the principle of the rule of law and the doctrine of the separation of powers—the legislative, the executive and the judicial. The judiciary is entrusted with general jurisdiction concerning legal disputes. The judiciary's orders are obeyed and enforced because the need to preserve the rule of law is generally recognized.

Although Malaysia is a federation of states, it has a centralized judicial system comprising superior and subordinate courts, except for state Native Courts found only in Sabah and Sarawak. The courts' fundamental role is to decide on constitutional, criminal and civil disputes between subjects, and between the government and its subjects. The courts also decide on disputes between the states, and between the Federal and State Governments.

The vast majority of civil and criminal cases are heard in the Magistrates' Courts located nationwide. Criminal cases that may involve the death penalty are heard in the High Court, as are certain civil matters such as divorce, bankruptcy and grants of probate.

Following Independence, the Privy Council in London served as the final court of appeal on all matters. The Malaysian government began to restrict this right in 1975, and abolished it in 1985. The Supreme Court then became the highest judicial authority and final court of appeal. In 1994, an intermediate superior court, the Court of Appeal, was created, and the Supreme Court renamed the Federal Court.

Cases that come before the Federal Court are heard by a panel of three judges. However, the Chief Justice may convene a bigger panel, with five or seven judges, under certain circumstances. The Federal Court first sat as a seven-person bench in 1996 to decide authoritatively on the law governing the standard of proof required for the prosecution of criminal cases. If the court is not unanimous in its opinion, the majority's views prevail.

In 1994, the government amended the Federal Constitution to enable the Yang di-Pertuan Agong, on the advice of senior judges and in consultation with the Prime Minister, to prescribe a written code of ethics applicable to every superior court judge. A judicial code of conduct was decreed later that year, the breach of which could result in dismissal.

Interpretation of the law

In theory, Parliament makes the law and judges merely interpret it when determining cases. In practice, however, through the normal process of interpreting statutes and applying existing rules to new sets of circumstances, judges help to develop the law by way of precedents.

The rule of law is based on the Constitution. Parliament enacts laws and cases are brought before the courts in reliance on the law. The courts interpret the law, and the Federal Court serves as the final arbiter of the law, including the Constitution.

In 1987, the Supreme Court held that a section of the Criminal Procedure Code was unconstitutional as it was an intrusion into judicial power. Parliament subsequently amended Article 121 of the Constitution, removing any reference to the vesting of judicial power in the judiciary; however, the right of the courts to review legislative and executive action on the ground of unconstitutionality remains, and is specifically provided for elsewhere in the Constitution.

Lord President and Chief Justice

When Malaysia was formed in 1963, the office of Lord President of the Federal Court of Malaysia was created to head the judiciary. The first Lord President was Tun Sir James Thomson, previously Chief Justice of Malaya, and a Scotsman. The position was named after the Scottish office of Lord President of the Court of Session.

In 1994, the position of Lord President was renamed Chief Justice of the Federal Court, and the Chief Justices of Malaya and Borneo renamed Chief Judges of the High Court in Malaya and the High Court in Sabah and Sarawak respectively.

Lord Presidents
1. Tun Sir James Thomson (1963–6)
2. Tun Syed Sheh Syed Hassan Barakbah (1966)
3. Tun Mohd Azmi Haji Mohamed (1966–74)
4. Tun Dr Mohamed Suffian Haji Mohd Hashim (1974–82)
5. Raja Tun Azlan Shah Ibni Almarhum Sultan Yussuf Izzuddin Shah (1982–4)
6. Tun Mohamed Salleh Abas (1984–8)
7. Tun Abdul Hamid Haji Omar (1988–94)

Chief Justices
8. Tun Haji Mohd Eusoff Chin (1994–2000)
9. Tun Mohammed Dzaiddin Haji Abdullah (2000–3)
10. Tun Ahmad Fairuz Dato' Sheikh Abdul Halim (2003–present)

The court system

The civil and criminal courts

Lowest court — **SUBORDINATE COURTS** — **SUPERIOR COURTS** — Highest court

Penghulu's Court

- Cases of a minor nature specifically enumerated in the letters of authority of the *penghulu* (village headman) and which can be adequately punished by a fine not exceeding RM25.

☐ Peninsular Malaysia
☐ Sabah and Sarawak

Native Courts

The Native Court building in Sapulut, Sabah.

A separate hierarchy of state Native Courts is found only in Sabah and Sarawak. These courts hear cases relating to the native customs of the indigenous people, and generally preside over matters concerning customary reserved land.

Magistrates' Court

Court for Children

Magistrates' Courts
- Criminal offences where the maximum term of imprisonment does not exceed 10 years; offences punishable by fines; robbery; housebreaking by night.
- Civil cases where the disputed amount does not exceed RM25,000; landlord-tenant disputes.

Courts for Children
- All offences except offences punishable with death, security offences, and when a child is charged jointly with an adult.

Magistrates' Court

Court for Children

Sessions Court

Sessions Courts
- All criminal offences not triable in the Magistrates' Courts other than those punishable with the death penalty.
- Civil cases where the disputed amount does not exceed RM250,000.

Sessions Court

High Court in Malaya

High Courts
- Criminal offences that carry the death penalty.
- Civil cases such as divorce and matrimonial cases; admiralty, bankruptcy and company cases; appointment and control of guardians of infants and their property; appointment and control of guardians of disabled persons and their estate; and grant of probates of wills and letters of administration.

High Court in Sabah and Sarawak

The Federal Court and the Court of Appeal moved to the Palace of Justice in Putrajaya in October 2003.

Court of Appeal

- Criminal and civil cases originating from the High Court, and criminal cases from the Sessions Court.

Federal Court

- Final judgments on legal matters, on appeal from the Court of Appeal.
- Interpretation of the Constitution and determination of the legality of legislative or executive acts when challenged.
- The ultimate court in civil, criminal and constitutional matters.

The mace of the Federal Court of Malaysia.

Inside the courts

1. Ipoh High Court interior.
2. Interior of one of the five Courts of Appeal.
3. Inside one of the four Federal Courts.

Special Court

The Special Court was set up on 30 March 1993 to deal with any offences committed by the Malay Rulers, including the Yang di-Pertuan Agong, in their personal capacity.

The court also hears all civil cases brought by or against the monarchies. It is chaired by the Chief Justice assisted by four other members: the two Chief Judges of the High Courts, and two persons (current or former judges) appointed by the Conference of Rulers.

The syariah court system

Parallel to the secular system, the *syariah* court administers Islamic laws for Muslims. With the *syariah* court's formation in 1988, the secular civil courts' jurisdiction over Islamic laws was removed. The administration of Islamic law has taken on common law forms, including precedents and a hierarchical system of courts. This was pioneered by the Federal Government which implemented a uniform model for *syariah* courts in the Federal Territories and formalized *syariah* offences and procedures in statutes. Outside the Federal Territories, *syariah* courts are established under state jurisdiction. At the national level, it is the Malaysian Department of Islamic Judiciary (Jabatan Kehakiman Syariah Malaysia) that coordinates the administration of the *syariah* courts.

The *Syariah* Court of the Federal Territories of Kuala Lumpur and Labuan, in Kuala Lumpur.

Key legal institutions

The legal profession and the Bar Council

The legal profession is 'fused'; that is, lawyers take on work as both advocate and solicitor. All advocates and solicitors are members of the Bar, a body corporate established in accordance with the Legal Profession Act 1976 and managed by the Bar Council, which comprises 36 elected members.

Amongst the declared objectives of the Bar is to uphold the rule of law and the cause of justice and to protect the interests of both the legal profession and the public.

The Bar Council organizes a legal aid scheme.

Pardons boards

The Yang di-Pertuan Agong has power to grant pardons for all offences committed in the Federal Territories of Kuala Lumpur, Labuan and Putrajaya, and the Ruler or Yang di-Pertua Negeri of a state has power to grant pardons in respect of all other offences committed in their respective states.

The Yang di-Pertuan Agong, Ruler or Yang di-Pertua Negeri, as the case may be, may only exercise his power on the advice of a Pardons Board comprising the Minister of Federal Territories, or Menteri Besar or Chief Minister of the relevant state, the Attorney General, and no more than three other members.

Attorney General's chambers

The Attorney General's chambers provides a number of legal services, these include:

- Provision of prosecution instructions for criminal cases.
- Provision of consultation services in international and *syariah* laws to the Federal and state governments.
- Representation for the government in civil cases.
- Drafting of all legislation for the Federal Government.
- Reference resource for the Federal Government.
- Management of law revision and review.

The administration of justice

The judiciary has responsibility for deciding cases brought before the courts on matters including those of constitutional, civil and criminal law. Procedures have been laid down for the fair process of all legal cases. In particular, criminal procedure from arrest to sentencing and beyond is subject to strict regulation.

The *syariah* court complex in Kuching, Sarawak, comprises Subordinate Courts, High Courts and an Appeal Court.

Syariah law

All persons, irrespective of race, religion or creed, are subject to the general criminal laws of the country. However, Muslims are further subject to religious provisions contained in State legislation. These primarily relate to personal behaviour and family matters. The Syariah Courts (Criminal Jurisdiction) Act 1965 expressly confers jurisdiction on the Syariah Courts to deal with offences under Islamic law.

The role of the courts

Part IX of the Federal Constitution provides for the exercise of judicial power by the courts. 'Judicial power' can be defined to include the power to resolve disputes between subjects, between the government and subjects, and between government bodies themselves. This power extends to the determination of the constitutionality of government actions and includes the declaration of legislation as null and void where it contravenes the Constitution. The courts serve as guardians of the Constitution's supremacy, and ensure that the three branches of government—legislative, executive and judicial—act within the bounds of the law.

Sources of law

The main source of law in Malaysia is written law. This consists of the Federal Constitution and State Constitutions, legislation enacted by Parliament and the State Assemblies, and subsidiary legislation made under powers conferred by Acts of Parliament or State Enactments. In addition, the Yang di-Pertuan Agong (Supreme Ruler or King) may make Ordinances during periods of emergency proclaimed under Article 150 of the Constitution.

Another important source of Malaysian law is unwritten law. This includes principles of common law that apply to local circumstances (in the absence of Malaysian statutes covering the matter in question), case law (judicial decisions of the superior courts, including those now superseded) and local customs (*adat*) accepted by the courts as law.

Islamic law is a further source of Malaysian law, but is applicable only to Muslims.

Criminal law

The main body of legislation relating to criminal offences is found in the Penal Code, itself adapted from India's colonial Penal Code. The code serves as the operating manual for enforcing the law. It covers a broad range of offences—including those against the State, the armed forces, or public tranquillity; theft; criminal breach of trust; cheating; murder; and rape. Over time, the Penal Code has been amended; it now includes offences that were not envisaged at its inception. The code also stipulates defences which can be invoked by an accused person, such as intoxication, provocation and self-defence.

Besides the Penal Code, other pieces of legislation deal with specific crimes including commercial crimes.

The criminal justice system

The High Court (Criminal Division) building in Kuala Lumpur.

Elements of a fair system

The fundamental principle underlying the criminal justice system in Malaysia is that an accused person is innocent until proven guilty by a competent court of law. In line with this principle, the criminal justice system provides various safeguards to protect accused persons. However, under some legislation, such as the Dangerous Drugs Act 1952 and the Prevention of Corruption Act 1961, certain statutory presumptions are applicable against the accused. Thus, when a person is charged under these laws, the burden is placed on the accused to rebut the presumptions that arise against him.

The right to counsel

The Federal Constitution guarantees all accused persons the right to be represented by a lawyer. In most cases the accused person seeks the services of a private practitioner. However, where the accused is charged with an offence which carries the death sentence, and is extremely poor, the state will appoint a lawyer to represent him.

Provision of bail

As a general rule, unless otherwise provided by law, an accused person who has been charged may apply to the court for bail. The amount of bail is at the court's discretion.

Protection against retrospective criminal laws and repeated trials

The Federal Constitution provides that no person shall be punished for an act or omission which was not punishable by law when it was committed, and no person shall suffer greater punishment for an offence than was prescribed by law at the time it was committed. It also provides that a person who has been acquitted or convicted of an offence shall not be tried again for the same offence, except in cases where the acquittal or conviction has been quashed and a retrial is ordered by a superior court.

Habeas corpus

The Federal Constitution provides that when a complaint is made to a High Court or any High Court judge that a person is being unlawfully detained, the court shall inquire into the complaint and, unless satisfied that the detention is lawful, order the detainee to be produced before the court and released. Applications are often made for an order of habeas corpus where persons have been preventively detained through administrative orders. However, once a person has been sentenced to imprisonment by a court, habeas corpus cannot be issued since such a person is not unlawfully detained.

The criminal legal process

Criminal offence
Generally dealt with under the Penal Code. Other pieces of legislation deal with specific crimes, such as the Sedition Act 1948 and the Anti-Corruption Act 1997.

Complaint from the public or a police officer
The police conduct preliminary investigations following allegations of offences, usually in a police report lodged by a complainant. In certain cases, investigations begin as a result of information obtained by the police.

Arrest
The police are empowered by the Criminal Procedure Code to arrest without a warrant. A person arrested must be brought before a Magistrate within 24 hours.

Charge
When the accused first appears in court, the charge is read and explained.

Trial
Trial by jury was abolished in 1994. All criminal trials are conducted before a single Judge or Magistrate. Most are conducted in the Magistrates' or Sessions Courts. The maximum sentence in such cases generally does not exceed 20 years imprisonment. Offences that carry the death sentence are tried before a High Court Judge.

The prosecution must prove to the satisfaction of the court each and every factual ingredient of the offence. The burden on the prosecution is proof beyond reasonable doubt. Where, however, certain presumptions apply against the accused, the accused has a duty to rebut the presumptions on a balance of probabilities. However, the duty to prove the commission of the offence remains with the prosecution.

Procedural safeguards
The Criminal Procedure Code (CPC) and the Evidence Act 1950, provide procedural safeguards in criminal proceedings.

Police investigations
The CPC spells out in detail the procedure for investigation of all offences and the manner and place of trying offences. The police carry out preliminary investigations of any offence.

Arrest and detention
Article five of the Federal Constitution provides that no person shall be deprived of his life or liberty save in accordance with the law, and that a person who is arrested by the police must be released within 24 hours, except where that person is produced before a Magistrate and the Magistrate makes an order for further detention. Section 117 of the CPC expressly provides that if the police are unable to complete their investigation within 24 hours, they may obtain a remand order from a Magistrate to detain the person for a further 15 days.

Statements by the accused
Statements made by an accused person while under police investigation are admissible as evidence in specified circumstances. Where such statements are tendered as evidence, it is for the court to determine whether such statements were made by the accused person voluntarily (i.e. without any inducement, threat, promise or oppression).

> **LAWS OF MALAYSIA**
> REPRINT
> **Act 593**
> **CRIMINAL PROCEDURE CODE**
> *Incorporating all amendments up to 31 January 2002*

In deciding whether any incriminating statements made by an accused ought to be admitted as evidence, the court takes into consideration whether the arrested person was aware of, and fully understood, the implications and consequences of making such statements. An accused person also has a right to silence.

Confessions
Generally, confessions made by an accused person are not admissible as evidence. However, section 27 of the Evidence Act provides an important exception which is frequently invoked by the prosecution. Under this section, any information given by an accused, even though it may amount to a confession, may be admissible if the confession leads to the discovery of facts relating to the commission of the offence. Since the section makes a serious inroad into the fundamental principles of criminal justice in Malaysia, the courts are cautious about admitting confessions made by accused persons. Unless satisfied of their credibility, the courts will not admit them as evidence.

The charge
After the police investigation, and once a decision is made by the Attorney General's Chambers to prosecute, the charge is framed.

A charge sets out in detail the specific offence and the law under which the person is being prosecuted. It must also mention the time, place and date on which the alleged offence was committed.

Refusal to plea or plea of not guilty
Where the accused refuses to plead or makes a plea of not guilty, the court proceeds with a trial.

Plea of guilt
If the accused pleads guilty, the plea is recorded. If the court is satisfied that the accused understands the consequences of the plea, an appropriate sentence is imposed.

A High Court criminal trial
1. The judge
2. The accused
3. The prosecution
4. The defence
5. A witness
6. Court staff
7. Police
8. Public gallery

Acquittal

Conviction

Federal Court appeals
are heard by a minimum of three judges.

Sentencing
The maximum sentence a court may impose on an accused person who is found guilty of an offence is stipulated in the law for that particular offence. The most common sentences imposed by the courts are fines, imprisonment, caning and the death sentence (for drug trafficking offences, kidnapping and murder). In imposing a sentence, the courts take into consideration public interest.

Prisoners being transported to Sungai Buloh prison, Selangor.

Right of appeal
The accused has a right to appeal against the decision of a Magistrate to a High Court Judge. Under certain circumstances, further appeals are allowed to the Court of Appeal and to the Federal Court. A High Court Judge also has the right to review and revise the decision of a Magistrate.

1. Inaugural meeting of the Public Service Appointments and Promotions Board, predecessor of the Public Service Commission, in 1954.

2. Police roadblock on the highway to Kuala Lumpur International Airport.

3. Entrance to Agricultural Department compound at Kota Bharu, Kelantan.

4. The Institut Tadbiran Awam Negara (INTAN or National Institute of Public Administration) main campus in Bukit Kiara, provides training for public sector officers.

5. Royal Malaysian Army troops of 10th Brigade Para on parade.

6. Teacher helping pupils at Subang Jaya National School.

7. Lecturer conducting a class at Universiti Tenaga Nasional's College of Engineering.

8. Jabatan Kerja Raya (JKR or Public Works Department) engineers working on a bridge in Perak

9. Doctors in the operating theatre at Hospital Kuala Lumpur.

10. MARDI (Malaysian Agricultural Research and Development Institute) scientist examining oil palm waste converted to chicken feed.

11. Dato' Zaibedah Haji Ahmad, Ambassador to Turkey (1991–6), inspecting a guard of honour before presenting her letters of credentials.

INSTITUTIONS OF STATE AND NATIONAL SECURITY

Some observers have described Malaysia as 'an administrative state', meaning that the core of government activity and the implementation of policy has been, and is, essentially the role of the public bureaucracy (the civil service and various government and quasi-government agencies), the police and the armed forces.

Legacies of British colonial rule, these organs have since undergone a process of institutional development. This has been an imperative of the government of the day since Independence, and has allowed the institutions to render continuous service to the nation. Even during the Emergency (1948–60) (see 'The Emergency' and 'The Emergency resolved'), public services were not interrupted, as the nature of government was basically an administrative operation.

At the apex of these institutions is the Malaysian Administrative and Diplomatic Service (Perkhidmatan Tadbir dan Diplomatik, PTD), whose members form the higher echelons of the public policy-making elite and staff the top posts of the various ministries and agencies. Successor to the Malayan Civil Service (MCS), the PTD carries on a long tradition of service and professionalism and continues to manage and lead the other public and technical services.

Together with the police and the armed forces, the public services have provided for a high degree of stability in government operations—in executive, regulative, penetrative, distributive and coercive functions. The Royal Malaysia Police has evolved into a federal agency charged with normal policing (criminal investigation and preservation of law and order), intelligence, and paramilitary and

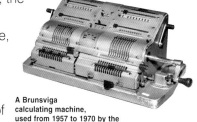

A Brunsviga calculating machine, used from 1957 to 1970 by the Survey and Mapping Department.

constabulary functions. The Malaysian Armed Forces (MAF) have developed into a credible, external defence force comprising army, navy and air force components, and continue to modernize to meet the demands of a changing security environment. More specifically, the MAF is being transformed into a conventional platform from what had essentially been a counter-insurgency force.

The provision of such services by the highly institutionalized organs of government has meant that government authority is a hallmark of Malaysian political development, that Malaysia is a 'closely administered' state, and that it continues to be a country poised to achieve the goals of a developed nation.

This section includes a discussion of the challenge of national security (which is more domestic in nature rather than comprising threats of external aggression), the system of local government, and the administration of the Federal Territories.

Provision of government services—spearheaded by the civil service, and undergirded by robust 'coercive' institutions in the police and armed forces—has meant Malaysia has 'strong' institutions which in turn are important contributors to government performance and political stability. Together, these institutions comprise the administrative machinery of the Malaysian 'state': the effective functioning of this machinery constitutes a significant factor in the state's politics, economy and society.

The Public Service

Providing the government's administrative machinery, the Public Service—which employs over one million Malaysians—can trace its history to the British colonial administration. As a result of privatization, some services, once part of the public sector, are now provided by the private sector.

Definition
The Public Service under Article 132 of the Federal Constitution includes:

- The armed forces
- The judicial and legal service
- The general Public Service of the Federation
- The police force
- The joint Public Services mentioned in Article 133
- The Public Service of each state
- The education service

Manpower allocation

	%
Education	26.31
Administration	17.26
Skilled	11.53
Armed forces	11.33
Medical	8.17
Police	6.96
Security	3.51
Financial	3.46
Engineering	3.14
Agriculture	1.81
Social	1.54
Science	0.97
Economy	0.68
Info. systems	0.61
Legal	0.60
Research	0.55
Transportation	0.45
PTD	0.42
Talent and arts	0.41
Maritime	0.30
TOTAL	**100.00**

–Structure

Members of the Public Service are organized into three main categories: the administrative, executive and clerical, commonly known as the general-user services or common-user services; the professional or specialist services, staffed by professional officers including doctors, engineers, dentists, architects, accountants, chemists, legal officers, and educationists; and departmental services that include customs and excise, immigration, survey and audit.

The Public Service is headed by the Chief Secretary to the Government, a post which continues from pre-Independence days. The Chief Secretary heads a hierarchy comprising a premier group, a professional and managerial group, and two groups of support staff. Within the premier, professional and managerial groups, a prominent role is played by the Malaysian Administrative and Diplomatic Service (Perkhidmatan Tadbir dan Diplomatik, PTD) which provides nearly all senior administrative officials to the Federal Government, and to the states under a secondment arrangement.

Independent Service Commissions—namely the Public Service Commission, the State Service Commission, the Judicial and Legal Service Commission, the Police Force Commission, and the Education Service Commission—ensure that appointments, confirmations, promotions, transfers, and discipline are based on established principles and are free from outside interference. A comprehensive,

Federal administration

The Federal administrative machinery consists of Ministries, each headed by a Minister, with a Secretary-General as administrative head (see 'The federal executive'). In addition, the Prime Minister's portfolios include the Public Service Department (PSD), the Public Service Commission (PSC), the Economic Planning Unit (EPU), the Malaysian Administrative Modernization and Management Planning Unit (MAMPU) and the Implementation and Coordination Unit (ICU) as well as the Attorney General's Chambers, the Auditor General's Office, the Keeper of the Ruler's Seal, the Election Commission, the Anti-Corruption Agency and Petroliam Nasional Berhad (PETRONAS).

The allocation of administrative responsibility for the Ministries and Federal Departments is in accordance with the Federal and Concurrent lists of the Constitution (see 'Federal-state relations').

Public Service personnel (2005)

Agency	Position			
	Higher management	Professional and managerial	Support	Total
Federal	780	216,203	827,621	1,044,604
States	101	5761	99,772	105,634
Federal Statutory Bodies	964	36,181	73,332	110,447
States Statutory Bodies	33	2816	19,415	22,264
Local Authorities	20	2587	51,827	54,434
TOTAL	**1898**	**263,548**	**1,071,967**	**1,337,413**

yet open appraisal system for performance of civil servants is used to determine annual work targets, and incorporates a mid-year review. Panels on Performance Appraisal and Salary Progression, as well as a review mechanism, ensure fair and just appraisals.

Conduct and discipline

Officers in Group 'A' (comprising premier group or higher management, professional and management personnel) are prohibited from taking part in or carrying on political activities or wearing any emblem of a political party. Officers in the support groups are allowed to participate in politics with prior written approval from the Government.

The Public Officers (Conduct and Discipline) Regulations 1993 and the Public Service Disciplinary Board Regulations 1993 form the legal

Head of the Civil Service

There have been 25 holders of the position of Chief Secretary (or its equivalent) since 1911. The functions and duties of the Chief Secretary to the Government extend beyond that of head of the Civil Service. In addition, the Chief Secretary is:

- Secretary to the Cabinet
- Administrative Head of the Prime Minister's Department
- Chairman of the Public Service Promotion Board
- Chairman of the Public Service Disciplinary Board
- Chairman of various high-level committees including:
  - Panel on Administrative Improvements
  - Committee on Rightsizing the Civil Service
  - Superscale Review Committee
  - Permanent Committee on Public Complaints
  - National Development Planning Committee

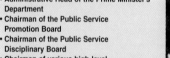

State and local government administration

The six states of Kedah, Kelantan, Terengganu, Johor, Sabah and Sarawak have State Civil Services. The majority of personnel employed by these states are recruited by the respective State Public Service Commissions, and the remainder by the national Public Service Commission. In all other states, administrative officials are provided by the federal administration. The state agencies have administrative responsibility for state matters under the Federal Constitution.

Local government is the third tier of government in Malaysia after the Federal and state governments (see 'Local government').

1. Kuala Lumpur's Bangunan Sultan Abdul Samad, pictured in 1906, has housed several Public Service offices including the Federal Secretariat and the Public Works Department.

2. Kedah State Secretary's Office, Alor Star, is one of the state departments responsible to the state government for carrying out state administration.

3. District Council building (foreground, formerly the District Office) and the current District and Land Office for Batang Padang in Tapah, Perak.

framework for the maintenance of discipline. Civil servants must also abide by laws applicable to all citizens, including the Official Secrets Act 1972, the Prevention of Corruption Act 1961 and the Emergency (Essential Powers) Ordinance No. 22 1970.

The accountability of public officials is part of good governance. The Secretary-General of a Ministry is appointed as the Controlling Officer of the Ministry's expenditure. This appointment clearly places responsibility for the financial management of the Ministry on the Secretary-General, who as Controlling Officer is answerable to Parliament through the Public Accounts Committee (PAC), the highest level of control on public expenditure. Its investigations focus on whether approved funds are disbursed for approved purposes and on whether expenditure has been properly incurred. It bases its investigation on the Auditor-General's Reports which are annually laid before Parliament. The Federal Constitution requires that any money that is to be spent by government agencies must be authorized by law and that the public accounts must be audited and reported by the Auditor-General.

Values, productivity and efficiency

Various programmes have been introduced over the years to instil and maintain professional values among members of the Public Service. In addition, a number of measures have been introduced to increase productivity and efficiency, including Quality Control Circles, Effective Counter Service, Total Quality Management, a Clients' Charter, Consumer Service Offices, and ISO 9000 Management Systems. In an attempt to further improve responsiveness and the capacity to serve the public, the government has adopted the E-Government Programme. This will see the greater use and application of information and communications technology in the Public Service. Projects have already been started, including electronic delivery of driver and vehicle registration, electronic licensing and summons services, electronic utility payments and electronic procurement of goods and services by government agencies. Other applications include human resources management information systems and case management systems in all Malaysian courts including the *syariah* courts.

The cover of a 1994 edition of *Khidmat* (Service) magazine documents the introduction of a Clients' Charter.

Public Service Values

The 'Bersih, Cekap dan Amanah' (Clean, Efficient and Trustworthy) campaign was introduced in 1981 to cultivate good working habits and internalize positive values. Courtesy and noble values are persistently instilled as the hallmarks of a responsive Public Service.

The National Integrity Plan has identified five priorities known as Target 2008:

- Effectively reduce corruption, malpractice and abuse of power
- Increase efficiency of the public delivery system and overcome bureaucratic red tape
- Enhance corporate governance and business ethics
- Strengthen the family institution
- Improve the quality of life and people's well-being

An Institute of Integrity Malaysia was established in 2004. It serves as the central vehicle for the coordination and implementation of the National Integrity Plan.

Chief Secretaries, Federated Malay States
1. Sir Arthur Henderson Young (1911)
2. Sir Edward Lewis Brockman (1911–20)
3. Sir William George Maxwell (1920–6)
4. Sir William Peel (1926–30)
5. Charles Walter Hamilton Cochrane (1930–1)
6. Sir Andrew Caldecott (1931–4)
7. Malcolm Bond Shelley (1934–5)
8. Marcus Rex (1935–6)

Federal Secretaries
9. Christopher Dominic Ahearne (1936–9)
10. Hugh Fraser (1939–42)*

Chief Civil Affairs Officer
11. H. R. Hone (1945–6)

Chief Secretary to the Malayan Union
12. Sir Alec T. Newboult (1946–8)

Chief Secretaries, Federation of Malaya
12. Sir Alec T. Newboult (1948–51)

13. Sir Vincent del Tufo (1951–2)
14. Sir David Watherston (1952–7)

Chief Secretaries (post-Independence)
15. Abdul Aziz bin Abdul Majid (Tun) (1957–64)
16. Abdul Jamil bin Abdul Rais (Tan Sri) (1964–7)
17. Tunku Mohamed bin Tunku Besar Burhanuddin (Tan Sri) (1967–9)
18. Abdul Kadir bin Shamsuddin (Tan Sri) (1970–6)
19. Abdullah bin Mohd Salleh (Tun) (1976–9)
20. Abdullah bin Ayub (Tan Sri) (1979–80)
21. Hashim bin Aman (Tan Sri) (1980–4)
22. Sallehuddin bin Mohamed (Tan Sri) (1984–90)
23. Ahmad Sarji bin Abdul Hamid (Tan Sri) (1990–6)
24. Abdul Halim bin Ali (Tan Sri) (1996–2001)
25. Samsudin Osman (Tan Sri) (2001–present)

* Photograph not available.

The other services
The introduction in 1983 of the policy of privatization led to the transfer to the private sector of activities and functions which had traditionally rested with the public sector (see 'Economic policies').

Alongside this, an appropriate regulatory framework has been established to regulate the privatized entities in order to ensure the protection of consumer interests.

Method of privatization	Examples
Sale of equity	Malaysia Airlines and Malaysian International Shipping Corporation
Lease of assets	Northport (Malaysia) Berhad and Westport Berhad, Malaysia Airports Berhad and Keretapi Tanah Melayu Berhad
Management buyout	Peremba Berhad, FIMA Group Berhad and PERNAS Berhad
Build–Operate–Transfer	North South Highway (PLUS), other road projects and the independent power generation plants

Regulatory agencies
- Bank Negara Malaysia
- Malaysian Communications and Multimedia Commission
- Companies Commission
- Securities Commission
- Labuan Offshore Financial Services Authority
- Energy Commission

Securities Commission building, Kuala Lumpur.

Local government

Local government is the third tier of government. Its main role is to provide people with basic amenities. A key event was the passing of the Local Government Act 1976 and other related measures. The entire structure was reorganized: local elections were abolished, the number of local authorities was reduced, and their roles and responsibilities were streamlined.

Three levels of government

The first two of the three tiers of government in Malaysia are those at federal and state level. Below these there are city, municipal and district administrations, and in Sarawak there are also divisional administrations.

Local government bodies operate under the exclusive jurisdiction of their respective state governments, apart from those within the Federal Territories of Kuala Lumpur, Labuan and Putrajaya, which come under the jurisdiction of the Federal Territories Ministry (see 'Federal Territories').

Before 1976, members of local government assemblies were elected into office. These district, municipal and town councils were plagued with problems, and in some cases their administrators were accused of malpractice, corruption and maladministration. Some councils ran into financial problems and could not discharge their duties and functions effectively. Their respective state governments were eventually forced to take over their administrative duties. This state of affairs prompted the Federal Government to re-examine the entire local government system.

The Athi Nahappan Report

In July 1965, a Royal Commission was formed to study the workings of local authorities in Peninsular Malaysia. The commission submitted its report to the Federal Government in December 1969. However, the Athi Nahappan Report—named after the commission's Chairman—was not publicly released until two years later.

Following the report, the Federal Government initiated steps to restructure local government. In 1974 it enacted an interim Local Government (Temporary Provisions) Act which introduced a 'board of management' structure for local authorities. The Street, Drainage and Building Act 1974 (Act 133) prescribed regulations for the building development of any area in a local authority. To prevent haphazard construction and design, the Act dealt with the control of buildings and the infrastructural facilities that should be provided in them.

Local Government Act 1976

This Act abolished elections at local government level. Although the Athi

Senator Dato' Athi Nahappan (left) submits his report to acting Minister of Housing and Local Government, Tan Sri Dr Lim Swee Aun. The report would form the basis for reforming local government.

Local government of the Federal Territories and cities

Local government functions in the Federal Territories are performed by distinct bodies. In Kuala Lumpur it is the Dewan Bandaraya Kuala Lumpur (Kuala Lumpur City Hall); in Labuan it is the Labuan Development Authority; and in Putrajaya it is the Putrajaya Corporation. Each operates under its own Act of Parliament, although they also utilize certain sections of the Local Government Act 1976. From 2004, these bodies are supervised by a newly established Ministry of Federal Territories.

Local government for other cities, such as Ipoh and Melaka, is in the hands of city councils or halls. These are governed by the Local Government Act 1976, and also make use of internal by-laws which are regulated by their respective state governments.

Cities
Listed in order of grant of city status

George Town	1957
Kuala Lumpur	1972
Ipoh	1988
Kuching North	1988
Kuching South	1988
Johor Bahru	1994
Kota Kinabalu	2000
Shah Alam	2000
Melaka	2003
Alor Star	2003
Miri	2005
Petaling Jaya	2006

Kuala Lumpur City Hall (DBKL) took over the old Sanitary Board and Town Hall building (above left) in 1972, before moving to new premises (left) in 1982.

Nahappan Report recommended maintaining and further developing local elections, the Federal Government decided that elections at state and federal levels were sufficient. The government wanted to end the problems of administrative inefficiency, ineffectiveness and limited finances within local government. With the abolition of local government elections, issues would not be politicized and those responsible could concentrate on providing amenities and services to the public.

The restructuring exercise, scheduled for completion within a year, was fraught with delays. State governments had to reorganize their operational infrastructure to facilitate the changes. Matters were made even more difficult by delays in the channelling of federal grants to local authorities via the respective State Governments.

The restructuring exercise in Peninsular Malaysia was completed in the mid-1980s. Meanwhile, in Sabah and Sarawak (to which states the Local Government Act 1976 does not apply) existing structures were mostly upgraded rather than revamped. A number of local authorities were elevated to the status of municipal councils.

Roles and responsibilities

Apart from obligatory functions such as 'housekeeping' or maintenance services, local governments may also provide discretionary services, which are developmental in nature. In 1976, the Federal Government introduced the Town and Country Planning Act (Act 172) (TCPA) to further define the functions of the local councils. The Act expanded local authority powers

Classification of local authorities

Local authority restructuring

Acts 133 (1974), 171 and 172 (both 1976) provided a comprehensive base for restructuring local government in Peninsular Malaysia. One of the most pronounced effects was a change in the number and size of local authorities. The previous 373 local councils were pared down to 90 in 1985—15 municipal councils, 74 district councils and one city hall in Kuala Lumpur. Most of the local authorities combined to form municipal and district councils. Some grew to encompass totally new and formerly non-local authority areas. Over the years, developments within local governments and changes in the economy have further redefined their status.

LEFT: The Majlis Perbandaran Subang Jaya (Subang Jaya Municipal Council) headquarters in USJ 5, Subang Jaya, Selangor. The council was upgraded from district council status in 1997.

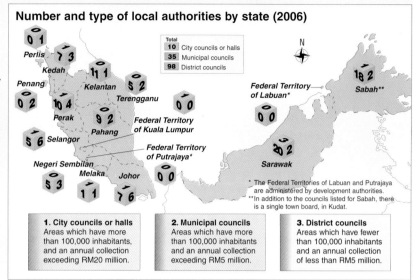

Number and type of local authorities by state (2006)

Total	
10	City councils or halls
35	Municipal councils
98	District councils

Perlis 0 1
Kedah 7 3
Penang 11 1
Kelantan 0 1
Terengganu 5 2
Perak 10 4
Pahang 9 2
Selangor 5 6
Negeri Sembilan 5 3
Melaka 1 1
Johor 7 6
Federal Territory of Kuala Lumpur 0 0
Federal Territory of Putrajaya* 0 0
Federal Territory of Labuan* 0 0
Sabah** 18 2
Sarawak 3 2

* The Federal Territories of Labuan and Putrajaya are administered by development authorities.
**In addition to the councils listed for Sabah, there is a single town board, in Kudat.

1. City councils or halls
Areas which have more than 100,000 inhabitants, and an annual collection exceeding RM20 million.

2. Municipal councils
Areas which have more than 100,000 inhabitants and an annual collection exceeding RM5 million.

3. District councils
Areas which have fewer than 100,000 inhabitants and an annual collection of less than RM5 million.

to include those related to planning. Local authorities thereby assumed the position of catalysts for local development. In accordance with the Act, they produce 'structure' and 'local' plans. Before local plans are adopted they are displayed to allow for public comment. Many local authorities have also adopted internationally accepted measures to engage the local community, with a view to improving local authorities' efficiency.

Following the introduction of the TCPA, the obligatory functions of a council are generally grouped into five sections: environmental, public health and cleansing; enforcement and licensing; public amenities; social services; development.

Local government finance

Local government is listed under the state list of the Federal Constitution (see 'Federal-state relations). Nevertheless, local authorities throughout the country receive financial assistance from both Federal and State (with the exception of the Federal Territories) Governments in the form of grants, subsidies and loans.

Local authorities are also empowered to collect taxes, rates, fees and other charges for their services. By far the most important source of local government revenue is assessment rates. Other sources include fees from trading licences, fines and compounds for offences such as illegal parking.

Roles and responsibilities of local authorities

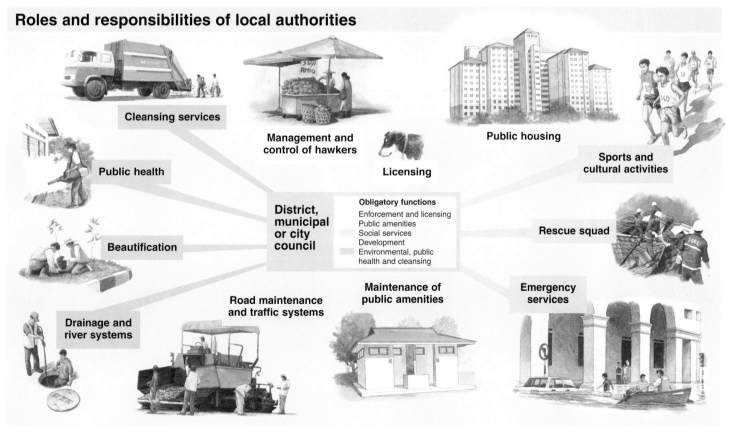

Cleansing services

Management and control of hawkers

Public housing

Public health

Licensing

Sports and cultural activities

District, municipal or city council

Obligatory functions
Enforcement and licensing
Public amenities
Social services
Development
Environmental, public health and cleansing

Beautification

Rescue squad

Road maintenance and traffic systems

Maintenance of public amenities

Emergency services

Drainage and river systems

Federal Territories

The Federal Government has created three Federal Territories listed in Article One of the Federal Constitution: Kuala Lumpur (incorporating the federal capital), Labuan and Putrajaya (the federal administrative capital). Their creation has involved the acquisition of state land by the Federal Government in accordance with the Constitution.

From state lands to Federal Territories

The concept of the first Federal Territory was intended to enable full administrative control over the geographical area in which the Federal Government agencies were located. To this end, an area of 243 square kilometres, including the municipality of Kuala Lumpur (which is the federal capital) was made the Federal Territory of Kuala Lumpur in 1973 by virtue of the Constitutional (Amendment) (No. 2) Act 1973.

Labuan, previously part of the state of Sabah, was made a Federal Territory in 1984. The Federal Territory of Labuan comprises seven small islands, of which Pulau Labuan is the largest, and lies some 10 kilometres off the northwest coast of Sabah. The islands cover an area of approximately 92 square kilometres and had a population of 58,900 in 2004. In 1989 the government declared Labuan an International Offshore Financial Centre.

The Federal Territory of Putrajaya, named after the first Prime Minister, Tunku Abdul Rahman Putra, was established in 2001. Putrajaya is the nation's new federal administrative capital. Built to relieve the pressure of growth on the federal capital of Kuala Lumpur, it is symbolic of the nation's development.

The Federal Territories return 13 Members of Parliament (MPs) to Parliament: 11 from Kuala Lumpur, and one each from Labuan and Putrajaya. A Ministry of Federal Territories was created in 2004.

The federal administrative capital

Tan Sri Ahmad Sarji Abdul Hamid, Chairman of the Putrajaya Development Committee, (second from right) and Prime Minister Dr Mahathir (third from right), who initiated the Putrajaya project, inspect a model of the completed project at its launch in August 1995.

Putrajaya

The Masterplan for Putrajaya, the new 4580-hectare administrative capital, is divided into 20 self-contained neighbourhood 'precincts', each with its own schools, shops, open spaces and other basic facilities. The administrative, commercial and cultural centres will be in the middle, surrounded by residential areas; the aim being to provide green and pleasant living conditions to encourage better productivity. Conceived as an 'intelligent city' with fibre-optic cables and the latest in information technology, Putrajaya will provide a paperless environment for electronic government at a final projected cost of US$8.1 billion.

Once completed in 2010, Putrajaya will accommodate 330,000 people in 52,000 housing units. It will function as the principal seat of government where 76,000 staff will occupy 1.5 million square metres of office space. Ultimately, 135,000 people will be working in Putrajaya's new office complexes.

The Putrajaya flag.

| 1 | Precinct number |
| | Area illustrated |

The three Federal Territories

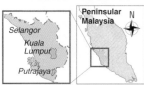

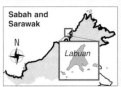

Tan Sri Azizan Zainul Abidin, first President of the Putrajaya Corporation.

Housing and public amenities

1. Putrajaya District Police Headquarters is flanked by the Federal Territory's Fire Station and Hospital.
2. Putrajaya Fire Station, in Precinct Seven.
3. The modern Putrajaya Hospital occupies an 11-hectare site.
4. Typical housing provided for government servants.

(1) Aerial view of central Kuala Lumpur. The city was until 1973 part of the state of Selangor. (2) Since being made a Federal Territory, Labuan has experienced rapid development. (3) Putrajaya is the newest Federal Territory.

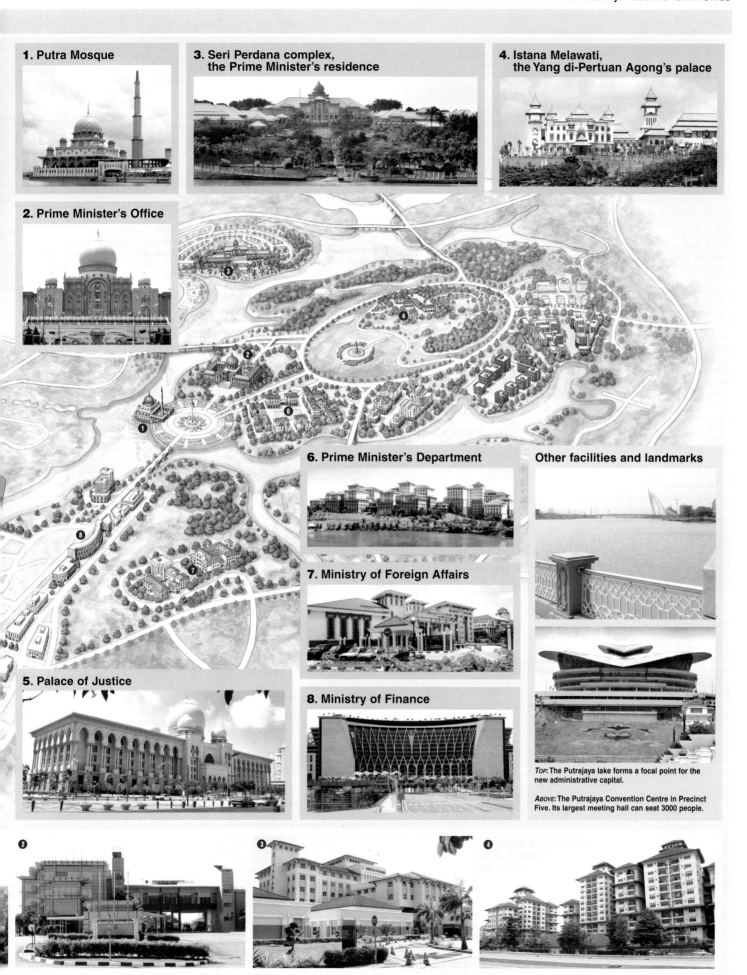

1. Putra Mosque

3. Seri Perdana complex, the Prime Minister's residence

4. Istana Melawati, the Yang di-Pertuan Agong's palace

2. Prime Minister's Office

6. Prime Minister's Department

Other facilities and landmarks

7. Ministry of Foreign Affairs

5. Palace of Justice

8. Ministry of Finance

TOP: The Putrajaya lake forms a focal point for the new administrative capital.

ABOVE: The Putrajaya Convention Centre in Precinct Five. Its largest meeting hall can seat 3000 people.

National security

Since Malaysia is a multi-ethnic nation, the need to maintain racial harmony is essential to maintain national security. In addition, the country's sovereignty was severely threatened by two episodes, namely the communist insurgency (1948–60) and the Indonesian Confrontation. Through strong governance, the government has ensured continued peace and stability.

A passenger having her passport scanned at the Kuala Lumpur international Airport immigration autogate. The Immigration Department is tasked with securing the nation's borders against illegal and unwanted immigrants.

Security concerns

In order to protect the independence and sovereignty of the country, the government is concerned with both external and internal security.

Internal security concerns arise as a result of the nation's multiracial and multi-religious society. The avoidance of communal conflict is always on the government's agenda. Harmony has been maintained through social and economic policies, not through the police. In the past, the internal security situation was different. Although the communist insurgency lasted from 1948 to 1960 (see 'The Emergency' and 'The Emergency resolved'), residual communist activities persisted until as late as December 1989 when the Malayan Communist Party (MCP) officially ended its armed struggle and effectively surrendered. The communist threat has profoundly influenced Malaysia's approach to security and its laws and policies up to the present.

The external security threat reached its peak between 1963 and 1966, during the *Konfrontasi* (Confrontation) with Indonesia (see 'External opposition to Malaysia'). Indonesian communist volunteers made incursions into Sarawak, Sabah and the Peninsular states, and were followed by regular Indonesian troops. The Malaysian Armed Forces, working with British and other Commonwealth troops, successfully repelled the invaders. While subsequent threats have been less dramatic, the government has taken active measures to ensure the nation's external security is maintained.

Communal conflicts

Communal relations in a multi-ethnic and multi-religious country are sometimes unpredictable and can turn volatile unexpectedly. Malaysia's government has always been aware that such tensions can be aggravated by factors such as extensive unemployment (due to a deterioration in the economy); exploitation of political, economic and social issues by political parties and other groups that impact upon communal relations;

Top: Anti-communist rally in Semenyih, Selangor, in 1957.

Above: Police with captured Indonesian insurgents during the Confrontation.

National Operations Council Director of Operations Tun Abdul Razak being briefed on the situation in Negeri Sembilan after the 13 May riots, June 1969.

and media treatment of sensitive issues and differences among the communities.

The major communal conflict that arose on 13 May 1969 precipitated a suspension of democratic governance and the imposition of emergency rule for 18 months. During this period, many aspects of national political, economic and security policy were modified (see 'The 13 May 1969 tragedy' and 'The National Operations Council'). Constitutional amendments (known as the 'entrenched provisions') were implemented, which put certain sensitive matters beyond debate, and the New Economic Policy was introduced (see 'Economic policies'). These measures enhanced national unity. There is a universal consensus, especially among officialdom and the generation that lived through the event, that such an outbreak should never be allowed to recur.

Maintaining security and public order

National security lies in maintaining racial harmony, religious tolerance and equality before the law. However, various laws are in place to reserve and protect the integrity of the nation and thereby reinforce national security. The government is unapologetic in its attitude to strong internal security laws. It considers them necessary for maintaining stability and public order in a multi-ethnic and multi-religious society that is vulnerable on many fronts, and has yet to mature as a unified nation state. The authorities have placed a premium on 'strong governance' without becoming illiberal. The fact that Malaysia has been relatively peaceful compared to other countries confronting similar issues can be seen as vindication of this approach. Ruling-coalition victories in successive general elections indicate that the population generally accepts such laws, considering them an acceptable price to pay for stability and general welfare.

Proclamations of emergency are designed to manage the most dire of crises. Article 150 of the Constitution empowers the Yang di-Pertuan Agong to proclaim an emergency when security, economic life or public order is threatened. New proclamations may be issued to meet different exigencies, even if other proclamations remain in force.

Emergencies have been declared on five occasions. The first was before Independence (in

1948) to fight the communist insurgency (see 'The Emergency'). Emergency was again declared in 1964 when Indonesia launched *Konfrontasi* (see 'External opposition to Malaysia').

In 1966, another emergency was declared for Sarawak when the Chief Minister, Stephen Kalong Ningkan, was dismissed and a short political crisis, albeit a peaceful one, followed (see 'The formation of Malaysia'). The fourth emergency was proclaimed following the events of 13 May 1969 (see 'The 13 May 1969 tragedy'). The fifth emergency was declared in respect of Kelantan in 1977 following another political crisis—the Menteri Besar of Kelantan refused to step down after a motion of no confidence was passed and demonstrations were held in the state capital, Kota Bharu (see 'Federal-state relations').

Only the last proclamation has been formally revoked. The rest remain technically in force, though it is likely the government will make a fresh proclamation should the situation warrant it.

Other laws relevant to the maintenance of security and public order include the Internal Security Act 1960. Among other things, this provides for preventative detention where swift action is necessary and for cases which cannot be brought before a court of law in order to protect secrets and the integrity of the country. The Emergency (Public Order and Prevention of Crime) Ordinance 1969 is another instrument that provides for preventative detention.

The Sedition Act 1948 seeks to punish seditious tendencies with respect to inciting hatred against the government or Ruler, contempt or hatred for the administration of justice, hostility between the various races or religions, or attempts to question the rights and privileges granted to the Bumiputera community under the Constitution.

The Societies Act 1966 is intended to regulate mass organizations. The Official Secrets Act 1972 protects the sanctity of state secrets. The Printing Presses and Publications Act 1984 checks abuse of the written word so as to preserve public order, morality and security.

LEFT: Police giving advice to school-children as apart of a campaign to address student social problems.

BELOW: Army and police personnel evacuating villagers near Kuching, Sarawak, during a flood. The armed forces play an active role in the provision of community services and relief efforts.

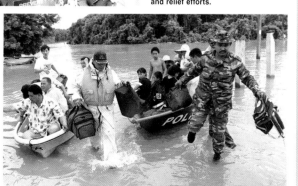

The security forces

1. Air base in Subang, Selangor, the location of the Royal Malaysian Air Force's Number One and Number Three Air Divisions.

2. Lumut naval base, Perak, home to the KD *Pelandok*, the Royal Malaysian Navy's main training centre.

3. Malaysian Army soldiers undergoing group training on jungle patrol techniques.

The Federal Reserve Unit

The Federal Reserve Unit (FRU) is a specially trained unit of the Department of Internal Security and Public Order of the Royal Malaysia Police (see 'The Royal Malaysia Police'). The main duties of the FRU involve controlling riots, dispersing unlawful assemblies, controlling crowds at festivals and assemblies, assisting other police units in their duties and assisting with rescue operations during natural disasters.

An FRU Command Vehicle on parade.

Ikatan Relawan Rakyat Malaysia

Commonly known as RELA, Ikatan Relawan Rakyat Malaysia (People's Volunteer Corps) is a voluntary organization under the Ministry of Home Affairs formed to recruit civilians for the defence of the country, both in times of peace and emergency. It was created through the reorganization, in 1974, of the Vigilante Units set up during *Konfrontasi*.

RELA's objectives are to assist the government in the maintenance of peace and stability in the country, to serve as a third line of defence and to assist other government agencies in times of natural disasters and crises.

RELA personnel taking a pledge during RELA Day celebrations in Kuala Lumpur, August 2004.

National service training

To enhance national security, citizens need to be instilled with patriotism. To this end, Malaysia's compulsory national service (*khidmat negara*) programme began in February 2004. Some 85,000 teenagers were chosen at random from more than 480,000 girls and boys born in 1986, for three-month stints in 41 camps around the country. Those selected reflected the country's ethnic mix.

The objective of the RM500-million pilot programme was to build a self-confident, patriotic younger generation and to enhance multiracial harmony.

The programme does not involve weapons handling, although its physical training element does include unarmed military-style exercises such as basic self-defence and jungle survival. Recruits also perform community service and are given classes on patriotism, nation- and character-building.

Pioneer national service trainees at Camp 'Building Spirit' at Kuala Kubu Bharu, Selangor.

The Royal Malaysia Police

The Royal Malaysia Police (RMP) or Polis Diraja Malaysia (PDRM) is entrusted with law and order functions that encompass civilian policing and paramilitary duties. A national police force, it is nevertheless organized territorially at the state and district levels. It is also organized in functional formations charged with specific policing duties. The RMP's role is integral to the rule of law.

Minister of Internal Security, Prime Minister Dato' Seri Abdullah Ahmad Badawi, accompanied by Inspector General of Police Tan Sri Mohd Bakri Haji Omar, inspecting a guard of honour during the 197th Police Day celebrations at PULAPOL, Kuala Lumpur, 25 March 2004.

Badges of rank

- Inspector General of Police
- Deputy Inspector General
- Commissioner of Police
- Deputy Commissioner
- Senior Assistant Commissioners I and II
- Assistant Commissioner
- Superintendent
- Deputy Superintendent
- Assistant Superintendent
- Chief Inspector
- Inspector
- Probationary Inspector
- Sub-Inspector
- Sergeant Major
- Sergeant
- Corporal
- Lance-Corporal

The badge of the Royal Malaysia Police.

TOP: Police cars are used to enforce traffic rules and as mobile patrol vehicles.

ABOVE: Mobile Police Stations are sent to crime-prone areas as a deterrent to criminal activities.

The history of Malaysia's police force

The Royal Malaysia Police traces its origins from March 1807, with the presentation of a 'Charter of Justice' by the British administration in Penang. The spread of police authority throughout the Malay Peninsula followed the advance of British colonization. In 1871, the Straits Settlements (Penang, Melaka, and Singapore) Police Force was formed, followed by the Federated Malay States Police Force (for Perak, Selangor, Negri Sembilan and Pahang) in 1896. Separate police forces were established for each of the Unfederated Malay States (Johor, Terengganu, Kelantan, Perlis and Kedah). These police forces had a distinct paramilitary or constabulary character, a trait that persists to the present. In Sabah and Sarawak, the police forces

Police functions and responsibilities

The functions and responsibilities of the Royal Malaysia Police (RMP) are defined by the Police Act 1967 and in broad terms include:

The maintenance of law and order.

The preservation of peace and security of the federation. This remit includes the prevention of inter-communal violence, the overthrow of the government by unconstitutional means, organized destruction of life and property, and subversion and insurgency.

The prevention and detection of crime.

The apprehension and prosecution of offenders.

The collection of security intelligence relating to any attempt to disrupt the peace and security of the federation, and to take counter-measures.

The regulation and control of traffic, and keeping order in public places.

The RMP is one of only three government agencies in which senior officers are empowered to conduct prosecutions in the courts. Equally notable is the dual function of the RMP, namely its combination of regulatory and non-regulatory roles. Regulatory roles include basic, conventional policing. Non-regulatory roles include collation of intelligence by the Special Branch, and the paramilitary role of the General Operations Force (part of the Internal Security and Public Order Department).

The Traffic Branch enforces traffic rules and regulations, and regulates traffic flow.

were respectively the North Borneo Armed Constabulary and the Sarawak Constabulary.

After World War II, the seven police forces that had existed in the Peninsula before the Japanese Occupation were combined to form a unified organization, the Malayan Union Police, with centralized jurisdiction for the whole of the Peninsula. With the establishment of the Federation of Malaya in 1948, the Malayan Union Police was renamed the Federation of Malaya Police. Singapore, which became a separate colony in 1946, established its own Singapore Police Force.

In 1963, with the formation of Malaysia, the Federation of Malaya Police was amalgamated with the Singapore Police Force, the North Borneo Armed Constabulary, and the Sarawak Constabulary. Then, with the separation of Singapore from Malaysia in 1965, the RMP was re-organized into three major formations: the Peninsular component and the Sarawak and Sabah contingents, the latter two with their own Commissioners, but all three under centralized control from Kuala Lumpur.

Structure and role

Centralization, consolidation and unification have been key themes of the RMP's development. It now operates as a national police force with state contingents and district formations with a uniform line of authority. Command and control is effected by the Federal Government through a gazetted officer corps and inspectorate.

The RMP is entrusted with onerous, complex and extensive law and order functions. These range from traffic control to intelligence and defence missions, and the enforcement of law and order under a wide array of legislation. The RMP played a key role in combating insurgency (particularly during the Emergency) and in external defence (for example, during the Indonesian Confrontation). It is primarily responsible for societal stability through its law and order duties, and it continues to serve as an authoritative institution of government.

The government received the Report of the Royal Commission to Enhance the Operations and Management of the Royal Malaysia Police on 29 April 2005. The report contained 10 strategies and 125 recommendations.

Organizational structure

National level

Inspector General of Police (IGP)

The Police Act 1967 established the position of the Inspector General of Police (IGP) as the head of the Royal Malaysia Police (RMP), reporting to the Minister of Internal Security. He is based at the RMP headquarters in Bukit Aman, Kuala Lumpur and is assisted by the Deputy Inspector General of Police, Directors of seven departments at federal headquarters, with the rank of Commissioner or Deputy Commissioner of Police, 13 state Chief Police Officers and the Commissioners of Police for the states of Sabah and Sarawak.

Commissioners of Police

1. E. Bagot (1939–42)
2. H. B. Longworthy (1944–8)
3. Col W. N. Gray (1948–52)
4. Col A. E. Young (1952–3)
5. W. L. R. Carbonell (1953–8)

Inspectors General of Police

6. Claude Henry Fenner (Tan Sri Sir) (1958–66)
7. Mohammed Salleh Ismael (Tun) (1966–73)
8. Abdul Rahman Hashim (Tan Sri) (1973–4)
9. Mohammed Hanif Omar (Tun) (1974–94)
10. Abdul Rahim Noor (Tan Sri) (1994–9)
11. Norian Mai (Tan Sri) (1999–2003)
12. Mohd Bakri Haji Omar (Tan Sri) (2003–present)

Federal police headquarters, Bukit Aman, Kuala Lumpur.

The Police Training Centre (Pusat Latihan Polis), commonly known as PULAPOL, at Kuala Lumpur.

Deputy Inspector General of Police

Federal headquarters departments

Internal Security and Public Order Department

The department has diverse functions, from basic policing to paramilitary activities. The Traffic Branch, Air Unit, Cavalry, and Marine Police undertake its basic police functions. Its paramilitary units are the Special Operations Force, the Federal Reserve Unit, and the General Operations Force, formerly known as the Police Field Force. The department is divided into five brigades, sixteen battalions, and forty-eight companies.

Management Department
Formulation of policies and servicing the human resources needs of the police force.

Special Branch
Acquisition, collation and dissemination of security intelligence to the government.

Criminal Investigation Department (CID)
Prevention and detection of crime; apprehension and prosecution of criminals.

Narcotics Department
Dealing with drug-related offences including forfeiture of properties acquired through drug transactions.

Logistics Department
Administration and control of finance, computer systems, and general logistical needs.

Commercial Crime Department
Investigation and prevention of white-collar crime, cyber-crime and money-laundering activities.

1. The General Operations Force patrols remote areas, borders, and coastal areas against armed threats to national security.

2. The Cavalry is used for crowd control, patrols and on ceremonial occasions.

3. The Special Operations Force is used for countering acts of terrorism and to provide security for dignitaries.

4. The Marine Police patrols Malaysia's territorial waters to enforce marine laws and prevent piracy, illegal immigrants, smuggling, and encroachment.

5. The Air Unit is primarily used in aerial surveillance operations.

State level

Contingents

The 13 states and the Federal Territories of Kuala Lumpur and Labuan are each termed a contingent. Each contingent is headed by a Chief Police Officer, except for the contingents of Sabah and Sarawak, which are each commanded by a Commissioner of Police.

District level

Police districts

A state comprises several districts and a district police chief known as the Officer-in-Charge of Police District (OCPD) heads each district. The OCPDs are responsible to their respective Chief Police Officers for the command and control of the police set-ups in their districts. There are altogether 134 police districts in the country and each is headed by a senior police officer. His rank, determined by the area and sensitivity of his district, ranges from that of Deputy Superintendent to Senior Assistant Commissioner.

Station area level

Police stations

Each police district is divided into a number of station areas under the charge of the Officer-in-Charge of Police Station (OCS). The OCS's rank may vary from Sergeant, Sergeant Major, and Sub-Inspector to an Inspector, depending on the importance of the station. There are 728 police stations throughout the country. The station areas are further divided into Police Beat and Patrol Areas to ensure that police personnel service every inhabited part of the country.

Section 6 Police Station, one of the five police stations in Shah Alam police district, Selangor.

101

The Malaysian Armed Forces

The Malaysian Armed Forces (MAF)—comprising the army, navy and air force—form the vanguard of Malaysia's defence and security. Each service is composed of commissioned volunteers and reservists; there is no compulsory military service. With proven counter-insurgency warfare experience, the MAF continue to be transformed and upgraded in line with the demands placed on a modern fighting force.

Diverse roles

The armed forces have several functions. They:
- Defend the sovereignty, territorial integrity and strategic interests of the nation against external threats.
- Support Malaysia's foreign policy by participating in United Nations peace-keeping operations such as the UN Protection Force (UNPROFOR).
- Assist civil authorities in combating internal threats.
- Assist civil authorities in restoring and maintaining public order.
- Assist in flood relief activities (see 'National security').
- Assist during national disasters.
- Assist in national development.

Military education

A class in session at the Armed Forces Academy, Sungei Besi, which offers engineering and management degrees from Universiti Technologi Malaysia.

In line with Malaysia's development, the MAF has emphasized continued educational opportunities and professional advancement for both its officer corps and the rank-and-file.

The Royal Military College is now complemented by a tertiary-level Armed Forces Academy, and post-graduate training offered at the staff and command colleges, including the soon-to-be-established National Defence Institute.

History

The MAF trace their origins from the Royal Malay Regiment (RMR), formed as an Experimental Company in 1933 to serve the various Malay states. The RMR, together with Allied forces, fought valiantly against the Japanese in World War II, and defended its positions in Singapore at great cost. After the war, the RMR was regrouped, reorganized and retrained, and remains to this day the mainstay of the Army and of the MAF. While the RMR is an entirely Malay unit, the MAF as a whole have been developed as a national, multi-ethnic force.

Until the formation of the RMR, non-indigenous paramilitary units were utilized for colonial security control; local volunteer military units were formed only in the early 20th century. The latter in part formed the basis of post-war military organization, spearheaded by the RMR and other army elements.

The Royal Malay Regiment crest.

Development

Following Independence, the MAF's development was initially driven by the nature of the security threats faced by the nation (communist insurgency, *Konfrontasi*, the May 13 tragedy, and trans-border transgressions). But since the end of the Cold War, the MAF have been transformed into a conventional fighting platform from its origins as an infantry-biased, counter-insurgency force with naval and air support elements. Specialization over time and the amalgamation of the Malaysian federation have resulted in the expansion of the army into a combat

The MAF have undertaken international peace-keeping operations around the globe. In November 1993, a contingent of 1489 officers and men were sent to be part of the UNPROFOR in Bosnia-Herzegovina.

force of corps and regiments (including armour, signals, engineer and intelligence units among others) and the organization of territorial commands at the level of field, divisions and brigades. Similarly, the navy and air force have expanded their operational capabilities to be a force to reckon with in the Southeast Asian military theatre.

Modernization of the MAF has been punctuated by need and circumstance. In the 1990s, a Rapid Deployment Force was developed to enhance the MAF's quick reaction, strike power and mobility, and also its joint operational efficacy.

Increased cooperation

To meet the security challenges of the 21st century, joint force development is proceeding with the establishment of a Joint Force Command to complement the existing MAF Headquarters, increasing further the MAF's war-fighting capabilities and tri-service operational effectiveness.

The MAF exercise regularly within the ambit of the Five-Power Defence Arrangements, and with neighbouring and friendly forces. Procurement has also become more broad-based, moving away from an earlier reliance on Anglo-American sources.

Chiefs of Armed Forces (known until 1970 as Chiefs of Armed Forces Staff)

Lt Gen. Tan Sri Dato F. H. Brooke (1956–9)

Gen. Tan Sri Sir Rodney Moore (1959–63)

Gen. Tan Sri Tunku Osman Tunku Mohd Jewa (1964–9)

Gen. Tan Sri Abdul Hamid Bidin (1969–70)

Gen. Tan Sri Ibrahim Ismail (now Tun) (1970–7)

Gen. Tan Sri Mohd Sany Abdul Ghaffar (1977–81)

Gen. Tan Sri Ghazali Mohd Seth (1981–5)

Gen. Tan Sri Ghazali Che Mat (1985–7)

Gen. Tan Sri Mohamed Hashim Mohd Ali (1987–92)

Gen. Tan Sri Yaacob Mohd Zain (1992–3)

Gen. Tan Sri Abdul Rahman Abd Hamid (1993–4)

Gen. Tan Sri Borhan Hj. Ahmad (1994–5)

Gen. Tan Sri Ismail Hj. Omar (1995–8)

Gen. Tan Sri Mohd Zahidi Zainuddin (1999–2005)

Admiral Tan Sri Mohd Anwar Mohd Nor (2005–present)

Major components of the armed forces

The Malaysian Armed Forces headquarters (MAF HQ)

Created in 1993, MAF HQ forms the highest level of military command in the armed forces, and coordinates their day-to-day running. It assists the Chief of Defence Forces to carry out his responsibilities as the commander of the armed forces; primarily to ensure that the armed forces are capable of defending Malaysia's sovereignty and strategic interests in accordance with the National Defence Policy. However, while it coordinates and controls all joint operations (through the Joint Chiefs' Committee chaired by the Chief of Defence Forces), MAF HQ does not directly command routine single service operations. These are placed under the jurisdiction of the respective service chiefs, with the MAF HQ merely monitoring such operations.

The MAF HQ is organized in line with a central joint staff concept in which each of the three services—army, navy and air force—receive policy guidance from the Chief of Defence Forces. To ensure better integration between the three services, a tri-service concept has been implemented such that appointments at headquarters are filled by selection based on rotation between the three services.

Organizational structure

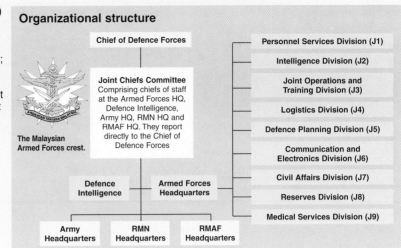

The Malaysian Armed Forces crest.

- Chief of Defence Forces
- **Joint Chiefs Committee** Comprising chiefs of staff at the Armed Forces HQ, Defence Intelligence, Army HQ, RMN HQ and RMAF HQ. They report directly to the Chief of Defence Forces
- Defence Intelligence
- Armed Forces Headquarters
- Army Headquarters
- RMN Headquarters
- RMAF Headquarters

- Personnel Services Division (J1)
- Intelligence Division (J2)
- Joint Operations and Training Division (J3)
- Logistics Division (J4)
- Defence Planning Division (J5)
- Communication and Electronics Division (J6)
- Civil Affairs Division (J7)
- Reserves Division (J8)
- Medical Services Division (J9)

The Malaysian Army

The Malaysian Army has undergone a process of conventional-ization since 1990, having served as a counter-insurgency warfare (CIW) organization for many years. Nevertheless, CIW and jungle warfare remain the army's trademarks.

The two main elements of combat power have been addressed in the restructuring of the army. With regard to manpower, emphasis has been placed on creating a balanced force combining combat, combat support and service support elements. The standard infantry weapon is the 5.56-mm Steyr AUG assault rifle. Additional firepower is provided by 155-mm field howitzers, surface-to-air missiles, multiple-launch rocket systems and anti-aircraft guns.

In addition, some 42 PT-91 Main Battle Tanks, together with associated equipment, have been ordered by the army.

In addition to its domestic military and security roles, the army provides support to government agencies during national disasters and assists in the implement-ation of socio-economic development projects (see 'National security').

Army corps

List of army corps with their respective dates of establishment.

Royal Malay Regiment (1933)
Royal Armoured Corps (1952)
Royal Signals Regiment (1952)
Royal Engineers Regiment (1953)
Royal Military Police Corps (1953)
Royal Artillery Regiment (1957)
Royal Services Corps (1957)
Royal Ordnance Corps (1957)
Royal Electrical and Mechanical Engineering Corps (1957)
Territorial Army (1958)
General Services Corps (1958)
Royal Rangers Regiment (1965)
Special Services Regiment (1965)
Royal Medical Corps (1967)
Royal Intelligence Corps (1969)
Armed Forces Religious Corps (1985)
Army Aviation Force (1995)

ABOVE LEFT: **Soldiers participating in a water-borne exercise in a canoe.**

LEFT: **Royal Rangers Regiment soldiers assemble before joining the National Day parade, 31 August 2004.**

FAR LEFT: **Royal Armoured Corps vehicles participate in the Merdeka Day parade.**

Royal Malaysian Air Force (RMAF)

The RMAF comprises four air force commands: two regional commands, a logistics command, and a training command.

The RMAF now operates nearly 200 aircraft. Among these are 28 BAE Systems Hawk Mk108 advanced jet trainers and Mk208 light multi-role fighters, purchased in 1990, and 18 MiG-MAPO MiG-29s and eight Boeing F/A-18D combat aircraft, purchased in 1993. These have provided the RMAF with greater capacity for conducting day-night offensive counter-air (OCA) and defensive counter-air operations and other important activities.

Light logistics support and aerial observation respon-sibilities have been gradually handed over to the Army and Navy Air Wings. The RMAF retains the roles of providing troop lift, combat search and rescue and military evacuation.

The RMAF's MiG-29N air superiority combat aircraft have been upgraded with in-flight refuelling probes and fire control radars.

The Royal Malaysian Navy (RMN)

The RMN is responsible for safeguarding 4490 kilometres of coastline, a 598,450 square-kilometre exclusive economic zone and 148,307 square kilometres of territorial waters.

The RMN boasts a fleet comprising two Jebat 2000 frigates and one training frigate; four Laksamana-class corvettes; two Musytari-class offshore patrol vessels; and four Spica M-class boats; four Combattantce-II and four Lerici-class missile gunboats; six Jerong-class patrol vessels; four AL-class minehunters; and eight auxiliary craft. The RMN also has the MM-38, MM-40 and Otomat II anti-ship missiles, six Super Lynx and six Fennac training helicopters in its aviation wing.

ABOVE: **The RMN naval base in Lumut, Perak.**
LEFT: **The corvette squadron, led by the KD *Kasturi*.**

1. The crowd awaiting election results at the Selangor Club padang, May 1969.

2. Banners and bunting festoon the drive leading to a polling station in Bandar Sunway, Selangor, March 2004.

3. Dato' Seri Abdullah Ahmad Badawi, President of UMNO, raises the UMNO standard before the 55th party General Assembly in 2004.

4. Voters queuing at a polling station in Terengganu, 2004.

5. Under police escort, members of opposition party PAS escort their candidates to a nomination centre in Kedah for the 2004 general election.

THE POLITICAL PROCESS

An orderly political process, in which the government mandate is decided by popular vote at both the national and state levels, has contributed to Malaysia's overall political development. Elections determine representation in Parliament, and the party with the majority of seats forms the government for up to five years. This makes political parties an institution for peaceful political change. Indeed, the manner in which political parties have thrived is a striking feature of the Malaysian political process. This is crucial to the spirit of democratic governance, and contrasts with some other post-colonial countries, which in the years following the achievement of independence were reduced to either military dictatorships or single party systems with little political competition.

The party system has endured due to three factors. First, its roots in the colonial past, where liberal-democratic ideas were infused into society. The British colonial administration exerted political control through a pluralistic framework—organizations were allowed to function, and sometimes even given support against traditional power bases. Second, the communist threat to the Alliance government following Malaya's Independence reinforced the ruling coalition's commitment to democracy, and hence the functioning of party politics. Third, a party system allowed for pluralism in a multi-racial society, enabling all races to be represented in government.

Newspaper headline announcing the registration of UMNO Baru (New UMNO) on 16 February 1988. The party was accepted into the Barisan Nasional on the same day.

It has been the ability to coalesce competing ethnic demands by mediation between political parties that marks out Malaysia's political process as a success. At the heart of this success is the power-sharing formula forged through the Barisan Nasional (BN), and its precursor the Alliance, successful in all eleven general elections since 1957 and, looking back even further, in the Malaya-wide elections of 1955 and the municipal elections of 1952. The reality of this winning combination is that even though a multi-party system exists, there is in effect a 'one-party dominant plus' party system.

Within the BN, it is the United Malays National Organisation (UMNO)—the party that spearheaded the quest for independence—that remains central and *primus inter pares*. Yet it is UMNO's willingness and ability to share power with the Malaysian Chinese Association (MCA), the Malaysian Indian Congress (MIC), Parti Bersatu Sabah, the Sarawak United People's Party and the other BN component parties that has ensured the coalition's continued ability to win control of Parliament and the various state assemblies.

Power-sharing among the multi-ethnic BN coalition is organized not after the fact of elections, but rather is agreed in advance by the nation's leaders (being heads of their respective ethnically-based parties). The success of this system, represented by the BN's repeated triumphs at the polls, demonstrates the effectiveness of the multi-ethnic coalition format in a plural society. The system has proved difficult for the disparate opposition parties to match, even if they have of late been able to attempt a similar coalition of forces.

The democratic electoral system

The broad principles underlying elections in Malaysia are similar to those of Britain's simple-majority system. Each elected government is given a five-year mandate. An independent Election Commission is responsible for the conduct of parliamentary and state elections, for defining electoral boundaries and maintaining electoral rolls.

Malayans queuing up to vote in the first federal elections, 1955.

Voters queuing up to cast their votes at a polling centre during the 2004 election. Voter turnout for parliamentary and state elections has averaged 75 per cent since Independence.

Political tutelage up to Merdeka

One of the most significant government reforms that took place in the post-World War II period in the Malay Peninsula was the introduction of local elections. Embodied in the Federation of Malaya Agreement, this initiative was part of the British government's preparation of Malaya for self-government and, eventually, independence. To ensure a smooth transfer of power, there was to be a gradual process of political tutelage, starting with elections at municipal level before progressing gradually to the election of legislatures at state and federal level.

With the passage of the Election Ordinance 1950, elections were held near-simultaneously for the municipalities of Penang, Melaka and Kuala Lumpur. The first elections were for the George Town Municipal Council in Penang on 1 November 1951, when Parti Radikal (Radical Party) gained a majority. In Melaka, all the candidates who contested won unopposed. In the Kuala Lumpur municipal elections of 16 February 1952 the UMNO-MCA's alliance won a landmark victory, an outcome that led to the development of the coalition concept that has characterized Malaysian party politics ever since (see 'The Alliance formula').

Elections were subsequently held for the legislative assemblies of certain states in the Federation. Then, faced with mounting demands by nationalist leaders, the British agreed to the first elections at federal level, which took place on 27 July 1955.

The electoral system

The Federal Constitution states that parliamentary (i.e. federal level) and state elections must be held every five years when Parliament and the State Legislatures are dissolved. Elections may be held sooner if the legislatures are dissolved earlier. Parliament is dissolved by the Yang di-Pertuan Agong on the advice of the Prime Minister (see 'The federal legislature'); State Assemblies are dissolved by their respective Sultans or Yang di-Pertua Negeri on the advice of the Menteri Besar or Chief Ministers.

A woman casting her vote for her parliamentary representative during the 2004 elections.

Elections must be held within 60 days of the date a seat is vacated. With the dissolution of Parliament, a general election is held; state elections are usually held concurrently if the State Assembly is dissolved within 60 days of Parliament's dissolution (as is usually the case in Barisan-led states). If an elected representative dies or resigns from his seat, a by-election is called. A notice of election is gazetted and the nomination day is set by the Election Commission.

'First past the post'

The electoral system, based on Britain's 'Westminster' model, works on a simple-majority, 'first-past-the-post' (FPTP) method. The candidate who wins the most votes in a constituency is declared winner, even if he wins by a single vote. Each constituency has one elected representative in the legislature.

FPTP provides a clear-cut choice for voters. It is simple and straightforward compared to alternative systems. One of its disadvantages, however, is that voters may not be represented proportionally.

The electoral rolls

Only registered voters, that is those listed in the electoral rolls, may participate in elections. Registration, which is open throughout the year, is neither compulsory nor automatic.

Citizens over the age of 21 may register in the constituency where they reside. They must do so in person and may use only the address stated on their identity cards. This helps address the problem of so-called 'phantom voters', those who vote in constituencies where they do not belong. Members of the military and police field force and their spouses, and students studying abroad, may vote by post.

The electoral rolls are revised annually, and the public so informed through the media. A revised register is prepared for public inspection and voters may lodge objections within 14 days of publication. Once these enquiries have been addressed, the rolls are certified by the Election Commission (EC).

Prime Ministers voting

1. Tunku Abdul Rahman waits for his turn to vote in the 1964 general election.
2. Tun Abdul Razak Hussein casts his vote in the 1969 election.
3. Dato' Hussein Onn joins the queue in the 1978 election.
4. Dr Mahathir votes in the 1999 election.
5. Dato' Seri Abdullah Ahmad Badawi and his wife Datin Seri Endon Mahmud cast their votes during the 2004 general election.

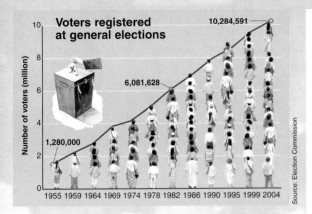

Voters registered at general elections

10,284,591

6,081,628

1,280,000

1955 1959 1964 1969 1974 1978 1982 1986 1990 1995 1999 2004

Source: Election Commission

The number of registered voters has been growing ever since 1955, rising from 1,280,000 in that year to over 10 million in 2004. Nearly half the voters in 2004 were women, and the percentage of young voters has also increased.

Delimitation of constituencies

By law, the EC reviews parliamentary and state constituencies every 8–10 years. There have been six delimitation exercises—1955, 1959, 1974, 1984, 1995 and 2003. The delimitation process follows the principles and recommendations contained in Lord Merthyr's report of 1955. The area of each constituency is based on its level of development and convenience to the electorate. The size of the electorates (the numbers of voters in each constituency) should ideally be about equal. However, special consideration is given to inland and rural constituencies due to their lack of communications and other socio-economic infrastructure. These may have as few as half the number of voters of an urban constituency. The disparity in electorate size between urban and rural constituencies has, however, narrowed with each delimitation exercise.

The result of power sharing

The Alliance and subsequently the Barisan Nasional have been in power without interruption ever since Independence. They have managed to draw support from both urban and rural constituencies, cutting across ethnic boundaries.

In the 2004 general election, the Barisan Nasional, led by Dato' Seri Abdullah Ahmad Badawi, won an unprecedented 199 of the 219 parliamentary seats, giving the coalition the largest majority in both its and the country's history.

Contesting election results

An election result can be challenged in court on grounds of bribery or illegality, breach of the law and election rules, disqualification of candidates or their agents, cheating and threats.

Election petitions must be filed in the High Court within 21 days of the announcement of the election result being gazetted. If the Election Judge decides that the election was invalid and cancels it, the Election Commission will hold a new election for the relevant constituency.

The Election Commission

During the colonial period elections were conducted by Supervisors of Elections, appointed by the state governments concerned. The Federal Constitution enacted upon Independence in 1957 created an independent Election Commission to conduct elections to the Dewan Rakyat (House of Representatives) in Parliament and to the state legislative assemblies. The Election Commission may also conduct elections for the Senate and local governments, when required. At present, members

An Election Commission officer checks the details of prospective voters at a Voter Registration Centre in Kuala Lumpur, 1999.

of the Senate are appointed by the state legislative assemblies and the Yang di-Pertuan Agong. Local elections were abolished in 1976 (see 'Local government').

The Election Commission comprises a chairman, deputy chairman and five members appointed by the Yang di-Pertuan Agong in consultation with the Conference of Rulers. A secretariat implements the commission's decisions through offices in every state. Members of the Election Commission have security of tenure and hold office until the age of 65. They can only be removed on the same grounds and in the same manner as a judge. This gives the Election Commission the power to act without fear or favour.

Chairmen of the Election Commission

1. Dato' Dr Mustapha Albakri (1957–67)
2. Tan Sri Dato' Ahmad Perang (1967–77)
3. Tan Sri Dato' Abdul Kadir Talib (1977–90)
4. Dato' Harun Din (1990–9)
5. Dato' Omar Mohd Hashim (1999–2000)
6. Tan Sri Abdul Rashid Abdul Rahman (2000–present)

Seats won by political parties in parliamentary elections

	1955*	1959*	1964*	1969**	1974	1978	1982	1986	1990	1995	1999	2004
Alliance/BN	51	74	89	74	135	130	132	148	127	162	148	199
PMIP/PAS	1	13	9	12		5	5	1	7	7	27	6
KeADILan											5	1
SF/PSRM/PRM		8	2						0	0	0	
PPP		4	2	4								
Parti Negara		1										
Parti Malaya		1										
Tindakan Ra'ayat				1								
Demokratik Bersatu				1								
DAP				13	9	16	9	24	20	9	10	12
Gerakan				8								
USNO				13								
Sabah Chinese Assn				3								
SNAP				9	9							
SUPP				5								
PESAKA/PBB				2								
Pekemas					1							
Sapo							1					
Semangat 46									8	6		
PBS									14	8	3	
Independents		3		1	2	8	4	4				1
Total	52	104	104	144	154	154	154	177	180	192	193	219

■ Party not yet formed, did not take part, or dissolved.

□ Election fought as part of BN.

SF/PSRM/PRM: Socialist Front, Parti Sosialis Rakyat Malaysia and Parti Rakyat Malaysia

*Malay Peninsula only

**Includes election results for Sabah and Sarawak that were postponed until 1970.

Source: Malaysiakini

The Alliance and the Barisan Nasional

The Alliance, a coalition of the political parties of different communal groups, first arose to fight the Kuala Lumpur municipal elections of 1952, at which it met with great success. In 1974 the Alliance was superseded by the Barisan Nasional, which has remained in power since then due to its ability to bring together political parties representing the nation's major ethnic groups.

Barisan Nasional Chairman Dato' Seri Abdullah Ahmad Badawi (right) and Deputy Chairman Dato' Sri Mohd Najib Tun Razak (centre) lead the counting of the seats won by the Barisan Nasional in the 2004 general election.

The Alliance manifestoes for the 1959 (front) and 1969 general elections.

Formation of the Alliance

On 8 January 1952, the Selangor branches of UMNO and the MCA made a joint declaration announcing that the two parties would contest the Kuala Lumpur municipal elections together in a common front. There was, however, no attempt to merge the two parties. The arrangement proved extremely successful. The Alliance won nine of the 12 seats contested, and went on to win 26 of the 37 municipal council seats contested in six cities in December 1952.

At their conference in March 1953, UMNO and the MCA agreed to set up a National Alliance Organization. This was formally established in August 1953. Liaison committees consisting of two representatives from each party were set up at local level. An Alliance National Council was formed in September 1954 which, among other things, allocated seats to be contested among the member parties. Tunku Abdul Rahman Putra was named 'Leader of the Alliance'. The MIC joined the Alliance in October 1954, and the Alliance National Council met for the first time in April 1955.

The election authorities considered the Alliance a political party for the 1955 Federal Legislative Council elections, but it was only officially registered as a political party with the Registrar of Societies in 1957, when it changed its name from the Alliance Organization to the Alliance Party.

A successful formula

In the 1955 federal elections, the Alliance won 51 of the 52 seats, capturing 81.7 per cent of the total vote cast.

A new draft constitution was prepared in May 1958 to strengthen the national organs of the party, and was first ratified at the UMNO General Assembly in June 1958, and then later by the MCA and the MIC.

The new constitution maintained the level of representation on the Alliance National Council as 16 for UMNO, 16 for the MCA and six for the MIC. On the Alliance Executive Council representation was UMNO six seats, the MCA five, and the MIC three. The constitution required that the chairmen of both bodies must be members of UMNO: both positions were held by Tunku Abdul Rahman Putra. Decisions made by both councils had to receive the unanimous agreement of all parties, but not of all individual members.

The Alliance National Council had full power to select Alliance candidates for federal office, while the Executive Council had the authority to expel any individual from the Alliance (and the respective member party) by a simple majority vote, subject to appeal to the National Council. The constitution stated that members had to be federal citizens.

In the 1959 federal elections, the Alliance's share of the vote dropped to a bare majority of 51.8 per cent, although it won 74 of the 104 seats.

Elections were held in the Peninsula in 1964, after the creation of Malaysia in 1963 (see 'The formation of Malaysia'). 'Alliance' coalitions were also formed around this time in Sabah and Sarawak, although these were fundamentally different from the Peninsular Alliance, as non-Muslim natives formed the dominant force rather than Malays. Following the election, the three Alliance coalitions between them held a total of 123 of the 159 seats in the newly expanded Parliament: the Peninsular Alliance held 89 seats, the Alliance (Sarawak) 18 seats, and the Alliance (Sabah) 16 seats.

The Alliance suffered a setback, however, in the 1969 elections. It won less than half of the votes polled, and secured fewer seats than in the 1964 elections: just 66 of 103 seats in the Peninsula.

In response to the events of 13 May 1969 (see 'The 13 May 1969 tragedy'), the Alliance took steps to widen its support base. In 1972, Parti Gerakan Rakyat Malaysia joined the Alliance at the federal

Alliance Chairman Tunku Abdul Rahman Putra addresses the 1965 Malaysian Alliance Convention at Kuala Lumpur.

The appeal of the Alliance

- The Alliance appealed to voters of all races, and took a moderate position on communal issues, although it did lean towards the Malay position of supporting Malay special privileges, at least temporarily in order to improve the position of the Malays.
- The Alliance gained support of the middle and upper income groups on economic issues, and also introduced wide-ranging rural development programmes to increase the living standard of the rural poor, mainly Malays.
- The Alliance's policies were rooted in its structure, being composed of communal political associations which took communal stands on political issues but were willing to compromise their position to preserve the Alliance's unity.
- By dominating the centre of the political spectrum on communal issues, the Alliance tended to force opposition parties to seek support at the political extremes.

level, and at the state level the Alliance was admitted as a partner in the Gerakan-controlled state government in Penang. Several months later, the People's Progressive Party (PPP) reached a similar agreement. In January 1973 Parti Islam Se-Malaysia (PAS) was also accommodated within the Alliance.

Formation of the Barisan Nasional

Prime Minister Tun Abdul Razak first used the term *barisan nasional* (national front) in his Independence day broadcast in August 1972. However, the term remained undefined until April 1974, when the scales of justice (*dacing*) were announced as the common symbol for all Barisan Nasional political parties. In early May of that year, a huge Barisan Nasional rally was held in Alor Star, Kedah, and it was announced that a selection committee had been formed to decide the Barisan Nasional candidates who would be fielded in the next general election.

The Barisan Nasional of Malaysia was officially registered with the Registrar of Societies on 1 June 1974. At that time it comprised nine political parties: UMNO, the MCA, the MIC, PAS, PPP, Gerakan, SUPP, Parti Pesaka Bumiputera Bersatu (PBB) and the Sabah Alliance Party. Its first constitution allowed only for organization at the national level. Administration was handled by a Supreme Council with members from each component party. Tun Abdul Razak was the first Chairman.

The 1974 general election provided the Barisan Nasional with a clear mandate, when it captured 135 of the 154 parliamentary seats available. The Cabinet announced by Tun Abdul Razak after the election contained representatives of every component party apart from Gerakan (which received a Deputy Ministership) and the PPP. After the 1974 election, the Barisan Nasional was broadened to include the Sarawak National Party (SNAP), an Iban-based party.

A new Barisan Nasional constitution was approved by the Supreme Council in 1975. It called for state and divisional coordinating committees, and empowered them to establish branch committees. Numerous amendments have since been made to the constitution, although these have been relatively minor in nature.

Barisan's 25th anniversary celebrations at the Bukit Jalil Stadium, Kuala Lumpur in 1999. Over 100,000 supporters turned out for the event.

Barisan organization
Barisan is essentially a confederation of 14 political parties. These represent almost all the people of Malaysia regardless of their race, religion, tribe, clan or ethnic group.

National level organization
At the national level, the Barisan Nasional is administered by the Dewan Tertinggi (Supreme Council), the supreme executive body which meets at least twice a year on the direction of the Chairman or acting Chairman.

Barisan Nasional leaders at a meeting in January 2004.

Decisions at meetings of the Dewan Tertinggi are made unanimously other than those relating to discipline and interpretation of the rules, which are by majority, with each member having one vote.

The Dewan Tertinggi formulates Barisan Nasional policies, coordinates matters connected with parliamentary and state elections, and decides on disciplinary measures affecting member parties.

The Dewan Tertinggi consists of a Chairman, Deputy Chairman, Vice Chairman, Secretary-General, Treasurer-General, three party representatives from each member party (including, if any, a member appointed as Vice Chairman), a representative of all Youth movements to be appointed by the coordinating committee of the Barisan Nasional Youth movement, and a representative of all women's movements to be appointed and decided by the coordinating committee of the Barisan Nasional Women's Movement. The Chairman of the Barisan Nasional, to date always the leader of UMNO, is also made Chairman of the Dewan Tertinggi.

State level organization
At the state level, the Barisan Nasional is administered by State Coordinating Committees, and at the parliamentary constituency level by Divisional Coordinating Committees.

Tun Abdul Razak meets with Barisan Nasional leaders to announce seat allocation for the 1974 general election. He is seen mapping out strategy with PPP President Dato' S. P. Seenivasagam. Looking on are (from left) MCA President Dato' Lee San Choon, Dato' Hamzah Abu Samah and PAS President Dato' Mohammad Asri Muda.

Objectives of the Barisan Nasional
• To foster and maintain a united and harmonious Malaysian nation

• To strive for material and spiritual development and maintaining Islam as the religion of the federation; but other religions may be practised in peace and harmony in any part of the federation; and to uphold and practise the principles of the *Rukunegara* (see 'The National Operations Council').

• To strive for the achievement of a fair and just society.

• To promote a closer relationship between the member parties.

Differences between the Alliance and Barisan Nasional
The Barisan and Alliance remain conceptually similar. Barisan is much larger than the Alliance, with many more coalition partners. Leaders of the Barisan member-parties do not enjoy the same close relationships that were enjoyed by those in the Alliance. This is partly as a result of the Barisan's size and the resulting increased range of social and educational backgrounds.

The Barisan has long-term socio-economic policies designed to eliminate the causes of ethnic hostility. The Alliance, on the other hand, had no firm policy and tended to respond to ethnic pressures as they arose. UMNO, dominant in the Alliance, has played an even more important role in Barisan.

TOP RIGHT: A scoreboard on the Selangor Club padang keeps count during the 1965 general election.

RIGHT: Dr Mahathir points out the Barisan Nasional's lead on election night during the 1999 election.

The United Malays National Organisation (UMNO)

Representing the interests of the country's Malays, the United Malays National Organisation has been the lynchpin of the Malaysian political system since the party's formation. It has dominated Malay politics and, more importantly, the multiracial coalition governments that have governed the nation from Independence to the present.

UMNO was founded by Dato' Onn bin Jaafar (standing). His desire to include non-Malays met with fierce opposition and prompted him to leave the party in 1951.

UMNO President Tunku Abdul Rahman Putra and his Deputy, Tun Abdul Razak, at the 1960 party General Assembly.

Dato' Hussein Onn lays the foundation stone for the new UMNO building, Kuala Lumpur, 1981.

Imperatives of formation

The United Malays National Organisation (or UMNO) was formed to lead the Malay nationalist campaign in opposition to the Malayan Union. In March 1946, delegates from 41 Malay organizations in the Peninsula met at the inaugural Pan-Malayan Malay Congress, held at the Sultan Sulaiman Club in Kuala Lumpur. A resolution was passed to form one central Malay organization to fight against the Malayan Union scheme. On 11 May 1946 during the Third Congress held at the Johor Grand Palace, UMNO was born with Dato' Onn Jaafar, Menteri Besar of Johor, chosen as the first Yang di-Pertua (President) (see 'Dato' Onn bin Jaafar').

For the first time, the Malays had been brought together in a political movement which was supported by virtually all the key components of Malay society, from aristocrats and civil servants to radicals and Islamic leaders. In this regard, *Utusan Melayu* and *Warta Negara*, two leading Malay newspapers based in Singapore and Penang respectively, played a vital role in bringing about assertive Malay political consciousness and unity, and eventually the birth of UMNO.

The UMNO flag.

Strong resistance from this young and vigorous Malay political movement eventually resulted in the revocation of the controversial Malayan Union plan by the British government. The British were forced to begin negotiations with the Malay Rulers and UMNO for a new constitutional arrangement. This ultimately led to the Federation of Malaya being instituted in February 1948.

The following decade saw UMNO playing a central role in the Alliance which negotiated independence for Malaya from the British in 1957.

UMNO principles and philosophy

UMNO's ideological imperative has always been to protect the primacy of Malay interests, without losing sight of the fact that it has to operate in a multiracial state built on democratic institutions and a free market economy. To burnish its Malay nationalist credentials, conditions set by UMNO for Malayan independence in 1957 involved investing the new state with Malay symbols of nationhood and ensuring the privileged status of the Malay community. Today, Islam is the religion of the federation, Malay serves as the official language, and the Yang di-Pertuan Agong (Paramount Ruler or King) is responsible for safeguarding the special position of Malays. UMNO's concessions on citizenship to non-Malays and guarantees to uphold non-Malay 'legitimate interests', meanwhile, underlined its commitment to a multiracial state.

UMNO's conservative, moderate and pragmatic ideological orientation has also been essential to its success in gaining the cooperation of its key non-Malay allies, first in the Alliance and then in the Barisan Nasional (BN). Although UMNO since 1946 has indisputably been the predominant political force in Malaya and Malaysia and has enough seats in Parliament to form the government on its own, it is willing to share power with its BN colleagues in the interests of national unity, peace, stability and progress.

UMNO leadership and the nation

UMNO's Presidents have led the Malays and the nation through key historical moments. Apart from Dato' Onn Jaafar, each UMNO President has also served as Prime Minister. Dato' Onn successfully mobilized Malay opposition to the Malayan Union. Tunku Abdul Rahman led the country to Independence in 1957, and presided over the formation of Malaysia in 1963. Tun Abdul Razak's leadership resulted in the establishment of the Barisan Nasional and the introduction of the New Economic Policy. Under Dato' Hussein Onn, national unity was greatly emphasized and the country continued to prosper. During Dato' Seri Dr Mahathir's tenure, Malaysia experienced unprecedented economic growth. Incumbent UMNO President and Prime Minister Dato' Seri Abdullah Ahmad Badawi achieved a resounding general election victory in 2004, with the largest parliamentary majority in Malaysian history.

Dato' Onn bin Jaafar (1946–51)

Tunku Abdul Rahman Putra (1951–70)

Tun Abdul Razak Hussein (1970–6)

Dato' Hussein Onn (1976–81)

Dato' Seri Dr Mahathir Mohamad (1981–2003)

Dato' Seri Abdullah Ahmad Badawi (2003–present)

Objectives

Clause 3, UMNO Constitution

• UMNO is a political party that strives to carry on the national aspirations of Malays and to maintain the dignity and status of race, religion and country. It also strives:

• To defend the independence and sovereignty of the nation

• To uphold and defend the nation's Federal Constitution, State Constitutions, and constitutional monarchy.

• To uphold, defend and spread Islam, the official religion of the nation while respecting national religious principles.

• To defend the peoples' sovereignty and social justice by practising parliamentary democracy and by improving the economy of the Malays and Bumiputera especially, and the Malaysian peoples generally.

• To guarantee the status of the national language (Malay) as the only official language and of the national culture, which is based on the Malay culture.

• To create cooperation among all races to give rise to a Malaysian race that is strong and united, and founded on basic human rights and the special rights of the Malays and Bumiputera.

Constitution and organization

The UMNO constitution provides that at the national level, the party's authority is vested in the General Assembly (GA). The GA's chief executive body, the Supreme Council (SC), is responsible for party administration nationally, and functions under the GA's authority. At the state and Federal Territory level are the state and Federal Territory Liaison Committees. At the Division and Branch level, authority is vested in the divisional Conference of Representatives (DCR) and the Branch General Meeting (BGM) respectively, with the Division Executive Committee (DEC) and the Branch Executive Committee (BEC) as the chief executive bodies. The DECs and BECs are responsible for party administration within their respective divisions and branches and function under the authority of their respective DCRs and BGMs.

The General Assembly

The General Assembly (GA) is the highest authority in the party and the functioning of the party derives from its power and directives. The Annual GA decides the policies of the party and elects the members of the SC, the Permanent Chairman and his Deputy. The Annual GA comprises the Permanent Chairman and his Deputy, members of the SC and delegates chosen by the annual DCR (one delegate for every 500 members; not more than seven from each Division). The Chiefs, Deputy Chiefs and Vice-Chiefs of the three UMNO wings, Pergerakan Pemuda UMNO (UMNO Youth), Pergerakan Wanita UMNO (UMNO Women) and Pergerakan Puteri UMNO (Daughters of UMNO), also attend, as well as their Division Chiefs and 10 delegates from each chosen by their respective General Assemblies (see 'UMNO and its constituent bodies').

The Supreme Council

The SC is the body that administers UMNO affairs under the authority and directives of the GA. It is empowered to carry out any measure on behalf of the GA. The SC consists of the President and his Deputy, six Vice-Presidents (including the Chiefs of the Youth, Women's and Daughters of UMNO wings), the Secretary-General, the Treasurer, the Information Chief, 25 members elected by the GA and 12 members

Dr Mahathir addresses UMNO delegates during a party briefing at PWTC in February 1995.

appointed by the President (including at least one person each from the Youth, Women's and Daughters of UMNO wings). The President, Deputy President, three Vice-Presidents and 25 members of the SC are elected by the GA triennially. The Chiefs of the Youth, Women's, and Daughters of UMNO wings are also elected by their respective GAs triennially and possess the rights and powers of Vice-Presidents. The Secretary-General, Treasurer and Information Chief are appointed by the President.

Liaison Committees

Liaison Committees (LC) are established by the SC in every state and Federal Territory. The LCs facilitate the running of the Divisions of a state or Federal Territory and select members to represent the party in any group or board at state or Federal Territory level.

Divisions

The SC is empowered to establish a Division in each federal electoral constituency. The running of a Division derives from the power and directives of the DCR. The DCR selects members of the DEC and Division delegates to the GA. The DCR also discusses party policies to be presented at the GA and proposes candidates to stand for SC positions. The DEC nominates candidates for elections and party representatives to participate in city, municipal, and district councils. It also ensures the smooth running of the branches.

Number of seats (2006)	
Parliament: 110	
State Assemblies: 303	
As at 31 May 2006	

Branches

The running of a Branch derives from the power and directives of the BGM. Duties of the BGM include discussion of party policies to be presented to the DCR, examination of work done by the BEC, organization of work plans to benefit the people and the selection of members of the BEC. The BGM also chooses the representatives to the DCR, proposes candidates to stand for DEC membership and puts forward seven names to be chosen as Divisional delegates to the GA.

Membership

UMNO membership is open to Malaysian citizens who are Malays or Bumiputera.

The BECs also carry out the party's directives as decided by the SC and DEC and examine and forward applications for membership to the SC through the DEC.

Divisions, Branches and membership of UMNO, 2004

State	Divisions	Branches	Members
Perlis	3	330	53,945
Kedah	15	1,963	293,686
Kelantan	14	2,119	207,645
Terengganu	8	910	210,070
Penang	13	640	150,761
Perak	24	1,590	307,048
Pahang	14	1,015	227,346
Selangor	22	1,826	393,421
Kuala Lumpur	13	571	135,332
Negeri Sembilan	8	563	146,904
Melaka	6	364	113,246
Johor	26	2,013	446,189
Sabah	25	5,328	426,040
Total	**191**	**19,232**	**3,111,633**

The election process

Candidates who stand for Supreme Council posts must be nominated by the divisions. For the President's post, they must be nominated by at least 30 per cent of the party's Divisions; for the Deputy President's post, by no less than 20 per cent; for a Vice-President's post, by at least 10 per cent; and for Supreme Council members, by at least five per cent.

Candidates who stand for positions in Division Executive Committees must be nominated as follows: for Division Chief, by at least 20 per cent of the total number of Branches in the Division; for Deputy Chief, 15 per cent; for Vice-Chief, 10 per cent; and for Committee members, by two branches. However, for Divisions with over 150 Branches, it is enough if a candidate for Division Chief receives the support of at least 30 Branches, while for 20 Branches are required, and for Vice-Chief, 10 Branches.

Ballot boxes being shown to delegates during the 2004 UMNO General Assembly.

UMNO's first headquarters in Kuala Lumpur (above) were a modest four-storey building, compared to the modern complex (right) completed in 1985, which has a six-storey exhibition and conference centre.

Deregistration and UMNO Baru

In 1987, the fourth UMNO President, Dr Mahathir Mohamad, faced a major test from Tengku Razaleigh Hamzah and Datuk Musa Hitam during the UMNO Annual General Assembly. Alleging electoral irregularities, Tengku Razaleigh challenged the party-election results in court. In a surprise decision, the High Court ruled that UMNO should be deregistered. Dr Mahathir regained the initiative by forming UMNO Baru (New UMNO) in 1988, which took over the defunct party's organizational network and financial resources.

Dr Mahathir Mohamad receiving memoranda of loyalty from UMNO Baru members, 1988.

Tengku Razaleigh subsequently formed rival party Semangat 46, and formed a pact with Parti Islam Se-Malaysia (PAS) to challenge UMNO in the 1990 general election; Barisan Nasional lost control of Kelantan. In 1996, after running into difficulties with PAS, Tengku Razaleigh disbanded his party and returned to the UMNO fold.

UMNO and its constituent bodies

Over the years, UMNO has adapted to changing circumstances and developments, yet retained its basic objective: to give political expression to Malay opinion. In meeting the exigencies of the times, the party has founded auxiliary political bodies, set up social organizations and moved into Sabah politics.

Kelab UMNO Luar Negara

Known as Overseas UMNO Clubs, Kelab UMNO Luar Negara were formed to cater for the welfare of students studying overseas. The first such club was established in 1956 in New York, and was set up to serve as a meeting place for Malays and students residing there. By 1970, several UMNO Clubs had been set up in the United Kingdom. From there, the clubs began to spread into other countries, serving as meeting centres for students and Malays furthering their studies or working overseas. As at 2004, there were 42 clubs in 14 countries with more than 4000 members. Overseas UMNO Clubs have their own Secretariat to co-ordinate club activities at UMNO headquarters.

UMNO organizations

To ensure its appeal to all sections of the community, UMNO has set up three auxiliary organizations: Pergerakan Wanita UMNO, Pergerakan Pemuda UMNO and Pergerakan Puteri UMNO. In particular, these organizational wings nurture and cultivate the younger generation, and provide them with guidance, advice and support.

Further, social organizations such as Kelab UMNO Luar Negara have been established to organize activities for Malays and other Malaysians living abroad. The Pertubuhan Alumni Kelab-kelab UMNO Luar Negara, for former members of Kelab UMNO Luar Negara and Malay students who have studied overseas, was launched in 2000. Kelab Maya UMNO, launched in 2002, has carried UMNO's aspirations into cyberspace.

UMNO at State level

Since Independence, UMNO and the Alliance, and then the Barisan Nasional (BN), have been in control, with a few exceptions, of Peninsular State Governments. Although UMNO is not represented in Sarawak, that state's Government has been receptive to federal directives. In Sabah, however, PBS's assertive defence of state rights and withdrawal from the BN just before the 1990 elections provided the justification for UMNO to set up branches in Sabah.

UMNO in Sabah

UMNO felt compelled to set up branches in Sabah in response to the influence of Parti Bersatu Sabah (PBS). As an opposition party, PBS won the Sabah state elections in 1985. It joined the Barisan in 1986 but the relationship was unstable from the start. PBS called for a review of the 'Twenty Points' which formed the basis for the participation of Sabah and Sarawak in the Malaysian federation (see 'The idea of Malaysia'). Frustrated by the lack of progress, PBS President Joseph Pairin Kitingan pulled the party out of Barisan Nasional on the eve of the 1990 state elections.

UMNO Sabah was formed in 1990 to represent the state's 40 per cent Malay-Muslim population, and represented a direct challenge to PBS. In the 1994 election, Barisan Nasional narrowly lost to PBS with 23 seats against the latter's 25. However, a series of defections to the Barisan tipped the scales against Kitingan, who lost control of Sabah a month later. UMNO and Barisan Nasional further consolidated their grip on Sabah in the 1999 election, winning 31 out of 48 state assembly seats. In the 2004 election, UMNO and Barisan Nasional won 59 out of 60 state seats.

Dr Mahathir, as UMNO President, launching an UMNO Sabah function in 1991.

UMNO wings

An UMNO Youth parade at the Sulaiman Club, Kuala Lumpur, in 1962.

Organization and administration

The party's three organizational wings are Pergerakan Wanita UMNO (UMNO Women's movement), Pergerakan Pemuda UMNO (UMNO Youth movement) and Pergerakan Puteri UMNO (Daughters of UMNO movement). Each has its own General Assembly and office-bearers. UMNO's Supreme Council makes the rules that govern the three wings; these provide for the organization, administration, duties and responsibilities of the various bodies within them. Leaders are elected following the procedures set down in the UMNO constitution.

The Executive Committee and leaders

The basic structure of the three wings is similar. At the apex is the Executive Committee or Exco. The Women's, Youth and Daughters of UMNO Excos each comprise 31 members, including each wing's Chief, Vice-Chief and the UMNO Secretary-General.

Each wing's Chief is elected by the respective wing's General Assembly triennially and becomes an UMNO Vice-President. Candidates who stand for posts in the Women's, Youth and Daughters of UMNO wings' Excos must be nominated by a fixed percentage of each wing's total number of divisions. The Exco of each wing is charged with implementing the movement's objectives and carrying out directives from the Supreme Council.

The General Assembly

The Annual General Assembly of each wing is held prior to the main UMNO General Assembly (see 'The United Malays National Organisation (UMNO)'). The General Assembly of each wing comprises an Exco, Division Chiefs and Vice-Chiefs and two representatives chosen by the wing's Division Delegates' Meeting.

The General Assembly of each wing elects for that wing the Permanent Chairman, Deputy Permanent Chairman, Chief and Vice-Chief, Exco members and 10 representatives to the UMNO General Assembly.

UMNO President Dato' Seri Abdullah Ahmad Badawi inspects a guard of honour comprising members of the party's three wings at the 55th Umno General Assembly, 2004.

The Liaison Committees

Each of the three wings has established Liaison Committees in every state and Federal Territory that has more than one Division.

The responsibilities of these Liaison Committees include working together with the main UMNO Liaison Committee to organize and facilitate the running of the Divisions and Branches of each wing in a state or Federal Territory. In addition, the Liaison Committees liaise between the Pemuda, Wanita and Puteri wings and their respective Divisions, and present and put into action

Pemuda UMNO
***Formed*: 1949**

Pemuda UMNO membership is open to male ordinary members of the party aged not more than 40. The wing initially took a more strongly communal line than its parent body. In the early 1950s, it featured prominently in decision-making related to the independence struggle. It remains a substantial force in UMNO politics.

Objectives
Article 3, Pemuda rules
- To encourage members to take an active part in religion, politics, education, economy, culture, sports and social welfare.
- To organize leadership and other courses to achieve the above objectives.

ABOVE: Hussein Onn (left) takes the salute at an UMNO Youth parade with Dato' Onn Jaafar.

BELOW: The 2004 UMNO Youth Executive Committee.

Ketua Pemuda UMNO

1. Captain Hussein Onn (1949–50)
2. Dato' Abdul Razak Hussein (1950–1)
3. Sardon Jubir (1951–64)
4. Senu Abdul Rahman (1964–70)
5. Dato' Harun Idris (1970–6)
6. Dato' Syed Jaafar Albar (1976–7)
7. Suhaimi Kamaruddin (1978–82)
8. Dato' Seri Anwar Ibrahim (1982–7)
9. Dato' Sri Mohd Najib Tun Abdul Razak (1988–93)
10. Tan Sri Abdul Rahim Thamby Chik (1993–6)
11. Datuk Ahmad Zahid Hamidi (1996–8)
12. Dato' Hishammuddin Tun Hussein (1998–present)

UMNO Putera
***Formed*: 2005**

UMNO Putera was launched by Prime Minister Dato' Seri Abdullah Ahmad Badawi at the Hang Tuah stadium, Melaka, in June 2005 as a bureau of UMNO Youth. It organizes activities for youths aged between 18 and 25 years.

UMNO Putera Pengerusi
Dato' Abdul Azeez bin Abdul Rahim (2005–present)

Pop star Asmawi bin Ani (left), better known as Mawi, on the occasion of his becoming a member of UMNO Putera. He is presenting a signed poster to UMNO Putera Pengerusi Dato' Abdul Azeez bin Abdul Rahim.

Objectives
- To give birth to a generation of young Malays with towering personalities, humanitarian values and who are highly confident to create a strong party and become heirs to the national leadership.

Wanita UMNO
***Formed*: 1949**

Membership of Wanita UMNO is open to female UMNO ordinary members.

The movement originated from Jabatan Kaum Ibu (Mothers' Group Department), formed in 1946. In 1949, Ahli-ahli Perempuan UMNO (Women Members of UMNO) was formed. It then changed its name to Pergerakan Kaum Ibu (Mother's Group Movement) in 1956, and in 1971, to its present name, Pergerakan Wanita UMNO.

Puan Sharifah Rodziah (front right) and Toh Puan Rahah (to her right), the wives of the Tunku and Tun Abdul Razak, at a Kaum Ibu function in 1963.

Objectives
Article 3, Wanita rules
- To encourage members to take an active part in religion, politics, education, law (especially women's rights), culture, economy, sports and social welfare.
- To organize leadership and other courses to achieve the above objectives.

LEFT: A scene at the Wanita UMNO 2004 General Assembly.

Ketua Wanita UMNO

1. Datin Puteh Mariah Ibrahim Rashid (1946–50)
2. Hajjah Zain Sulaiman (1950–3)
3. Khatijah Hj Sidek (1954–6)
4. Datin Fatimah Hashim (1956–72)
5. Tan Sri Aishah Ghani (1972–84)
6. Dato' Seri Rafidah Aziz (1984–96) and (2000–present)
7. Datuk Dr Siti Zaharah Sulaiman (1996–2000)

Puteri UMNO
***Formed*: 2001**

Membership of Puteri UMNO is open to women below 35 years of age and not yet Wanita UMNO members. The wing was formed in 2001 to attract young women into the fold and to complement the Women's and Youth Movements.

Ketua Puteri UMNO
1. Azalina Othman Said (2001–4)
2. Noraini Ahmad (2004–present)

Objectives
Article 3, Puteri rules
- To encourage members to take an active part in voluntary, religious, political, economic, educational, health, social service and cultural activities.
- To organize leadership and other courses to achieve the above objectives.

Datuk Azalina Othman Said (fourth from right) and the Puteri UMNO executive committee taking a pledge during the 2002 Puteri UMNO general assembly.

---

directives issued by the national-level wings and the main UMNO Liaison Committee to the wings' Divisions in each state or Federal Territory.

Divisions and Branches
Divisions for each wing are established in every UMNO Division. The wings' Annual Division Delegates' Meetings (DDMs) are held before the main Annual UMNO Divisional Conference of Representatives (DCR). Each DDM elects a Division Committee, and representatives to the DCR and to the wing's General Assembly. They also nominate candidates to serve as Exco members.

Branches for each wing are established by the UMNO Branch Executive Committee in UMNO Branches that have at least 15 wing members. Each of the wings' Branches has a Branch Committee. The Branch Committees meet before the main UMNO Branch Executive Committee meeting (see 'The United Malays National Organisation (UMNO)').

The duties of the wings' Branch Committees include the election of each wing's Branch Committee members and two representatives to each wing's DDM. The Committee also nominate candidates to serve as Division Committee members, and propose two Division representatives to each wing's General Assembly.

The MCA and the MIC

The Chinese and Indians constitute the second and third largest ethnic groups respectively after the Malays. This position is reflected in two of the three longest-serving member parties of the ruling coalition; political parties in Malaysia being primarily communal in nature. The Malaysian Chinese Association (MCA) and the Malaysian Indian Congress (MIC) were both formed prior to Independence, and have a long history of furthering the aims of their members and of the nation as a whole.

Malaysian Chinese Association President Dato' Seri Ong Ka Ting (left) and Malaysian Indian Congress President Dato' Seri S. Samy Vellu confer prior to a Barisan Nasional Supreme Council meeting, March 2004.

Malaysian Chinese Association (MCA)

Formed: 1949

History

Founded as the Malayan Chinese Association, the party changed its name to the Malaysian Chinese Association in 1963. In its early days during the Emergency, the MCA helped win over Chinese supporters from the communists by providing aid and offering a moderate alternative to the insurgents. At its core was a group of prominent figures from the Chinese Chambers of Commerce.

The MCA formed an alliance with UMNO in 1952 to contest the Kuala Lumpur municipal elections, a relationship that was subsequently formalized in the guise of the Alliance Party (see 'The Alliance and the Barisan Nasional'). The MCA met with considerable electoral success until the general election of 1969, at which it won just 13 of the 33 seats that it contested. This decline was caused in part by the departure of Tun Dr Lim Chong Eu in 1968 to form Parti Gerakan Rakyat Malaysia.

The MCA nevertheless managed to overcome this setback, as well as several other internal challenges. The party remains a key member of Barisan Nasional.

Tun Tan Cheng Lock addressing an MCA Annual Delegates Conference in the 1950s.

Organization

Elected party officials include the President, Deputy President, six Vice Presidents (including the National Chairmen of the Youth and Wanita sections), and 33 Central Committee members. In 2003, the party's constitution was amended to prevent the same person holding the office of President for more than nine years. Appointed party officials include the Secretary-General, the Treasurer-General and the National Organizing Secretary.

Party affairs are directed, managed and controlled by the General Assembly. However, the General Assembly may delegate its powers as it deems fit (other than the power to effect changes to the party's constitution) to a committee. An annual meeting of the General Assembly is held, and extraordinary meetings may also be held at any time. The General Assembly consists of the members of the Central Committee, delegates elected by their respective Divisional Assemblies, Members of Parliament and State Legislative Assemblies, all State Liaison Committee Chairmen, and all Division Chairmen.

The Central Committee, which acts on behalf of the General Assembly, consists of the President, Deputy President, Secretary-General, the Vice Presidents, the Treasurer-General, the National Organizing Secretary, 25 delegates to the General Assembly (elected by the General Assembly) and not more than eight members appointed by the President. A Presidential Council, established from among the members of the Central Committee, is responsible for the administration of party affairs under the authority and direction of the party's General Assembly and Central Committee.

The Central Committee may establish in each state a State Liaison Committee to supervise the Divisions and Branches in the state. Divisions are established in each parliamentary electoral constituency, with executive authority vested in annual Divisional Assemblies. Divisional Committees run Division affairs and exercise all functions on behalf of the Divisional Assembly. Branches may be set up with a minimum of 50 members.

Central Committee members (seated, from left) Dato' Seri Chan Kong Choy, Dato' Seri Ong Ka Ting (President), Datuk Wira Dr Fong Chan Onn and Datuk Dr Ting Chew Peh (now Tan Sri), at the 2003 MCA General Assembly.

Number of seats (2006)

Parliament: 31
State Assemblies: 76
As at 31 May 2006

Membership

Membership of the party is open to Malaysian citizens of Chinese descent aged at least 18 years.

Party Presidents

Tun Tan Cheng Lock (1949–58)

Dr Lim Chong Eu (now Tun) (1958–9)

Dato' Dr Cheah Toon Lok (acting, 1959–61)

Tun Tan Siew Sin (1961–74)

Datuk Lee San Choon (now Tun) (1974–83)

Dato' Dr Neo Yee Pan (acting, 1983–5)

Tan Koon Swan (1985–6)

Dato' Seri Dr Ling Liong Sik (now Tun) (1986–2003)

Dato' Seri Ong Ka Ting (2003–present)

Aims and objects

Article 6, constitution of the Malaysian Chinese Association

- To safeguard and defend the independence and sovereignty of Malaysia.
- To safeguard and uphold the Constitution of Malaysia.
- To uphold and safeguard the system of parliamentary and democratic government on a multi-racial basis.
- To secure and maintain the enforcement of human rights and interests of Malaysians of Chinese descent and the legitimate rights and interests of all other communities as provided under the Malaysian Constitution.
- To maintain, foster and promote goodwill and harmony among the citizens of various races in Malaysia so as to ensure the peaceful progress and growth of a strong and united nation.
- To foster, safeguard, advance and secure the political, social, educational, cultural, economic and other interests of Malaysians of Chinese descent by legitimate and constitutional means;
- To consider, assist and deal with problems affecting its members as a whole and to take such steps as may be necessary for their welfare and advancement.
- To promote the development and utilization of the economic assets of the country for the benefit of the citizens of the country as a whole.
- To promote full and equitable employment for all citizens of the country.
- To work for and promote a high standard of living by increasing and improving the productivity of the country.
- To promote and maintain social justice, economic security and equal opportunities for every citizen of this country.
- To encourage, establish and develop cooperative activities.
- To work with other political organizations with similar aims and objectives registered within Malaysia so as to encourage the healthy development of party politics.
- To preserve and sustain the use and study of the Chinese language, and to ensure that its use, teaching or learning shall not be prohibited or prevented in the context of Article 152 of the Malaysian Constitution.
- Generally to do all such acts and things not enumerated above for the well being of the Party and its members.

Representing the Chinese and Indians

The MCA and the MIC have emerged alongside UMNO as the leading communal political parties in the Barisan Nasional (see 'The Alliance and the Barisan Nasional'). Primarily based in the Peninsula, the MCA and MIC each boast sizeable memberships harnessed by well-developed branch and divisional networks.

Since the defeat of the radical Chinese Left, contemporary ethnic Chinese politics has been dominated by the MCA and other Chinese-based political parties such as Parti Gerakan Rakyat Malaysia (Gerakan) and the Sarawak United People's Party (SUPP) (see 'Barisan component parties' and), both also members of the Barisan Nasional, and the opposition Democratic Action Party (DAP) (see 'Opposition parties').

Meanwhile, the MIC dominates Malaysian Indian politics. Smaller Indian-based parties also exist, including the People's Progressive Party (see 'Barisan component parties (continued)').

Both the MCA and MIC have managed to appeal to—and indeed unite—the diverse subgroups that comprise their respective ethnic groups.

The Malaysian Indian Congress (MIC)
Formed: 1946

History
During its formative years, the MIC was not part of the 'establishment', being involved with the All Malaya Council of Joint Action (AMCJA) and the Independence of Malaya Party (IMP). It joined the Alliance in 1954.

Initially viewed as a party of elites, the MIC did not receive grassroots support from the Tamil majority of Indians in the Malay Peninsula until Dato' V. T. Sambanthan became President in 1955.

Throughout much of its earlier history, the party was beset by leadership tussles, the most intense of which was that between President Sambanthan and Vice President, Tan Sri Dato' V. Manickavasagam. Mediation was required on the part of Prime Minister Tun Abdul Razak. Dato' Seri S. Samy Vellu took over the leadership in 1979 and has managed to retain the post for over two decades.

Organization
The MIC's General Assembly, which meets once a year, is the core component of the party. It directs and controls the Central Working Committee. Those entitled to attend the General Assembly include all office bearers and members of the Central Working Committee, delegates from Divisional Congresses who are elected to attend (one for every 250 members), and 35 delegates each from the Youth section and the Women's section who are elected for that purpose. The maximum size allowed for the General Assembly is 1500. If the need arises, the Central Working Committee may order an extraordinary General Assembly at any time subject to at least 14 days notice.

The Central Working Committee administers the affairs of the party, and consists of the President, Deputy President, three Vice Presidents and 29 members including the Youth leader, Women's leader, and two members each from the Youth and Women's sections. The committee's functions and powers include the implementation of decisions made at the General Assembly. It is also responsible for discipline.

The Central Working Committee may also establish, where necessary,

The MIC women's wing with an election candidate, 2004.

Dato' V. T. Sambanthan addresses delegates at the party's 1963 Delegates' Conference.

State Liaison Committees in each state. These have specific powers including those required to settle disputes at Division and Branch level.

The party is further organized into Branch Congresses which are grouped into Divisional Congresses. A Divisional Congress is established by the Central Working Committee in each Parliamentary electoral constituency. Each Divisional Congress must have at least five Branch Congresses. A secret ballot is held triennially at the divisional level to elect a Divisional Chairman and other position holders including delegates to the General Assembly. In addition, each Branch Congress too holds a triennial secret ballot to elect its leaders.

Membership of the party is through admission to an MIC Branch. Office bearers include the President, Deputy President, three Vice Presidents, the Secretary-General, the Treasurer-General and the Information Officer. The President is elected by a secret ballot of the Branch Chairmen. Once elected, an incumbent holds office for three years.

Membership
Malaysian citizens of Indian origin who are above 18 years of age.

Number of seats (2006)
Parliament: 9
State Assemblies: 19
As at 31 May 2006

Party Presidents

John A. Thivy (1946–7)

Budh Singh (1947–50)

K. Ramanathan (1950–1)

K. L. Devaser (1951–5)

Dato' V. T. Sambanthan (later Tun) (1955–73)

Tan Sri Dato' V. Manickavasagam (1973–9)

Dato' Seri S. Samy Vellu (1979–present)

Aims and objects
Article 6, constitution of the Malaysian Indian Congress
• To safeguard and defend the independence and sovereignty of Malaysia.
• To uphold and preserve the Constitution of Malaysia and the principles of *Rukunegara*.
• To safeguard and promote the political, economic, educational, cultural and social interests of Indians in Malaysia.
• To represent, express and give effect to the legitimate aspirations of Indians in Malaysia.
• To promote and maintain inter-racial harmony and goodwill.
• To consider, assist and deal with all matters affecting the interests of the whole or any section of the community in a fair and just manner.
• To cooperate or work with other organizations whose interests and objects are similar to those of the MIC.
• To promote the advancement of Malaysia in cooperation with other communities.
• Generally to do all such acts and things as may be conducive to the furtherance of all or any of the objects of the MIC.

Barisan component parties

In addition to the United Malays National Organisation (UMNO), the Malaysian Chinese Association (MCA) and the Malaysian Indian Congress (MIC) there are some 11 other parties that make up the Barisan Nasional coalition. The largest of these, in terms of the number of elected representatives returned to the Federal Parliament and State Assemblies, are Parti Pesaka Bumiputera Bersatu, Parti Gerakan Rakyat Malaysia, the Sarawak United People's Party, Parti Bersatu Sabah and the United Pasokmomogun Kadazandusun Murut Organisation.

Barisan Nasional Chairman Dr Mahathir Mohamad arriving to address a gathering of members of the Barisan Nasional's Sarawak component parties, 1998.

Parti Pesaka Bumiputera Bersatu (PBB)
Formed: 1974
Presidents: Abdul Rahman Yakub (later Tun) (1974–81); Pehin Seri Tan Sri Haji Abdul Taib bin Mahmud (1981–present)

Parti Bumiputera (which represented Muslims) and Parti Pesaka Sarawak (which represented the Iban) merged to establish PBB. This consolidated Iban and Muslim political support behind a single party and strengthened the Malay-Melanau hold on Sarawak politics. PBB's role in the Sarawak Barisan Nasional (BN) is similar to that of UMNO in Peninsular politics, with the President of PBB becoming the state Chief Minister and Chairman of Sarawak BN. Since its formation the party has steadfastly maintained two wings: Bumiputera and Pesaka.

Abdul Rahman Yakub

The party operates under the authority of the General Assembly (GA), which is itself bound by the party's constitution and rules, and which meets every three years. The GA is made up of the members of the Supreme Council, representatives chosen by the Divisions into which the party is organized (each representative representing at least 500 members), and no more than five members from each of the Youth and Women's movements.

Selected aims and objects
Article 4, constitution of Parti Pesaka Bumiputera Bersatu (PBB)
- To look after and defend the independence, sovereignty and personality of Malaysia.
- To support the Constitution of Malaysia and the constitution of Sarawak and to look after and defend the principles contained in the Constitution of Malaysia and the constitution of Sarawak especially relating to the position and basic rights and special rights of the Bumiputera of Malaysia and to guarantee the livelihood of the Bumiputera of Sarawak for the future.
- To perform whatever for the welfare and development of the Bumiputera in particular and Malaysian citizens that are loyal and faithful generally in the fields of education, economy, society and culture.
- To encourage and look after the feelings, harmony and solidarity among the citizens of Malaysia so as to express one race that is strong and united.
- To guard and look after the foundation of parliamentary democratic rule.
- To support and defend the charter of united races.
- To take any steps that are effective to eradicate subversive movements that may threaten the security of Malaysia.

The party is administered, under the GA's authority, by a Supreme Council which comprises a maximum of 53 members including the President and the two Deputy Presidents. The Supreme Council meets once every three months.

PBB has incorporated a Parliamentary Caucus made up of those party members who are Sarawak State Assemblymen, Members of Parliament and Senators. From among them a Chief Whip is appointed.

At a lower level, the party is organized into Divisions and Branches.

Number of seats (2006)
Parliament: 11
State Assemblies: 35
As at 31 May 2006

Membership
Membership of the party is open to all Malaysian citizens who are Bumiputera and are at least 18 years of age.

Sarawak Chief Minister Abdul Taib Mahmud fixes a plaque on the foundation stone of the new PBB headquarters, May 1992.

Parti Gerakan Rakyat Malaysia (Gerakan)
Formed: 1968
Presidents: Professor Syed Hussain Alatas (pro-tem Chairman); Dr Lim Chong Eu (later Tun) (1968–80); Dato' Seri Dr Lim Keng Yaik (1980–present)

Positioned as a non-communal party with a multi-ethnic composition, Gerakan was founded by former members of the dissolved United Democratic Party and the Labour Party. It extended its support base by wooing trade unionists and took control of Penang in the 1969 elections as an opposition party, before joining the Alliance (now Barisan Nasional) coalition in 1972. The party is predominantly Penang-based. In an attempt to broaden its reach, it moved its headquarters to Kuala Lumpur in 1996.

Dr Lim Chong Eu

Selected aims and objects
Article 7, constitution of Parti Gerakan Rakyat Malaysia
- To honour and uphold the Constitution of Malaysia and sustain the tenets of the *Rukunegara*.
- To strive for an egalitarian Malaysian Society based on humanitarian and democratic principles and to ensure social and economic justice....
- To preserve and strengthen the unity and the happiness of the people in a spirit of understanding, tolerance and goodwill.
- To promote and ensure the economic and cultural advancement of all communities in the development of national identity.
- To eliminate the conditions which cause economic backwardness among our people; to protect the economically weak from exploitation and to encourage, assist and strengthen their participation in economic activities.
- To ensure well organized and efficient civil and other services.
- To uphold the institution of the family.
- To encourage and promote respect and tolerance for the religious life of all communities.
- To eliminate corruption in all forms.
- To uphold Bahasa Malaysia as the national language, to preserve and sustain the use and study of the Chinese, Tamil, English and other languages of the Malaysian communities....

The party is organized into Branches, Divisions and State-level Delegates' Conferences. The National Delegates' Conference, through the Central Committee, has the power to supervise and direct the activities of all Branches, Divisions and State-level Delegates' Conferences.

Membership
Membership of the party is open to all Malaysian citizens of at least 18 years of age.

Number of seats (2006)
Parliament: 10
State Assemblies: 30
As at 31 May 2006

RIGHT: Alliance Chairman Dato' Hussein Onn officiates at the 1978 Gerakan National Delegates' Conference in Kuala Lumpur.

BELOW RIGHT: Gerakan booklet, 2004.

BELOW: Dr Lim Keng Yaik (centre) and party leaders celebrate Gerakan's success in the 2004 elections.

Parti Rakyat Bersatu Sarawak (Sarawak United People's Party, SUPP)

Formed: 1959

Presidents: Tan Sri Ong Kee Hui (1959–82); Tan Sri Stephen Yong Kuet Tze (1982–90); Tan Sri Dr Wong Soon Kai (1990–6); Tan Sri Dr George Chan Hong Nam (1996–present)

SUPP was the first political party established in Sarawak. In its early years, it derived most of its political support from the left, including the communist movement in the state. Although it had substantial Iban support, the leadership has always been Chinese. After failing to stop the formation of Malaysia (it wanted Sarawak to be independent), it entered into a coalition government led by Abdul Rahman Yakub in 1970. By then, most of the leftist elements in the party were purged, deported or under detention.

Today SUPP is seen as a well run Chinese party although the party philosophy is multiracial. The party has been successful in retaining the support of the Chinese community, especially at the state level.

At the core of the party's structure is the Central Committee which may approve the formation of a Branch in any area corresponding to a state constituency or a parliamentary constituency or other such area as it decides.

Ong Kee Hui

Sarawak United Peoples' Party President Ong Kee Hui is sworn in as Minister Without Portfolio in Tun Abdul Razak's (seated right) Cabinet in 1976.

The Central Committee comprises some 21 party members, in addition to all members who are Members of Parliament. Unless the Central Committee decides otherwise, a Branch shall have at least 500 members. A Delegates' Conference—constituting the supreme authority of the party—is held once every three years, and a Special Delegates' Conference whenever the Central Working Committee deems it desirable.

Number of seats (2006)
Parliament: 6
State Assemblies: 11
As at 31 May 2006

Membership
Party membership is open to Malaysian citizens of at least 18 years of age.

Objects
Article 5, constitution of the Parti Rakyat Bersatu Sarawak
- To establish by constitutional means a fair, just and equal society for all people irrespective of their racial origin or creed.
- To secure and maintain the establishment of a government based on parliamentary democracy.
- To promote and ensure economic, educational and cultural advancement of all races and particularly to improve the economic condition of those who are economically backward.
- To maintain, foster and promote goodwill, racial harmony and unity of all races and to inspire the people with the spirit of self-reliance and endeavour.
- To promote and safeguard the interests Sarawak within the context of Malaysia.
- To cooperate with other political organisations with similar aims and objectives on a Malaysian basis in joint political activities....

Aims and objectives
Article 5, Parti Bersatu Sabah constitution
- To uphold, maintain and ensure the continued and proper process and practice of parliamentary democracy.
- To uphold the dignity of man.
- To promote goodwill and work towards peace, progress, harmony and understanding so as to ensure a proper process of integration and unity among all the races in Malaysia, particularly in Sabah.
- To preserve and to protect the rights and interests of Sabah within the federation of Malaysia.
- To protect and safeguard the rights and special privileges of the local Bumiputera and the legitimate interests of other Malaysian citizens of Sabah.
- To protect, preserve and to promote the traditional customs and cultures of all the people of Sabah.
- To ensure and uphold without conditions the practice of religious freedom.
- To promote awareness of being a Malaysian and loyalty to the King and Country.
- To uphold and maintain the principles of the *Rukunegara* in the true sense of the word and its noble spirit.
- To work with other Malaysian registered political organisations with similar aims and objects so as to ensure and encourage the healthy development of party politics; and to do all that is necessary and incidental to the above aims and objects towards a just, stable, harmonious and prosperous society.

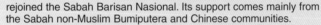

Parti Bersatu Sabah (PBS)

Formed: 1985

Presidents: Datuk Seri Panglima Joseph Pairin Kitingan (1985–present).

After being sacked from the ruling Berjaya Party in 1984 for championing the rights of the Kadazandusun, Joseph Pairin Kitingan won re-election as an independent candidate. Shortly afterwards he registered PBS and won a snap election, and became Chief Minister of Sabah in 1985. PBS went on to win the 1986, 1990, and 1994 state elections. However, defections saw PBS fall from power just days after winning the 1994 state elections. The party joined the Barisan Nasional in 1986, but left in 1990. In 2003 it rejoined the Sabah Barisan Nasional. Its support comes mainly from the Sabah non-Muslim Bumiputera and Chinese communities.

The party is administered by a Supreme Council under the authority and direction of the Annual Delegates Conference. Divisions of the party are established in every State Assembly constituency. Branches, with at least 30 members, are established in each polling district, and other places approved by the relevant Divisional Committee. The party also has Youth and Women's movements.

Joseph Pairin Kitingan is also Huguan Siou (Paramount Chief) of the Kadazandusun.

Number of seats (2006)
Parliament: 4
State Assemblies: 13
As at 31 May 2006

PBS President Joseph Pairin Kitingan (left) greets Dato' Seri Abdullah Ahmad Badawi after a BN Supreme Council meeting, January 2004.

Membership
Membership of the party is open to all Malaysian citizens residing in Sabah or the Federal Territory of Labuan who are not less than 18 years of age.

United Pasokmomogun Kadazandusun Murut Organisation (UPKO)

Formed: 1994

President: Tan Sri Datuk Seri Panglima Bernard Giluk Dompok (1994–present)

The original UPKO was formed in 1964 as a result of the merger of the United National Kadazan Organisation (UNKO) and the United Pasok Momogun Organisation (see 'Nationalism in northern Borneo') and represented the Kadazandusun and Murut peoples of Sabah. However, UPKO was defeated in the Sabah state election of April 1967, and was dissolved in December of that year.

In 1994, following the state elections, Parti Demokratik Sabah (PDS) was established by several Kadazandusun leaders who had won seats under the PBS. It sought to represent the Kadazandusun community but attracted limited support. Nevertheless, its leader Bernard Dompok served—albeit briefly—as Sabah's Chief Minister from 1998–9. He was then defeated by a PBS candidate in the 1999 state election. Later that same year, the party changed its name to United Pasokmomogun Kadazandusun Murut Organisation.

Central administration of the party at the party's headquarters is by an Executive Committee comprising 18 party officials, with the President responsible for the party's day-to-day running. The party's Supreme Council is responsible for the administration of party affairs under the authority and direction of the Annual Delegates' Conference. It is the Supreme Council that formulates party policy. Divisions are established in every State Assembly constituency, and must have at least 500 members. Branches, with a minimum of 30 members, are established in each polling district. The party has a Youth Movement and a Women's Movement.

Bernard Dompok

Number of seats (2006)
Parliament: 4
State Assemblies: 5
As at 31 May 2006

Bernard Dompok displays the logo with which the party was first registered, 1994.

Membership
Membership of the United Pasokmomogun Kadazandusun Murut Organisation is open to all Malaysians whose place of abode or origin is Sabah or the Federal Territory of Labuan.

Selected aims and objects
Article 5, constitution of UPKO
The aims and objects of the party include:
- To uphold, maintain and ensure the continued and proper practice of parliamentary democracy.
- To promote and preserve national unity and national integration in line with the tenets of the *Rukunegara* and objectives of Vision 2020.
- To uphold the dignity of man.
- To promote goodwill and work towards peace, progress, harmony and understanding so as to ensure a proper process of integration and unity among all races in Malaysia, particularly Sabah.
- To preserve and to protect the rights and interest of Sabah within the Federation of Malaysia.
- To protect and safeguard the rights and special privileges of the local Bumiputera and the legitimate interests of other Malaysia citizens in Sabah.
- To protect, preserve and to promote the traditional customs, and cultures of all the people of Sabah.
- To endure and uphold without conditions the practice of religious freedom.
- To promote awareness of being a Malaysian and of loyalty to King and country.
...
- To be the vehicle for the indigenous people of Sabah to actively contribute towards the achievement of a developed status for our community, Sabah and Malaysia as envisioned by Vision 2020.
- To promote and defend the dignity, identity and image of the Pasokmogun tribe.

Barisan component parties (continued)

Six smaller political parties, five of them from Sabah and Sarawak, complete the list of members of the 14-party Barisan Nasional. They are the Sarawak Progressive Democratic Party, Parti Rakyat Sarawak, the Sabah Progressive Party, Parti Bersatu Rakyat Sabah, the People's Progressive Party and the Liberal Democratic Party. The majority of them are of recent origin.

People's Progressive Party supporters mark the party's golden anniversary, 2003.

Sarawak Progressive Democratic Party (SPDP)

Formed: 2002
President: Datuk William Mawan Ikom (2002–present)

The Sarawak Progressive Democratic Party (SPDP) was formed as a breakaway from the Sarawak National Party (SNAP). When SNAP was deregistered in November 2002 and dropped from Barisan Nasional, its incumbent assemblymen banded together to form the SPDP, led by Datuk William Mawan Ikom. SPDP was registered just three days after SNAP's deregistration and took over SNAP's place in the Sarawak BN. The party openly proclaims itself as the successor to SNAP.

In the 2004 general election, the party won in all four of the parliamentary constituencies that it contested. Its core support comes from the Iban community.

The party's General Assembly, which is held annually, constitutes the party's supreme authority. In the absence of the General Assembly, the party's Supreme Council serves as the supreme authority. The Supreme Council is empowered to review, decide, formulate and implement party policy. Members of the Supreme Council are elected, determined and appointed every three years.

Like other political parties, SPDP has established Divisions, not more than one

Former SNAP member Dunstan Meling (left) hands in his application to join SPDP to President Datuk William Mawan Ikom, March 2004.

for each state parliamentary constituency, and Branches which cover at least one electoral district. Each Division has at least three Branches, and each Branch has a minimum of 100 members. The party has also established a Women's Movement, known as Pergerakan Wanita, as well as a Youth Movement, Pergerakan Pemuda.

William Mawan Ikom

Number of seats (2006)
Parliament: 4
State Assemblies: 7
As at 31 May 2006

Membership
Membership of the party is open to all Malaysian citizens of at least 18 years of age, irrespective of race, sex and religion.

Aims and objectives
Article 2, SPDP constitution
The objects of the party include:
- To promote the political advancement of Malaysia with the aim of maintaining the principles of parliamentary democracy through constitutional means.
- To ensure the constitutional rights and freedom of assembly, speech and religion and to secure and to protect the civil liberty of citizens.
- To promote the social, economic and cultural development of the inhabitants of Malaysia and particularly to improve the earning power of individuals thereby raising their standard of living.
- To promote the league of friendship and racial harmony between all races and to inspire all persons to live in a true spirit of tolerance, cooperation, understanding, self-reliance and honest endeavour.
- To cooperate or affiliate or ally with any political organization or party in any part of Malaysia having similar views, principles, policies and objectives for the benefit and in the interest of the people and country.

Aims and objectives
Article 2, constitution of Parti Rakyat Sarawak
- To preserve and protect the sovereignty of Malaysia.
- To advance the political development of the people of Sarawak with the aim of maintaining the principle of parliamentary democracy through constitutional means.
- To protect the constitutional rights and freedom of assembly, speech and religion and to secure the civil liberty of all citizens in Malaysia, especially the people of Sarawak.
- To ensure a responsible, fair and dynamic government which is free of corruption, partiality and favouritism.
- To promote the social, economic, educational, *adat* (customary law) and cultural development of the people of Sarawak particularly the earning power of individuals and thereby raising their standard of living.
- To safeguard the interests and welfare of the people of Sarawak in general and especially to protect the socio-economic rights of individuals.
- To imbibe amongst the *rakyat* (people) a sense of friendship and racial harmony towards all races and to inspire all communities to live in the true spirit of tolerance, cooperation, understanding, self reliance and honest endeavour.

Parti Rakyat Sarawak leaders at a party Women's Division function in Sarawak, 2004.

- To cooperate with any political organization or party in any part of Malaysia, having similar views, principles, policies and objects of the benefit and in the interest of the people and country.
- To work for the establishment of a truly democratic government for the federation of Malaysia based on the concept and principle of parliamentary democracy.
- To encourage active participation of the people of Sarawak in the political, social and economic development of Malaysia.
- To take necessary steps to eliminate any subversive elements which threaten the safety and sovereignty of Malaysia....

Parti Rakyat Sarawak (PRS)

Formed: 2004
President: Dato' Seri Dr James Jemut Masing (2005–present)

PRS was established to replace Parti Bansa Dayak Sarawak (PBDS) which was deregistered in October 2004. Its first elected President was James Jemut Masing, former senior Vice President of PBDS, with Sng Chee Hua as his deputy. Nine of the 14 elected members from the defunct PBDS joined the party.

James Jemut Masing

The party joined the Sarawak Barisan Nasional in October 2004 and was accepted into the Federal Barisan Nasional in June 2005.

The governing bodies of the party are the Triennial Delegates' Conference (TDC) and the Supreme Council. The TDC comprises primarily of delegates chosen by each of the party's main Divisions, as well as from the Youth Division. The Supreme Council consists of 34 members including the President, the Deputy President and the seven Vice Presidents. Its role includes policy formation and the implementation of decisions reached by the TDC.

The party is divided into Divisions formed subject to the approval of the Supreme Council where not fewer than 500 party members are registered. Division General Meetings are normally held annually. Branches may be established in a combination of two or more polling districts where not fewer than 25 party members are registered.

Membership
Membership of the party is open to all Malaysian citizens domiciled in Sarawak who are at least 18 years of age.

Number of seats (2006)
Parliament: 4
State Assemblies: 6
As at 31 May 2006

Parti Maju Sabah (Sabah Progressive Party, SAPP)

Formed: 1994
President: Datuk Yong Teck Lee (1994–present)

Yong Teck Lee

SAPP is a Chinese-based party with its core support in urban areas. Most of its founding leaders are Chinese leaders who left PBS just prior to the 1994 state elections. One of these leaders, Yong Teck Lee, was then a Deputy Chief Minister as well as a Minister in the PBS State Government of Chief Minister Joseph Pairin Kitingan. Yong himself served as Chief Minister between 1996 and 1998.

The supreme authority of the party is the Annual General Congress, while the party's Supreme Council is responsible for general administration, and an Executive Committee administers party headquarters. Constituency Liaison Committees coordinate activities of the party within constituencies. Branches are established for polling districts.

Number of seats (2006)
Parliament: 2
State Assemblies: 4
As at 31 May 2006

Membership
Membership of the party is open to all Malaysian citizens irrespective of race, sex and religion.

Yong Teck Lee announcing the registration of SAPP at a press conference, 1994.

Objects
Article 4, SAPP constitution
- To establish a democratic, responsible and fair government which is firm, decisive and disciplined.
- To establish a fair, free and just society for all peoples irrespective of race, religion, creed or sex.
- To protect, promote and safeguard the rights and interest and aspirations of the people of Sabah in the federation of Malaysia.
- To uphold and promote the principles of parliamentary democracy and the constitutional rights and civil liberties of all citizens.
- To promote and protect the rights and interests of local natives and other citizens in Sabah and Malaysia.
- To protect, preserve and promote the cultures and traditional customs of all peoples of Sabah and Malaysia.
- To uphold, protect and promote religious freedom in Sabah and Malaysia.
- To promote harmony, understanding, goodwill and unity among all the peoples of Sabah and Malaysia, with the spirit of self-reliance, endeavour and cooperation....

Parti Bersatu Rakyat Sabah (PBRS)

Formed: 1994
President: Tan Sri Datuk Seri Panglima Joseph Kurup (1994–present)

Joseph Kurup

Parti Bersatu Rakyat Sabah (PBRS) was formed in March 1994 by a group of PBS Kadazandusun leaders who left the latter party immediately after the 1994 state election. In June 1994, PBRS was officially accepted as one of the component parties in Sabah Barisan Nasional.

The supreme authority of the party is the Annual Delegates' Conference; executive authority is vested in a Supreme Council. The decisions of both are implemented by an Executive Committee. Divisions are established in State Assembly constituencies having not less than 150 subscribing members. Polling districts are represented by Branches.

Number of seats (2006)
Parliament: 1
State Assemblies: 1
As at 31 May 2006

Membership
Membership of the party is open to any Malaysian citizen above 18 years of age.

PBRS President Joseph Kurup (second from left) displays the flag of the new party, 1994.

Aims and objectives
Article 5, PBRS constitution
The aims and objectives are to:
- Preserve, protect and promote the continued and proper process and practice of parliamentary democracy.
- Preserve, protect and promote the honour and dignity of man.
- Preserve, protect and promote goodwill and understanding among men and work for peace and harmony to ensure a realistic process of integration and unity among all races in Malaysia and Sabah.
- Preserve, protect and promote the rights and interests of Sabah within the federation of Malaysia.
- Preserve, protect and promote the special privileges of Bumiputeras.
- Preserve, protect and promote the traditional customs and cultures of Sabah.
- Preserve, protect and promote awareness among Malaysians of loyalty to King and Country.
- Preserve, protect and promote the noble principles of the *Rukunegara*.
- Preserve, protect and promote development of politics in Malaysia and to work peaceably with other Malaysian political parties having similar aims and objectives towards a healthy, harmonious and prosperous nation.

Parti Progresif Penduduk Malaysia (People's Progressive Party, PPP)

Formed: 1953
Presidents: D. R. Seenivasagam (1953–69); S. P. Seenivasagam (1969–75); Khong Kok Yet (1975–8); S. I. Rajah (1978–82); acting 1988–93); Dato' Paramjit Singh (1982–5; 1986–8); Tee Ah Chuan (1985–6); Dato' Mak Hon Kam (1988); Datuk M. Kayveas (1993–present)

M. Kayveas

A formidable force under the leadership of the Seenivasagam brothers, the PPP was part of the Alliance briefly in 1954 but left after one year because it was not allocated any seats in the Federal Legislative Council elections. In 1969, the PPP won 12 Perak State Assembly seats, just two short of a majority. This was the party's zenith. It joined Barisan Nasional in 1973, but in the 1974 elections, lost nearly every seat it contested. This multiracial party has yet to regain its former prominence.

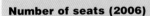

Number of seats (2006)
Parliament: 1
State Assemblies: 0
As at 31 May 2006

Membership
Membership of the party is open to all Malaysian citizens who are 18 years of age and above.

Victorious Perak PPP candidates after the 1969 Parliamentary elections.

Aims and objectives
Article 3, PPP constitution
PPP is a political party that strives to uphold the aspiration of a multiracial Malaysia and to strengthen the pride and dignity of all Malaysians.
- To further the political, domestic, economic, cultural and aesthetic interests of its members.
- To promote and assist all charitable objects in connection with its members and the citizens of Malaysia in general.
- To defend the independence, pride and sovereignty of the nation.
- To uphold and defend the nation's Constitution, state constitutions and constitutional monarchy.
- To strengthen, defend and honour the principles of freedom of religion.
- To defend the rights of citizens and social justice by practising the system of parliamentary democracy and to improve the economic position of its members and the citizens of Malaysia in general.
- To instil cooperation amongst the various communities to establish one Malaysian race that is strong united and founded on basic human rights.

Liberal Democratic Party (LDP)

Formed: 1989
Leaders: Hiew Ming Kong (1989–90); Tan Sri Datuk Chong Kah Kiat (1991–2005)

The LDP was established in Sabah by two former Berjaya leaders, Hiew Min Kong and Chong Kah Kiat, as a multiracial but predominantly Chinese-based party to oppose PBS. The party targeted Chinese professionals with the hope of becoming the state's main Chinese party. It fared poorly in Chinese areas in the July 1990 state elections, forcing Hiew to make way for Chong as party leader.

The LDP's fortunes changed dramatically with the pullout of PBS from the Barisan Nasional (BN) coalition in October 1990. Immediately, the LDP was accepted into the BN, and subsequently it won several seats in Chinese areas.

Number of seats (2006)
Parliament: 0
State Assemblies: 3
As at 31 May 2006

Membership
Membership of the party is open to any Malaysian citizen who is not a member of any other political party.

LDP party leaders with Dr Mahathir Mohamad (centre) at the party's General Assembly, 1992.

Aims and objectives
Article 5, LDP consitution
The objects of the Party include:
- To honour and protect the Constitution of Malaysia and to uphold the principles of the *Rukunegara*.
- To strive for and establish a fair, just and equal society regardless of racial origin or creed and to inculcate into the people the spirit of mutual respect, tolerance and goodwill in a multiracial, multicultural and multireligious society.
- To eliminate corruption in all forms in the government and to ensure the establishment of a government fully accountable to the people.
- To promote and ensure the socio-economic, educational and cultural advancement of all races in the creation of a just and stable society.
- To promote and safeguard the interests of Sabah within the context of Malaysia.
- To cooperate with other political organizations with similar aims and objectives on a Malaysian basis in joint political activities.
- To carry out such activities as are necessary or incidental to or in furtherance of any or all the above objects including the collection of funds for the maintenance of the party.
- Generally to do all such acts and things not enumerated above for the well-being of the party.

Opposition parties

Malaysia's opposition parties actively contest elections but face significant obstacles in competing with the long-entrenched ruling coalition. They have not formed any alternative coalitions to rival the Barisan Nasional. Instead, they have attempted to form electoral pacts, without any significant or lasting success.

Following the 2004 general election, DAP President Lim Kit Siang became the leader of the opposition in Parliament.

The opposition

As a fractionated group, the opposition lacks the ability to shape public opinion or influence the ruling elite on national policies. It is marginalized by the ruling coalition's continued success: in particular the government's generous spending on development projects has gained the Barisan Nasional (BN) more supporters.

The opposition is also beset with internal problems such as organizational weaknesses and limited financial resources to contest elections effectively. Further, they have very little control over the national media. Privately owned newspapers are closely linked to the ruling coalition and further controlled by legislation concerning printing and broadcasting (see 'Information and the news media'). In addition, the government wields the power to declare a state of emergency, which, theoretically, could be used to overthrow an opposition-held State Government (see 'National security').

At present, there are three major opposition parties in Peninsular Malaysia—PAS, DAP and Parti Keadilan Rakyat. Electoral pacts between opposition parties, such as the Barisan Alternatif established in 1998, have not proved resilient.

Opposition politics in Sarawak and Sabah

There are no significant opposition parties in either Sabah or Sarawak. Most of the successful opposition parties have tended to join the state BN after winning an election. In Sabah, the ruling parties tend to start out as opposition parties: for example, Berjaya toppled the USNO government in 1976, and PBS in turn toppled Berjaya in the 1985 state election. In Sarawak, the most significant opposition parties have been the Sarawak National Party (SNAP) and Parti Bansa Dayak Sarawak (PBDS), which joined the Sarawak BN in 1976 and 1994 respectively.

PAS President Dato' Haji Fadzil Mohd Noor was leader of the opposition from 1999 until his death in 2002.

Parti Islam Se-Malaysia (Islamic Party of Malaysia, PAS)

Formed: 1951
Presidents: Haji Ahmad Fuad (1951–3); Dato' Dr Haji Abbas Alias (1953–6); Dr Burhanuddin Al-Helmi (1956–69); Tan Sri Dato' Mohammad Asri Haji Muda (1969–82); Ustaz Dato' Haji Yusof Rawa (1982–8); Ustaz Dato' Haji Fadzil Mohd Noor (1988–2002); Dato' Seri Tuan Guru Haji Abdul Hadi bin Awang (2002–present)

PAS's origins may be traced to an early attempt by UMNO to gain greater support from Islamic leaders. In 1950, UMNO sponsored a national meeting of religious leaders in Johor. At this meeting, the Persatuan Ulama-ulama Sa-Malaya (Pan-Malayan Union of Scholars) was formed, as a body within UMNO. In 1951, at the Union's second and final meeting in Kuala Lumpur, it was decided to form an independent Islamic political party and the Pan-Malayan Islamic Party (PMIP) came into being the same year

Haji Ahmad Fuad

in Penang. In 1963, the party was renamed Parti Islam Se-Malaysia.

PAS is UMNO's biggest rival for the Malay vote, especially in Kelantan and Terengganu. In the 1955 general election,

it was the only non-Alliance party to win a seat. In 1959, PAS captured Kelantan and Terengganu and ruled the former until 1978 when the state came under the control of UMNO. Terengganu was recaptured by UMNO in 1962. PAS itself joined the Barisan Nasional in 1974, but left in 1977 when threatened with expulsion.

In 1990, PAS recaptured Kelantan from the Barisan, and in 1995, Terengganu too. The party also made inroads into Kedah, Selangor and Pahang by winning a number of state seats. The Barisan won Terengganu back from PAS in 2004.

PAS positions itself as an Islamic party and desires to impose *hudud* (Islamic criminal law) in the country. This has posed problems in forming lasting alliances with non-Muslim parties committed to a secular state.

Membership
Malaysian Muslims are entitled to join the party if they have attained puberty according to *syariah* law.

Objectives
- To strive for the establishment of a society and government with Islamic living values and whose laws lead towards Allah's blessings.
- To defend the purity of Islam and the independence and sovereignty of the nation.

(1) Dato' Haji Yusof Rawa addresses the 1987 PAS Annual Congress. (2) Party supporters on nomination day, 2004. (3) A 2004 election poster featuring the party's spiritual advisor Ustaz Dato' Haji Nik Aziz Nik Mat (left) and President Dato' Seri Tuan Guru Haji Abdul Hadi Awang.

Party structure
Supreme authority is vested in the PAS Annual Congress. This authority is safeguarded by a Majlis Syura Ulamak (Scholars' Consultative Council) headed by the Mursyidul 'am (Spiritual Advisor). The PAS Annual Congress comprises Majlis Syura Ulamak and Central Working Committee members and 15 delegates each from the Central Scholars Council Congress, the Central Youth Council Congress and the Central Women's Council Congress. The PAS Annual Congress elects the office bearers of the 35-member Central Working Committee biennially.

The Central Working Committee is the national executive body and subject to selection procedures laid down by the Majlis Syura Ulamak, selects candidates for parliamentary and State Assembly posts. Each state and Federal Territory has a Liaison Committee headed by the State or Federal Territory Commissioner respectively. PAS areas are administered by Area Working Committees under the directives of Area Council General Meetings. Each area sends to the PAS Congress between four and 10 delegates. The basic party unit is the Branch, which is administered by the Branch Working Committee, following the directives of the Branch General Meeting.

Number of seats (2006)
Parliament: 6
State Assemblies: 35
As at 31 May 2006

Democratic Action Party (DAP)

Formed: 1966
National Chairmen: Dr Chen Man Hin (1966–99); Lim Kit Siang (1999–2004); Karpal Singh (2004–present)

The DAP was the Malaysian wing of Singapore's People's Action Party when Singapore was part of Malaysia. It is arguably the most significant non-Malay opposition party. Its support comes primarily from non-Malays, particularly urban Chinese. The DAP has been outspoken on civil liberties and non-Malay rights. Nevertheless, it is non-communal in principle and has even nominated Malay candidates for election.

Dr Chen Man Hin

Internal conflicts over the years have led to the departure of several party leaders and weakened its electoral support. The party has been involved in several electoral pacts without much success, including the Barisan Alternatif. Accused of compromising its commitment to a secular state, the party fared poorly in the 1999 general election and lost its position as the leading opposition party in Parliament, a role it held for many years. It regained this position, however, in 2004.

Objects
- To strive by constitutional means for the establishment of a democratic socialist pattern of society in Malaysia.
- To advance and protect the integrity and independence of the national state of Malaysia.To preserve the democratic state of Malaysia based on universal adult suffrage of all those who are citizens.
- To abolish the unjust inequalities of wealth and opportunities existing in the present system; to establish an economic order which gives all citizens the right to work and full economic returns for their labour and skill; to ensure a decent living, and social security to all those who through sickness, infirmity or old age can no longer work.
- To infuse into the people of Malaysia a spirit of national unity, self-respect and self-reliance, and to inspire them with a sense of endeavour in the creation of a prosperous, stable and just society.
- To propagate the above objectives through all lawful and constitutional means available including the publication and distribution of journals, newsletters and newspapers.

Party structure
The work of the party is under the direction and control of the Party Congress and the Party Conference. The Party Congress meets once in three years, when it is called the Party National Congress, or at such times as it is convened by the Central Executive Committee or at the request of 60 per cent of the party's Branches. Delegates to the Party Congress are selected by their respective Branches. In addition, the party's Members of Parliament, State Assemblymen and Central Executive Committee members are entitled to attend the Party Congress as additional delegates. The business of the Party National Congress includes the election of the Central Executive Committee, the passing of resolutions and declarations presented by the Central Executive Committee, and the consideration and adoption of proposed amendments to the party's constitution.

The Party Conference is held once every 18 months except when in between there has been a Party National Congress, in which case a Party Conference shall be held not later than 18 months after the Congress. Delegates are selected in the same manner as for the Party National Congress. Business conducted at the Party Conference is similar to that at the Party National Congress other than the election of the Central Executive Committee.

The Central Executive Committee (CEC) consists of 20 members. These members elect from among themselves a National Chairman, a National Deputy Chairman, up to five National Vice-Chairmen, a Secretary-General and other office holders. Among its duties, the CEC has to present to the Party National Congress and Party Conference a report covering the work and progress of the party during its term of office (and for the Party Conference, during the preceding period following the Party National Congress), it also organizes and maintains a fund to finance elections and to spread among the people the aims and ideals of the party. The CEC forms, and delegates duties and responsibilities to, a 10-member Central Working Committee.

At state level, the party is under the direction and control of the respective State Ordinary Convention, State Annual Convention and the CEC. Other important bodies within the party hierarchy are the Parliamentary Liaison Committees which assist State Committees to coordinate Branch activity within each parliamentary constituency.

Number of seats (2006)
Parliament: 12
State Assemblies: 20
As at 31 May 2006

Membership
Party membership is open to Malaysian citizens not less than 17 years of age.

Parti Keadilan Rakyat (People's Justice Party)

Formed: 2003
President: Datin Seri Dr Wan Azizah binti Wan Ismail

Parti Keadilan Rakyat was formed by the merger in 2003 of Parti Rakyat Malaysia (Malaysian People's Party or PRM), and Parti Keadilan Nasional (National Justice Party or KeADILan).

PRM was one of the oldest parties in the country. It started life as Parti Rakyat, a founding member of the Socialist Front. This pact against the Alliance was not to last, however, and the Front was dissolved in the late 1960s. Despite its longevity, the party was unable to make any headway in the general elections. It tried to woo voters through several name changes and remodellings, settling on Parti Rakyat Malaysia in 1974. Upon the merger with KeADILan, PRM President Dr Syed Husin Ali became the new entity's Deputy President.

KeADILan was formed in 1998 to articulate protests over the arrest and subsequent conviction for corruption, and later sodomy, of former Deputy Prime Minister Dato' Seri Anwar Ibrahim. Led by Dato' Seri Anwar's wife, Datin Seri Dr Wan Azizah, the party attracted support primarily from young educated Malays and secured five parliamentary seats (in Penang, Kelantan and Terengganu) and four state legislature seats (in Selangor, Penang, Pahang and Perak) in the 1999 elections. The party secured a fifth state legislature representative in a by-election in 2001. At the 2004 general election, Datin Seri Wan Azizah became Parti Keadilan Rakyat's sole Member of Parliament seat. In September 2004, Dato' Seri Anwar Ibrahim was acquitted by the Federal Court of the sodomy charge and released from prison.

A 2004 election poster for Mustaffa Kamil Ayub, KeADILan Secretary-General.

Objectives
- To establish a society that is just and a nation that is democratic, progressive and united.
- To promote respect for the system of constitutional monarchy, strengthen parliamentary democracy and support the rights of the people, whilst endeavouring always to improve the nation's political framework in line with the wishes and interests of the people.
- To establish and promote the rule of just law, an independent mass media and judiciary, and institutions for security that uphold principles of professionalism.
- To guarantee freedom of conscience, speech, movement, public assembly and association for all.
- To espouse Islam as the religion of the Federation whilst ensuring that the rights of non-Muslims to freedom of religion and conscience are guaranteed.
- To promote the role of religious and universal values to uphold truth, justice, ethical conduct, humanitarianism and human dignity.

Membership
Party membership is open to Malaysian citizens above 18 years of age.

Party structure
The National Congress is the ultimate authority in the party and meets annually. The Annual National Congress (ANC) comprises the Permanent Chairman and his Deputy, Supreme Leadership Council members, Division Chiefs and their Deputy- and Vice-Chiefs, Division Youth and Women's Chiefs, five delegates chosen by each Divisional General Meeting and 30 delegates each from the Youth and Women's wings chosen by their own national congresses. The ANC elects the President, her deputy, three Vice-Presidents and 20 ordinary members of the 62-member Supreme Leadership Council (SLC) triennially.

The SLC administers the affairs of the party under the directives of the ANC. The SLC also establishes the party's State and Federal Territory Liaison Committees, Divisions and Branches. Divisions are established in parliamentary constituencies and must have a minimum of 30 members. Each Annual Division General Meeting elects divisional delegates to the ANC. Branches need a minimum of 15 party members before they can be set up and are headed by an elected Branch Committee. The Annual Branch General Meeting elects delegates to the Division general meeting.

Number of seats (2006)
Parliament: 1
State Assemblies: 1
As at 31 May 2006

The official launch of Parti Keadilan Rakyat in August 2003.

THIS IS MALAYA

SOCIAL DEVELOPMENT

An understanding of indigenous political control requires an examination not only of the travails of power, but also of its impact, and of how, in turn, social change affects political behaviour and national advancement.

Social development has been concomitant with political development over the course of the past four decades; and as the developing nation of the 1950s has changed into the middle income country of the 21st century, the nation has undergone a social transformation. Given the pervasive role of government, social change and development have been contrived as much as they have been generated by the people.

The logo of one of several lifestyle programmes promoted by the Ministry of Youth and Sports as part of its Rakan Muda (Young Partners) project.

Education is a key element of modernization—as a tool of economic upliftment, as a means to undergird national competitiveness, as an incubator of positive values, and as a crucible of national unity in a multi-ethnic society. Unsurprisingly, education has been a key element of governance, with annual allocations of government spending averaging a quarter of the national budget. This section surveys the education sector at the primary, secondary and tertiary levels and records the achievements that have resulted from the changes effected in this critical sector (see 'Primary and secondary education' and 'Higher education').

As literacy and education levels have advanced, there has been a corresponding increase in awareness among the public of their rights and responsibilities, as well as greater participation in civic and leisure activities. There has been a marked increase in the availability of information in the print and electronic media; in particular, advantage has been taken of improving information technology (see 'Information and the news media'). As society has grown more complex, non-governmental organizations (NGOs) have emerged, often with specialized interests, advocating social and political causes with ramifications for the body politic (see 'Non-governmental organizations').

Government and quasi-government efforts have been made to educate and benefit the public in certain crucial areas, notably finance. Institutions such as the Employees Provident Fund (EPF), the Social Security Organization (SOCSO), Permodalan Nasional Berhad (National Equity Corporation, PNB), Majlis Amanah Rakyat (Council of Trust for Indigenous People, MARA) and Lembaga Tabung Haji (Pilgrims Fund Board) have been at the

With the push of a button, Tunku Abdul Rahman Putra launches Radio Televisyen Malaysia, the national broadcasting agency, in December 1963.

forefront of these efforts. They provide services that include pension fund schemes, worker compensation schemes, pilgrimage programmes, educational funds and trust fund investment schemes. These undertakings have served as agents of social change, developing awareness and large-scale participation in activities that contribute to individual, group and public welfare. Not only are they vital contributors to changes in social values, but they also reinforce the social pillars of political development and civil society.

Primary and secondary education

Malaysia offers a comprehensive, national education system at primary and secondary levels. With roots traceable to an amalgam of religious schools, missionary schools, secular British colonial schools and vernacular schools, Malaysian schools today cater to the needs of a diverse, multi-ethnic population.

In 1996, the Smart Schools initiative became a flagship application of the Multimedia Super Corridor project, designed to produce a thinking, technology-literate workforce.

A selection of textbooks used in national secondary schools.

Penang Free School, established in 1816, was the first English school in Southeast Asia.

Before Independence

Prior to Independence, education in Malaya followed a variety of different school systems: Malay, English, Chinese, and Tamil. As Independence approached, the authorities tried to bring order to the situation, and remedy the lack of a uniform structure. In 1950, Malay was proposed as the primary medium of instruction. This was so unpopular among the Chinese that a team from the United Nations was commissioned to study the situation. Their report merely added fuel to the controversy when it advocated the preservation and improvement of Chinese schools.

An education ordinance of 1952 provided for eventual free and compulsory primary education for children of all races between the ages of six and 13, the establishment of an inspectorate and local education authorities, and the introduction of religious instruction. The issue of Malay as the main medium of instruction was not addressed.

A national education system

In 1955, the Razak Education Committee laid down some foundations for a national education system, and in 1959, a new committee headed by Minister of Education Abdul Rahman bin Talib endorsed these proposals. The latter report also recommended, among other things, that free primary education be provided in Malay, English, Chinese and Tamil schools, that the school-leaving age be raised to 15, and that a new type of post-primary education with a vocational content be introduced for those who

failed the Malayan Secondary School Entrance Examination (MSSEE). The recommendations of both the Razak and Rahman Talib reports were codified in the Education Act 1961.

The government reviewed secondary education policy in 1965 and introduced the 'comprehensive' system. The MSSEE was abolished; unimpeded schooling was extended from six to nine years. Courses in secondary schools were diversified and students could choose from mandatory subject electives. After the Lower Certificate of Education, they could choose to move on to the academic, technical or vocational streams.

Phasing out English

On 21 July 1969, the government announced that all English-medium schools in Peninsular Malaysia would use Malay by 1982. Secondary schools would use solely Malay. This requirement would not be extended to Sabah and Sarawak until 15 years later.

Tamil and Chinese primary schools were not affected, although pupils had to undergo a one-year 'remove class' intensive Bahasa Malaysia course before progressing to National Secondary Schools.

The Mahathir education policy

In 1974, as Minister of Education, Dato' Seri Dr Mahathir Mohamad headed a committee to evaluate every aspect of education. In 1979 it made 173 recommendations. Stress was laid on the 'Three Rs' and inculcating 17 'noble values' across the curriculum: the broad thrust of six-year elementary schooling under a reform programme, the New Primary School Curriculum (also known by its Malay acronym, KBSR). The New Secondary School Curriculum (KBSM) enshrined similar values, which continue to form the basis of the school system at the beginning of the 21st century.

The Razak Report

In 1955, a special committee headed by Dato' Abdul Razak bin Hussein, then Minister of Education, studied the education system. The committee produced a report, commonly known as the Razak Report, which made several key recommendations, including that common syllabuses be used in all schools in the Federation—an essential element in the development of a united Malayan nation; and that Malay and English be compulsory subjects in both primary and secondary schools.

Dato' Abdul Razak bin Hussein chairing the first special committee meeting in 1955.

The committee recommended a school system providing six years primary, three years lower secondary, two years upper secondary and two years pre-university education. Examinations would be held at the end of each stage: Malayan Secondary School Entrance Examination (MSSEE) at the end of the primary stage, the Lower Certificate of Education (LCE) examination, after lower secondary, and the Federation of Malaya Certificate of Education Examination (MCE) after upper secondary. This would, for many students, be the end of formal education. However, those who did well in the MCE could proceed to a further two years of schooling, after which they would sit for the Higher School Certificate of Education—mandatory for university entry.

Tamil vernacular schools were first started in 1816. The photograph shows the Vivekananda Tamil school in Brickfields, Kuala Lumpur in the 1950s.

The school system today

The national education philosophy

All schools operate according to a national education philosophy that seeks to develop individual intellectual, spiritual and physical potential within the context of social unity and nation building.

As a federal matter, education policy-making and administration come under the purview of the Ministry of Education, although State Education Departments also play a role in the management of schools and students. A national curriculum and public examination regime ensures that consistency is maintained in both teaching and learning.

Malaysia's racial and cultural diversity makes policy-making and implementation complicated. Concerns about a growing divide between the rural and urban populations, and growing signs of racial and social polarization, have resulted in attempts to improve the system via information and communication technology in the Smart School Project, a limited reintroduction of English into the curriculum, and the establishment of a small number of Vision Schools.

Most government school buildings follow a standard architectural plan. The photograph shows a secondary school in Belaga, Sarawak.

Primary education

Primary schooling in Malaysia (Standards One to Six) runs from age seven to age 12. The New Primary School Curriculum (Kurikulum Baru Sekolah Rendah, KBSR) promotes the child's overall development, with primary focus on the 'Three Rs'. At the end of Standard Six, students take a common public examination, the Primary School Achievement Test (Ujian Penilaian Sekolah Rendah, UPSR). Primary schools fall into three categories:

ABOVE: Kampong Bharu National School in Kuala Lumpur.

RIGHT: Science class at a Chinese vernacular school in Melaka.

National schools

The majority of primary schools, in which the medium of instruction is the national language, Malay. Since 2003, however, a new initiative has seen the introduction of English as the medium of instruction for teaching science and mathematics.

National-type schools

The Chung Hwa Confucian School in Penang, founded in 1904, is one of the oldest Chinese schools.

Descended from the Chinese and Tamil vernacular schools of the British colonial era, national-type schools are a feature of the Malaysian education system. These Federal Government-funded schools parallel the national curriculum, but use Mandarin or Tamil, rather than Malay, as the main medium of instruction.

Private schools

These include those schools that follow the national curriculum, those with an emphasis on Islamic instruction, and a number of international schools aimed principally at expatriate children.

Secondary education

The New Secondary School Curriculum (Kurikulum Baru Sekolah Menengah, KBSM) provides a five-year course of secondary education (Forms One to Five) for the age range 13–17. The system has a '3+2+2' structure: three years of lower secondary, two years of upper secondary and a possible further two years of pre-university studies in Form Six. After Form Three, students sit for a diagnostic evaluation, the Lower Secondary Assessment (Penilaian Menengah Rendah, PMR), before proceeding to Form Four and Form Five. Form Five ends with a GCSE or 'O' level-equivalent examination, the Malaysian Certificate of Education (Sijil Pelajaran Malaysia, SPM).

After Form Five, eligible students can proceed to secondary schools which offer Form Six studies, and sit for the 'A' level-equivalent examination, the Malaysian Higher School Certificate (Sijil Tinggi Persekolahan Malaysia, STPM). Alternatively, students can leave school to pursue pre-university, matriculation and other programmes in public and private higher education institutions. Secondary schools fall into the following main categories:

National schools

These include the mainstream 'academic' schools offering a general education in the arts and sciences, as well as a handful of Technical, Vocational and Special Education schools and religious schools.

All national schools use Malay as the medium of instruction, although English has been used for the teaching of science and mathematics since 2003. Other recent initiatives include the setting up of Smart Schools, aimed at incorporating the latest information technology tools for teaching and learning.

St Thomas' School, Kuching, founded in 1848, is the oldest school in Sarawak.

Chinese independent schools

Employing Mandarin as the medium of instruction, and largely funded by the Chinese community, these 60 schools offer a distinct syllabus which culminate with the Unified Examination Certificate (Senior Middle Level) examination. They do, however, follow Ministry of Education guidelines and require a licence from the Ministry in order to operate.

Private schools

As at primary level, these include those that follow the national curriculum, those with an emphasis on Islamic instruction and a selection of international schools catering to expatriate children.

The Vision School concept

Despite numerous education reports and the Education Act 1961, the ambition of a single system for all races remains unfulfilled, as three types of ethnic-based schools still exist. The Education Ministry's 'Vision School' concept sets up three ethnic-based schools (Malay, Chinese and Tamil) within a single location: all pupils share a common playground and canteen. The hope is that close proximity will foster a sense of togetherness and understanding, and hence a sense of oneness as a nation. As at 2004, there were five Vision Schools in the country.

The first Vision School was established in Subang Jaya, Selangor, in 2002.

Growth in national school enrolment

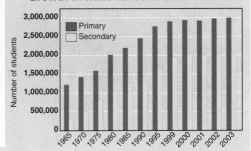

Number of students: 0, 500,000, 1,000,000, 1,500,000, 2,000,000, 2,500,000, 3,000,000

Primary / Secondary

1965, 1970, 1975, 1980, 1985, 1990, 1995, 1999, 2000, 2001, 2002, 2003

Higher education

Malaysia's higher education sector provides opportunities for both its own citizens and for scholars from abroad. Tertiary education is delivered through 17 public institutions, supplemented by private colleges, private universities and university colleges, and branch campuses of foreign universities. The system offers everything from certificates and diplomas to first degrees and professional, technical and postgraduate qualifications.

Malaysia's institutions of higher learning seek to produce a competent workforce equipped with the skills and knowledge to meet the demands of the cyber age.

Higher education participation rates: ages 17–23

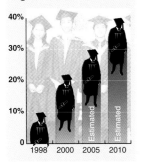

Public tertiary education: rapid growth

Viewed as the primary means of producing qualified and competent personnel, higher education has proved central to the government's aim to reposition Malaysia as a developed nation in a globalized world. As a result there has been a gradual democratization of higher education.

Options for higher education in Malaysia were once very limited—confined to an elite at Universiti Malaya (established in 1949). In the late 1960s, graduates still accounted for only one per cent of the population. The 1970s, however, witnessed a big expansion of tertiary education; new public universities such as Universiti Kebangsaan Malaysia were set up and enrolment increased dramatically.

The overseas and private options

One notable development was the large increase of students studying overseas. By 1980, an estimated 39,908 Malaysian students were studying abroad, of whom 60.5 per cent were Chinese, 23 per cent Malays, 15.9 per cent Indians and 0.6 per cent other Malaysians. By 2004, this had risen to an estimated total of 112,000 students overseas, with 5,809 of them sponsored by the government.

Public institutions of higher education

Public universities and university colleges offer Bachelor degree courses for Malaysians only, while postgraduate studies are also open to foreign students. International Islamic University Malaysia is the only public university that allows foreign students at both undergraduate and graduate level.

Universiti Malaya

Universiti Malaya is the oldest local public university. Its predecessors were the King Edward VII College of Medicine (founded 1905) and Raffles College (1929), established in Singapore to meet the need for doctors and teachers. The two institutions joined to form the University of Malaya in October 1949 as a national institution serving the Federation of Malaya and Singapore. Growth was rapid during the first decade of its establishment, hence the setting up of two autonomous divisions in 1959, one in Singapore and the other in Kuala Lumpur.

In 1960, the governments of the two territories decided to give the divisions the status of national universities. Legislation was passed in 1961 formally founding the University of Malaya, now known as Universiti Malaya, on 1 January 1962.

Universiti Malaya's Dewan Tunku Canselor (Chancellory).

Public universities and university colleges in Malaysia

The International Islamic University Malaysia is under the direction of a Board of Governors with representatives from eight sponsoring governments and the Organisation of Islamic Conference (OIC).

Universities and university colleges	Year established
1. **Universiti Malaya** University of Malaya	1962
2. **Universiti Sains Malaysia** University of Science Malaysia	1969
3. **Universiti Kebangsaan Malaysia** National University of Malaysia	1970
4. **Universiti Putra Malaysia** Putra University Malaysia	1971
5. **Universiti Teknologi Malaysia** University of Technology Malaysia	1972
6. **Universiti Islam Antarabangsa Malaysia** International Islamic University Malaysia	1983
7. **Universiti Utara Malaysia** Northern University of Malaysia	1984
8. **Universiti Malaysia Sarawak** University of Malaysia Sarawak	1992
9. **Universiti Malaysia Sabah** University of Malaysia Sabah	1994
10. **Universiti Pendidikan Sultan Idris** Sultan Idris University of Education	1997
11. **Kolej Universiti Islam Malaysia** Islamic University College of Malaysia	1998
12. **Universiti Teknologi MARA** MARA University of Technology	1999
13. **Kolej Universiti Teknologi Tun Hussein Onn** Tun Hussein Onn University College of Technology	2000
14. **Kolej Universiti Teknikal Kebangsaan Malaysia** National Technical University College Malaysia	2000
15. **Kolej Universiti Kejuruteraan Utara Malaysia** Northern University College of Engineering Malaysia	2001
16. **Kolej Universiti Kejuruteraan dan Teknologi Malaysia** University College of Engineering and Technology Malaysia	2001
17. **Kolej Universiti Sains dan Teknologi Malaysia** University College of Science and Technology Malaysia	2001

However, the spiralling of overseas education costs in the 1980s (particularly when the United Kingdom abolished grant support for overseas students), coupled with the effects of an economic recession, stimulated the growth of local private education. In 1996, a raft of education-related Acts was passed, which provided for the establishment of 'branch campuses' and the setting up of a national accreditation board (Lembaga Akreditasi Negara, LAN). Private education enrolments climbed steadily during the 1990s before reaching a plateau in 2005 of over 310,000 students, despite increased capacity in the public institutions.

Blueprint for the future

At the end of 2000, the Ministry of Education issued a draft educational 'blueprint' outlining some key issues affecting higher education and strategies for the future. At the heart of the new proposals was a massive expansion of tertiary education, further increasing student choices.

Students from overseas represent an important revenue stream. Indeed, the government aims to make Malaysia a 'regional centre of educational excellence': education (along with engineering and architecture, construction and related services, healthcare, and printing and publishing) constitutes one of the key service sectors identified as foreign exchange earners. In 2005, approximately 32,000 foreign students were among the students enrolled in private tertiary institutions.

Tan Sri Dato' Dr Wan Mohd Zahid Mohd Noordin, Chairman of the Committee to Study, Review and Make Recommendations Concerning the Development and Direction of Higher Education in Malaysia commissioned by the Ministry of Higher Education in January 2005. The committee completed its task in July 2005, making 138 recommendations.

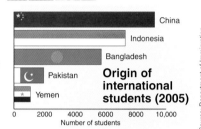

Origin of international students (2005)

China
Indonesia
Bangladesh
Pakistan
Yemen

0   2000   4000   6000   8000   10,000
Number of students

Source: Department of Immigration

Programmes in the private sector

External programmes
Students apply to register as an 'external' candidate of a university. Entry requirements, syllabus and examinations are determined and conducted by the university, which ultimately awards the degree. Standards are identical to those applied to 'internal' students; however, the university has no active role in the actual teaching. Students can opt for self-study or attend classes at colleges offering tuition support. The most established foreign external programme is offered by the University of London in the United Kingdom.

Many private colleges were established with the primary purpose of imparting computing and other skills in high demand in the private sector.

Twinning programmes
These programmes involve one or two years in Malaysia before going to the twinning partner institution overseas for one or two years to complete the degree ('1+2' or '2+1'). Programmes known as '3+0' and '4+0' are an extension of the '1+2' and '2+1' model, with the entire degree completed locally in collaboration with a foreign university.

Credit transfer advanced standing
Unlike twinning, students do not pursue the syllabus of any specific foreign university. Instead, the foreign institution agrees to transfer credits studied locally. This is the norm for most American degree programmes. Many British and Australian universities now also offer 'advanced standing' into Year Two or Three of their degree programmes.

Foreign university branch campuses
These campuses are an integral part of the parent university, even though located in Malaysia. Theoretically, they offer the same syllabus, courses and awards delivered to the same standards as in the home country. The five fully-fledged foreign university campuses in Malaysia are: Monash, Nottingham and De Montfort in the Peninsula and Swinburne and Curtin in Sarawak.

Established in December 1997, Universiti Tun Abdul Razak was Malaysia's first university to be granted MSC status.

Open, virtual, and distance learning
Here, the university uses a variety of delivery methods such as correspondence course notes and television. Electronic-learning is the 21st century version of distance learning. For example, Malaysia's first virtual university, Universiti Tun Abdul Razak (UNITAR) uses a comprehensive package of study materials and CD ROMs, interaction through video conferencing, e-mail and Intranet, supplemented by 'real' contact with lecturers and peers. METEOR, a consortium comprising 11 public universities, launched Open University Malaysia in 2000.

Professional and vocational courses
Conducted by local and foreign professional examination bodies, these courses can be completed without going overseas. Most of these qualifications are vocational as opposed to academic in nature, and are designed to produce technically skilled members of the work force. Popular foreign professional courses include ABE (Association of Business Executives), City and Guilds courses, ICSA (Institute of Chartered Secretaries and Administrators), as well as accounting qualifications.

Established in 1950, Stamford College was one of the nation's first private higher education providers. It has since evolved from a small institute into a multi-disciplinary college with eight campuses.

Private local universities and university colleges
In addition to local public universities, quasi-private local universities owned by corporations such as Telekom Malaysia, Tenaga Nasional Berhad and Petronas offer degree courses mainly in business, engineering, information technology and management. Some private colleges have been upgraded to 'university college' status, enabling them to award degrees in their own right, thereby reducing dependence on foreign partners.

Universiti Tenaga Nasional, awarded university status in 1997, was one of the first private universities.

Local university franchise programmes
Some public universities, such as UPM and USM, have been active in 'franchising' their programmes to (mainly Bumiputera-owned) private colleges. The private college is responsible for the teaching but the university is tasked with monitoring standards and academic quality.

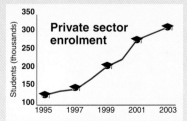

Private sector enrolment

Students (thousands)

350
300
250
200
150
100

1995   1997   1999   2001   2003

Source: 1999 figures from JPT; 2001 figures JPS statistics December 2001; 2003 figures Ministry of Higher Education.

Non-governmental organizations

People interested in a range of causes have formed politically oriented but non-governmental advocacy groups in modern-day Malaysia. They have made issues such as environmentalism, women's rights and human rights more visible to the public and policymakers. However, the tradition of non-governmental advocacy is still a young one in Malaysia, and its influence has often been limited.

Non-governmental organizations have succeeded in persuading the government to change or reconsider its decisions. In this way, for example, the proposed demolition of the Merdeka Stadium, Kuala Lumpur, was avoided.

The Malaysian Human Rights Report 2002 published by Suaram, a Malaysian human rights organization working for a free, equal, just and sustainable society. For its part, the government in 1999 established, by Act of Parliament, a Malaysian Human Rights Commission (SUHAKAM) with some functions similar to those of NGOs, including the promotion of awareness of human rights.

Civil society

Under Article 10 of the Federal Constitution, every citizen has the right to form associations subject to various laws such as the Societies Act.

As societies develop, people take an interest in issues beyond survival and attaining basic needs. People who share a certain belief, attitude, value or concern tend to form interest or advocacy groups, commonly termed non-governmental organizations (NGOs), to raise public awareness or persuade the government of the need for change. Not all NGOs are political, but even non-political ones have a sphere of influence or 'social capital' (through networks, reciprocal obligations, reputations and trust) which can be mobilized for political ends.

NGOs are legally registered associations which are not part of the government machinery. They are part of 'civil society'. Defined broadly as the realm between the family and the state, civil society encompasses all sorts of non-electoral political engagement, including organized lobbying for particular policies; demonstrations and other forms of protest; and the provision of welfare services.

History and development

Many colonial-era associations evolved into political parties. Others remained or developed into voluntary welfare organizations, professional associations and advocacy groups.

NGOs began to gain prominence in the 1970s. Prior to that, they had a relatively low profile, being active primarily in urban areas and among non-Malays (with the exception of Islamic NGOs). That changed with high-profile campaigns to protest against detention without trial, to criminalize domestic violence and to oppose the construction of large-scale dams, among other issues.

Women's rights: non-governmental pressure groups

Women have been struggling to assert their presence and exercise their rights since the 1920s. Many grievances stemmed from cultural practices and laws that were discriminatory and insensitive. In the colonial period, the struggle for women's rights was carried on within the larger struggle for Independence. Women leaders formed auxiliary bodies within UMNO and the Malayan Nationalist Party. Teachers formed informal groups such as the Johore Teachers Association to persuade the government and public to allow girls entry to schools. Indian women estate workers were vocal in demanding fair wages, maternity leave, better working conditions and an end to sexual harassment.

Women's activism began to intensify in the 1960s, when urban and educated women formed several associations. In 1963, these came together to form an umbrella organization, the National Council of Women's Organizations (NCWO). From 1969 to 1980, the NCWO successfully lobbied for laws to ensure equal pay (in the public sector) and separate taxation for women; helped institute civil family law for

RIGHT: A participant at the 'Speak Out Against Rape (SOAR)' campaign during International Women's Day, 2002.

BELOW LEFT: Women's groups participate at a 'Citizen Against Rape' rally in 1987, highlighting the rape and murder of Ang May Hong.

BELOW RIGHT: A march to protest 'Violence Against Women' and to express the rights and freedom of women and children to walk the streets without being violated, 2001.

non-Muslim women; and urged state governments to codify and standardize Islamic family law.

In the 1980s, several other women's groups, such as the Women's Aid Organisation (WAO), All Women's Action Society (AWAM), Women's Crisis Centre (now the Women's Centre for Change), Women's Development Collective, Sabah Women Action Resource Group (SAWO), Sarawak Women for Women Society (SWWS) and Sisters in Islam (SIS) were formed. These newer groups, which came under the banner of the Joint Action Group against Violence against Women (JAG-VAW), expanded the scope of women's rights by setting up women's shelters and research centres, providing legal services and lobbying for laws to deal with issues related to violence against women. The call for advocacy and social change culminated in the late 1990s in the creation of a document advocating changes, the Women's Agenda for Change (WAC), endorsed by 88 NGOs in the country. The WAC fights for gender equality, sustainable development and participatory democracy for men and women.

Types of NGO

Politically-oriented groups either create social capital or engage the government directly on issues such as consumer protection and conservation.

Some groups provide services (such as providing for the physically disabled or helping victims of rape or domestic violence) to supplement the government's efforts while suggesting policy remedies. Community-based groups such as those supporting Chinese vernacular education, plantation workers and the Orang Asli, for example, also have a political agenda. Professional organizations for physicians, lawyers, academics, and so forth, concern themselves with both the status of their profession and broader questions such as the provision of healthcare, judicial independence and academic freedom.

Since the mid-1980s, clusters of organizations have come together in broad coalitions, campaigning for specific issues, such as preventing the privatization of healthcare, systemic political changes and the welfare of aboriginal people.

Prominent non-governmental organizations

Organizations	Established
Conservation and environmental groups	
Malaysian Nature Society (MNS)	1940
World Wildlife Fund (WWF)	1972
Friends of the Earth, Malaysia	1977
Heritage of Malaysia Trust (Badan Warisan Malaysia)	1983
Professional bodies	
Bar Council Malaysia	1947
Malaysian Medical Association	1959
Social rights groups	
Malaysian Youth Council	1948
Peninsular Malay Students Association	1948
Malaysian Trade Unions Congress (MTUC)	1949
Malaysian Muslim Youth Movement (ABIM)	1971
Federation of Malaysian Consumers' Associations	1973
The Malaysian AIDS Council	1992
Human rights groups	
Peninsular Malaysia Orang Asli Association	1977
National Consciousness Movement (Aliran)	1977
Women's Aid Organisation	1982
Women's Centre for Change	1985
All-Women's Action Society of Malaysia	1988
Sisters in Islam	1988
Voice of the Malaysian People (Suaram)	1989
Centre for Orang Asli Concerns (COAC)	1989
Borneo Resources Institute Malaysia, Sarawak	1993
Partners of Community Organisations, Sabah	1996
International Movement for a Just World	1999

Top: The Bar Council offers free legal advice to the public during its Law Awareness Week, 1997.
Above: Malaysian Youth Council members take part in Merdeka day celebrations, 2003.

Selected non-governmental organizations

Malaysian Nature Society

Established in 1940, the Malaysia Nature Society (MNS) is the oldest and largest environmental NGO in Malaysia. Its mission is to promote the study, appreciation, conservation and protection of Malaysia's natural heritage, focusing on biological diversity and sustainable development.

The MNS advocates methods such as education, scientific research and the promotion of sustainable management of natural resources. Its efforts have led to the creation of a number of new protected areas in Malaysia, including the Endau Rompin National Park, the Kuala Selangor Nature Park, the Belum State Park and the Pulau Pinang National Park.

In 2003, the Malaysian Nature Society organized a campaign to save the Botanical Park of Kota Damansara, Selangor, part of the country's oldest regenerated forest, from development.

Malaysian AIDS Council

The Malaysian AIDS Council (MAC), formed in 1992, is an umbrella organization for 37 NGOs involved in HIV and AIDS-related programmes focusing on treatment, care and support, advocacy, education and prevention. MAC is also the avenue for liaison between the government and NGOs operating in this field.

Through the Council's efforts, the Malaysian AIDS Charter was published in 1995 setting out the rights and responsibilities of all sectors of society in relation to HIV and AIDS. MAC was given the task of organizing the Fifth International Congress on AIDS in Asia and the Pacific (ICAAP) in October 1999.

In conjunction with World AIDS Day 2002, the Malaysian AIDS Council organised an AIDS awareness campaign called 'Stop the AIDS Stigma—Move from Fear to Hope'.

Badan Warisan Malaysia

Badan Warisan Malaysia (Heritage of Malaysia Trust) was established in 1983. It aims to promote the conservation and preservation of Malaysia's built heritage.

It has undertaken restoration and adaptive re-use projects involving both urban and vernacular structures. It has also initiated documentation of heritage areas—these have included an urban inventory covering towns and cities throughout Malaysia, a rural inventory covering selected states, and area conservation studies.

Badan Warisan Malaysia has persisted in promoting comprehensive heritage legislation; it has worked closely with the Government in this initiative.

No. 2 Jalan Stonor, Kuala Lumpur, the 1925 bungalow that houses Badan Warisan Malaysia's headquarters, is an example of the adaptive use of a heritage building.

FOMCA

The Federation of Malaysian Consumer Associations (FOMCA) was founded by seven state-level consumer associations in 1973. A further five state-level associations have since joined.

The organization aims to strengthen the growth and spread of the organized consumer movement in Malaysia, and also plays an active role at the international level, having been elected three times to serve on the Board of Directors of Consumer International. FOMCA's role includes researching consumer issues and their implications, promoting and conducting consumer education, advocating for better consumer protection, and, where required, conducting product testing.

FOMCA President N. Marimuthu giving a speech at the launch of the National Consumer Complaints Centre at Petaling Jaya, July 2004.

Information and the news media

The broadcast and print media have flourished in Malaysia, having grown from modest beginnings. Although freedom of speech is enshrined in the Federal Constitution, there are legal and other controls regulating the discussion of sensitive issues in the mass media. Nevertheless, the internet is unrestricted, and public debate is served by a wide spectrum of freely expressed opinion.

Government broadcaster Radio Televisyen Malaysia (RTM), moved into the Angkasapuri complex at Bukit Putra, Kuala Lumpur on 6 October 1969. The complex is also home to the Ministry of Information.

Radio Televisyen Malaysia (RTM) first paired newscasters for its news programme, *Berita Nasional*, in 1973.

Freedom with responsibility

The mass media thrives in Malaysia, with a profusion of local and foreign newspapers, magazines and journals vying for attention. Niche-market publications, television and radio stations have mushroomed in recent years. Rising affluence has created a great demand for information.

The Federal Constitution contains a section entitled 'fundamental liberties' that guarantees free speech and expression. However, following the events of 1969 (see 'The 13 May 1969 tragedy'), the government made media licensing subject to certain terms and conditions so as to prevent the raising of sensitive issues. Furthermore, no film is allowed to be publicly screened in Malaysia unless approved by the Censorship Board, which vets films to ensure that they do not show offensive or harmful material.

Print media in Malaysia has a long history. Among the major newspapers are the *New Straits Times* and *The Star*, published in English, *Utusan Malaysia* and *Berita Harian* in Malay. These newspapers are free to publish any news and reports in accordance with the Printing Presses and Publications Act 1984. Like any other free press, each newspaper is free to editorialize any issues and express views and opinions which may differ from each other. Editors are generally aware of sensitive and inflammatory issues and practise self-censorship.

There have, of course, been occasions when offensive articles have been published or broadcast, and editors have been summoned to explain their actions to the authorities. In 1987, the government detained several people under the Internal Security Act following controversy over the promotion of non-Chinese educated headmasters in Chinese

Beginnings of the print media

The first newspaper published in the Malay Peninsula was the *Prince of Wales Gazette*, in 1806 in Penang. Among the plethora of early papers, only a few survived the tests of time and World War II. One of these, still published today, is *The Straits Times*, which started in Singapore in 1845. The organization was split up in 1972, some years after Singapore's separation from Malaysia. The Singapore edition retained its name while the Malaysian version, published by The New Straits Times Press (Malaysia) Bhd (NSTP) was renamed the *New Straits Times*.

The 1896 first edition of *The Malay Mail*. The newspaper is still published in 2006.

Another long-lived paper is *The Malay Mail*, first published in 1896 in Kuala Lumpur. The Straits Times Press acquired it for the use of its printing facilities and to distribute *The Straits Times* 'upcountry'. To differentiate the papers, *The Malay Mail* was made into a vehicle for classified advertisements with very cheap rates.

The Star was first published in 1971 as a regional newspaper catering to Penang. By 1976, it had become the largest selling English-language paper in Penang. It became a national newspaper that year. *The Star* was the first Malaysian, and the third Asian, newspaper to publish an Internet edition.

The *News Straits Times* press room at Jalan Riong, Kuala Lumpur.

The Borneo Post, established in 1978, is headquartered in Kuching. In Sabah, The Daily Express first incorporated colour into its pages in 1992.

Publications in Sabah and Sarawak

In addition to national newspapers flown to Sabah and Sarawak, where they have a slightly higher cover price, these states also have homegrown publications, such as the *Borneo Mail*. In Sabah, the trilingual *Daily Express* was established in 1963; the *Sabah Times*, founded in 1949, was re-launched as the *New Sabah Times* in 1998. *The Borneo Post* is published in both Sabah and Sarawak.

The vernacular press

The doyen of the vernacular press is *Utusan Melayu*, once published in the Jawi script. First published in 1938 by Utusan Melayu Press Ltd in Singapore, the newspaper reflected and encouraged the stirrings of Malay nationalism. The company moved to Malaya in 1958. Six years later it introduced a weekly romanized Malay edition, *Mingguan Malaysia*. A daily edition, *Utusan Malaysia*, followed three years later. Utusan's Romanization was in response to the *Straits Times*'s publication of the Romanized *Berita Harian* coinciding with Malaya's Independence.

The market for Chinese-language newspapers is fiercely competitive. They typically vie for attention with sensational headlines and graphic images. *Sin Chew Daily* (established in 1928), the current market leader, and *Nanyang Siang Pau* (founded in 1923) are the only publicly-listed publishers among the Chinese presses.

Tamil-language dailies *Tamil Nesan* (started in 1924) and *Malaysia Nanban* (founded in 1980) compete to serve the Indian community.

Popular vernacular publications (from top): *Utusan Malaysia*, *Sin Chew Daily*, and *Tamil Nesan*.

schools. Coverage of this event in *The Star* and *Sin Chew Jit Poh* was deemed excessive, and both newspapers were suspended for five months.

For the most part, however, the local media have struck a reasonable balance between the government's views and their audience's desire for more objectivity, and they do enjoy commercial success.

The growth of media influence today

The main newspapers have diversified considerably within their core business, reflecting the diverse interests of an economically more developed population. They cater to niche markets with editorial supplements on education, property, information technology and motor vehicles as part of their regular fare.

To reduce cost and compete better, *Business Times*—a national daily since 1976—was incorporated into the *New Straits Times* on 1 June 2002. *The Sun*, a relative newcomer, has embarked on a different strategy, choosing to distribute the paper free of charge, and relying on advertisement revenue to keep it viable.

Local newspapers, in keeping pace with developments, have set up their own websites and gained global reach to keep Malaysians and others abroad abreast of events in the country.

Bernama and the internet

Berita Nasional Malaysia (Malaysian National News or Bernama) was set up by the government under the Bernama Act 1967, as a news agency to serve local needs. It was supported by a consortium of newspaper publishers that welcomed its help in news-gathering.

BERNAMA

In 1984, Bernama was made the sole local distributor of news and features from foreign news agencies. The idea behind the move was to make Bernama a gatekeeper of news and so curb 'inaccurate and biased' reporting by Western media on Third World events. Practical difficulties led the government to abandon this arrangement in 1998. The government's Multimedia Super Corridor (MSC) initiative, with a focus on information technology, was one of the factors behind the decision. As the MSC is a vehicle intended to attract foreign investment, the government decided not to impose censorship on the Internet—and the Internet rendered Bernama's gatekeeping role ineffective.

The Internet itself has created new government concerns over the dissemination of information detrimental to national security and racial harmony. *Malaysiakini*, an online 'newspaper' run by former journalists from *The Sun*, takes advantage of the government's flexibility on the Internet. It is noted for carrying critical articles.

The broadcast explosion

Radio broadcasting began in 1921 with the first successful Morse code radio transmission in Peninsular Malaya. In 1940, the government took over the privately operated British Malaya Broadcasting Corporation (established in 1937) and named it the Malayan Broadcasting Corporation, which broadcast multilingual programmes. Following the Japanese surrender, the radio service adopted the name 'Radio Malaya' in 1946.

The RTM logo: the first logo (left) was introduced in 1957, when the service was known as Radio Malaya. The logo was changed (right) in 1963, adopting elements of the national flag.

Television was introduced in Malaysia after Prime Minister Tunku Abdul Rahman Putra visited Thailand, where he saw how people took to television. Two experts from the Canadian Broadcasting Corporation arrived in July 1962 to set up the service. Transmissions began in December 1963 and so Radio Malaya became Radio Televisyen Malaysia (RTM). There was initially just one channel, broadcast from Dewan Tunku Abdul Rahman in Jalan Ampang, Kuala Lumpur. It ran for four hours daily, starting at 6.30 p.m., in four languages: Malay, English, Chinese and Tamil.

Malaysia's pilot television service was inaugurated by Tunku Abdul Rahman Putra on 28 December 1963 at the Radio Televisyen Malaysia studios.

RTM moved to its permanent location at Angkasapuri, Kuala Lumpur, in 1969. A second channel was commissioned in November of that year. Channel One (now RTM 1) went over to colour in 1978. Transmission times were extended to near-midnight and television ownership and viewer numbers climbed.

Radio IKIM

IKIM.fm, Malaysia's first Islamic digital radio station, began broadcasting on 6 July 2001. The station is operated by the Institute of Islamic Understanding Malaysia (IKIM), a think tank launched by Dato' Seri Dr Mahathir Mohamad in 1992 to promote better understanding of Islamic principles. IKIM.fm promotes Islam as a way of life.

Private stations and channels

Private radio stations were first introduced in the early 1980s. Most private stations broadcast in English and Chinese, languages which are more popular with urban audiences.

The first private television channel, TV3, then owned by Sistem Televisyen Malaysia Bhd, came into being in 1983, broadcasting initially only to the Klang Valley area. This paved the way for Metrovision, the second private station, to enter the market in early 1995, followed by Mega TV, Sistem Televisyen Malaysia Bhd's pay-television station, a few months later. However, both of the latter two stations were badly affected by competition and the economic downturn of 1997 and ceased operations.

One of the biggest broadcasters is Astro, which introduced cable and satellite services in September 1996. Run by MEASAT Broadcast Network System Sdn Bhd, it boasts over 40 television channels and 17 radio channels in digital format. Undaunted, NatSeven TV Sdn Bhd launched its digital, terrestrial television station in April 1998. The nationwide service is called ntv7. NatSeven TV Sdn Bhd was sold to TV3 parent company Media Prima Berhad in 2005. Terrestrial television station 8TV was launched in January 2004. Malaysia's second pay-television network, MiTV, was launched in September 2005. Channel 9, which operated from 2003 to 2005, was relaunched in April 2006 as TV9. Both 8TV and TV9 are owned by Media Prima Berhad.

Malaysia's first satellite, the Malaysia East Asia Satellite (MEASAT–1), was launched on 13 January 1996 from the European Space Centre in French Guyana, South America.

The foreign press

Offering a global perspective, many world and regional news magazines are readily available in Malaysia. Indeed, for some years *The Asian Wall Street Journal* and *International Herald Tribune* were printed in Malaysia for local distribution.

Imported publications are subject to Malaysian law including the Sedition Act 1948, Part IV of the Printing Presses and Publication Act 1984, which deals with the control of undesirable publications, and the Printing Presses and Publications (Importation of Publications) (Deposit) Rules 1985, which empower the Minister of Information to require publishers of publications originating outside Malaysia to pay specified deposits before such publications may be imported.

FOREIGN AFFAIRS

Malaysia has conducted its foreign affairs in broadly the same way as many other newly independent nations: its priorities have been to protect its sovereignty and independence. The formulation and execution of Malaysia's foreign policies are directly related to these goals. Perhaps due to the continuity of the political regime, the nation's approach to foreign affairs has been remarkably consistent ever since Independence.

Newly independent Malaya was caught in the midst of a communist insurgency backed by the People's Republic of China. The world was in the midst of a Cold War between the United States and the Soviet Union. Both these superpowers tried to influence and win over new nation-states in pursuit of their respective strategic interests. Malaya tried to stay clear of this and resisted attempts to draw it into military alliances, such as the Southeast Asia Treaty Organisation (SEATO). It also tried to keep the region peaceful and neutral, but did not always find this easy—indeed, the formation of Malaysia antagonized neighbouring Indonesia and the Philippines.

This section explores Malaysia's place in the world and the instruments it uses to pursue its foreign policy. It covers Malaysia's work within the Association of Southeast Asian Nations (ASEAN) to maintain a peaceful and neutral region. Malaysia also plays an active role in the Non-Aligned Movement (NAM), the Organisation of the Islamic Conference (OIC), the Commonwealth and the United Nations, among other bodies.

Each succeeding premiership has seen Malaysia's foreign policy interests extending further abroad, reflecting the desire to become a global player and the confidence to achieve it. During Tunku Abdul Rahman Putra's premiership, the country fought

The 2003 Organisation of the Islamic Conference (OIC) Expo, held concurrently with the OIC Conference, served as the focal point for the convergence of cultural values, arts and historical fellowship among OIC member states.

militant communism and fended off communist influence. The Tunku's successor, Tun Abdul Razak, promoted a zone of peace and neutrality through ASEAN and saw Malaysia establishing diplomatic ties with China. Dato' Hussein Onn's premiership was notable for Malaysia's extended diplomatic coverage in the South Pacific, which helped it win support at the United Nations Conference on the Law of the Sea. Dato' Seri Dr Mahathir Mohamad took the nation to greater international prominence. He was an outspoken critic of certain policies and international institutions that he considered to be unfair to the poorer nations of the globe. An experienced diplomat, Prime Minister Dato' Seri Abdullah Ahmad Badawi, on assuming office, became Chairman of NAM and the OIC, which will see him play a dominant role in international affairs.

Since joining the international community of nations, Malaysia has become a very audible and recognized voice, speaking on behalf of the countries of the Third World and the Muslim community. Malaysia's previous chairmanship of the United Nation's Security Council, and its chairmanship of NAM and the OIC, have provided—and continue to provide—the country opportunities to contribute towards a more peaceful and equitable world.

Early foreign policy

At Independence, Malaya found itself in a world dominated by the so-called Cold War between the West and the Communist Bloc led by the then Union of Soviet Socialist Republics (USSR). Although Malaya initially leaned toward the West, Prime Minister Tun Abdul Razak sought increasingly to maintain a neutral, equidistant stand, working as far as possible through international associations.

Wisma Putra (above) at Bukit Petaling in Kuala Lumpur in 2006 houses the Institute of Diplomacy and Foreign Relations, having housed the Ministry of Foreign Affairs from 1966 to 2001.

End of colonization

The era of formal colonization in Asia effectively ended after World War II. There was a climate of change. The United Nations made a push to end colonization. The old colonial powers had lost their image of superiority, in part as a result of losses and defeats sustained during the war. They were also economically weakened. In Bandung, Indonesia, in April 1955, a conference of 29 African and Asian nations was held to promote economic and cultural cooperation, and to oppose colonialism. This led to the formation of the Non-Aligned Movement (NAM) in 1961.

Choosing sides

It was a priority for the emerging new independent nations to maintain a neutral posture as the world's two superpowers—the United States of America (USA) and the USSR—continued to embrace opposing ideologies.

When Malaya gained Independence in 1957, its priorities were the safeguarding of its sovereign status, as well as internal and external development. It was under pressure to choose sides.

The nation adopted an anti-communist stance, partly because it was still facing a domestic communist insurgency (see 'The Emergency' and 'The

Tunku Abdul Rahman Putra (front row, second from right) at the Commonwealth Prime Ministers' Meeting in May 1960 in London. Malaysia joined the Commonwealth in 1957.

Emergency resolved'). Although Malaya considered the insurgency as an issue separate from international communism, the Malayan Communist Party (MCP) did receive tacit support from the People's Republic of China. Furthermore, Malaya did not recognize China and had no diplomatic relations with Eastern Europe.

Prime Minister Tunku Abdul Rahman Putra was inclined towards the West. However, unlike Thailand and the Philippines, which showed similar leanings, Malaya did not enter any bilateral military agreements with the United States, including the US-dominated Southeast Asia Treaty Organization (SEATO) (see 'External opposition to Malaysia').

The United States was content to leave Malaya under the strategic influence of its ally, Britain. Malaya had entered the Anglo-Malayan Defence Agreement (AMDA) in 1957, which granted it military assistance from Britain, Australia and New Zealand. British troops were stationed in Malaya (later Malaysia) and Singapore to ensure political stability and protect British economic interests.

Strength through association

Malaya positioned itself as an impartial actor in world affairs, looking upon the United Nations and the NAM as rallying points. It was also active in the Commonwealth, a grouping of countries formerly under direct or indirect British rule (see 'A global role').

At the regional level, the Tunku promoted a broad grouping known as the Southeast Asia Friendship and Economic Treaty (SEAFET). He wanted to protect the independence of member nations by means of economic and security cooperation.

SEAFET was sternly rebuffed by Indonesia. Instead, there was formed in 1961 the Association of Southeast Asia (ASA), which proved to be short-lived (see 'Association of Southeast Asian Nations (ASEAN)').

Policy of neutrality

Even during the Tunku's time, Malaysia was gradually shifting to a more neutral stance. As Minister of Foreign Affairs, Tun Abdul Razak (who would later succeed the Tunku as Prime Minister) wanted Malaysia recognized as a non-aligned state, notwithstanding AMDA, and sought solidarity with NAM countries. Diplomatic missions were sent to Africa and Asia to win friends and gain influence. Malaysia overcame objections to its joining NAM by proposing that the concept of non-alignment be construed as meaning non-involvement in superpower rivalry.

Malaysia's efforts paid off when it took its seat at the 1970 NAM conference in Lusaka. NAM and ASEAN provided multilateral avenues for promoting one of its key foreign-policy objectives: a Zone of Peace, Freedom and Neutrality (ZOPFAN) in Southeast Asia (see 'Association of Southeast Asian Nations (ASEAN)').

Membership of NAM helped Malaysia maintain its neutral stand when it reviewed AMDA in 1968–9 and signed the pro-Western Five Power Defence Arrangements (FPDA) in 1971 involving Britain, Australia, Malaysia, New Zealand and Singapore. Following the FPDA, Britain gradually withdrew its forces from Malaysia.

The guiding principles of Malaysia's foreign policy were friendship with all countries, neutrality and neutralization in the face of superpower rivalry and regional cooperation.

The 1961 Association of Southeast Asia (ASA) Conference in Kuala Lumpur. The Chairman of the Conference and leader of the Malayan delegation, Raja Mohar Raja Badiozaman, addresses the Conference.

Major political blocs in 1961

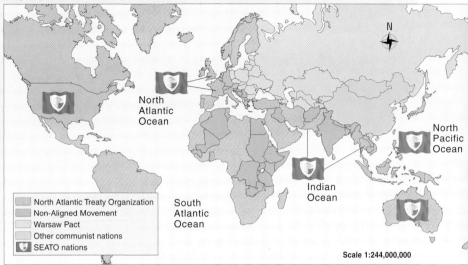

North Atlantic Ocean

North Pacific Ocean

Indian Ocean

South Atlantic Ocean

- North Atlantic Treaty Organization
- Non-Aligned Movement
- Warsaw Pact
- Other communist nations
- SEATO nations

Scale 1:244,000,000

The Non-Aligned Movement (NAM)

The first Conference of Non-Aligned Heads of State, at which 25 countries were represented, was convened at Belgrade in September 1961, mainly through the efforts of Yugoslavian President Tito. He had expressed concern that an accelerating arms race might result in war between the Soviet Union and the United States of America.

Subsequent conferences involved ever-wider participation by developing countries. The 1964 conference in Cairo, with 47 countries represented, featured widespread condemnation of Western colonialism and the retention of foreign military installations. Thereafter, the focus shifted away from essentially political issues to the advocacy of solutions to global economic and other problems.

Malaysia became chair of NAM in 2003 and hosted the Ministerial Meeting of the NAM Committee on Palestine in May 2004.

Neutralization proved to be unattainable. In addition to the two superpowers, Japan and China both had a strong interest in the region, particularly in the Strait of Melaka. Malaysia's policy was to encourage the big powers to play a stabilizing role in the region. There were disparities in the power equation among the big powers. The United States, the USSR and Japan had their respective spheres of influence. But Malaysia could not ignore China, and in pursuit of its policy of equidistance, the government under Tun Abdul Razak decided to recognize China.

Rapprochement with communist countries

In 1974, Prime Minister Tun Abdul Razak visited Beijing to resolve the issue of some 200,000 'stateless' Chinese residents in Malaysia. Also during this period, Malaysia began to realize that the United States was keen to end its presence in Indochina.

Against this background, Malaysia acted quickly to normalize relations with China and the nations of Indochina as a means of securing their non-interference in the region. Diplomatic relations were established with China in 1974. China relinquished its claims on the *huachiao* (overseas Chinese) population in Malaysia and agreed to cease supporting the Malayan Communist Party (MCP).

After the end of the Vietnam War, Malaysia also made moves to establish relations with Vietnam, Laos and Cambodia, and was a strong supporter of their applications to join ASEAN (see 'Association of Southeast Asian Nations (ASEAN)').

Chinese Premier Chou En Lai greets Tun Abdul Razak on his historic visit to China in 1974.

BELOW: In the 1974 talks, headed by Tun Abdul Razak (seated third from left) and Chou En Lai (seated third from right), China agreed to stop helping the Malayan Communist Party and to drop its claims on the Chinese in Malaysia.

Expanding ties

Under Dato' Hussein Onn's leadership, the scope of Malaysia's foreign policy expanded. Establishing friendly ties with more nations was a priority as the world's power balances shifted. Dr Mahathir Mohamad's premiership saw Malaysia dealing with any and all of the big powers that could help its economic development, while remaining careful not to 'take sides' or participate in military alliances.

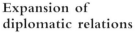

Malaysia hosted the 1998 Asia Pacific Economic Cooperation Forum (APEC) Summit in Kuala Lumpur. APEC opened avenues of trade between Malaysia and the Hispanic market, which represents one-third of the world economy.

Convention on the Law of the Sea

The United Nations attempted to write a comprehensive treaty for the oceans and their resources at the Third United Nations Conference on the Law of the Sea in 1973. This turned out to be a nine-year process, culminating in the Convention on the Law of the Sea in 1982.

Of importance was the need to define the ocean boundaries of a coastal country. Coastal states wanted a 20 nautical mile border; other nations feared this would affect shipping passages. Indonesia made a claim to all waters separating its 13,000 islands, which would have affected Malaysia's interests. Malaysia depended on the support of other nations, not least of which were the Pacific islands, in achieving a more equitable solution.

The Convention gave Malaysia the rights to its rich undersea oil reserves.

Expansion of diplomatic relations

The mid-1970s to the 1990s saw a rapid expansion of Malaysia's network of foreign missions abroad. Under Dato' Hussein Onn, Malaysia's foreign policy was kept on an even keel, based on his predecessor Tun Razak's efforts to forge new relationships with a broader range of countries. Diplomatic missions were established with Fiji, Samoa, Vanuatu, the Solomon Islands and Micronesia. His efforts paid off when the Pacific islands, among others, supported Malaysia's case at the Third United Nations Conference on the Law of the Sea.

After the Cold War

The end of the Cold War brought new challenges in Malaysia's relations with the major powers, and particularly the superpowers. Russia, the largest component of the now-defunct Union of Soviet Socialist Republics (USSR), was too preoccupied with domestic problems to play a very active international role, leaving the United States to become the sole 'superpower'.

Malaysia maintained relations with both Russia (including the purchase of arms), and the United States (with which economic and educational ties were strong). The United States even considered Malaysia an important ally in its 'war against terrorism'. However, diplomatic ties became strained when the United States and Britain invaded Iraq in 2003 citing as justification the threat from the Iraqi regime's 'weapons of mass destruction', without the specific backing of a United Nations resolution, and without any clear links having been established between Iraq and terrorist groups. The war was seen by many in Malaysia as symptomatic of an imbalance in the American approach to world affairs in general, and to the world of Islam in particular, especially when considered in the context of the continuing Israeli-Palestinian conflict.

The government was mindful of the dangers of 'neo-colonialism', forms of behaviour on the part of the big powers which imply a colonialist world view. Whereas formerly colonialism took the form of direct military and political control, powerful countries were now seen as having the potential to exert undue influence through the mass media and international institutions, and, in the case of the United States, by seeking to extend the reach of domestic laws beyond their own borders.

China poses both an opportunity and a challenge for Malaysia. Its economy began to grow rapidly when it adopted an open-door policy in 1978 and the process accelerated after the Cold War ended. It represents a huge market for Malaysian goods and a potential source of investment. However, China also has the ability to divert inward foreign investment away from Southeast Asia, including Malaysia; and Chinese-made goods compete with Malaysian products in international markets.

Japan, a rising power during the Cold War, has always been considered an important source of investment and trade for Malaysia. Such was Malaysia's admiration for Japan's success that the government launched a 'Look East' policy in 1982 to emulate Japan's economic model. However, economic stagnation in the 1990s took some of the shine off the Japanese model.

Malaysia was initially reluctant to accept a major role for India in Southeast Asia. However, given India's increasing political and economic clout, and its prowess in certain areas of high technology, this position softened somewhat.

BELOW: Dr Mahathir greets Palestinian President Yasser Arafat at the NAM Summit, February 2003.

BELOW RIGHT: Deputy Prime Minister Dato' Seri Abdullah Ahmad Badawi welcomes Russian president Putin to the OIC Conference, October 2003.

Trade and cooperation have been increasing between Malaysia and India as a result.

East Asia Economic Caucus

Under Dr Mahathir's leadership, Malaysia mooted the formation of an East Asia Economic Caucus (EAEC), an economic entity to encompass both ASEAN and the nations of Northeast Asia. Essentially, this was just a formalization of ASEAN's existing relationship with China, Japan and South Korea. These countries have been engaged through a form of association dubbed 'ASEAN Plus Three' since 1997.

The EAEC met with immediate resistance from the United States, which did not want to be excluded from such a grouping. It urged Malaysia to participate in the Asia–Pacific Economic Cooperation Forum instead. Malaysia eventually joined APEC in 1989.

Relations with other groupings

The European Union, in particular Britain, Germany and France, is considered a very important economic partner, with whom Malaysia maintains close links. Malaysia supports the Asia–Europe Dialogue between the heads of governments of the European Union and ASEAN Plus Three countries.

ASEAN leaders and the leaders of China, Japan and South Korea prior to their ASEAN Plus Three group meeting during the 10th ASEAN Summit at Vientiane, Laos, 2004.

Malaysia's top 10 trading partners (2003)

United States	Singapore	Japan	China	Hong Kong
RM126.76bil	RM100.07bil	RM96.92bil	RM53.62bil	RM34.36bil
17.69%	13.96%	13.52%	7.48%	4.79%

Thailand	Taiwan	South Korea	Germany	Indonesia
RM32.09bil	RM30.05bil	RM28.86bil	RM23.93bil	RM19.26bil
4.48%	4.19%	4.03%	3.34%	2.69%

Others
RM170.72bil
23.82%

Source: MATRADE

Asia-Pacific Economic Cooperation Forum (APEC)

Member Economies of APEC

RUSSIA

CANADA

North Pacific Ocean

JAPAN
KOREA
CHINA
HONG KONG
TAIWAN
THAILAND
VIETNAM
MALAYSIA
PHILIPPINES
BRUNEI DARUSSALAM
INDONESIA
PAPUA NEW GUINEA
SINGAPORE

UNITED STATES
OF AMERICA

MEXICO

AUSTRALIA

NEW ZEALAND

APEC

PERU

CHILE

N

Scale 1:176,000,000

Breaking down trade barriers

In 1989, Australia proposed setting up an Asia-Pacific economic cooperation forum, which did not include the United States. However, the United States was permitted to attend the forum's first-ever meeting and in due course, the group was expanded to include the Americas.

The Asia-Pacific Economic Cooperation Forum (APEC) comprises 21 'member economies' spanning the Pacific Rim, including Malaysia. APEC is the only inter-governmental grouping that operates on non-binding commitments, open dialogue and equal respect for the views of all participants. Unlike those of the World Trade Organisation (WTO) and other multilateral trade groups, APEC members are not treaty-bound to adopt decisions made within APEC; commitments are voluntary.

Since its inception, APEC has worked on reducing tariffs and other trade barriers across Asia-Pacific. At the 1994 APEC meeting in Bogor, Indonesia, leaders outlined an agenda of trade and investment liberalization, with the prospect of creating a Free Trade Area by 2010 for developed economies, and 2020 for other members.

Prime Minister Dato' Seri Abdullah Ahmad Badawi with Mexican president Vicente Fox (left), Hong Kong chief executive Tung Chee-Hwa (right) and Thai prime minister Thaksin Shinawatra (bottom right) at the APEC 2004 Leaders' Summit in Chile.

Association of Southeast Asian Nations (ASEAN)

The Association of Southeast Asian Nations (ASEAN) provides Malaysia with an important means of pursuing national foreign policy objectives with regard to neutrality and neutralization, regional co-operation, Indochina and nuclear non-proliferation.

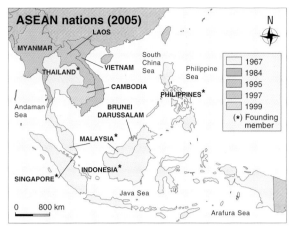

ASEAN nations (2005)

LAOS
MYANMAR
THAILAND*
VIETNAM
South China Sea
Philippine Sea
CAMBODIA
PHILIPPINES*
Andaman Sea
BRUNEI DARUSSALAM
MALAYSIA*
SINGAPORE*
INDONESIA*
Java Sea
Arafura Sea

1967
1984
1995
1997
1999
(*) Founding member

0   800 km

Thai foreign minister Thanat Khoman (second from left) broached the idea of forming ASEAN at a banquet marking the reconciliation between Indonesia, Malaysia, and the Philippines after a dispute over Sabah, in 1966.

The origins of ASEAN

In 1961, Thailand called for the formation of the Association of Southeast Asia (ASA). In the event, only Malaya and the Philippines participated in the group. ASA was never able to fulfil its objectives, because, soon after its inception, diplomatic ties between Malaya and the Philippines (see 'External opposition to Malaysia') were severed. Tensions in the region were later reduced when Indonesia ended *Konfrontasi* and recognized Malaysia's sovereignty in a peace treaty brokered by Thailand.

Thailand's foreign minister, Thanat Khoman, concerned that the future of Southeast Asia would remain uncertain without cooperation between the nations of the region, proposed the idea of the Association of Southeast Asian Nations (ASEAN). It came into being in 1967, as a result of the Bangkok Declaration, following a meeting of five foreign ministers.

Through ASEAN, Malaysia pursued its regional foreign policy: it was able to tilt regional policies toward neutrality and neutralization, particularly by the endorsement of a 'Zone of Peace, Freedom and Neutrality' (ZOPFAN). ASEAN was especially important in charting and disentangling relationships among Southeast Asian nations during and immediately after the Cold War.

The formation of ASEAN: the five foreign ministers signing the Bangkok Declaration in 1967.

The Bangkok Declaration

The Bangkok Declaration that gave birth to ASEAN on 8 August 1967 was a short and simply worded document signed by the foreign ministers of Indonesia, Malaysia, the Philippines, Singapore, and Thailand. It announced the establishment of an association for regional cooperation among the countries of Southeast Asia and spelled out the aims and purposes.

They include cooperation in economic, social, cultural, technical, educational and other fields; and the promotion of regional peace and stability through respect for justice, the rule of law and adherence to the principles of the United Nations Charter.

Although the initial membership was five nations, ASEAN was open to participation by all Southeast Asian nations that subscribed to its aims, principles, and purposes. Brunei Darussalam joined the Association in 1984 and Vietnam became the seventh member of ASEAN in 1995. Laos and Myanmar were admitted into ASEAN in 1997.

ASEAN represents 'the collective will of the nations of Southeast Asia to bind themselves together in friendship and cooperation and, through joint efforts and sacrifices, secure for their peoples and for posterity the blessings of peace, freedom and prosperity'.

ASEAN in a central role, 1976–80

From its inception, ASEAN was intended to encompass all Southeast Asian countries, including the states of Indochina. Tun Abdul Razak once said it was his 'fervent hope' that these countries would join ASEAN to 'build a strong foundation of regional cooperation and regional peace'. (His wish was fulfilled only in the late 1990s, more than 20 years after his death.)

The First ASEAN Heads of Government Meeting was held in Bali in 1976. The nations represented were (from left) Singapore, Malaysia (by Dato' Hussein bin Onn), Indonesia, the Philippines, and Thailand.

Important events in the region, namely the withdrawal of United States troops from South Vietnam and the subsequent fall of Saigon to North Vietnam in 1975, prompted ASEAN to hold its first heads of government meeting in Bali, Indonesia on 23 February 1976. The Bali Summit produced two important documents: the Declaration of ASEAN Concord and the Treaty of Amity and Cooperation (TAC).

One of the positive results of this summit was the initiation of a general rapprochement with Vietnam, Laos and Kampuchea (now Cambodia). In 1977, Malaysia offered Vietnam technical assistance to help reconstruct its war-torn economy.

Kuala Lumpur hosted the second ASEAN Summit in August 1977, the highlight of which was the announcement by the Philippines president Ferdinand Marcos that his country would drop its claim to Sabah. However, elation in Malaysia proved premature, as Marcos later redefined his position as merely 'making definite steps' to drop the claim.

Laos and Myanmar were admitted as members of ASEAN at the 30th ASEAN Ministerial Meeting in Malaysia, 1997.

The Kuala Lumpur Summit also made further overtures and 'an offer of peace' to Indochina, with the intention of establishing peaceful relations and securing support for ZOPFAN. However, this idea was shelved when Vietnam invaded Kampuchea (now Cambodia) in 1978. The Vietnamese occupation of Kampuchea became a delicate diplomatic issue for ASEAN as it tried to safeguard the principles of ZOPFAN and TAC.

The Mahathir period, 1981–2003

The period from 1981 to 2003 saw the end of the Cold War and progress in rapprochement with Indochina. ASEAN pushed for a United Nations-sponsored conference on Kampuchea and demanded negotiations for a comprehensive political settlement. Malaysia remained closely involved throughout the ensuing peace process.

Malaysia strongly supported the inclusion of Vietnam and Laos in ASEAN at the 1992 ASEAN Summit in Singapore. This meeting reiterated support for the United Nations' role in the Cambodian peace process and ASEAN's willingness to help in the reconstruction of Vietnam, Laos and Cambodia.

The ASEAN Summit of July 1994 in Bangkok saw the inauguration of the ASEAN Regional Forum (ARF) that gave a much-needed platform for handling conflicts and engaging in dialogue and collaboration with other global powers. The following year, the Asian-European Meeting (ASEM) was established by which this dialogue was extended to the European Union.

A further development was the Bangkok signing of a draft treaty in December 1995 for the Southeast Asian Nuclear-Weapon-Free Zone (SEANWFZ). In all these instances, Malaysia was in full support.

ASEAN and ZOPFAN

The 'Zone of Peace, Freedom and Neutrality' (ZOPFAN) proposal reflected Malaysia's desire for neutrality in the Cold War. In its original form, it called for Southeast Asian countries to adopt non-aggression principles in resolving conflicts; for the region to be kept out of the Cold War; and for guarantees from the United States, Soviet Union and China to that end.

Although the proposal initially received a lukewarm response within ASEAN, a modified version was eventually agreed upon at the 1971 ASEAN Foreign Ministers Meeting in Kuala Lumpur. The Zone of Peace, Freedom and Neutrality Declaration was signed by the foreign ministers of Indonesia, Malaysia, the Philippines and Singapore, and by Thanat Khoman representing Thailand's National Executive Council.

The concept of neutrality was to be approached in three ways: national cohesiveness and resilience; regional cohesiveness and resilience; and a policy of equidistance vis-à-vis the major powers. To avoid provoking the big powers, ASEAN countries would only 'exert initially necessary efforts to secure the recognition of, and respect for, Southeast Asia as a Zone of Peace, Freedom and Neutrality, free from any form or manner of interference by outside powers'.

ZOPFAN was formally adopted by the heads of government at the First ASEAN Summit in Bali in February 1976. Its spirit was further embodied in the Treaty of Amity and Cooperation (TAC) and Declaration of ASEAN Concord, both signed in 1976. Among other points of economic, political, social, cultural, security and educational cooperation, all disputes would be settled through a High Council comprising representatives at ministerial level. The High Council acts only in an advisory capacity and cannot compel conflicting parties to abide by its findings.

SEANWFZ

At the ASEAN Foreign Ministers' meeting in Jakarta in July 1984, a proposal was tabled for a Southeast Asian Nuclear-Weapon-Free Zone (SEANWFZ). A treaty was signed by ASEAN states at the Bangkok Summit meeting in December 1995. The idea received especially strong backing from Malaysia, which strongly supported the Non-Proliferation Treaty and the Comprehensive Test Ban Treaty aimed at reducing the nuclear threat on a global level. Under the treaty provisions, ASEAN states undertook not to produce, possess or allow the transit of nuclear weapons in Southeast Asia, while expecting nuclear-weapon states to sign protocols respecting such a zone.

Heads of government at the Bangkok Summit, 1995. From left: Dr Mahathir Mohamad, Fidel Ramos (the Philippines), Goh Chok Tong (Singapore), Banharn Silpa-Archa (Thailand), Vo Van Kiet (Vietnam), Sultan Hassanal Bolkiah (Brunei) and Suharto (Indonesia).

ASEAN symbols

The current ASEAN logo represents the concept of a stable, peaceful, united and dynamic ASEAN. The colours of the logo: red, yellow, blue and white, represent the main colours of the crests and of the flags of the ASEAN member countries. Blue represents peace and stability, red depicts courage and dynamism, white denotes purity and yellow symbolizes prosperity.

The ten stalks of paddy represent the dream of ASEAN's founders for an ASEAN comprising all the ten countries in Southeast Asia bound together in friendship and solidarity. ASEAN's earlier logos depicted five and then six stalks of paddy. The circle represents the unity of ASEAN.

PEACE
STABILITY
COURAGE
DYNAMISM
PURITY
PROSPERITY

FAR LEFT: Dato' Seri Abdullah Ahmad Badawi (third from right) meets with other ASEAN leaders during the 10th ASEAN Summit at Vientiane, Laos in November 2004.

LEFT: Indonesian president Susilo Bambang Yudhoyono greets Dato' Seri Abdullah Badawi before the Special ASEAN Leaders' Meeting on the aftermath of the earthquake and tsunami, Jakarta, January 2005.

A global role

Each successive Prime Minister has extended Malaysia's diplomatic reach to engage various countries throughout the world, at times through associations such as the Commonwealth, the OIC and the United Nations, and sometimes through direct diplomatic contact. Notably, Malaysia has often spoken up for Third World and Islamic countries, speaking out against what it perceives to be double standards imposed by developed nations.

The Wisma Putra complex in Putrajaya, home to the Ministry of Foreign Affairs. The ministry moved to its new location in September 2001.

The United Nations

Since Independence, Malaya had been fully committed to the United Nations (UN), on the basis that the UN embodied the aspirations of small, developing countries, and that the enhancement of UN authority would concomitantly increase that of Third World states.

The most significant foreign policy action taken during Tunku Abdul Rahman Putra's premiership was Malaya's contribution of 1413 personnel to the Congo peacekeeping operations in 1960. This was done as a show of support for the UN's Secretary-General, Dag Hammaerskjold, whose position then was under threat. The Soviet Union had challenged the authority of the Secretary-General and wanted the office replaced by a three-man 'troika' secretariat.

Three years later, it was the Tunku's turn to ask for help. He sought the UN's endorsement of the creation of the larger federation, Malaysia (see 'The formation of Malaysia').

A Ferret armoured car of the Malayan Special Force on patrol in Leopoldville shortly after the first unit landed in the Congo, 1960.

Reform of the United Nations

In 1991, as a non-permanent member of the United Nations Security Council, Malaysia was in the thick of decision-making concerning the First Gulf War. Malaysian Minister of Foreign Affairs Dato' Abu Hassan Omar argued that the 'all necessary means' clause of Resolution 678 did not sanction the destruction of Iraq, only the recapture of Kuwait. After the subsequent bombardment of Iraq, Malaysia criticized the United States' notion of a so-called New World Order and the domination of the UN Security Council by Western powers. It argued for reform to include more Third World states and Japan as permanent members. In his final speech at the United Nations in 2003, Dr Mahathir urged the Security Council to abolish the veto power of the council's permanent members, calling it part of an outdated system formed by the countries that had won World War II.

ABOVE: Brochure for a conference on the UN Convention on Biological Diversity held in Malaysia in 2004.

LEFT: Tan Sri Razali Ismail calls to order the 51st session of the UN General Assembly in New York. He was elected President of the General Assembly in 1996.

The Commonwealth

The Commonwealth comprises nations which were previously under either direct or indirect British rule. Malaysia has contributed to the Commonwealth in many ways. In 1960, Tunku Abdul Rahman Putra raised the issue of apartheid at the Commonwealth Prime Ministers' Meeting; the Republic of South Africa withdrew from the association the following year. (South Africa rejoined in 1994 after apartheid was abolished). It was Malaysia that chaired a high level appraisal group to review the roles and structures of the Commonwealth at heads of government and senior official level in 1990. The nation also chaired the first steering committee of senior officials meeting in 1993 that formulated policy guidelines and strategic direction for the Commonwealth Secretariat. Malaysia was also part of the Commonwealth Ministerial Action Group (CMAG) that reconstituted the Harare Declaration in 1999. The CMAG was established in 1995 to deal with persistent violations of these principles. The nation has participated in observer missions with regard to elections in several Commonwealth countries. It is a part of a 12-member Intergovernmental Group on the Criteria for Membership. This body examines applications to join the Commonwealth. Perhaps most visibly, Malaysia hosted a highly successful Commonwealth Games in 1998.

The 1989 Commonwealth Heads of Government Meeting at Kuala Lumpur reiterated its support for the independence, sovereignty and non-aligned status of Cyprus.

53 countries of the Commonwealth

Scale 1:192,000,000

Speaking up for Third World nations

A major theme during Dr Mahathir's period of office as Prime Minister was support for the causes of the so-called South and Third World nations. Malaysia has used various international platforms to highlight 'North-South' issues. It proposed the setting up of a South-South Commission at the Non-Aligned Movement (NAM) conference in Harare, in 1986. Tanzania's Julius Nyerere became the commission's first chairman that year, with Malaysia's Tan Sri Muhammad Ghazali Shafie working as its Secretary-General.

Malaysia has addressed several environmental issues from the Third World's perspective. Dr Mahathir observed that developed countries

The South-South Commission's first Chairman and Secretary-General, Julius Nyerere (left) and Tan Sri Muhammad Ghazali Shafie.

tended to blame the earth's dismal state on the less developed South, while hindering the South's ability to protect the environment through sustainable development. He took the North to task for its role in carbon monoxide emissions and blaming the problem primarily on disappearing tropical forests. Malaysia was particularly prominent in articulating the views of the South at the 1992 Rio de Janeiro Earth Summit.

North and South

Since Independence, Malaya—subsequently Malaysia—has identified itself with the 'South', a term applied to a group of relatively poor, developing countries pitted against the developed, richer 'North'.

Malaysia played host to the South-South Summit in 1990.

Malaya was historically a raw material exporter, dependent on tin and rubber for up to 60 per cent of its external revenue. Accordingly, Malaya signed international tin agreements in 1960 and 1965 and in the 1970s to operate buffer stocks with the purpose of fixing and stabilizing tin prices in the world market.

Malaysia was also among the original 75 countries—later to be known as the Group of 77—that called for a United Nations Conference on Trade and Development (UNCTAD) in 1964. UNCTAD's agenda was to create trading conditions that would favour the systematically disadvantaged South through measures such as the removal of Northern trade barriers and improvement of invisible trade within the South (such as payments for freight and insurance).

When UNCTAD II was held in 1968, Malaysia served on its Trade and Development Board. UNCTAD II introduced a Generalized System of Preferences (GSP) for developing countries. The inconclusiveness of UNCTAD IV in 1976 drove Malaysia towards a policy of national self-reliance, and a shift from global to regional instruments such as ASEAN.

Champion of Islamic causes

Malaysia has been a vocal critic of the West of what it perceives to be double standards and bias against Islamic nations.

Issues related to Islam came to a head during the Bosnian conflict, where scores of Muslim Bosnians were massacred in an 'ethnic cleansing' programme. Malaysia contributed personnel for the United Nations Protection Force (UNPROFOR) peacekeeping operations in 1995.

When the United States extended its 'war on terror' and invaded Iraq without the backing of a specific UN resolution, Malaysia actively consolidated the voice of Third World and Islamic countries in protest.

Malaysian troops were deployed as part of the United Nations Protection Force in Bosnia and Herzegovina.

Organisation of the Islamic Conference (OIC)

The OIC was established in Morocco on 25 September 1969, when the first meeting of leaders in the Islamic world met to discuss an attack on Islam's third holiest shrine, the Al-Aqsa mosque in Jerusalem, a month before. They united behind a common cause: the liberation of Jerusalem and Al-Aqsa from Israel.

Six months after the meeting, a permanent general secretariat was established in Jeddah to coordinate the activities of member states, with Tunku Abdul Rahman Putra appointed as secretary general. In 1972, the OIC issued a charter, which refined its purpose—to strengthen solidarity and cooperation among Islamic countries in political, economic, cultural, scientific and social fields.

Members of the Organisation of the Islamic Conference

N

KAZAKHSTAN
UZBEKISTAN
TURKMENISTAN
KYRGHYZSTAN
TAJIKISTAN
ALBANIA AZERBAIJAN
TUNISIA TURKEY SYRIA
LEBANON IRAQ IRAN AFGHANISTAN
MOROCCO PALESTINE JORDAN KUWAIT
ALGERIA LIBYA EGYPT SAUDI ARABIA PAKISTAN
MAURITANIA MALI NIGER U.A.E. BAHRAIN BANGLADESH
SENEGAL SUDAN YEMEN QATAR
GUYANA GAMBIA CHAD OMAN MALAYSIA BRUNEI
GUINEA BISSAU NIGERIA DJIBOUTI
GUINEA CAMEROON SOMALIA INDONESIA
IVORY COAST BENIN GABON MALDIVES
SURINAME SIERRA LEONE TOGO UGANDA COMOROS
BURKINA FASO
MOZAMBIQUE

☐ 57 countries of the OIC

Scale 1:158,000,000

1. Foreign Minister Datuk Seri Syed Hamid Albar chairs the plenary session of the 27th Islamic Conference of Foreign Ministers at Kuala Lumpur, 2000.

2. OIC delegates listen to Dato' Seri Dr Mahathir's opening address at the 10th OIC Summit at Putrajaya, 2003. Malaysia became chair of the OIC in 2003.

3. OIC Chairman Dato' Seri Abdullah Ahmad Badawi with OIC delegates at a special meeting on the Middle East at Putrajaya, April 2004.

Glossary

A

Alliance: Coalition of political parties which began as an ad hoc alliance between the MCA and UMNO in 1952, and was formalized in 1953. In 1954, the MIC joined; other Peninsula-based parties joined in the early 1970s. It was officially registered as a political party, known as the Alliance Party, in 1957, and secured parliamentary majorities at each general election until it was superseded by the Barisan Nasional in 1974.

Api rebellion: Uprising that began in Api (as Jesselton, now Kota Kinabalu, had been renamed by the Japanese) against the Japanese Occupation by youths known as the Kinabalu Guerrilla Defence Force in 1943.

Attorney General: A civil servant, qualified to be a judge of the Federal Court, who is appointed by the Yang di-Pertuan Agong on the advice of the Prime Minister. The Attorney General's role includes advising the Yang di-Pertuan Agong, Cabinet or any Minister on legal matters, and the institution, conduct and discontinuation of proceedings for an offence, other than proceedings before a *syariah* court, a Native Court or a court-martial. The Attorney General is also the Public Prosecutor, empowered to commence and carry out prosecutions in criminal proceedings.

B

Bangkok Declaration: Document signed in 1967 that gave birth to ASEAN. Also known as the ASEAN Declaration.

Barisan Nasional: Coalition of political parties that superseded the Alliance in 1974. Has secured a majority of parliamentary seats at the general elections of 1974, 1978, 1982, 1986, 1990, 1995, 1999 and 2004.

BARJASA (Barisan Rakyat Jati Sarawak): Coalition of Native Sarawak People. A Malay-based party formed in 1962.

Berjaya: A Sabah multi-ethnic party formed in 1975 to oppose the Sabah Alliance.

Briggs Plan: The 'Federation Plan for the Elimination of the Communist Organisation and Armed Forces in Malaya' report, popularly named after Lieutenant General Sir Harold Briggs, who was appointed as Director of Operations in March 1950 during the Emergency.

British Military Administration: System of government introduced into the Malay Peninsula in September 1945 following the Japanese surrender. Ended in October 1946 with the introduction of the Malayan Union.

Bumiputera: Malays and all other indigenous peoples of Malaysia.

C

Chief Justice: The president of the Federal Court, styled the 'Chief Justice of the Federal Court', appointed by the Yang di-Pertuan Agong acting on the advice of the Prime Minister after consulting the Conference of Rulers.

Chief Minister: The Chairman of the Council of State Ministers, and head of the state government, in each of the four states of Melaka, Penang, Sabah and Sarawak. See also Menteri Besar

Conference of Rulers: Body comprising the nine Rulers of the Malay states, a major function of which is the election of the Yang di-Pertuan Agong and his Timbalan (deputy).

Confrontation: Indonesian President Sukarno's policy of *Konfrontasi* from 1963–6 when Indonesia attempted to disrupt the newly formed nation of Malaysia.

Crown colony: Overseas territory that is under the sovereignty and formal control of the United Kingdom but is not part of the United Kingdom.

D

Dataran Merdeka: Independence Square, where, at 12.01 a.m. on 31 August 1957, the Federation of Malaya flag was raised for the first time and the Union Jack lowered for the last time.

Dato', Datuk, Dato' Seri and other variations: Titles awarded by the Yang di-Pertuan Agong, Malay Rulers and Yang di-Pertua Negeri.

Datu: A hereditary title in Sabah.

Dewan Negara: The Senate, one of the two Houses of Parliament.

Dewan Rakyat: The House of Representatives, one of the two Houses of Parliament.

E

Emergency: The period from June 1948 to July 1960 during which the British colonial administration and, later, the Malayan government fought against the insurgency of the Malayan Communist Party.

F

Federated Malay States: A federation of four states—Pahang, Perak, Selangor, and Negeri Sembilan—established by the British government in 1895 and survived until the Japanese Occupation of World War II.

G

Group of 77: Group established by 77 developing countries in 1964 that provides the means for developing nations to articulate and promote their collective economic interests and enhance their joint negotiating capacity on major international economic issues in the United Nations system, and promote economic and technical cooperation among developing countries. In 2005 there were 132 member states.

H

Harare Declaration: Reaffirmation by heads of government of Commonwealth countries in 1991 of their confidence in the Commonwealth as a voluntary association of independent sovereign states.

Hari Raya Aidilfitri: Festival to mark the end of Ramadhan, the Muslim month of fasting.

Hari Raya Qurban: Muslim festival of sacrifice.

Hartal: A form of passive resistance involving closing shops and stopping work.

I

Indonesia Raya: The Malay term, used in Indonesia, for the concept of a 'Greater Indonesia' that was to include the Netherlands Indies as well as Portuguese Timor, northern Borneo and the Malay Peninsula. See 'Melayu Raya'.

Internal Security Act: Legislation enacted in 1960, based on the colonial administration's Emergency Regulations of 1948, that provides for preventive detention for up to two years with the possibility of renewal every two years.

L

Laksamana: Admiral

LDP: Liberal Democratic Party.

M

Malayan Democratic Union (MDU): Initially moderate political party inaugurated in December 1945 by a group of professionals. Initially moderate, it turned more radical after co-operating with communist fronts. In 1948, the colonial authorities began clamping down on these fronts, and the MDU dissolved itself.

Malayan Union: Confederation of the Malay States and the Straits Settlements states excluding Singapore introduced by the British in 1946, which survived until the inauguration of the Federation of Malaya in 1948.

Malaysia Plans: Five-year economic plans, the first of which was published in 1966, devised and adopted by the government to achieve economic and socio-economic goals.

MCA: Malaysian Chinese Association, originally the Malayan Chinese Association. The major ethnic-Chinese based political party.

Melayu Raya: The Malay term, used in Malaysia, for the concept of a 'Greater Indonesia'. See Indonesia Raya.

Menteri Besar: The Chairman of the Council of State Ministers and head of the state government in each of the nine states of Malaysia ruled by a Sultan.

Merdeka: Independence; usually refers to the independence of the Federation of Malaya from British Rule on 31 August 1957.

MIC: Malaysian Indian Congress, originally the Malayan Indian Congress. The major ethnic-Indian based political party.

Multimedia Super Corridor: Government sponsored initiative to create a hi-tech business corridor between Kuala Lumpur City Centre and Putrajaya.

N

Nanyang Communist Party: Established in Singapore in 1928. Outlawed and harassed by the Singapore police, the party was reorganized in 1930 as the Malayan Communist Party.

National Operations Council: Joint civilian-military body that governed Malaysia for 21 months following the 13 May 1969 tragedy.

New Villages: Fenced and patrolled villages set up by the colonial administration for Chinese squatters during the Emergency.

P

PANAS (Parti Negara Sarawak): Sarawak National Party. Formed in 1960, it was the first pro-Malaysia Borneo party.

PAP (People's Action Party): Ethnic Chinese-based Singaporean party formed in 1954.

Partai Komunis Indonesia (PKI): Indonesian Communist Party, founded in 1920.

Parti Kebangsaan Melayu Malaya (PKMM): National Malay Party of Malaya; it was the first Malay political party to be formed after the Japanese Occupation.

Parti Pesaka Anak Sarawak (PESAKA): Sarawak Peoples' Ancestral Party.

PBB: Parti Pesaka Bumiputera Bersatu (United Ancestral Bumiputera Party).

PBDS: Parti Bansa Dayak Sarawak (Sarawak Native People's Party).

PBRS: Parti Bersatu Rakyat Sabah (United Sabah People's Party).

PBS: Parti Bersatu Sabah (United Sabah Party).

Penghulu: Village headman.

Pusat Tenaga Rakyat: PUTERA or Nucleus of the People's Energy. A coalition of Malay organizations established in 1947 to oppose the Federation proposals.

Putrajaya Corporation: Established to develop, administer and manage the federal administrative capital of Putrajaya on behalf of the Federal Government. Also serves as local authority and local planning authority.

R

Raja Permaisuri Agong: The consort to the Yang di-Pertuan Agong, immediately after whom she takes precedence.

S

SAPP: Sabah Progressive Party.

Sook ching: Clean-up. Purge of anti-Japanese elements during the Japanese Occupation of World War II.

Southeast Asia Treaty Organisation (SEATO): Alliance of Australia, France, Great Britain, New Zealand, Pakistan, the Philippines, Thailand and the United States organized in 1954 to oppose further communist gains in Southeast Asia.

SPDP: Sarawak Progressive Democratic Party.

Straits Settlements: The name given to the three British East India Company territories of Penang, Singapore and Malacca (Melaka) upon being given a unified administration in 1826.

T

Tan Sri: The second highest federal honorific title.

The Tunku: Familiar way of referring to the nation's first Prime Minister, Tunku Abdul Rahman Putra.

Tun: The highest federal honorific title.

Tunku, Tengku: Malay hereditary title indicating royalty.

Twenty Points: List of points published by the Inter-Governmental Committee in 1963, designed to safeguard the rights of Sabah and Sarawak within the Malaysian federation.

U

UMNO: The United Malays National Organisation. The main ethnic-Malay political party.

Unfederated Malay States: A former group of five states—Johor, Kedah, Kelantan, Perlis and Terengganu—under indirect British control.

Y

Yang di-Pertua Negeri: The appointed Heads of State of the four states of Melaka, Penang, Sabah and Sarawak. Formerly known as Governors.

Yang di-Pertuan Agong: The Paramount Ruler or King, elected from among the nine Malay Rulers for five years by the Conference of Rulers.

Z

ZOPFAN: Zone of Peace, Freedom and Neutrality, espoused in a declaration signed by the foreign ministers of Indonesia, Malaysia, the Philippines and Singapore, and a representative of the Thai National Executive Council in 1971. It was formally adopted by the heads of government at the First ASEAN Summit held in Bali in 1976.

Bibliography

Abdullah Abdul Rahman (1995), 'Malaysia Incorporated: Private Sector-Public Sector Collaboration', in Ahmad Sarji (ed.), *Malaysia's Vision 2020: Understanding the Concept, Implications and Challenges*, Petaling Jaya: Pelanduk Publications.

Abdul Latiff Abu Bakar (1996), *Melaka dan Arus Gerakan Kebangsaan Malaysia*, Kuala Lumpur: Penerbit Universiti Malaya.

—— (1998), *Peranan Media dalam Pilihanraya Persekutuan*, Petaling Jaya: Fajar Bakti.

Abdul Razak bin Hussein and Morais, John Victor (1969), *Strategy for Action; the selected speeches of Tun Haji Abdul Razak bin Dato' Hussein al-Haj*, Kuala Lumpur: Malaysian Centre for Development Studies, Prime Minister's Dept.

Ahmad bin Abdullah (1969), *The Malaysian Parliament (Practice & Procedure)*, Kuala Lumpur: Dewan Bahasa dan Pustaka.

Ahmad Sarji Abdul Hamid (1993), *The Changing Civil Service: Malaysia's Competitive Edge*, Petaling Jaya: Pelanduk Publications.

—— (1996), *The Chief Secretary to the Government*, Petaling Jaya: Pelanduk Publications.

—— (1996), *Circulars on Administrative Reforms in the Civil Service of Malaysia*, Kuala Lumpur: Percetakan Nasional Malaysia Berhad.

—— (1996), *Civil Service Reforms: Towards Malaysia's Vision 2020*, Petaling Jaya: Pelanduk Publications.

ALIRAN (1987), *Reflections on the Malaysian Constitution*, Penang: Persatuan Aliran Kesedaran Negara.

Andaya, Barbara Watson and Andaya, Leonard Y. (2001), *A History of Malaysia*, London:

Palgrave Publishers.

Bowie, A. (1991), *Crossing the Industrial Divide: State, Society and the Politics of Economic Transformation in Malaysia*, New York: Columbia University Press.

Cheah Boon Kheng (1983), *Red Star Over Malaya: Resistance and Social Conflict during and after the Japanese Occupation, 1941–1946*, Singapore: Singapore University Press.

—— (2002), *Malaysia: The Making of a Nation*, Singapore: Institute of Southeast Asian Studies.

Chin Kee Onn (1977), *Malaya Upside Down*, Kuala Lumpur: Federal Publications.

Chin Ung Ho (1997), *Chinese Politics in Sarawak*, New York: Oxford.

—— (1999), *'Kataks', Kadazan-Dusun Nationalism and Development*, Canberra: ANU.

Comber, L. (1983), *13 May 1969: A Historical Survey of Sino-Malay Relations*, Kuala Lumpur: Heinemann Asia.

Crouch, Harold (1996), *Government and Society in Malaysia*, Ithaca: Cornell University Press.

Crouch, H., Lee Kam Hing and Michael Ong (eds) (1980), *Malaysian Politics and the 1978 Elections*, Kuala Lumpur: Oxford University Press.

Donnison, F. S. V. (1963), *British Military Administration in the Far East 1943–1946*, London: HMSO.

Esman, Milton J. (1972), *Administration and Development in Malaysia, Institution Building and Reform in a Plural Society*, Ithaca: Cornell University Press.

Faaland, Just, Parkinson, J. R., and Rais Saniman (1990), *Growth and Ethnic Inequality: Malaysia's New Economic Policy*, New York: St. Martin's Press.

Firdaus Haji Abdullah (1985),

Radical Malay Politics, Petaling Jaya: Pelanduk Publications.

Foong, James (2002), *Malaysian Judiciary: A Record*, Petaling Jaya: Sweet and Maxwell Asia.

Funston, John (1980), *Malay Politics in Malaysia: A Study of UMNO and PAS*, Kuala Lumpur: Heinemann Educational Books (Asia).

Gale, Bruce (1981), *Political and Public Enterprise in Malaysia*, Kuala Lumpur: Eastern Universities Press.

Gill, Ranjit (1987), *ASEAN: Coming of Age*, Singapore: Sterling Corporate Services.

Goh Cheng Teik (1971), *The May Thirteenth Incident and Democracy in Malaysia*, Kuala Lumpur: Oxford University Press.

Gomez, E. T. and Jomo K. S. (1999), *Malaysia's Political Economy*, New York: Cambridge University Press.

Hajrudin Somun (2003), *Mahathir, The Secret of the Malaysian Success*, Petaling Jaya: Pelanduk Publications.

Hanna, W. (1964), *Formation of the Federation of Malaysia*, New York: American Universities Field Staff.

Hanrahan, Gene Z. (1971), *The Communist Struggle in Malaya*, Kuala Lumpur: University of Malaya Press.

Harding, Andrew (1996), *Law, Government and the Constitution in Malaysia*, The Hague: Kluwer Law International.

Heng Pek Koon (1988), *Chinese Politics in Malaysia*, Singapore: Oxford University Press.

Hng Hung Yong (2004), *5 Men & 5 Ideas—Building National Identity*, Petaling Jaya: Pelanduk Publications.

Ho Khai Leong and Chin, James (2001), *Mahathir's Administration: Performance and Crisis in Governance*, Singapore: Times Books International.

Hussin Mutalib (1990), *Islam and ethnicity in Malay Politics*, Singapore: Oxford University Press.

Hwang, In-Won (2003), *Personalized Politics: The Malaysian state under Mahathir*, Singapore: Institute of Southeast Asian Studies.

Ismail Kassim (1979), *Race, Politics and Moderation: A Study of the Malaysian Electoral Process*, Singapore: Times Books International.

Ismail Noor (2003), *Pak Lah: A Sense of Accountability: An Insight into Effective Stewardship*, Kuala Lumpur: Utusan Publications and Distributors.

Jayum A. Jawan (1994), *Iban Politics and Economic Development*, Bangi: Penerbit Universiti Kebangsaan Malaysia.

Josey, Alex (1980), *Lee Kuan Yew*, Singapore: Times Books International.

Kahn, J. and Loh, K. W. (1992), *Fragmented Vision: Culture and Politics in Contemporary Malaysia*, Sydney: Allen & Unwin.

Khoo Boo Teik (1995), *Paradoxes of Mahathirism: An Intellectual Biography of Mahathir Mohamad*, Oxford: Oxford University Press.

Kratoska, Paul H. (2002), *Southeast Asian Minorities in the Wartime Japanese Empire*, London: Routledge Curzon London.

Lau, Albert (1991), *The Malayan Union Controversy 1942–1948*, Singapore: Oxford University Press.

—— (1998), *A Moment of Anguish: Singapore in Malaysia and the Politics of Disengagement*, Singapore: Eastern University Press.

Loh Kok Wah and Johan Saravanamuttu (eds) (2003), *New Politics in Malaysia*, Singapore: ISEAS.

Luping, Herman (1994), *Sabah's Dilemma: the Political History of*

Sabah (1960–1994), Kuala Lumpur: Magnus Books.

Mackie, J. A. C. (1974), *Konfrontasi: The Indonesia-Malaysia Dispute 1963–1966,* Kuala Lumpur: Oxford University Press.

Manderson, Lenore (1980), *Women, Politics, and Change: The Kaum Ibu UMNO, Malaysia, 1945–1972,* Kuala Lumpur: Oxford University Press.

Mauzy, Diane K. (1983), *Barisan Nasional: Coalition Government in Malaysia,* Kuala Lumpur: Marican & Sons.

Means, Gordon P. (1976), *Malaysian Politics,* London: Hodder and Stoughton.

—— (1991), *Malaysian Politics: The Second Generation,* Singapore: Oxford University Press.

Miller, Harry (1982), *Prince And Premier: A Biography of Tunku Abdul Rahman Putra,* Singapore: Eastern Universities Press.

Milne, R. S. and Mauzy, D. K. (1978), *Politics and Government in Malaysia,* Vancouver: University of British Columbia Press.

Mimi Kamariah Majid (1999), *Criminal Procedure in Malaysia,* Kuala Lumpur: University of Malaya Press.

Mohamed Abid (2003), *Reflections of Pre-Independence Malaya,* Petaling Jaya: Pelanduk Publications.

Mohamed Noordin Sopiee (1974), *From Malayan Union to Singapore Separation: Political Unification in the Malaysia Region, 1945–65,* Kuala Lumpur: Penerbit Universiti Malaya.

Mohammad Redzuan Othman (2001), *Jendela Masa,* Kuala Lumpur: Penerbit Universiti Malaya.

Mohammad Sufian and others (eds) (1978), *The Constitution of Malaysia Development 1957–77,* Kuala Lumpur: Oxford University Press.

Morais, J. Victor (1981), *Hussein Onn: A Tryst With Destiny,* Singapore: Times Books International.

Muhammad Ghazali Shafie (1998), *Ghazali Shafie's Memoir on the Formation of Malaysia,* Bangi: Penerbit Universiti

Kebangsaan Malaysia.

Nair, Shanti (1997), *Islam in Malaysian Foreign Policy,* New York: Routledge.

National Operations Council (1969), *The May 13 Tragedy: A Report,* Kuala Lumpur: National Operations Council.

Nik Abdul Rashid bin Nik Abdul Majid (1997), *A Century of the Conference of Rulers: 1897–1997,* Kuala Lumpur: Office of the Keeper of the Ruler's Seal.

Nik Anuar Nik Mahmud (1999), *Tok Janggut: Pejuang atau Penderhaka?,* Bangi: Jabatan Sejarah, Universiti Kebangsaan Malaysia.

Nordin Yusof, Dato' and Abdul Razak Abdullah Baginda (1994), *Honour & Sacrifice: The Malaysian Armed Forces,* Kuala Lumpur: Malaysian Armed Forces, Ministry of Defence.

Ongkili, James P. (1986), *Nation-Building in Malaysia,* Singapore: Oxford University Press.

Oong Hak Ching (2000), *Chinese Politics in Malaya 1942–55: The Dynamics of British Policy,* Bangi: Penerbit Universiti Kebangsaan Malaysia.

Parker, W. C. (1979), *Communication and the May 13th Crises: A Psychocultural Interpretation,* Kuala Lumpur: Penerbit Universiti Malaya.

Puthucheary, Marvis (1978), *The Politics of Administration: The Malaysian Experience,* New York: Oxford University Press.

Rabushka, Alvin (1973), *Race and Politics in Urban Malaya,* Stanford: Hoover Institution Press, Stanford University.

Rais Yatim (1995), *Freedom under Executive Power in Malaysia,* Kuala Lumpur: Endowment.

Rashid Rahman, A. (1994), *The Conduct of Elections in Malaysia,* Kuala Lumpur: Berita Publishing.

Ratnam, K. J. (1965), *Communalism and Political Process in Malaya,* Kuala Lumpur: University of Malaya Press.

Rawlings, Joan (1965), *Sarawak 1839–1963,* London: Macmillan.

Reece, R.H.W. (1982), *The name of Brooke: The End of White Rajah*

Rule in Sarawak,* Kuala Lumpur: Oxford University Press.

—— (1998), *Masa Jepun: Sarawak under the Japanese, 1941–1943,* Kuching: Sarawak Literary Society.

Roff, W. R. (1967), *The Origin of Malay Nationalism,* Kuala Lumpur: University of Malaya Press.

Saravanamuttu, J. (1983), *The Dilemma of Independence: Two Decades of Malaysian Foreign Policy, 1957–1977,* Penang: Penerbit Universiti Sains Malaysia.

Sothi Rachagan, S. (1993), *Law and the Electoral Process in Malaysia,* Kuala Lumpur: University of Malaya Press.

Shafruddin, B. H. (1987), *The Federal Factor in the Government and Politics of Peninsular Malaysia,* Singapore: Oxford University Press.

Shaw, William (1976), *Tun Razak, His Life and Times,* Kuala Lumpur: Longman Malaysia.

Short, Anthony (2000), *In Pursuit of Mountain Rats: The Communist Insurrection in Malaya,* Singapore: Cultured Lotus.

Singh, Gurmit K. S. (1984), *Malaysian Societies: Friendly or Political?,* Petaling Jaya: Environmental Protection Society Malaysia and Selangor Graduates Society.

—— (ed.) (1987), *No to Secrecy: The Campaign against 1986's Amendments to the OSA,* Kuala Lumpur: Aliran, et al.

Sullivan, Anwar and Leong, Cecilia (eds) (1981),

Commemorative History of Sabah 1881–1981, Kuala Lumpur: Sabah State Government Centenary Publications Committee.

Suntharalingam, R. and Abdul Rahman Hj. Ismail (eds) (1985), *Nationalisme: Satu Tinjauan Sejarah,* Petaling Jaya: Penerbit Fajar Bakti.

Tan Boon Kean and Bishan Singh (1994), *Uneasy Relations: The State and NGOs in Malaysia,* Kuala Lumpur: Gender and Development Programme, Asian and Pacific Development Centre.

Tilman, Robert O. (1964), *Bureaucratic Transition in Malaya,* Durham: Duke University Press.

Tregonning, K. G. (1967), *A History of Modern Sabah,* Kuala Lumpur: University of Malaya Press.

von Vorys, Karl (1976), *Democracy without Consensus: Communalism and Political Stability in Malaysia,* Kuala Lumpur: Oxford University Press.

Weiss, Meredith L. and Saliha Hassan, (eds) (2003), *Social Movements in Malaysia: From Moral Communities to NGOs,* London: Routledge Curzon.

Welsh, Bridget (2004), *Reflections: The Mahathir Years,* Baltimore: John Hopkins University.

Wu Min Aun (1978), *An Introduction to the Malaysian Legal System,* Kuala Lumpur: Heinemann Educational Books.

Zakaria Haji Ahmad (ed.), (1987), *Government and Politics of Malaysia,* Singapore: Oxford University Press.

Index

Picture Credits

Agence France-Presse, p. 7, Technology City; p. 80, EAEC; p. 82, 'Malaysia Boleh'. Ahmad Sarji, p. 35, Crest; p. 59, Report; p. 72, The Tunku presents report; p. 74, The Tunku and President Johnson; The Tunku and Prince Sihanoukh; p. 77, Alliance Cabinet; First day cover; p. 83, Book launch; p. 92, Ahearne, Ahmad Sarji. 'Abdullah Ahmad Badawi–Revivalist of an Intellectual tradition', p. 84, Ahmad Badawi, Abdullah Fahim. All Women's Action Society, p. 123, March; p. 128, 'Speak Out Against Rape', 'Citizens Against Rape', March. Arkib Negara Malaysia, p. 10, Proclamations; p. 12, Road block, Duke of Gloucester; p. 14, Sultan Abdullah, Birch; p. 16, College, Sultan Ibrahim, The Tunku; p. 17, Sheikh Tahir, Burhanuddin Al-Helmi; p. 18, Nehru; p. 19, S. N. Veerasamy, Kong See Boo Poe, Dr Lim Boon Keng, Parade; p. 22, Lieutenant Adnan, Japanese Army, Johor Bahru, Penang, Mini-sub; p. 24, Force 136, Tokugawa Yoshichika; p. 25, Sultan of Selangor; p. 28, General surrenders, Parade; p. 29, Soldiers, Hawkers, Onlookers; p. 30, Agreement; p. 31, UMNO formed; p. 32, Malay Congress; p. 33, Dato' Onn resigns; p. 34, 12-man committee, Working committee; p. 35, Seal; p. 37, Road blocks; Body searches; p. 38, Sultan of Kedah, Poster, Public display; p. 39, J. L. H. Davis, David Marshall, Tan Cheng Lock and the Tunku, Parade, Relocation; p. 40, The Tunku returns, Independence Agreement; p. 41, Pen; p. 42, Foreign Correspondents Association, Sarawak Tribune; p. 43, Temenggong Jugah, Lord Lansdowne; p. 44, Document; p. 46, Caricature (14 September 1963), Caricature (Sukarno), Weapons; p. 47, Treaty; p. 49, First Agong, Communist surrenders; p. 52, The Tunku; 'Sail-boat' logo; p. 53, The Straits Times; p. 54, FRU; p. 55, The Straits Times; p. 56, NOC; p. 57, Rukunegara; p. 68, Opening of Parliament; p. 69, Mahmud Mat, Raja Uda; p. 70, First Cabinet; p. 71, First Prime Minister, The Tunku and Cabinet; p. 76, Rural development; p. 77, Opening conference; p. 92, Arthur Young, Edward Brockman, William Maxwell, William Peel, Charles Cochrane, Andrew Caldecott, Malcolm Shelley, Marcus Rex, Hugh Fraser, H. R. Hone, Alec Newboult, Vincent del Tufo, David Watherston; p. 93, Magazine; p. 94, Athi Nahappan; p. 98, Briefing; p. 101, Mohammed Salleh Ismael; p. 103, Naval base; p. 105, Newspaper; p. 108,

Manifestoes; p. 113, Hussein Onn, Abdul Razak; p. 114, Dr Cheah Toon Lok; p. 115, John Thivy, Budh Singh, K. Ramanathan, K. L. Devaser; p. 124, Meeting; p. 130, The Malay Mail; p. 134, 'The Prompter'. Associated Press, p. 83, Langkawi Dialogue, OIC Chairman; p. 103, Royal Rangers; p. 104, PAS members; p. 132, Dr Mahathir and Kofi Annan. Auger, Timothy, p. 9, Putra Mosque; p. 13, Memorial, First-day cover; p. 37, Car; p. 58, PNB; p. 60, Signboard; p. 66, First-day cover; p. 68, First-day cover. Badan Warisan, p. 129, No. 2 Jalan Stonor. Bernama, p. 9, Handing over; p. 61, Abdullah Badawi and party leaders; p. 71, Oaths of office; p. 108, Counting seats; p. 109, Dr Mahathir on election night; p. 121, Launch; p. 132, Abdullah Badawi at UN; Abdullah Badawi and ASEAN leaders; p. 136, Dr Mahathir and Yasser Arafat; p. 137, Abdullah Badawi at APEC Summit; p. 139, Bangkok Summit, Abdullah Badawi with ASEAN leaders; p. 141, Plenary session, OIC Summit. Bowden, David, p. 122, Lembaga Tabung Haji. Central Office of Information, London, p. 40, Panglima Bukit Gantang. Chai Kah Yune, p. 5 and p. 66, Royal Regalia; p. 96–7, Putrajaya. Chang, Tommy, p. 58, Wisma SEDCO. Chen Ko Ting, p. 27, Circular. Chief Justice of the Federal Court of Malaysia, p. 86, Syed Sheh Syed Hassan Barakbah, Mohd Azmi Mohamed, Dr Mohamed Suffian Mohd Hashim, Raja Tun Azlan Shah, Mohamed Salleh Abas, Mohd Eusoff Chin, Mohammed Dzaiddin Abdullah, Ahmad Fairuz Sheikh Abdul Halim; p. 87, Mace; High Court, Court of Appeal, Federal Court. Chief Secretary to the Government of Malaysia, p. 92, Abdul Aziz Abdul Majid, Abdul Jamil Abdul Rais, Tunku Mohamed Tunku Besar Burhanuddin, Abdul Kadir Shamsuddin, Abdullah Mohd Salleh, Abdullah Ayub, Hashim Aman, Sallehuddin Mohamed, Abdul Halim Ali, Samsudin Osman. Chin, Steven, p. 87, Syariah court. Chung Hwa Confucian School, Penang, p. 125, School. Cross, Martin, p. 48, Parliament, Shah Alam complex; p. 58, RISDA; p. 62, Prime Minister's Department; p. 90, INTAN, Agricultural Office; p. 93, District Office, Securities Commission; p. 94, City Hall (old and new premises); p. 95, Majlis Perbandaran Subang Jaya; p. 97, Lake, Police HQ, Fire Station, Hospital, Housing, p. 100, Mobile Police Station; p. 101, Training Centre; p.104,

Banners; p. 140, Wisma Putra. Department of Museums and Antiquities, Malaysia, p. 40, The Tunku announces date of Independence. Dewan Bahasa dan Pustaka, p. 17, Za'ba; p. 48, Poster. EDM Archives, p. 14, British forces; p. 15, British attack, Weapons; p. 17, Protest, Ibrahim Yaakob, First congress; p. 18, Peranakans, Tin mine, Indian women; p. 20, Anti-cession protesters; p. 22, HMS Prince of Wales; p. 25, 'Banana money', Cartoon; p. 27, Expedition; p. 29, Straits Dollar; p. 45, Proclamation in Kuching; p. 49, Muslim prayers; p. 65, 20 Ringgit note; p. 67, Seal; p. 75, Prime Ministers' meeting; p. 93, Bangunan Sultan Abdul Samad. Education Quarterly, p. 124, Smart School; p. 126, Competent workforce; p. 127, KLIUC, Computing skills, Stamford College. Election Commission Malaysia, p. 49, Vote tallying; p. 107, Dr Mustapha Albakri, Ahmad Perang, Abdul Kadir Talib, Harun Din; Omar Mohd Hashim. Federal Information Department, Sabah, p. 21, Fuad Stephens, Support for Malaysia; p. 43, Mustapha Harun; p. 45, Proclamation in Kota Kinabalu. Federal Information Department, Sarawak, p. 7, Billboard; p. 20, Painting; p. 21, First rally; p. 42, Protests in Kuching, Anti-Malaysia protests, Communist propaganda; p. 43, Anti-Malaysia slogans; p. 47, Tebedu. Federation of Malaysian Consumer Associations, p. 129, Consumer Complaints Centre. Foong, Dato' James, p. 86, Lord Chancellor, James Thomson, Abdul Hamid Omar, Opening of Court of Appeal. Foreign and Commonwealth Office, p. 32, Onn and Azizah Jaafar; p. 35, Signing of Agreement; Sultan of Kelantan. Goh Seng Chong, p. 3 and p. 97, Prime Minister's Office; p. 87 & p. 97, Palace of Justice; p. 88, High Court; p. 96, Putrajaya; p. 97, Putra Mosque, Seri Perdana, Istana Melawati, Prime Minister's Office, Prime Minister's Department, Ministry of Foreign Affairs, Ministry of Finance, Convention Centre; p. 125, Kampong Bharu School, Vision School. HBL Network Photo Agency (M) Sdn Bhd, p. 141, Abdullah Badawi with OIC delegates. HSBC Group Archives, London, p. 23, Sandakan (before and after). Imperial War Museum, London, p. 28, Mountbatten (SE4708); p. 30, MacMichael (SE5192);

p. 31, MacDonald and Gent (SE7474), Gent taking salute (SE7112); p. 36, Stage bus (KI5269), Fuel depot (KI3101), Rubber trees (KI5631), Train derailment (KI2991); p. 39, Resettlement village (KI3796). Internal Security Department, Singapore, p. 37, Lai Tek. Jabatan Kerja Raya, p. 90, Engineers. Jabatan Perkhidmatan Penerangan Malaysia, p. 6, Home Guard; p. 12, MacGillivray; p. 13, Yang di-Pertuan Agong; p. 31, Onn Jaafar; p. 33, Templer and Onn Jaafar; p. 41, 'Merdeka!'; p. 49, Masjid Negara; p. 51, Ethnic groups; p. 52, UMNO conference, Tun Razak, V. Manickavasagam, Tan Siew Sin; p. 53, The Tunku seated in boat; p. 56, Heads of State Operations Councils; p. 60, Abdul Razak at BN meeting; p. 61, Dr Mahathir at MCA AGM; p. 62, Wisma Bapa Malaysia; p. 63, Opening ceremony; p. 64, The Tunku, Abdul Razak, Hussein Onn, Dr Mahathir, Abdullah Badawi, Court of Appeal; p. 65, Prime Minister's Department; p. 66, Tuanku Syed Sirajuddin, Conference of Rulers in 2004; p. 67, First to 12th Yang di-Pertuan Agongs; p. 69, Dewan Negara; Abdul Malek Yusof; p. 75, Last Cabinet meeting; p. 77, Abdul Razak at Bangkok conference; p. 78, Press conference; p. 79, Hussein Onn with guest; p. 83, Factory, First car; p. 88, Syariah court, p. 93, State Secretary's Office; p. 99, Trainees; p. 104, Voters; p. 106, Woman voter; Dr Mahathir votes; p. 106–7, Background; p. 108, The Tunku at convention; p. 109, 25th anniversary, Scoreboard; p. 111, First headquarters; p. 113, Senu Abdul Rahman, Abdul Rahim Thamby Chik, Hishammuddin Tun Hussein, Wanita UMNO, Rafidah Aziz; p. 114, Tan Siew Sin, Tan Koon Swan, Dr Ling Liong Sik, Ong Ka Ting; p. 115, Women's wing, V. T. Sambanthan; V. Manickavasagam, S. Samy Vellu; p. 116, Hussein Onn; p. 120, Supporters; p. 121, Dr Chen Man Hin; p. 125, Chinese school; p. 130, Angkasapuri; p. 131, Satellite; p. 132, NAM Conference; 10th Session of OIC; p. 133, OIC Expo; p. 134, Wisma Putra; p. 135, ASA Conference, Chou En Lai and Abdul Razak, 1974 talks; p. 136, APEC Summit; Abdullah Badawi and Putin; p. 140, Commonwealth Heads of Government Meeting; p. 141, South-South Summit, Julius Nyerere and Muhammad Ghazali Shafie. King-Holford, Ian, p. 55, Curfew pass. Kuala Lumpur General Hospital, p. 90, Doctors. Kyodo News, p. 25, Masanobu Tsuji. Lembaga

151